Indonesia's Small Entrepreneurs

Small enterprise studies in developing countries are still often framed within 'informal sector' theoretical approaches or broader industrial paradigms. This book moves beyond such approaches and explores the potential use of a new framework, the 'small enterprise integrative framework'. This framework is used to examine the organisation and operations of small enterprises in developing countries, to reach a greater understanding of their micro-level activities, as well as their interactions on a range of scales.

The book explores the socio-economic and cultural relationships that make life for small entrepreneurs in Makassar, on the eastern Indonesian island of Sulawesi, so distinctive. The application of this new framework for research reveals the diversity of labour flexibility, networking and cluster styles among the enterprises studied, and the constraints they face for growth. Applied in the context of Makassar, it allows us to gain an in-depth understanding of what life is like for the small-scale entrepreneurs who operate in the city. The analysis begins with an examination of the internal dynamics of the enterprise studies, concentrating on their history, production processes and labour flexibility. It then moves to explore inter-firm dynamics, focusing upon the networks, trust and clusters that have evolved amongst the enterprises, and also with other local economic factors. These insights give us a clear understanding of the constraints that small-scale entrepreneurs face in trying to attain their own versions of 'success'.

While the recent Southeast Asian economic crisis has been heralded by certain commentators as a new era for small enterprises in the region, the book concludes that local realities for the small enterprises in Makassar mean that while for some it has been a time of shifting fortunes, others have continued trading on the margins.

Sarah Turner is an Assistant Professor in the Department of Geography at McGill University, Canada.

Indonesia's Small Entrepreneurs

Trading on the margins

Sarah Turner

RoutledgeCurzon
Taylor & Francis Group

LONDON AND NEW YORK

First published 2003
by RoutledgeCurzon
11 New Fetter Lane, London EC4P 4EE

Simultaneously published in the USA and Canada
by RoutledgeCurzon
29 West 35th Street, New York, NY 10001

RoutledgeCurzon is an imprint of the Taylor & Francis Group

© 2003 Sarah Turner

Typeset in Times by
M Rules
Printed and bound in Great Britain by
Antony Rowe Ltd, Chippenham, Wiltshire

British Library Cataloguing in Publication Data
A catalogue record for this book is available from the British Library

Library of Congress Cataloging in Publication Data
Indonesia's small entrepreneurs: trading on the margins / Sarah
Turner.
  p. cm.
Includes bibliographical references and index.
1. Small business – Indonesia. 2. Business networks – Indonesia. 3.
Corporate culture – Indonesia. 4. Entrepreneurship – Indonesia. 5.
Small business – Indonesia – Makassar – Case studies. 6. Indonesia –
Economic conditions – 20th century. I. Title.
HD22346.I6 T87 2002
338'.04'09598 – dc21   20002069799

ISBN 0–7007–1569–X

Contents

List of illustrations

Figures

Plates

Tables

Preface

On my arrival in Makassar in 1996 I visited a small enterprise making gold jewellery. After striking up a conversation with the owner, Amir, he detailed the way his business was run. He talked about the difficulties in finding and then maintaining a team of skilled workers, the networks he used to gain raw materials as well as to market his finished goods, and the barriers which were limiting his ability to expand the business in the way he dreamed of doing. This book then, is about Amir, his goldsmith neighbours, and many other small-scale entrepreneurs operating in Makassar, the largest city in Sulawesi, Eastern Indonesia. It seeks to explore the internal dynamics of small enterprises like Amir's, while also gaining an understanding of their interactions with other enterprises and actors in their contextual environment.

There are numerous arguments as to why small enterprises have an important role to play in the economies of peripheral areas of developing countries. Most are without exception heralded as a means by which production output may be improved, employment increased and general development enhanced (Hill, 2001). Yet, I argue in this book that we still do not have an appropriate, critical framework with which to understand small enterprise production organisation in developing countries, with past 'informal sector' theories and industrial paradigms proving problematic in their application.

In attempting to rectify this problem, I also aimed to find out the key organisational features of the small enterprises in the Makassar sample. Also of interest were what the small scale entrepreneurs themselves interpreted as 'success' in relation to their enterprise operations, and what, if any, were the constraints they maintained were prohibiting them from reaching this.

As the analysis utilising the *small enterprise integrative framework* developed here unfolds, close attention is paid to the social, cultural and gender aspects which influence and are influenced by how the entrepreneurs operate within their political and economic environment. It becomes clear that for many small enterprises in Makassar subsistence and a daily concern for survival offers perhaps the most relevant appraisal of the entrepreneurs' situation, restraints on reaching emically defined full potential being imposed by local conditions and constraints. Barriers which impede the operations of many small enterprises in Makassar usually come from either within them or are associated with the local socio-cultural and political environment. The integrative framework is then further tested through an examination of the impacts of the economic crisis on small enterprises in Makassar.

This book is based largely on the content of my Ph.D. thesis, undertaken at the Centre for Southeast Asian Studies, University of Hull, and completed in 1998. However, after its examination I wanted to present the findings somewhat differently from that found in the thesis, especially so that information gathered after the beginning of the Southeast Asian economic crisis in mid-1997 could be included, and the whole made more readily available to a much wider readership. I have therefore shortened and rearranged the theoretical chapters, added more information from a return trip to Makassar after the economic crisis had begun, and hopefully have created a more exciting product.

Not surprisingly, then, the people who have assisted in the development of this book span a number of regions of the world. During my time based in England as a Ph.D. student I was particularly grateful to Lynda Johnston, Morten Pedersen, Luxmon Wongsuphasawat and Denise Hill for their valuable ideas, support and friendship. In Indonesia I am indebted to Tunru, Hasbi and Dias for all their help and information, and especially to Aco for his support and patience in helping me with my initial questionnaire translations. Special thanks also to the entrepreneurs I interviewed who were kind enough to spare the time to talk and open a window into their world. Thanks, too, to the numerous other people in Sulawesi with whom I had formal and informal conversations. *Terima kasih banyak.* From New Zealand I would like to thank Professor Richard Bedford for his encouragement and advice which have traversed the globe with me since my University of Waikato days. I also acknowledge the generous financial support of the Commonwealth Scholarship Commission in the United Kingdom, and the New Zealand Federation of University Women.

This book has taken shape in the Department of Geography, at the University of Otago, New Zealand. My gratitude there to my colleagues for their friendship and support. Particular thanks to Associate Professor Brian Heenan for his perceptive suggestions, sense of humour and friendship, and my gratefulness to my friends Andrea Howard and Sarah Johnsen for their assistance. Special thanks are also due to my parents for their unfailing encouragement and friendship, and for introducing me to Southeast Asia initially, and to Jean Michaud for making me see the bigger picture.

List of abbreviations

ABRI	*Angkatan Bersenjata Republik Indonesia*	Former name for the Indonesian Armed Forces, now *Tentara Nasional Indonesia*
ASEAN		Association of South East Asian Nations
BAPPEDA	*Badan Perencanaan Pembangunan Daerah*	Local planning development agency. Has regional (*Tingkat* I) and municipal (*Tingkat* II) offices
BIPIK	*Bimbingan dan Pengembangan Industri Kecil*	Programme for Guiding and Developing Small Industry
BLK	*Balai Latihan Kerja*	Work training centre
Bosowa*	*Bone, Soppeng, Wajo*	Large trading company based in South Sulawesi
BPS	*Biro Pusat Statistik*	Central Bureau Of Statistics
BUMN	*Badan Usaha Milik Negara*	State-owned enterprises
CEFE		Competency-based economies through formation of enterprise
ESCAP		Economic and Social Commission for Asia and the Pacific

*Many Indonesian constructions are not acronyms, but are condensed forms of words, often compromising the first syllable or first few letters of the composite words. These are shown in lower case.

FDI		Foreign direct investment
Golkar	*Golongan Karya*	Functional groups
GRP		Gross regional product
ILO		International Labour Office
IMF		International Monetary Fund
JICA		Japanese International Co-operation Agency
KADIN	*Kamar Dagang dan Industri*	Chamber of Commerce and Industry
KADINIA	*Kamar Dagang dan Industri Daerah*	Provincial Chamber of Commerce and Industry
KAS	*Konrad Adenauer Stiftung*	German non-govemmental organisation working with small enterprises in Indonesia and other parts of Southeast Asia
KIMA	*Kawasan Industri Makassar*	Company that owns an industrial estate in Makassar
Krismon	*krisis moneter*	Monetary crisis
KUK	*Kredit Usaha Kecil*	Small business credit
LDCs		Lesser developed countries
MNCs		Multinational corporations
MPN		Minimum physical needs
MPR	*Mejelis Permusyawaratan Rakyat*	People's Consultative Assembly
NICs		Newly industrialised countries

NIEs		Newly industrialising economies
PDI	*Partai Rakyat Demokrasi*	People's Democratic Party
PPP	*Partai Persatuan Pembangunan*	United Development Party
PPPK or 'P^{3}K'	*Pusat Pembinaan Pengusaha Kecil*	Centre for the Establishment of Small Entrepreneurs
PUKTI	*Pusat Pengembangan Usaha Kecil Kawasan Timur Indonesia*	Centre for the Development of Small Businesses in the East Indonesia Region
Repelita	*Rencana Pembanganan Lima Tahun*	Five Year Development Plan
Rp.	*Rupiah*	Unit of Indonesian currency
Sl	*Stratum Satu*	Undergraduate programme, nearly equivalent to a British university Bachelor's degree
SITU	*Surat Izin Tempat Usaha*	Licence for a business place/site
SIUP	*Surat Izin Untuk Perusahaan*	Licence for a business or enterprise to operate
SMA	*Sekolah Menengah Atas*	Upper secondary school
SME		Small and medium enterprises
SPSS		Statistical Package for the Social Sciences
SSI		Small-scale industry
UNHAS	*Universitas Hasanuddin*	Makassar State University

Note on exchange rate

The Indonesian currency is the *Rupiah*. The exchange rate has fluctuated throughout the period that is the focus of this book. The following table gives an indication:

	USD$1=	*GBP£1=*
December 1995	Rp.2308.00	3581.57
December 1996	2383.00	4036.98
May 1997 (prior to the General elections)	2415.00	3956.00
December 1997	4650.00	7708.79
December 1998	8025.00	13,335.97
December 1999	7100.00	11,494.92

Sources: Asiaweek (2 May 1997), Bank of Indonesia (online).

1 Introduction

Thirty-seven-year-old Amir operates a small enterprise producing gold jewellery. He was born in a *kampung* (village) north of Makassar city, Sulawesi, to which he moved in 1987, and is married with four children. There are 14 people living with him, in his city home, including his immediate and extended family who work for him, as well as those employed by his wife, a tailor. He has been a goldsmith for 13 years, and makes rings, bracelets and necklaces, the skills for which his father taught him.

Amir designs most of his jewellery, fairly unusual among the small scale goldsmiths in the city, a majority of whom copy designs shown to them by the Chinese goldshop owners from whom they gain their gold supplies. Instead, Amir likes to use a magazine a friend brought back from Singapore as a basis for new designs and when interviewed was attempting to create a bracelet from a chain of linked, stylised, gold turtle shapes. Amir, a Bugis, has had a fairly good level of trust with his Chinese suppliers, having worked for them for three years, however, things became a bit tense during the economic crisis when the price of gold rose and Chinese shop keepers in general became more suspicious of the local non-Chinese community, and visa versa.

Although Amir is considered a fairly successful goldsmith in his local community, he has not had any luck gaining a loan from the bank. He tried to obtain one in 1998, but the paperwork was too complicated and he did not want to have to 'tip' the staff, as they requested. Instead he borrowed from his brother, and is happy with the arrangement as he does not have to pay interest. Nevertheless, he is increasingly concerned about the future of his enterprise, especially the impact on it of the economic crisis, yet believes that this has not been felt as hard in Makassar as elsewhere in Indonesia.

(Amir, interview notes, 16 January 1999)

As we begin the new millennium, small enterprises such as Amir's are increasingly endorsed as a means by which peripheral areas of developing countries might improve production output, employment and general development

(Hill, 1997b; Schmitz and Nadvi, 1999; Tambunan, 2000). There are a number of persuasive reasons for this optimistic appraisal. Among these, such enterprises represent a seed-bed for indigenous entrepreneurship which mobilises capital that would otherwise remain unused. They are labour intensive as well, employing more labour per unit of capital than large enterprises, and they enhance indigenous technological learning, while contributing to the decentralisation of industry. In addition, as users of predominantly local resources, small enterprises have low foreign exchange requirements, they cater for the basic needs of the poor, and they contribute to the more equitable distribution of income and wealth (Schmitz, 1989). Moreover, this set of positive qualities suggests that small enterprises are less inclined to produce negative socio-cultural effects so often associated with foreign ownership of firms, while filling niches usually ignored by larger enterprises (Echtner, 1995).

Not surprisingly, along with such endorsements, a range of academic work concerning small enterprises in developing countries has been identified. Indonesia is one such country in which these studies have concentrated. The small enterprise sector there, in the world's fourth most populous nation, is large and diverse. Most recent work on small enterprises in the archipelago has explored family enterprises in Jakarta and issues of intra- and inter-firm linkages (van Diermen, 1997), investigated the transformation of employment patterns in small enterprises through time (Tambunan, 2000), and researched the operations of small and cottage industry clusters in Java (Sandee and van Hulsen, 2000). This book, then, is designed to complement such earlier works, but places more emphasis on local cultural elements, as it strives for a greater understanding of the micro-level activities involving small enterprises, and of enterprise interactions at a range of scales. This is undertaken in the course of an examination of the shifting fortunes of small enterprises in Makassar, South Sulawesi.[1]

In the process it became obvious that, as Schmitz (1989: 3) argued more than a decade ago, 'we still lack a convincing theory of small-scale industrialisation'. For this reason, this book develops a new conceptual structure, the *small enterprise integrative framework*, as a tool with which to examine the organisation and operations of small enterprises in developing countries, one largely devoid of the limitations of previous approaches outlined in Chapter 2.[2]

The field site that informs this study is Makassar, the capital and administrative centre for the province of South Sulawesi (Figure 1.1). It is also a busy port city, with over one million inhabitants. For centuries Makassar has been the gateway to the famous 'spice islands' of Eastern Indonesia, while the Bugis, the most widely known of the local inhabitants, are recognised for their magnificent trading ships that still ply the waters of the Indonesian archipelago. Since previously there has been only limited empirical and even less theoretical research on small enterprises in peripheral locations of Indonesia like Makassar, this book not only details small enterprise organisation and

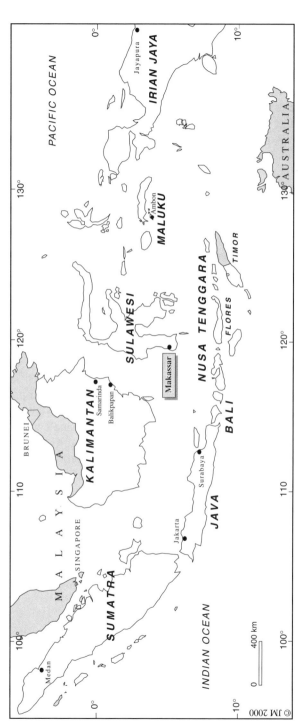

Figure 1.1 Makassar in the Indonesian context.

Source: adapted from De Koninck (1994: 3)

advances an important theoretical enquiry, it also contributes to knowledge about the regional economic and human geography of South Sulawesi.

In exploring the internal dynamics of small enterprises in Makassar, while also seeking to understand their contextualised interactions with other enterprises and actors, this book develops a critical framework with which to understand small enterprise production in developing countries. It examines the key organisational features of the small enterprises in Makassar, while grappling with the difficult question of assessing 'success', particularly to determine whether or not it is an emic, locally defined objective. The task at that point is to identify what, if any, constraints hindered the small enterprises in achieving their objectives.

A fundamental need at the outset however is to establish a working definition of what constitutes a 'small enterprise' for the purposes of this book. In this regard, the theoretical literature is not consistent in its definition of 'small', while the use of what previously was the all-encompassing term 'informal sector' has been largely rejected in more recent theorisations concerning such enterprises, an aspect discussed in detail in Chapter 2. Here, the distinction between 'informal' and 'formal' in the definition of small enterprises is not made, largely because of the fluidity of the legal/illegal position of many of the enterprises in Makassar. In developing a contextually appropriate definition, therefore, the first step was to review the multiple definitions of small enterprises that have been proposed and utilised by Indonesian Government[3] departments and institutions.[4]

Such an experience was rather less helpful than anticipated. Official definitions were, in general, vague and uncertain, a lack of clarity compounded by continuing debates among scholars in this field (for an overview see Dahles, 1999). For this reason, a single consistent definition of small enterprises has been developed and used in this book to avoid ambiguity. The definition adapts the Indonesian Central Bureau of Statistics definition by merging their categories of 'cottage' enterprises (those which employ one to four people), and 'small' enterprises (those which employ five to nineteen people), to construct a single category of enterprises with fewer than twenty workers. Preliminary investigations in Makassar showed that those enterprises officially categorised as 'cottage' or 'small' did not vary significantly in their internal structure due to labour size differences, nor in the entrepreneurs' own understandings of their operational differences.

Thus the chief characteristics of small enterprises according to the working definition preferred here are six in all, as follows:

1   fewer than twenty workers;
2   family workers, or a mixture of family and wage workers;
3   the owner of the enterprise works directly in the production process;
4   flexible working conditions;
5   low profits (certainly less than Rp.1000 million);[5]
6   frequently unlicensed by the Government.

It should be recognised, however, that small enterprises may meet some of these conditions to varying degrees rather than satisfy all of them. For example, many use family as well as some wage labour, provide no employment security, yet require skilled workers and pay wages higher than their larger competitors. In addition, if taxes are paid, this may be in part only. Bribery may also occur as well as the building of patron–client relationships with those in positions of authority. Therefore it is important that differences *among* small enterprises are explicitly recognised, all the more so when one understands that enterprises exist in a diversity of environments and fulfil a very broad range of roles. This means that small enterprises incorporate into their basic organisation the imprint of the setting in which they emerge and operate, 'making it difficult to hammer out a neat definition' (Kabra, 1995: 221).

Uncertainty also surrounds the term 'entrepreneur'. Here it is used with reference to the owner of a small-scale enterprise, or more specifically, to the owner of an independent small enterprise who directs or organises production on a regular basis, and who makes decisions about styles, materials, capital and marketing (Thamrin, 1993). Although one could make a link between an entrepreneur and 'entrepreneurship' in terms of innovation, the connection made in this book is as an enterprise *owner* and *organiser* of production. While consideration was given to substituting what could be seen as a problematic term with a more appropriate Indonesian equivalent, no such generic term was in use. Instead, the interviewees called themselves *tukang mas* (goldsmith), *tukang kayu* (wood craftsperson) and so on, or preferred the English language word 'entrepreneur' themselves. Although the terms *pengusaha* (business owner), *usahawan* (industrialist) or *usahawan industri kecil* (small-scale industrialist) could have been employed, this would have meant adopting a term not used locally to describe the interviewees. Consequently it was decided to use the term 'entrepreneur', as defined above.

This study is based predominantly on field work undertaken in Makassar during 1996 and 1997. During this, a 'multiple method' approach was used to focus on the diversity of the linkages, networks and competition within the small enterprise sector and to explore the significance of the specific socio-cultural environment in which the enterprises operated. Follow-up field work was undertaken during January 1999 in order to assess changes which may have occurred to small enterprises in Makassar since the original research.

Initially, information was collected from 100 in-depth questionnaire interviews with owners of small enterprises (Group A), undertaken by researchers from *Universitas Hasanuddin* (*UNHAS*, a State University in Makassar). After collection, I translated and analysed the information, and used it to complement my own intensive, empirical research based on 200 semi-structured interviews (Group B) with small enterprise owners, of whom Amir was one. Further information was derived from discussions with members of a range of government and non-government agencies involved with small enterprises in the city. Such agencies included the *Departemen Koperasi dan Pembinaan Pengusaha Kecil, Ujung Pandang* (Department of Co-operatives and Small Enterprise Development, Ujung Pandang), *Departemen Perindustrian dan Perdagangan, Tingkat II* (Department for Industry and Trade, Ujung Pandang Municipal Region), and *Kamar Dagang dan Industri Sulawesi Selatan (KADINIA)* (South Sulawesi Chamber of Commerce and Industry).

Of the 100 Group A interviews, fifty each were with 'informal' and 'formal' small enterprises respectively, as defined by the Department of Industry and Trade which supplied information regarding the licences held by enterprises in the city. Promoted by the Department of Industry and Trade, the 'informal' businesses were members of *sentra* (clusters) of small enterprises, often operating without licences, whereas 'formal' businesses held at least a *Surat Izin Tempat Usaha* (licence for a business place, commonly referred to as *SITU*). All the enterprises were further divided into five product categories defined by the Department, namely food, clothing and leather, building materials and chemicals, metals, and handicrafts. Hence, using a stratified sampling procedure, the entrepreneurs of ten officially defined 'informal', and ten 'formal' small enterprises from each of these five categories were interviewed.

Within the food category, *tempe* (deep-fried fermented soya bean 'patties') producers were interviewed in the largest numbers, while others made bread, syrup drinks, sauces, rice flour, soya bean milk and *bakso* (meat ball soup). Most numerous in the clothes and textiles category were general clothes makers (sixteen), while others produced underwear, songkok (traditional Indonesian hat for men) and shoes. The building materials and chemicals category was very general. It included small-scale entrepreneurs who made cement, chairs, glass moulded for windows, fibreglass products, office equipment, floor tiles, general furniture, building materials, harvest threshing machines, rattan products and building lime. The metals category was again broad, ranging from welding, lathe work, blacksmithing and foundry, to oven and stove production, as well as metal car-part fabrication. Finally, the handicraft sector had a significant number of gold and silver producers (sixteen), but there was also a coppersmith, craftspeople producing wooden carved objects and traditional weaving as well.

For the second, Group B, set of interviews the same five product categories were utilised, forty small enterprise entrepreneurs from each being interviewed to give a total of 200 in all. These interviews were undertaken using a loose snowballing technique. Generally one informant knew of many others whom s/he thought would like to be interviewed. As I was particularly interested in examining socio-economic networks and linkages, this gave me the opportunity to talk to many people interacting with each other on a daily basis. These interviews revealed a significant number of 'general tailors' (17 per cent), goldsmiths (15 per cent), window frame, door frame and fence constructors (10 per cent), savoury food producers (7 per cent), as well as building pillar, flowerpot and paving block producers (5 per cent).[6] More 'unusual' enterprises, not found among the initial questionnaire interviews, included traditional ice-cream, candles, aquariums and wooden frames for the back sections of small trucks.

The different sampling methods resulted in Group B entrepreneurs tending to represent the more 'flexible', unorganised and unrecognised of the small enterprises in the city, whist those in Group A had gained some level of formal recognition. In effect this multiple method approach made it possible to gain a detailed picture of a cross-section of small enterprise operations, structures and production methods in Makassar.[7]

Observation, description and discussion, undertaken whenever possible, complemented the interview data discussed above. Significant relevant information was gained from impromptu discussions in shops, street stalls and restaurants, markets, on *pete pete* (minibuses) and in taxis. In this way information was gained regarding welfare, economic status, interaction among family members, safety and conditions in the work place, and so on.

Non-participatory direct observation was undertaken while interviewing members of small enterprises and moving about the areas of the city where small enterprises were concentrated. Participant observation was not undertaken as I did not immerse myself in the everyday affairs of my research subjects, interpersonal interactions with most informants being relatively brief (Howard, 1994; see also Bernard, 1995; Lal, 1996). Although repeat visits were made to the communities where interviews were carried out and observations and discussions undertaken with these people, as well as weddings and parties attended with Hasbi (my assistant and in his own right an owner of a small enterprise), participant observation occurred more with the people connected with the guesthouse where I lived. There I was accepted as a family member, 'sister' or 'cousin', and participated in two weddings, a funeral, numerous Islamic festivals and family parties, and followed the fasting month of *Ramadan*. Many discussions were undertaken covering a wide range of topics from local traditions, impressions of Western lifestyles, Islamic beliefs, to local food favourites.

Many discussants such as these are in the list of key informants (see Appendix 1).[8] As well as Indonesians, expatriates in Makassar are included in this list. The few expatriates whom I came to know and associate with in the city were either development aid workers or academics, and the many evenings spent discussing aspects of our work, local politics and current events provided me with further insight into the city and the life of those who lived there.

The majority of field work for this book was undertaken before the Southeast Asian economic crisis began in 1997, the impacts of which, for small enterprises in Makassar, have been surprisingly varied. In general, nonetheless, as detailed in Chapter 8, it was found during a return visit in 1999 that the impacts on the majority of those studied were not as severe as in other parts of Indonesia due, in part, to Sulawesi's isolated position in the Indonesian economy. The organisational properties of the enterprises studied, as detailed in this book, certainly remained valid.

This exploration of small enterprises in Makassar is presented in nine chapters. The story continues in Chapter 2 with a review and critique of literature on the 'informal sector' and existing theories on petty commodity production. During this discussion it becomes apparent, in the light of more recent debates, that such theories have a number of flaws which make them increasingly problematic as frameworks with which to investigate small enterprises in developing countries. Consequently, some researchers have turned to industrial production theories in a search for greater theoretical validity, and within this context craft production and mass production are contrasted.

The more recent literature on globalisation is also briefly discussed as a way of bringing theories of production closer to the needs of current research on small enterprises. However, problems relating to the globalisation framework are then identified, concerns that highlight the increasingly urgent need to find a more insightful framework with which to examine small enterprises.

In particular, three different approaches have been recognised as giving more agency to those operating at the local level: the post-Fordist, regulationist and flexible specialisation paradigms. Each is introduced as a potential candidate to fill the theoretical gap noted above. Of the three, however, flexible specialisation has attracted increasing support as a possible tool with which to analyse small enterprises in developing countries (Hirst and Zeitlin, 1991; Knorringa, 1996). Yet, following a critique of the approach accompanied by an investigation of past applications of the flexible specialisation approach to developing countries, it is argued that a new framework is required. This must be sufficiently robust to enable meaningful analysis of small enterprises while also acknowledging inter-enterprise linkages, understanding the role of their broader contextual environment, and utilising emic definitions of 'success'.

Chapter 3 therefore proposes a new conceptual approach, the *small enterprise integrative framework*. Within a broader contextual framework than has been proposed previously, this involves the incorporation of the small enterprise parameters of flexible specialisation, namely subcontracting, flexibility in labour relations, networks and trust, as well as clusters and collective efficiency. The essential characteristics of each of these parameters are then reviewed in terms of how they might contribute to a more detailed understanding of the internal dynamics of the enterprises themselves, as well as the interactions among them and other actors in their contextual environment.

Chapter 4 provides essential background details and completes the integrative framework. The economic and political environment of Indonesia is briefly examined, before discussing the multitude of Government policies that have been, at various times, introduced to help small enterprises, and considering the problems involved in their application. The geographical focus then shifts to South Sulawesi and Makassar, to concentrate our attention on the political, economic, social and cultural environment in which the small-scale entrepreneurs were operating.

The first part of the analysis utilising the proposed integrative framework

is undertaken in Chapter 5. This examines the internal dynamics and organisational features of a range of small enterprises in Makassar. Throughout
this, close attention is paid to social, cultural and gender aspects which influence and are influenced by how the entrepreneurs operate within their
political and economic environment. Then, in Chapter 6, an analysis of interactions and networks among enterprises and with other actors in their
contextual environment is undertaken. As the analysis progresses, it becomes
clear that for some small enterprises in Makassar, subsistence and a daily concern for survival offers perhaps the most relevant appraisal of the situation of
entrepreneurs such as Amir. For this reason aspects of 'survivalism' must be
considered, local conditions and constraints limiting some small enterprises
from reaching their emically defined full potential.[9]

Such barriers to the operations of many small enterprises in Makassar are
then analysed in Chapter 7. Some of these came from within the enterprises,
while some were associated with the local socio-cultural and political environment. Chapter 8 then analyses the shifting fortunes of the enterprises
studied as a consequence of the economic crisis or *krismon*. This exploration
again highlights the usefulness of the integrative framework. It is found that
due to specific local conditions, the responses of small enterprises to the
changes have been more varied than interpretations using other frameworks
would have revealed. While the fortunes of a few small enterprises have
shifted, the majority continue to trade on the margins within the archipelago,
not only economically, but also geographically.

2   Approaches to small enterprise research

To understand the choices we face today, we must clarify the choices made in the past.

(Piore and Sabel, 1984: 4)

The purpose of this chapter is to lay the theoretical foundation for a discussion of the organisation and operations of small enterprises in Makassar. Initially it provides a critical understanding of previous and current theoretical debates concerning small enterprises and industrial organisation. We begin this journey with a brief critique of the informal/formal sector and petty commodity production approaches, as conceptualised in developing countries. Following the realisation of the limited utility of these dualistic perspectives, some small enterprise researchers have turned to industrial production theories in the quest for theoretical validity. Such theories are outlined, and the concepts of craft production and mass production are introduced.

The focus then turns to more recent literature on globalisation, the argument advanced being that this should bring discussions closer to the needs of current research concerning small enterprises. Problems arising from the globalisation framework are raised in the context of the global/local nexus, highlighted by recent theorists who have examined the importance of local agency and context for industrial change, so emphasising an increasing need for a more rigorous and comprehensive framework. Thus, the theoretical discussion culminates in the identification of a number of different paradigms which have emerged to fill the theoretical impasse. From these, the flexible specialisation approach emerges as a framework from which potentially useful *building blocks* for examining small enterprise organisation in developing countries might be gained.

DUALISTIC PERSPECTIVES

The 'informal sector'

Since their initial appearance in the 1940s and 1950s, dualistic models have tended to occupy centre stage in research on small enterprises in developing countries. At that time the informal sector was regarded as the 'declining remnant of pre-capitalist economies' in a number of such countries (Dewar and Watson, 1990: 1). The informal sector was believed to refer to the activities of 'local' people in colonised countries which were not integrated into the colonial economic and social structure (Dewar and Watson, 1990). As a result, the sector was seen as backward, irrational and inefficient. Indeed, according to McGee (1978), it was not until the late 1960s that the importance of informal sector activities to the economic survival of a large proportion of the population was recognised.

Writing in 1953, Boeke introduced an early concept of dualistic production systems based on an examination of the Dutch East Indies. He defined two social systems: the capitalist, imported from abroad; and the domestic social system. This model was to provide a starting point for much subsequent work in Southeast Asia (Evers and Mehmet, 1994), including that of Clifford Geertz, who in 1963 identified the 'firm-centred' and 'bazaar' economies in his work focusing on two towns in Java and Bali, Indonesia (see also Jackson, 1978). The 'firm-centred' economic sector was where 'trade and industry occur through a set of impersonally defined social institutions which organize a variety of specialized occupations with respect to some particular productive or distributive end' (Geertz, 1963: 28). The 'bazaar economy' was, in turn, 'the independent activities of a set of highly competitive commodity traders who relate to one another mainly by means of an incredible volume of *ad hoc* acts of exchange' (ibid.: 29). This two-sector model was subsequently utilised by McGee and Yeung in their book on the informal sector in Southeast Asia. In this, they argue that although Southeast Asian cities are 'the outposts of modernization in their societies, they often contain sizeable traditional sectors in which the pattern of economic activity and life are very different from the so-called modern sector' (McGee and Yeung, 1977: 20).

In 1971, at the 'Conference on Urban Unemployment in Africa' held at the University of Sussex, Keith Hart coined the specific term 'informal sector' (Hart, 1973; Moser, 1978). Hart saw the informal sector as being distinct from wage-earning employment (the formal sector), the distinction between the two sectors being the 'degree of rationalization of work' (Roberts, 1990: 33). Labour within the formal sector was recruited on a permanent basis for fixed wages, whereas the informal sector consisted of irregular forms of employment and self-employment (Roberts, 1990, 1994). Despite its relative complexity however, Hart developed a classification of the two sectors based

Table 2.1 Income opportunities in a Third World city

Formal income opportunities
• Public sector wages.
• Private sector wages.
• Transfer payments: pensions, unemployment benefits.

Informal income opportunities: legitimate
• Primary and secondary activities: farming, market gardening, building contractors and associated activities, self employed artisans, shoemakers, tailors, manufacturers of beer and spirits.
• Tertiary enterprises with relatively large capital inputs: housing, transport, utilities, commodity speculation, rentier activities.
• Small-scale distribution: market operatives, petty traders, street hawkers, caterers in food and drink, bar attendants, carriers, commission agents, dealers.
• Other services: musicians, launderers, shoeshiners, barbers, night soil removers, photographers, vehicle repair and other maintenance workers, brokerage and middlemanship, ritual services, magic and medicine.
• Private transfer payments: gifts and similar flows of money and goods between persons; borrowing, begging.

Informal income opportunities: illegitimate
• Services: hustlers and spivs[1] in general; receivers of stolen goods; usury and pawnbroking (at illegal interest rates); drug-pushing, prostitution, poncing[2] ('pilot boy'), smuggling, bribery, political corruption Tammany Hall style, protection rackets.
• Transfers: petty theft (e.g. pickpockets), larceny (e.g. burglary and armed robbery), speculation and embezzlement, confidence tricksters (e.g. money doublers), gambling.

Source: adapted from Hart (1973: 69)

Notes
1 Hustlers and spivs: People who make a living by underhand dealings; black marketeer.
2 Poncing: The act of obtaining customers for a prostitute or brothel, in return for a share of the earnings (the role of a ponce, 'pilot boy' or pimp).

on the income opportunities available to people in a city (Table 2.1). It should be noted that his division made it possible for members of the same household to gain employment in different sectors of the economy.

International Labour Office

Within a year, Hart's dualistic concept of the informal sector was adopted by the International Labour Office (ILO) in their 1972 Kenya Mission Report (ILO, 1972), and was used in much of their subsequent urban research, as it was also by other international organisations (Bromley, 1978; Peattie, 1987). The ILO's widely quoted interpretation and classification of the contrasting characteristics of the informal and formal sectors is shown in Table 2.2.

Table 2.2 The informal and formal sectors as classified by the ILO

Informal sector	Formal sector
• ease of entry	• difficult entry
• reliance upon indigenous resources	• frequent reliance on overseas resources
• family ownership of enterprises	• corporate ownership
• small scale of operations	• large scale of operation
• labour intensive and adapted technology	• capital intensive and often imported technology
• skills acquired outside the formal school system	• formally acquired skills, often expatriate
• unregulated and competitive markets	• protected markets (through tariffs, quotas and trade licences)

Source: Bromley (1978: 1033)

From the early 1970s, however, other researchers produced their own interpretations of the dualistic approach. One was the more sharply focused perspective suggested by Mazumdar (1976) and his colleagues working at the World Bank. They perceived the informal sector as a labour market phenomenon (Mazumdar, 1976; Moser, 1978; Lubell, 1991), identifying a specific dichotomy between the unprotected informal sector and the protected formal sector. Formal sector protection arose from the actions of unions, governments or both acting together (Mazumdar, 1976), whereas by comparison, the informal sector was characterised by industries that were 'unprotected' by company policy, government regulations or trade union action, and to which entry was relatively easy (Lubell, 1991). Nonetheless, as in Indonesia, there are substantial difficulties in relating such definitions to developing countries which commonly have strict controls over union activities.

Critical assessment of the dualistic framework

Almost immediately after the informal sector concept first appeared, criticism of the approach also emerged. One of the strongest concerns was that by placing the informal sector in opposition to the formal sector an artificial dichotomy was created (DiGregorio, 1994). There was also much criticism from authors working with other perspectives concerning this formal/informal sector dichotomy (see e.g. Slater, 1973; Bromley, 1978; Kahn, 1978, 1980; Forbes, 1981b; Guinness, 1986; Murphy, 1990; Turner, 1994; Kabra, 1995). Dos Santos (1979: 25) for one, questions the contemporary relevance, contending that 'the "modern"/"traditional" dichotomy, prevalent and perhaps valid in the past, has no place in a world now dominated by innovation, diffusion and rapidly changing consumption patterns'. Indeed, what has been conceptualised as a dichotomy between informal and formal is in reality 'a continuity, not only in static but also in dynamic terms', as will be investigated in the case of small enterprises in Makassar (Huq and Sultan, 1991: 149).[1]

Petty commodity production

While the approach based on the informal/formal sector dichotomy was being developed by Hart, the ILO and others from the 1970s, the increasing wealth of information linking small enterprises in the 'informal sector' to those involved in other sectors of the economy forced many researchers to seek alternative frameworks. The most prominent of these emerged from a neo-Marxist critique of utilising informal sector terminology in developing countries, and subsequently the 'modes of production' approach became popular.[2]

Neo-Marxists saw informality as 'the product of the unequal development of capitalism in non-industrialised urban areas' (Chickering and Salahdine, 1991: 10) with the 'informal sector' playing an essential role in providing a low-wage reserve of labour. While essentially still dividing the urban economy into two parts - the capitalist and pre-capitalist modes of production - the neo-Marxist 'modes of production' approach also paid closer attention to inter-firm relationships, and was more pluralistic in nature (Kahn, 1974). Several forms of pre-capitalist mode of production were recognised, one being labelled 'petty commodity production'. This aspect of the model became increasingly popular as a tool with which to examine the development of, and relationships surrounding, what had previously been called the 'informal sector' (van Diermen, 1997), which following this approach, was stated by Murphy (1990: 164) to be 'neither autonomous nor complementary to the formal sector; rather, it is subordinate and exploited by the latter'.

The subordinate position that the petty commodity production sector occupied within the 'modes of production' approach formed an integral dimension of the conceptual framework formulated by Gerry (1977, cited in McGee, 1978) and reproduced in Table 2.3. Similarly, McGee (1978: 17) contended that the dualistic model was too simplistic and masked 'the real economic relationships which operate in Third World cities'. It could also be argued that the classifications used were an attempt to break down the rigid Marxist categories of bourgeoisie, proletariat and lumpenproletariat, so as to be more applicable to the situation found in developing countries (McGee, 1976).

Those who studied petty commodity production from a neo-Marxist perspective also maintained that over a period of time the capitalist mode of production would eventually replace pre-capitalist modes of production. This period of transformation was of specific interest to neo-Marxists concerned with developing countries, including Moser (1978), Forbes (1981a, 1981b) and Gerry (1987). Of these, Forbes (1981b: 111) argued that the transition to capitalism from pre-capitalist modes of production was 'not a straightforward one of invasion and succession' but a complex process involving interdependence and qualitative change. Forbes claimed this meant that only petty commodity producers assisting in the reproduction of capitalism survived, while those who were competing for markets and labour were dissolved (van Diermen, 1997). This simultaneously produced development and under-

Table 2.3 Labour markets' relationships in capitalist and peripheral capitalist
societies

Section of labour force	Mode of reproduction of labour power	Capital–labour relationship
1. Workers in capitalist industry (i.e.'formal sector')	Repetitive sale of labour power in the capitalist production process	Real subjection of labour by capital
2. Casual workers in capitalist industry (i.e. industrial reserve army)	Intermittent sale of labour-power plus some petty commodity production and/or services	Real (but intermittent) subjection of labour by capital, alternating with formal subjection of labour by capital
3. Workers exercising skills within a coexisting mode of production (marginal pole of the economy) subordinated to the capitalist mode of production (i.e. the 'informal' sector)	Petty commodity production, including some apprentice exploitation	Typically formal subjection of labour to capital on a relatively permanent basis
4. Unsuccessful sellers of labour power, the 'unemployed' urban 'lumpenproletariat', Marx's 'dangerous class'	Combined elements of 1, 2 and 3, but also possibly begging, extortion, political 'employment', family parasitism, 'illegal transfers'	Minimal relations with organised capital

Source: adapted from Gerry (1977, in McGee, 1978: 18)

development, allowing productive enterprises using advanced technology to exist alongside low-productivity enterprises dependent on labour power and primitive technology (Forbes, 1981b).

It was argued by McGee (1978) that capitalist production had not resulted in the disappearance of non-capitalist modes of production for several reasons. First, the goods and services produced by the petty commodity production sector were often unprofitable for the capitalist mode of production to produce. Second, the existence of a large petty commodity sector with underemployment and low incomes was an important factor in maintaining low wage levels and providing extra labour when necessary. Third, a petty commodity sector based around family employment was important for governments of developing countries, as it reduced social welfare needs, resulting in more capital being available for the capitalist 'formal' sector. The latter thus gained direct benefits from the existence of the petty commodity production sector (Davies, 1979; Evers and Mehmet, 1994), for, as Moser (1978: 1060) observes:

Petty production is dependent on capitalism while at the same time the capitalist mode of production benefits from the existence and relative viability of petty production for the maintenance of a low level of subsistence and a low cost of labour reproduction.

Followers of the petty commodity production approach reached conclusions which challenged the informal sector theorists' perceptions of the nature of informal sector growth. They pointed out that the levels of capital accumulation in the petty commodity production sector were constrained by factors which related to the whole socio-economic system. Thus, instead of the relationship between the two sectors being benign, it was exploitative (Moser, 1978). Legislation relating to small enterprises and petty traders in Southeast Asia provides evidence of this type of strategy, with periods of general laxity towards participants often followed by forceful restrictions on activities. As Davies (1979: 101) notes:

> The optimum capitalist strategy is not one of elimination but rather of keeping the [petty commodity] sector an optimum size, not too big so as not to represent dangerous competition to the formal sector, but not so small as to have no influence on wages.

Accordingly, many neo-Marxists believed that only radical change could improve the position of the poor in developing countries (Bromley, 1978). They dismissed positive, marginal government reforms towards the petty commodity sector as naive in their approach or 'cynical in their intent' (Gerry, 1987: 112).

Although many of the conceptions of the position of petty commodity producers in the economy upheld by the neo-Marxists appear to be still relevant, there are a number of issues which need to be addressed when contemplating the use of this perspective. The assumptions made by many neo-Marxists about the dominant–subordinate relationships and conservation–dissolution forces introduced by McGee (1979) are now being questioned by those working in this field. In particular, they query whether petty commodity producers will ever be replaced by capitalist producers (Teltscher, 1994; van Diermen, 1995, 1997). It has also been suggested that the approach tends to downplay the importance of local activities and has been accused of disallowing 'traditional' sectors in developing countries a history of their own (Corbridge, 1986; see also McGee, 1991, 1995).

The informal sector and petty commodity production approaches have become increasingly recognised as inadequate when one requires a conceptual framework with which to explore, in the current world environment, the structures and interactions of small enterprises in developing countries. Many such economies, especially in Southeast Asia, have grown and diversified significantly since the 1970s, and a number of small enterprises have emerged that do not fit within frameworks formulated earlier (van Diermen, 1997). To take account of this change, there has been a shift among some small enterprise researchers towards adopting an 'industrial production' perspective to provide an acceptable theoretical foundation.

INDUSTRIAL PRODUCTION PERSPECTIVES

Recently, increased interest in examining small enterprises from an industrial production approach has led to a re-investigation of the historical development of industrial paradigms and the position of small enterprises within these paradigms. An appropriate starting point for such an examination is *craft production*, followed by consideration of mass production, and its subsequent decline in predominance as *globalisation* tendencies have strengthened their influence over industrial production. Understanding each of these aspects is critical to our comprehension of why one specific industrial production approach, flexible specialisation, has in recent years gained favour among some small enterprise researchers.

Craft production

Craft production, or 'craft systems' as Piore and Sabel (1984: 5) have identified them, were associated with small enterprises operating in Western Europe in the nineteenth century. In the most advanced of such enterprises, 'skilled workers used sophisticated general-purpose machinery to turn out a wide and constantly changing assortment of goods for large but constantly shifting markets' (ibid.: 5; see also Goody, 1982). 'Craft systems' were founded on the premise that machines could enhance a craftsperson's skills, allowing a worker to utilise such skills across a wider range of products. Hence the more flexible the machine, the wider the scope for the craftsperson's production. Success of these enterprises relied heavily on co-operation, rather than on competition, with the overall picture being of 'small producers, each specialized in one line of work and dependent on the others' (Piore and Sabel, 1984: 20).

   In the nineteenth century there were a number of industrial districts in Europe and the United States of America that experienced significant success following such patterns of production. Among these were 'silks in Lyon; ribbons, hardware and speciality steel in Solingen, Remscheid, and Sheffield; calicoes in Alsace; woollen and cotton textiles in Roubaix; cotton goods in Philadelphia and Pawtucket' (Piore and Sabel, 1984: 28). Firms in these Marshallian industrial districts (named after their initial theorist, Alfred Marshall) often developed or exploited technologies without expanding. The larger firms in the districts, while utilising sophisticated machinery, usually did *not* produce standardised goods, a feature that placed them in direct contrast to mass production systems discussed below. The craft-based industrial districts of the kinds listed above were characterised by three main features:

first, the district's relationship to the market, with a wide range of goods being produced for the local and overseas market, goods being adapted in response to changes in taste, and new markets being established; second, widely applicable technology used in a flexible manner; and third, organisations created that counterbalanced co-operation with competition among firms, encouraging consistent innovation (Piore and Sabel, 1984; Sunley, 1992).[3]

Mass production

The 'First Industrial Divide' in the mid-nineteenth century saw mass production displace craft production as the predominant mode of manufacturing, initially in Britain and the United States of America. This shift in the dominant production mode subsequently prevented craft production systems from expanding in Continental Europe as well (Piore and Sabel, 1984).

Mass production has been defined by Hirst and Zeitlin (1991: 2) as 'the manufacture of standardised products in high volumes using special-purpose machinery and predominately unskilled labour'. The more standard the goods produced, the wider the potential market and yet, at the same time, the more specialised became the machinery of production. This in turn required a parallel increase in demand for the goods produced and hence the mass production of standardised goods was linked with mass consumption. Early examples of such transformations in Britain occurred in the craft sector of Birmingham metalwork shops, which responded to the increase in demand for bicycles in the 1890s by turning to mass production methods (see Lorenz, 1991, 1992; Sabel and Zeitlin, 1997).

Mass production became especially dominant and successful in the United States of America and Western Europe from the 1920s until the end of the post-war boom in the late 1960s.[4] According to Piore and Sabel (1984: 49): 'Mass production offered those industries in which it was developed and applied enormous gains in productivity – gains that increased in step with the growth of these industries.' This system relied on a division of labour marked by a high fragmentation of tasks and a split between skilled and unskilled workers (Graham, 1991). Industrial society was thus based on 'a homogeneous, male, full-time working class, concentrated in large plants in large industrial cities' (Hirst and Zeitlin, 1991: 9).

Despite the initial strengths of mass production, from the 1960s onwards a number of social and economic changes eroded the mass production pattern of development and the hegemony of the model was threatened. The result was a crisis of deindustrialisation, rising unemployment and capital flight (Scott and Cooke, 1988; Storper and Scott, 1989). Concurrently, however, the number of flexible, labour and skill intensive industries continued to grow. These were either producing inputs for mass consumption industries or directly serving the consumer market. Indeed, it has been argued that the very machinery required to undertake mass production makes visible a paradox in the argument of the overall significance of mass production, since the machinery required was highly specialised. The production crisis impacted on businesses throughout the world and initiated a restructuring of production on a global scale.

Globalisation

Since the 1960s then, the world economy has undergone a process of restructuring that has redefined capital–labour relationships and the role of the state. This transformation has been labelled globalisation, defined by Dieleman and Hamnett (1994: 357) as 'the growing integration of various parts of the world into a global economy and global financial system'. Increased interdependency across national boundaries has occurred with new links developing, especially among multinational corporations, banks and states.

Restructuring was a reaction to a number of crises which coincided with widespread social unrest. Among such crises, raw material shortages, rising oil and commodity prices, rising wage costs in developed countries, the increasing instability of the Bretton Woods monetary system, and the increasing fiscal deficits faced by many governments, all contributed (Piore and Sabel 1984; see also Gordon, 1988; Hettne, 1995; Preston, 1998). As a result, a new model of capitalist development emerged with multinational corporations (MNCs), banks and states all striving to gain maximum advantage while at the same time promoting economic recovery (Thrift, 1989; Fagan and Le Heron, 1994). The new world economy included the globalisation of production, trade, services, labour flows and financial circuits, all processes which altered the links between developed and less developed countries and many of the conditions within these countries (Gilbert and Gugler, 1992).

During the past thirty to forty years therefore, a notable global redistribution of industrial production has occurred, two key factors being the increasing dominance of MNCs and the geographical relocation of labour intensive production (Clairmonte and Cavanagh, 1983; Dicken, 1993). Newly industrialised countries (NICs), for instance in Southeast Asia, historically perceived as being at the periphery of global production, have become major focal points for changes in labour intensive manufacturing (Douglass, 2001).[5] In reality:

> The world economy is changing in fundamental ways. The changes add up to a basic transition, a structural shift in international markets and in the production base of advanced countries. It will change how production is organized, where it occurs and who plays what role in the process.
>
> (Cohen and Zysman, 1987: 79)

Part of this fundamental transition has been connected to the operations of multinational companies which have been able to locate and relocate industries at an international scale. They have been able to do so, in part at least, because of a number of technological developments including improvements in communications, transport technology and labour organisation (Dicken, 1993; Hettne, 1995). These developments have also included an increasingly dynamic and diverse number of inter-firm production arrangements involving vertical and/or horizontal linkages, such as subcontracting and homework, that increase the flexibility demanded of labour. The latter has been important in a number of developing countries in supporting rapid economic growth through the encouragement of international business linkages. However, as will be seen in the case of Makassar, many of these flexible forms also appear to be residuals of past labour structures, albeit increasingly modified.

There is no doubt that over the past three decades dramatic transformations have occurred in the global economy. Significant changes to production organisation have accompanied technological advances, a major restructuring of global markets, and changes of economic management policy at all levels of organisation (Hirst and Zeitlin, 1991). Much has been written about the nature of the processes at work. Some contend that a number of generalisations have been made concerning the homogeneity of these processes. It is argued that, in reality, globalisation is 'creating neither a stable nor a homogeneous globalized economy or society' (Luke, 1994: 620). This viewpoint is sound, as is the assertion that 'there is no single wave of globalisation washing over or flattening diverse divisions of labour in regions and industrial branches' (Mittelman, 1995: 279).[6]

In contrast to many past perspectives examining small enterprises, the globalisation approach considers regions in terms of their place in a broader, more encompassing environment. In adopting this approach, small enterprises have typically been generalised as having roles either as subcontractors or petty producers, while continuing to undertake the reproduction of the poorer sectors of the community (Aeroe, 1992; Lipietz, 1993). Thus it may be argued that the globalisation paradigm lends itself to interpretations which tend to hide local processes occurring during broader global changes. On this point Lipietz (1993: 12) argues that globalisation approaches deal 'too lightly with the irreducible specific characteristics of local society, of the role of the local state, of the nature of links and local social arrangements'. Instead it must be emphasised that the processes of globalisation are generating 'many unusual new effects at the local, regional and international levels of operation' (Luke, 1994: 620).

Because of the dynamic nature of globalisation processes, previous literature concerning such changes and the role of small enterprises within the global environment is now coming under close scrutiny as more locally based studies are undertaken. These are revealing that while globalisation is indeed a diverse and complex process, these qualities are intensified in subtle ways by local contextual differences. This point is well made by Mittelman (1995: 273) who argues that 'although globalisation is frequently characterised as a homogenising force, it fuses with local conditions in diverse ways, thereby generating, not eroding, striking differences among social functions'. Local development may be closely linked to globalisation forces, but it is not solely determined by them (Douglass, 1998).

It has been suggested that the empirical grounding of the globalisation discourse has not kept pace with its theorisation since the validity of the globalisation approach can only stand when tested by empirical studies in specific contexts (Cox, 1993, 1995). In reaction to this concern, there has been increasing attention paid to the interface between global and local processes currently underway. This has given rise to terms such as 'global–local nexus' (Dicken, 1994: 102), 'global–local dialectics' and 'glocalisation' in order to explain the alignment of local–global relations in the 1990s (Peck and Tickell, 1994b: 282).

The globalisation approach can alert us to a number of factors, often overlooked by previous approaches, that are highly significant in contextualising small enterprises within developing countries. These include the degree of flexibility apparent in production methods and labour, as well as the varied and numerous linkages between large and small enterprises. Nonetheless, there are still additional issues which need to be focused upon for such a paradigm to be of direct relevance while examining the current dynamics occurring in and around small enterprises in developing countries, not least in Southeast Asian NICs. The relevance of this assertion is well captured by Amin and Robins (1990: 28) who observe that:

> As far as the geography of change is concerned, it is necessary to grasp the coexistence and combination of localising and globalising, centripetal and centrifugal forces. The current restructuring process is a matter of a whole repertoire of spatial strategies, dependent upon situated contexts and upon balances of power.

There are thus a number of uncertainties still to be resolved in the debate about globalisation which in turn means that the concept 'must be regarded as problematic, incomplete and contradictory' (Mittelman, 1995: 273). At the local scale it is now being recognised that there are a host of actors, such as local power-holders, as well as ordinary citizens and workers able to respond to, facilitate or reject external forces of change. These actors belong to a category described by Dicken (1994: 122) as being the 'really seriously local' which plays a key role in the development and performance of small enterprises in developing countries. Perhaps, therefore, it is necessary to 'rethink globalization and therefore rework the relationships it establishes' (Kelly, 1999: 386). Indeed, as Douglass (1998: 307) argues, there has come

> a growing recognition of the importance of local context, of historically

specific, socially produced differences in the ways that larger global forces are filtered, challenged, manipulated, ignored and embraced by the constituent social, political and economic forces within each local setting.

THREE POTENTIAL APPROACHES

Perhaps the most important point to emerge from the above discussion on globalisation is that an approach is still required for examining small enterprises in developing countries that gives agency to all the players involved. Three potential approaches have emerged from recent debates on restructuring: the *post-Fordist*, *regulationist*, and *flexible specialisation* paradigms. While many uncertainties still surround these perspectives, DiGregorio (1994) has suggested that each is a potential advance on previous approaches applied to small enterprises. In this regard, the emerging perspectives appear to focus both on concerns largely ignored by 'informal' sector and petty commodity production theorists of the past, and on acknowledging those participants who have received little attention from followers of broader globalisation approaches.

Post-Fordism

Post-Fordism, a much less coherent concept than Fordism and the associated mass production literature, might best be described as 'a way of bundling together a series of economic and social changes' (Hirst and Zeitlin, 1991: 10). Among other concerns, post-Fordist research encompasses analyses into the uses of production methods considered to be more flexible and diverse than those used in Fordist production. These methods may include programmable machinery, more flexibly deployed labour, vertical disintegration of large firms and a greater reliance on inter-firm relations, such as subcontracting (Gertler, 1994).

The literature on post-Fordism is broad in its interpretation of economic and social change. Indeed, there is still much debate about the extent to which the shift from a Fordist regime to more adaptable structures is a permanent change and how far-reaching any such changes will be in their long-term impacts. Not surprisingly therefore, there is no one version of post-Fordism, but a diverse range of varied and contradictory arguments surrounding the concept's interpretation. This complexity demonstrates why the literature on post-Fordism 'must be considered as a debate rather than an achieved or universally accepted theory of transition' (Amin, 1994: 3). Nevertheless, even if that is the case, 'few would deny that there has been a significant change in industrial organisation' (Rasmussen *et al.*, 1992: 2).

Although post-Fordist approaches often attempt to highlight local differences in economic, social and cultural arenas, many proponents emphasise, at the same time, capitalist production and nation state control, hence marginalising non-capitalist production (Graham, 1992). Post-Fordism, in effect, often privileges capitalism as the site of fundamental change, while changes in non-capitalist settings are seen to be less influential or significant. Like many other knowledges of industrial society,

> post-Fordist theory provides a distinctive and partial story of those complexities; by highlighting certain processes, it inevitably suppresses others, creating in its emphasis a knowledge of social aspects while attempting – by virtue of its macro-orientation – to embrace the social whole.
>
> (Graham, 1992: 398)

Proponents of post-Fordism have been accused of using the paradigm to offer 'an embracing narrative of post-1980 capitalist development, modified for different national settings' (Graham, 1992: 405). The economy takes the lead, with culture responding. Yet as Gartman (1998) argues, the development of the economy and culture are more complex and uneven than this allows. In addition, while post-Fordists usually acknowledge differences within and between societies, they allow no room for diverse and contrasting *approaches* to contemporary development. Instead, post-Fordism 'subsumes theoretical diversity to an (admittedly complex) common story, narrated from a "universal" (that is, unsituated) point of view' (Graham, 1992: 405). Yet it has been argued that it is inappropriate to support a totalising description of the changes occurring to the political economy of capitalism (Rustin, 1989). More specifically, as Leborgne and Lipietz (1988: 263) contend, 'it must be understood that future spatial configurations cannot be deduced from the features of any one model'. Capital does not operate as a single entity, and individuals operate different strategies in their quest for further accumulation (Morris, 1988).

Due to such conceptual shortcomings, a number of different 'schools of thought' have emerged. While these have been influenced by the broad post-Fordist literature, each nevertheless comes to its own conclusions about the current directions and processes of production, including those of small enterprises. Of these schools, the most often discussed are the regulationist, the flexible accumulation and the flexible specialisation models.

Regulation school

It has been suggested that between the proponents of the post-Fordism and flexible specialisation approaches stand the followers of regulation theory. According to Hirst and Zeitlin (1991: 18) they comprise:

> a large but elusive 'middle ground' which seeks to combine the openness and contingency of the flexible specialisation approach with a continuing insistence on the systematic nature of capitalism as a mode of production and the centrality of class struggle in its development.

The French 'regulation school', regarded as the most developed and important representative of this approach, proposed an analysis of capitalist development which took as its point of departure the concepts of *regime of accumulation* and *mode of regulation* (Hirst and Zeitlin, 1991). In this view, a regime of accumulation describes the 'stabilization over a long period of the allocation of the net product between consumption and accumulation' (Lipietz, 1986: 19), a process similar to that associated with Fordism, whereby mass production and mass consumption grew at similar rates (Graham, 1992). A mode of regulation is 'a complex of institutions and norms which secure, at least for certain periods, the adjustment of individual agents and social groups to the overarching principles of the accumulation regime' (Hirst and Zeitlin, 1991: 19; see also Aglietta, 1979; Murdoch, 1995; Gartman, 1998).

Although it has been argued that an emergent post-Fordist regime of accumulation is yet to be fully determined (Hirst and Zeitlin, 1991), Harvey (1989) has defined the specific process in the context of the transition to post-Fordism. He labels this *flexible accumulation,* which he defines as resting 'on flexibility with respect to labour processes, labour markets, products, and patterns of consumption' (Harvey, 1989: 147).

Harvey's flexible accumulation regime raises questions about the 'potential role of flexible production technologies in extricating the advanced industrial economies from their present predicament' (Schoenberger, 1988: 246). The current trend in developed countries, Harvey (1989) suggests, is towards an increase in subcontracting arrangements and a reduction of core workers. Such subcontracting increases opportunities for small business formation and encourages the re-emergence of a range of previous labour systems including 'domestic, artisanal, familial (patriarchal), and paternalistic ("godfather", "gov'nor" or even Mafia like)' (Harvey, 1989: 152). Paralleling this has been a rapid growth in other forms of industrial organisation including the '"black", "informal" or "underground" economies' (ibid.). These have included the introduction of immigrant groups into flexible labour organisational modes, as well as other groups often discriminated against, among them the unemployed.

Drawing on dual market theory, Harvey (1989) argues that at the *core* of any one economic sphere there is a group consisting of a shrinking number of employees with full-time permanent jobs. This group enjoys job security and relatively generous pension and insurance rights. The *periphery*, on the other hand, consists of two (Harvey, 1989) or three groups (Atkinson, 1985) depending on the explanation followed. One, offered by Atkinson (1985), contends that the first peripheral group consists of people with jobs which may be full-time and flexible but which can be easily filled from the external labour market due to the lack of firm-specific skills involved. The second peripheral group consists of those on contracts who are called upon to match the changing requirements of production, while a third peripheral group has jobs which are not firm-specific, such as subcontractors, self-employed 'jobbers', outsourcing and temporary workers (Thompson, 1995). Such flexible employment arrangements in themselves do not cause employment dissatisfaction, as flexibility can sometimes be mutually beneficial (Harvey, 1989). Nonetheless, when insurance, pension rights, wage levels and job security are taken into account, the situation does not appear to be at all positive for the general working population (Graham, 1992).

In addition, according to Harvey (1989), although Fordist firms could adopt new technologies, what has tended to occur instead has been the rise of entirely new networks of industrial forms or the integration of Fordism into a system of subcontracting and outsourcing, thereby producing greater flexibility. This has been paralleled by an increase in the turnover time of products so that goods, especially textiles, clothing and computer software are outdated more rapidly than was possible under Fordism. This has been coupled, on the consumption side, by increasing attention to changing fashions, a point acknowledged by Harvey (1989: 156) who observes that relatively stable Fordist modernism 'has given way to all the ferment, instability, and fleeting qualities of a postmodernist aesthetic that celebrates difference, ephemerality, spectacle, fashion, and the commodification of cultural forms'.

In a critical assessment of these core–periphery models proposed by Harvey (1989) and others, Christopherson (1989: 132) contends that they have serious limitations, because 'multiple sources of labour segmentation (both old and new) are obscured by a dualistic model'. Driven by the relations between capital and labour, the model is limited in its ability to interpret changes in power relationships *within* the workforce, as it neglects to examine the actual formation of labour classes. This is a key factor that highlights the inappropriateness of the approach in developing countries where such class formation often remains a highly politicised issue. In addition, because the focus is on the firm as a self-contained unit, work patterns tend to be explained in terms of changes in individual firm requirements (Christopherson, 1989; Murdoch, 1995). Tickell and Peck (1995) are also sceptical that it is possible to make assumptions concerning a future regime of accumulation, since there are so many reservations concerning the sustainability of such a regime. Not only that, Murdoch (1995: 735) argues regulationists have an inclination to 'fall back on the general tendencies of capitalism as a mode of production to explain the likely shape of the "new order"'. It is with such criticisms in mind that we turn now to a close scrutiny of flexible specialisation as an approach which offers greater potential for the examination of small enterprises in developing countries, such as those enterprises comprising the Makassar sample in Indonesia.

Flexible specialisation

> the flexible specialisation paradigm has blasted open a new trail in small enterprise research.
>
> (Rasmussen *et al.*, 1992: 4)

The flexible specialisation paradigm was originally proposed by Piore and Sabel in their seminal work *The Second Industrial Divide* (1984). Espousing views that were somewhat related to regulation theory, they argued that the Fordist mass production system would be followed by a regime based upon flexible specialisation. This would incorporate a return to craft production, albeit via the application of computer technology (Graham, 1991). Writing later in the 1980s, similar conclusions were reached by Scott (1988), as well as by Storper and Scott (1989) who drew on the French regulationist perspective informed by neo-Marxist literature to examine the division of labour and 'the external effects of agglomeration' (Lipietz, 1993: 13; see also Amin and Robins, 1990). However, at a broader level of generalisation, Hirst and Zeitlin (1991: 2) considered there to be significant differences between post-Fordist approaches and the flexible specialisation paradigm. They suggested that while 'post-Fordism sees productive systems as integrated and coherent totalities, flexible specialization identifies complex and variable connections between technology, institutions and politics'.

Flexible specialisation, then, 'has been used to capture new ways of organising industrial production, which allegedly differ from the general Fordist pattern of post-war industrial development', and hence resulted in the 'Second Industrial Divide' (Rasmussen *et al.*, 1992: 2). In their work, Piore and Sabel (1984) did not provide a clear definition of flexible specialisation, an omission that has allowed room for numerous interpretations of the concept. Similarly, there has also been a range of suggestions concerning how it relates to specific situations in both developed and developing countries (Aeroe, 1992). Thus the concept of flexible specialisation has been used in various ways – as a general theoretical model of industrial change, as well as a specific model of the organisation of production – that add to the complexity surrounding current debates (Schmitz, 1989; Hirst and Zeitlin, 1991; Morris and Lowder, 1992).

Furthermore, it is also important to recognise that the flexible specialisation concept has been used to examine change at both the macro and micro levels. At the macro level, the term has been related to an examination of the move away from mass production systems to more diversified systems where flexibility and innovation are vital aspects. At the micro level on the other hand, flexible specialisation has been used to explore an innovative style of industrial organisation, one able to respond to demands for increasing innovation and flexibility. In this latter respect, the term has been related to skilled workers using general purpose machinery, able to respond to changing market demands (Rasmussen *et al.*, 1992). An extension of this flexibility to the inter-firm level allows for the 'discovery of dense webs of inter-firm linkages [that] outdate analyses which focus on the enterprise as an isolated unit' (Rasmussen *et al.*, 1992: 2). For this reason, the concept of flexible specialisation may be used to explain linkages among firms of equal status, as well as those involved in vertical subcontracting arrangements. This is one of the major strengths of the approach.

Due to the broad variety of industrial organisation that the flexible specialisation term attempts to address, further disaggregation is required (Schmitz, 1992). Hence it has been suggested that two variants of flexible specialisation exist – a large firm variant, and a small firm variant – as well as combinations of the two (Rasmussen *et al.*, 1992). In the context of our sample of small enterprises in Makassar, it is the *small firm variant*, characterised by clustering and networking, that is of particular interest.

Generally, flexible specialisation relies on a number of *key defining variables*. These include a **broadly trained workforce** which can undertake a number of production tasks; an emphasis on the virtues of **craftspersonship**, **flexible and informal management**, and the **close integration** of the processes of conception and execution; **general or multi-purpose machinery**; **just-in-time delivery systems** of inputs; and designs and varied products which respond to an **increasingly specialised and fragmented market**, and the **pursuit of niche rather than mass markets** (Piore and Sabel, 1984; Schmitz, 1989; Morris and Lowder, 1992; Storper and Scott, 1995).

Critical to the success of the *small firm variant* of flexible specialisation are a range of *small enterprise parameters*. These facilitate the integration of small enterprises, involving the establishment of **networks, clusters** and **linkages** and other forms of interaction and interdependence. There is a **balance between competition and co-operation** in areas such as design, innovation and the introduction of new technology, a form of integration that allows small enterprises to enjoy '**collective efficiency**'- economies of agglomeration – which would be unobtainable by individual firms (Piore and Sabel, 1984; Schmitz, 1989).[7]

In the general context, Schmitz (1989) argues that flexibility in technology and labour are two key factors that highlight the differences between flexible specialisation and mass production, the latter being distinguished by specific machinery and purpose trained workers.[8] Schmitz (1989: 15) also contends that there are four areas in which flexibility is essential to the application of the flexible specialisation approach. These include *flexibility in technology* (multi-purpose machine), *worker* (wide range of skills), *individual firm* (wide range of products), and *groups of firms* (wide range of products and volumes). The first two factors provide a clear contrast with mass production, while the second two factors – especially flexibility within groups of firms – are important when examining small enterprises, as their strength often lies in clustering (Schmitz, 1989).

The flexible specialisation approach emphasises four specific factors, largely ignored in past theories of small enterprise organisation, that need to be addressed in the current research agenda. These are, first, the importance of location variables, since geographical proximity to suppliers, competitors and distributors will have different impacts on firms; second, socio-cultural factors such as relationships between entrepreneurs that are influenced by non-economic factors such as trust and reciprocity, emphasising that social relations go beyond the market and formal structures; third, the role of local institutions; and fourth, the need to emphasise that small-scale entrepreneurs are not passive victims of changes occurring in the broader economy, but are agents who facilitate change themselves, taking chances and making decisions in their own right (Hirst and Zeitlin, 1991; Rasmussen *et al.*, 1992).

Consideration of these four factors implies that it is important not to assume that small enterprises in one geographical location are homogeneous. In fact, it is an extremely heterogeneous sector, with sweat-shop-style conditions found alongside highly flexible and enterprising small firms with good labour conditions (Spath, 1992). In some locations and production sectors small enterprises have flourished, in others they have stagnated or collapsed completely. Nonetheless, it has been pointed out by Hirst and Zeitlin that there is a growing possibility that flexible specialisation, unlike mass production, could be increasingly successful in *developing countries* in the future as an industrial paradigm, if the conditions of volatility in the global economy experienced in the 1990s continue.[9] As Hirst and Zeitlin (1991: 36) contend,

> the claim is not that international competition imposes a single form of productive organization on economic actors, given the plurality of institutional frameworks and the possibilities of hybridization, but rather that tendencies can be observed towards the displacement of mass production by flexible specialization as the dominant paradigm of the late twentieth century.

Among small enterprises, defensive responses to changes in the market, to raw material supplies, as well as labour supplies and so on, do not set the stage for flexible specialisation. According to Schmitz (1989: 26), 'in the informal sector literature one finds numerous passing references to the ability of small firms to survive crises, but many of these would add little to our case for flexible specialisation'. Thus, when examining the circumstances of small enterprises, a distinction between survival and growth must be made. Enterprises that utilise defensive coping mechanisms cannot be considered to be following a flexible specialisation approach. Indeed, as Das and Panayiotopoulos (1996: L59) maintain, 'for flexible specialisation to become a new paradigm for developing countries it needs to achieve the objectives of growth. . . . The growth has to be continual. It is not enough for this to be a transient phenomenon.' Accordingly, the 'success' of an enterprise following flexible specialisation is seen in terms of obtaining collective efficiency and continued growth (Sabel and Zeitlin, 1997).[10] This pre-defined definition of 'success' is but one of a range of criticisms directed at the approach, and outlined later in this chapter. Next however, given the advantages offered by flexible specialisation over previous small enterprise approaches, it is necessary to review the work of authors who have attempted to adopt the flexible specialisation approach in the context of developing countries.

Flexible specialisation in developing countries

In recent years there has been a substantial growth in the literature focusing specifically on the applicability of flexible specialisation concepts to small enterprises in *developing* country contexts. Perhaps best known of the initial attempts are those of Schmitz (1989), Rasmussen *et al.* (1992), and Pedersen *et al.* (1994). Others include Storper (1990) who questions the prospects for flexible specialisation within a number of South American countries; Kaplinsky (1991, 1994) who looks at the shift from mass production to flexible specialisation in Cyprus; Morris and Lowder (1992) who examine flexible specialisation and its application in Leon, Mexico; and Holmstrom's (1993) examination of the possibility of applying a flexible specialisation paradigm to small and medium-sized firms in India. In addition, James and Bhalla (1993) have investigated micro-electronics production in the context of flexible specialisation in a number of developing countries, while Smyth *et al.* (1994) examine small-scale industries and the applicability of flexible specialisation in Indonesian case studies. Moreover, writing in the mid-1990s, Galhardi (1995) and Knorringa (1996) have raised further questions about the applicability of the flexible specialisation paradigm to small enterprises in India and developing countries generally.

Due to the diversity of articles available, I have limited the focus here to Indonesian studies, the context in which my research has been undertaken.[11] First, in a comparative study, van Dijk (1994) concentrated on examining how small enterprises in Indonesia and Burkino Faso related to the new competition and flexible specialisation approaches to industrial transformation. He argued that the new competition approach, designed by Best (1990), was not as easy to adopt as the flexible specialisation approach. Nonetheless, he was critical of the way in which the flexible specialisation approach did not necessarily take into account relevant events occurring in the broader global economy. Van Dijk then looked very briefly at the evidence from Indonesia for flexible specialisation or new competition. In his view, although there had been rapid diversification in production, this had been mainly in the capital intensive industries because small enterprises had been largely excluded from any dynamic growth. He believed that if the country could continue to increase its exports and strengthen intra-sectoral linkages, then Indonesia might be able to pursue industrial development following the new competition or flexible specialisation approaches. In the case of Burkina Faso, van Dijk expanded on his previous 1992 article, applying a range of variables to determine whether flexible specialisation was occurring. He found that the firms which did show evidence of flexible specialisation were operated by private entrepreneurs in the modern industrial sector who had made substantial initial investments, and who 'stressed innovation, subcontracting and competitiveness with each other and with imported products' (van Dijk, 1994: 63).

In his examination of rattan production in Tegalwangi, a small town in

West Java, Indonesia, Smyth (1992) discussed the applicability of collective efficiency, a concept which is central to the flexible specialisation paradigm. She stated that the rattan industry had grown rapidly, aided by government intervention, which introduced laws initially banning exports of unprocessed rattan cane, and later all exports of semi-finished rattan goods, as well as introducing special credit facilities. Subcontracting was the most common form of inter-firm relationship followed within the industry, which, while supporting the collective efficiency approach, maintained a relationship of powerful control by large parent firms over small subcontractors. This resulted in skewed benefits from collective efficiency, reflected in the benefits which accrued to labour, with differing degrees of job security and regulation being apparent. Thus she concluded that the polarisation of wealth in the area, and the lack of evidence to suggest that there had been an increase in general living standards, indicated that collective efficiency would not necessarily bring an equal distribution of the benefits to the community involved.

Smyth *et al.* (1994) expanded on Smyth's (1992) study by examining the applicability of the small-scale variant of flexible specialisation to the textile, batik, footwear, metal products and rattan furniture manufacturing sectors in Java, Indonesia. They argued that although a number of flexible specialisation characteristics were identifiable among the small enterprises studied, there was still a distinct lack of information, and adequate access to appropriate, improved technology for the enterprises, reducing their ability to innovate and expand production. The authors found that employment within such sectors was divided between core and periphery workforces, those in the periphery – including a high proportion of women and older workers – undertaking the lowest paid activities and being the first to be displaced. The study also found that a number of the small enterprises were highly dependent on larger firms, with the greater the dependency, the less the range of tasks undertaken by the small enterprises as well as the skills of their workers.

Clusters of enterprises producing roof tiles in Karanggeneng, Central Java were investigated by Sandee (1994) in search of evidence of inter-firm linkages and the impact of new technology. Inter-firm linkages were embedded in local networks which incorporated relations between producers and traders, suppliers, middlepeople and institutions. His research revealed that flexible specialisation was limited among firms which were using low technology, while clusters of higher technology firms had more forward and backward linkages, with a greater division of tasks and labour within the cluster (Sandee, 1994). Technological change within a cluster of enterprises could result in a number of patterns: innovation tended to continue along traditional inter-firm linkages, with local leaders remaining in control; there was growing inequality among firms within networks, making the distribution of the benefits from innovation less equal; and production tended to occur on a larger scale, with a decline in the number of firms in a cluster and an increase in the number of small enterprises working for larger firms. In the case of the tile producers in Karanggeneng, the adoption of new technology, in this case hardpress technology, led to new forms of co-operation among leading firms. However, these were only temporary, newly established networks dissolving over time as the technology was incorporated into the traditional networks.

Writing in the same year, Weijland's (1994) research on how rural cottage industries in Indonesia were being incorporated into flexible industry enabled him to argue that there was a possibility that poor producers were able to gain from unequal alliances with the modern sector. Weijland argued that rural cottage industries were becoming increasingly involved in providing flexibility within production organisation through supplying a labour reserve, becoming part of industrial networks and forming clusters. However, these aspects were also determined by the local context, and with economic, cultural and natural endowments varying significantly throughout Indonesia, regional differentiation was seen to be significant. Weijland (1994) thus divided Indonesia into four broad regions: the densely populated centre provinces; the settled outer island provinces (which included South Sulawesi); the resource-rich provinces; and the isolated provinces. It was argued that all the regions apart from the isolated provinces have had favourable conditions for rural cottage industries to become incorporated into wider trade systems. In the isolated provinces rural cottage industries were limited by a local labour supply and poor local markets, with isolation inhibiting wider marketing. In contrast, the other regions have had more favourable conditions such as dense trade networks and active middlepeople, low transport and transaction costs, and so on. Weijland therefore concluded that the success of rural cottage industries in Indonesia was heavily dependent on wider market networks and the middlepeople who made these more accessible.

This review of literature on small enterprises in Indonesia, then, provides some evidence in support of the applicability of flexible specialisation in a number of regions. Nevertheless, it is also clear that a number of conditions limited the full development of successful flexible specialisation strategies in these study areas. Such conditions included the immense power of large businesses, unfavourable government regulations, low linkages with an expanding market and inequalities in the gains from growth and innovation. Thus although there may be practices and processes that underpin the success of flexible specialisation in parts of the *developed* world which appear to have been paralleled in a few *developing* countries, the evidence as yet is fairly limited. In addition, the flexible specialisation paradigm in developing countries has been subject to a range of criticisms and it is to an examination of these that we now turn.

Criticisms of the flexible specialisation approach

The flexible specialisation approach has been criticised from a number of perspectives, among them the 'new competition approach' which has emerged as a major challenge to the dominance of flexible specialisation (Pedersen *et al.*, 1994). Followers of flexible specialisation have also been criticised for transferring a paradigm to developing countries and the assumptions made in doing so, and for using the term 'success' in a non-Western environment, without thorough deconstruction of the term.

The new competition approach refers to the rise of industries that are organised to 'pursue strategies of continuous improvement in product and process within a regulatory framework that encourages industrial restructuring' (Best, 1990: 252). The new competition approach is more general than the flexible specialisation paradigm, in that while the latter focuses principally on the interactions among firms and the way they use their technologies primarily at a local level, the former examines worldwide markets and stresses the different modes of organisation which are possible within vertical integration (Pedersen *et al.*, 1994). In particular, according to van Dijk (1994), the new competition approach has three advantages over flexible specialisation in that it allows technologies and innovations to be defined more broadly, it highlights the importance of organisational innovations to a more adequate degree, and it regards a broader range of organisational forms.

Nonetheless, it may also be argued that by concentrating on examining clusters and networks, as well as environments prone to innovation, the flexible specialisation approach highlights the importance of location-specific factors. It does so more adequately than the new competition model which stresses the significance of shaping markets and of targeting strategic sectors instead (Pedersen *et al.*, 1994). Hence, it appears that aspects of the flexible specialisation approach offer a way forward in exploring an important range of interrelated issues which have so far received only limited attention in small enterprise discourse. Of particular interest in this respect are the internal dynamics of small enterprises, as well as linkages with other enterprises and organisations within a specific region.

Yet it remains that important criticisms have been made of the dynamics of the flexible specialisation approach. Among these are the dualistic nature of the initial paradigm; the means by which internal contradictions are disregarded; how the relationship between class and flexible specialisation is ignored; and the limited consideration given to the position of casual labour. Ethnicity, gender and local politics are also factors that have been neglected to a large extent by proponents of the approach, yet they are ones which I believe must be incorporated into a framework for examining the organisation and accomplishments of small enterprises in Makassar.

One of the most common criticisms of Piore and Sabel's (1984) work is the dichotomy they see between mass production and flexible specialisation (see Pollert, 1988; Schmitz, 1989; Amin and Robins, 1990; Best, 1990; Graham, 1991; Amin, 1994). Instead of allowing a variety of organisational forms, Piore and Sabel narrow production into two possible forms (Best, 1990), so that 'mass production and flexible specialisation become twin conceptual monoliths rather than completely constituted social processes under-going continual change' (Graham, 1991: 51). In addition, there is no room in Piore and Sabel's discussion for an examination of diversity or contradictions *within* these models (Amin, 1994). By focusing on stability and homogeneity instead of on contradiction and continual change, the approach at present 'obscures the scope for social contestation and potential rupture that a complex conception of contradiction can bring to light' (Graham, 1991: 54). There is also a danger of emphasising a duality, or a 'then and now' approach to Fordist and post-Fordist production systems which fails to grasp the continuities of industrial development (Amin and Robins, 1990; Gertler, 1992; Curry, 1993). Indeed, as Amin and Robins (1990: 25) remark: 'The new is not marked by an absolute and fundamental break from the old: the old order of things does not, cannot, simply and conveniently disappear.'

Research on flexible specialisation highlights the importance of industrial districts. Nonetheless, Amin and Robins (1990: 13) have difficulty with the conceptualisation of the term 'industrial districts'. They contend that Storper and Scott (1989), like Piore and Sabel (1984), are caught up 'in the idealisation of flexible specialisation and industrial districts and the demonisation of Fordism and mass production'. Accordingly, Amin and Robins (1990: 21) argue against such 'an all-embracing and epochal interpretation of the "new-industrial spaces", on the grounds that the processes of change behind these experiences are highly differentiated and also less epochal than is made out by the new orthodoxy'. However, I believe that the work of Pedersen (1994b), described in Chapter 3, does go some way towards breaking down the concepts of clusters and industrial districts into differentiated segments, so giving implicit recognition to the variation involved.

Casual labour is not seriously considered in Piore and Sabel's initial model of flexible specialisation. Rather, they suggest that in *developed* countries 'squeezing' labour is not an option and thus permanent innovation must be undertaken instead. They suggest that pushing labour to gain economic competitiveness is usually blocked by government regulations. Hence the flexible specialisation model is seen to be 'good for all' (Schmitz, 1989: 17). This view has been challenged by Graham (1991) who maintains that in developed countries (as in developing countries too) there is often a large labour surplus, so that the focus *is* on 'squeezing' labour rather than innovation. Previous examinations of flexible work practices show that exploitation, or 'flexible casualties', are prevalent within this industrial paradigm (see Hakim, 1988; Fernandez Kelly, 1989; Schmitz, 1989; Phizacklea, 1990). Indeed, the extent to which flexibility may be 'just a code word for casualization, involving decreased protections for workers and an increase in part-time, temporary, and unbenefitted jobs' has been questioned (Christopherson, 1989, in Graham, 1992: 397).

It has also been pointed out that an important deficiency in Piore and Sabel's (1984) discussion is that they did not explore the relationship between flexible specialisation and class. On this point, Annunziato (1989, in Graham, 1992) asserts that although flexible specialisation may improve the position of workers, in that they can have greater control over work, this does not necessarily mean they gain increased control over the capitalist class processes of production, appropriation and the distribution of surplus value. Thus exploitation may escalate unless flexible specialisation is accompanied by an increase in necessary labour, so that the level of surplus labour declines (Graham, 1991). Essentially, flexible production not only entails flexible machinery and multi-skilled workers, it also requires workers to be flexible concerning working hours, and to endure unrestricted hiring and firing practices as well as other casual labour practices (Schmitz, 1989).

In terms of social reproduction, flexibility of production brings together a socially differentiated population in response to various labour demands of the production system while, at the same time, the population may be spatially differentiated by dissimilar social customs, individual characteristics and social class formation (Storper and Scott, 1989). In developing their argument, Storper and Scott (1989: 34) maintain that 'the distinctive neighbourhoods and communities that emerge within any agglomeration become integral to the legitimation and stabilization of socio-economic divisions in the local area'. As a consequence, social stratification and polarisation may arise as two significant outcomes of growing flexibility (Douglass, 1992). It is possible that as well as divisions arising between those involved with small enterprise production on the basis of class and ethnicity, the divide between an 'elite' and a mass of casually employed workers within the labour market will become even more enhanced in the future than that presently occurring. As documented in chapters 5 and 6, which highlight the cultural and social divisions among small-scale entrepreneurs and workers, an examination of the role played by social relations and ethnicity is crucial to understanding small enterprises in Makassar.

While flexible specialisation may be seen by some to be a panacea for the ills of societies dealing with the remains of a Fordist regime, the incongruities that occur within this mode of organisation still need to be fully explored. Piore and Sabel do not advance this process because they 'present flexible specialization as having universal rather than gendered, racial, class, or other differentiated effects' (Jenson, 1989, in Graham, 1991: 55). They are therefore adding to common assumptions concerning the traditional dichotomies between male/female, industrial workplace/household, and production/other forms of work (for example, reproduction).

Class, ethnicity, gender, consumption and leisure have become increasingly popular entry points for discussions regarding the nature of work. The interactions among place, people and the environment, and the specific history of a location make every industrial setting unique. Where increasing flexibility in the workforce has been paralleled with the deregulation of labour, this has often resulted in a renewed growth of the feminisation of the labour force (Wilson, 1993). Nonetheless, proponents of regulation theory and flexible specialisation have been accused of being gender blind by McDowell (1991), as have followers of previous informal sector theories (Wilson, 1993). Here, then, it is important to stress that 'industrialization based on the workshop or other concealed forms of production has different implications for gender relations than the trajectory of factory-based industrialization', with specific locational socio-cultural factors also being highly significant (Wilson, 1993: 69).

Indeed, according to Pollert (1988: 59), the flexible specialisation model is a 'complacently male sex-blind view'. McDowell expands on this perspective, maintaining that followers of currently popular industrial paradigms 'assume women's secondary positions in the labour market, neglect the question about the gendering of skills and ignore the so-called masculine attributes in the labour market' (McDowell, 1991: 400). Within the flexible specialisation par-adigm, she argues, the jobs undertaken are gendered, with the skill content continually redrawn to assert the inferiority of women. In some cases women working in small enterprises may not be recognised as 'true workers' at all, as production takes place under servile relations or within the domestic realm. Such women have been given 'a different social identity and a different status as workers' (Wilson, 1993: 72).

Nonetheless, while McDowell (1991) has argued that increasing flexibility has had a largely negative impact on women and those outside the paid work-force, the current production models have to some extent broken down the gender division which was so important under the Fordist regime. In devel-oped countries it is now possible to find increasing numbers of men in peripheral employment, where they endure terms and conditions that in the past were regarded as female dominated. Clearly, this aspect needs to be fur-ther explored in terms of the conditions found within developing countries.

It is evident that those who have been placed on the periphery because their experiences fail to conform to the overarching story must be included in any proposed model of flexibility for it to be appropriate for future discussions. Part of the challenge set for this book, is thus to examine the dynamics of workplaces and flexible labour processes, while at the same time highlighting the situation and experiences of those who are often excluded from mass consumption, paid employment and capitalist class processes (Graham, 1991).

A 'politics of place' – the 'social construction of those institutional-regulatory structures that must be present in order to secure economic order and continuity' – moulds the structure and growth of industry in a regional economy (Scott and Storper, 1992: 15). Policy, involving a range of external economic agencies such as trade associations, labour education facilities, joint marketing arrangements and regulatory commissions, has significant consequences for industrial organisation and strategies for small-scale indus-trial growth (Best, 1990). However, what actually prevails in many developing countries 'is a legal and regulatory environment which is badly distorted, and an administrative and institutional setting which is hardly supportive

and often discriminatory' (Spath, 1992: 10). For this reason, an understanding of local political factors and the regulatory and developmental
roles they play with regard to industry is crucial to gaining a fuller understanding of the contextual basis of this debate. It would be unwise to
assume that small enterprises have always occupied the same position in
developing countries in the past, and that in the future the same policies will
be suited to all such enterprises. Small enterprises exist in a wide variety of
situations, diversely affected by the extent of large firm domination, changing state policies and differences in the local socio-cultural environment
(Rasmussen, 1992). In this respect, then, it is important to know whether
specific local governments act as regulators, ensuring certain standards of
labour use are kept; whether they provide assistance through training
schemes and advice; whether they stifle small enterprise growth through
corrupt and biased practices; or whether they have an insignificant relationship with small enterprise structures.

Of increasing concern in recent years has been the ways in which 'Western
thought' has made assumptions about developing countries (Crush, 1994; see
also Said, 1979; Simon, 1998). The deconstruction and decolonisation of
Western intellectual traditions is now gaining momentum as increasing numbers of scholars consider the possibility of producing a decolonised and
post-colonial knowledge (Crush, 1994). There has been a proliferation of
meanings relating to the term 'post-colonialism' and as Jacobs (1996: 22)
contends, 'the term refers not only to formal political status, but also to certain subject positions, political processes, cultural articulations and critical
perspectives'. Here I focus primarily on the potential use of the concept as a
critical theoretical and analytical perspective relating to small enterprise
research. Nonetheless, each of the dimensions of post-colonialism articu-
lated by Jacobs (1996) remains relevant to this discussion.

In particular, I argue that intellectual neo-colonialism has occurred by
taking a paradigm (flexible specialisation) initially designed for utilisation in
developed countries and applying it to developing countries. Therefore what
is required is 'the transgression of "the norms of (western) knowledge production"' (Crush, 1994: 350). The developing countries did not become rich
or industrialised during the initial formation of the existing world order, so
that their histories differ significantly from developed countries (Wolf-
Phillips, 1979). Clearly, developing countries cannot be treated as an
homogeneous group because of the diversity and distinctiveness to be found
among and within such countries. In short, this means that future approaches
to small enterprises must avoid past dualistic tendencies.[12] Therefore, while
abstraction is necessary if a paradigm is to be adopted in a number of different contexts, such abstraction must take account of the characteristics of
the people and processes involved and the fundamental relations among
actors, as required by a post-colonial approach.[13]

Also of considerable concern is the definition of 'success' as used in the
flexible specialisation approach when examining small enterprises in a

developing country context, where 'success' may mean a range of very different things among entrepreneurs. For those using non-paid family labour, 'success' may be seen in terms of values such as rising social status in the community, providing employment for family members as well as their livelihood needs, being self-reliant, building up an enterprise for the next generation to continue, and worker welfare. For those using a mixture of family labour and non-family labour, 'success' might refer to a more evident resolve to accumulate capital to reinvest into the enterprise. For those employing totally non-family labour, perhaps the tendency will be for 'success' to be seen more in terms of capitalist 'profits'.

No doubt there will also be other definitions of 'success' as conceptualised by small-scale entrepreneurs. What is important here is that one recognises that small-scale entrepreneurs in developing countries may well be operating in a contextual environment in which economic ideas of profit and loss are not the only markers of 'success' (or indeed failure) and cultural aspects may hold important consequences for the definition. This certainly does not sit well with the use of the economic concept of 'growth' which, along with collective efficiency, is seen as the key focus or objective for enterprises within the flexible specialisation approach (Schmitz, 1989; Sabel and Zeitlin, 1997).

CONCLUSION: A WAY FORWARD

As already detailed, the flexible specialisation approach has a number of strengths not found in previous approaches to small enterprise research. However, this critique has uncovered a fundamental concern regarding the use of the flexible specialisation paradigm in developing countries; that is, the use of a paradigm based on 'Western' economic rationale, in non-Western circumstances. Instead, local cultural interpretations are highly significant, much as Upadhya and Rutten (1997: 32) contend:

> The actions of entrepreneurs, like those of any other social group, cannot be understood in terms of their economic 'interests' alone. Like everyone else they are also driven by the desire for prestige, social status, or political influence . . . all non-tangible goals which are nonetheless salient for them.

For this reason, it is most important that the choices of entrepreneurs 'are not assumed to be reducible to the neo-classical paradigm of rational decision-making – i.e., abstracted from their social and cultural context' (Booth, 1993: 62).[14] In other words, the goals of flexible specialisation are rendered problematic in the developing world context, where much greater consideration of local ideologies and strategies is essential to an understanding of the objectives of small-scale entrepreneurs.

This critique of the flexible specialisation approach leads me to believe that one must not adopt the approach in its entirety when examining small enterprises in developing countries. Instead, perhaps flexible specialisation should be regarded as 'a valuable addition to the ongoing critical development discourse' (Sverrisson, 1992: 28). Indeed, there may be several types of new production organisational forms emerging, as enterprises experiment with a range of different strategies (Amin, 1989). These are all diverse routes to finding suitable strategies for the future, and their 'development is not guided by one overarching structural transformation' (Amin and Robins, 1990: 23). Because of this I develop, in Chapter 3, an integrative framework for examining small enterprises, one which takes these factors into consideration, and offers what is believed to be a more viable way forward.

3 Small enterprise research in developing countries

New directions

> For a long time now the study of the viability of small scale industries has been marred by theoretical and methodological problems.
>
> (Smyth, 1992: 52)

From the critique of small enterprise research presented in Chapter 2 it becomes clear that, in its entirety, flexible specialisation should not be used as an approach with which to examine such enterprises in developing countries. Yet there does not appear to be an alternative paradigm or theoretical approach robust enough to fill the gap in the theorisation process concerning such enterprises. What we need now is a framework that allows local agency to be taken seriously, while at the same time giving due weight to macro-level, structural constraints (Booth, 1993).

The development of a coherent theoretical lens through which to focus upon small enterprises in developing countries is yet to take place. Such a lens should take into account local contextual factors, and incorporate actors at different levels. Perhaps, however, its construction might well have to await the resolution of the general impasse in development and industrial development theories.[1] For this reason, I argue, the most immediate need and viable objective is to formulate a *conceptual framework* within which to examine small enterprises in developing countries. One quality of such a tool is that it should be instrumental in advancing empirical investigations and enlightening further theoretical debate.

A SMALL ENTERPRISE INTEGRATIVE FRAMEWORK

Given the deficiencies of existing theories and approaches documented in Chapter 2, I propose an integrated framework that builds upon the strengths of the flexible specialisation approach with its focus on inter-firm linkages. But more than that, my framework also incorporates a heightened sensitivity to the significant role of contextual factors in determining the 'success' of small enterprises in developing countries. Here I use the concept as an emic, locally defined objective based on the entrepreneurs' own experiences/points of view, because, to an 'outsider', these explain their behaviour and actions to the best degree possible (see Evans, 1993). Above all, it is imperative that such a framework be placed within the realm of post-colonial discourse.

Nevertheless, it must be acknowledged that operating within the same clusters and informal networks in developing countries may well be enterprises that, while all small, extend across a number of enterprise types, and display a range of organisational structures and labour flexibilities. It is important therefore to move well beyond the limited perspectives of existing dualistic models, and the deficiencies of the flexible specialisation approach, to look much more closely at intra-enterprise and inter-enterprise relationships and the role played by the contextual environment in shaping these. To achieve this, we need a conceptual framework that recognises the variation of interconnected processes both within and among small enterprises that are integrated and embedded in systems of cultural behaviour, social relationships, networks and linkages.[2] A model designed to achieve this objective is presented in Figure 3.1.

In arrangement, this framework brings together a number of key factors. First, it embraces the local and regional socio/economic/political/cultural contextual environment. This is influenced and moulded by the local historical context, as the basis of 'place' for a small enterprise, and incorporates components which have been ignored by proponents of a range of previous small enterprise approaches, including the flexible specialisation paradigm. Second, towards the centre of the contextual environment sit the building blocks that make up the immediate structure and organisation of a small enterprise. These all influence each other – hence the permeable/dashed lines in Figure 3.1 – as well as being strongly influenced by the contextual factors, emphasised by the inward flowing arrows. In turn, each and every contextual environmental factor may influence the different building blocks, hence one should imagine the smaller circle 'spinning' inside the larger, outer one. Third, these 'circles' are influenced in their construction by post-colonial discourse and concepts which emerged from the flexible specialisation approach. The result is that Figure 3.1 offers a more holistic perspective on the structure and organisation of the small enterprise and an enhanced understanding of what constitutes 'success', as a locally defined emic objective for the entrepreneur.

While the model reflects my rejection of the use of flexible specialisation as a suitable approach to the analysis of small enterprises in developing countries, it is sensible to retain the small enterprise parameters of the approach as the building blocks of this new framework, to be discussed in more detail below. Conceiving the model in this way allows for an examination of the organisation of small enterprises while taking into full account the dense web of inter-firm linkages and clusters. In effect, by placing greater emphasis on inter-firm relationships, flexible specialisation has improved markedly on previous theories and paradigms that have in general been focused at the level of the specific enterprise.

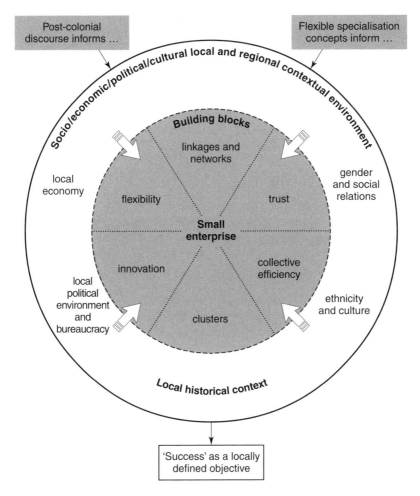

Figure 3.1 The small enterprise integrative framework.

Nonetheless, in terms of Figure 3.1, I am not suggesting that all the building blocks must be evident when examining an enterprise for it to fit conceptually within the notion of a 'small enterprise'. Instead, I propose that these building blocks should be investigated and their form explored, whichever way one chooses to define a small enterprise, which as the political history of small enterprise policies in Indonesia has shown, could be any of a myriad ways. Such an exploration is essential if one is to gain a more comprehensive understanding not only of the manner in which such enterprises operate, but also how they are influenced by and shaped within their contextual environment.

The building blocks of the framework (Figure 3.1) are contextualised by the locational factors to be found in the socio-economic, political and cultural environments that surround them. These factors all influence, and are often influenced by, the small enterprises in various complex ways according to both the internal structure of the enterprises themselves and the other contextual factors involved. In turn, it is impossible to separate the small enterprises from their historical context, and therefore one must have a broad understanding of the local history to comprehend how the resultant contemporary processes affecting the enterprises have emerged (Mathew, 1997).

The small enterprise integrative framework I present in Figure 3.1 is designed to ensure that all the features within it are taken into due consideration when small enterprises are being examined. When this is done, the output achieved should be a comprehensive analysis of the structure and success of the small enterprises studied. In this analysis, the contextual environment is fully incorporated, and 'success' appears as an emic, locally defined objective. Only then will the organisation and functioning of small enterprises in developing countries begin to be fully appreciated in terms of the circumstances in which they operate.

At this point, it has to be recognised that my integrative framework is still influenced by researchers operating within a post-Fordist framework. Despite criticism that this might raise when examining the organisation of small enterprises that have never reached a Fordist production strategy, this incorporation is necessary because post-Fordist researchers are concerned with studying aspects of both industrial development *and* local development, rather than one or other of these *per se*, as has generally been the case in the past (Smyth *et al.*, 1997). Nonetheless, to avoid working within a contextual vacuum, I argue for a greater emphasis on the specifics of placing research on small enterprises in developing countries within a locally contextualised setting than has been done traditionally by post-Fordist theorists.

I also argue that it is necessary to avoid the problems of previous theoretical binaries relating to entrepreneurship theory in which forms of entrepreneurship have been explained in terms of either cultural or political/economic imperatives, often based on European assumptions. Such a binary division is unworkable in a developing country location, where both sets of causative features are likely to be influential and powerful decision-making determinants, neither being mutually exclusive. At the same time, the role of human agency cannot be neglected. Indeed, there must be an exploration into the interconnectedness between individual agency, broader social structures and cultural traditions to avoid a deterministic approach (Upadhya and Rutten, 1997). Given these imperatives, the body of ideas emerging within post-colonialist discourse offers a potentially illuminating way forward.

In the past, post-colonial perspectives do not appear to have been engaged seriously by those analysing small enterprises in developing countries (Simon, 1998). It is now time that those involved should explore how post-colonialism could advance and strengthen the effectiveness and relevance of their work. It is my view that an effective post-colonial analysis would require the acknowledgement of a set of processes in which cultural formation is dispersed along a number of axes of potentially *commensurate* importance – class, certainly, but also sexuality and gender, racism, familial relations, religious discourses . . .

(Rattansi, 1997: 482; italics in original)

Such processes are among those highlighted in Figure 3.1 – the vital components of a framework that can take the reality of daily life for small-scale entrepreneurs in developing countries fully into account. The inappropriateness of the flexible specialisation paradigm, initially proposed in the 'West' as a tool with which to examine small enterprises in developing countries, emphasises the need to de-centre the 'West' and reduce its hegemony in geographical thought (Rattansi, 1997). Post-colonial studies would appear to be a viable field within which to situate such a challenge.

Clearly then, the potential of post-colonial theory for small enterprise research is an emerging field of study. For this reason, the discussion in this book is of necessity tentative and speculative. However, a number of potentially useful directions have been identified. First, the attention that post-colonialism pays to agency, and how individual agency is understood in the developing world context, is important in gaining a greater understanding of the lives of small-scale entrepreneurs (Crush, 1994). Second, issues concerning representation, writing and self-reflexivity are raised. In recognition of this, I have given careful consideration to how my writing is implemented in the prevailing world system of power (Watts, 1995; Childs and Williams, 1997).[3]

Keeping these useful directions in mind, the remainder of this chapter moves back to the smaller circle of Figure 3.1 and explores in detail the *building blocks* of the small enterprise integrative framework, namely **flexibility in labour relations, networks and trust, collective efficiency and clusters,** and **innovation**. These are subsequently adopted throughout the analysis of small enterprises in Makassar in chapters 5, 6 and 7.

FRAMEWORK BUILDING BLOCKS

Flexible labour relations

The notion of flexibility has two basic dimensions in the industrial production literature: flexibility in *work,* and flexibility in *employment* (Curry, 1993). Growing flexibility in production methods and technology is in turn leading to increasingly flexible work schedules, with a need to move rapidly among a variety of tasks, in turn raising stress levels for workers. The latter may easily end up with greater responsibilities, without parallel increases in authority or autonomy (Schoenberger, 1988). Hence, following one interpretation, flexibility may be considered as the 'presence of skilled, versatile workers who are able to perform various parts of the labour process' (Wilson, 1992: 57). Alternatively, workers are made 'flexible' in their employment, in that they are not protected by labour contracts or labour legislation, and thus are often working in 'sweat-shop' conditions (Wilson, 1992). Labour flexibility in this sense assumes two forms: first, functional flexibility, illustrated by job mobility in the workforce; and second, numerical flexibility, characterised by temporary and part-time workers (Morris, 1988; Curry, 1993). Such forms of flexibility will become apparent later in the case of small enterprise workers in Makassar.

Currently, the use of flexible forms of work and employment in small enterprises raises serious doubts about earlier assumptions that certain enterprises, previously defined as traditional 'informal' ones, constitute a residual sector of the economy (Mitter, 1994). Rather, it appears that global economic transformations have provided additional avenues through which labour can be exploited outside the domain of formal employment contracts. Firms are reducing their costs of production through the addition of labour from extended family networks, and by entering into flexible labour arrangements with small enterprises (Fernandez Kelly, 1989; Phizacklea, 1990).

Flexible labour is 'typically associated with high levels of external accelerated turnover, part-time work, short-term labour contracts, homeworking, and so on' (Storper and Scott, 1989: 32). Such increasing signs of versatility of labour deployment, as well as rapid advances in technological development have facilitated a significant spread of flexibility into sub-contracting enterprises and increased homework activities (Moser, 1978). This development signals a re-emergence at the local scale of enduring practices from 'homeworking and street vending (which inherently blend production and reproduction spheres), through [to] contemporary arrangements such as sub-contracting and outsourcing' (Hays-Mitchell, 1993: 1094.

Very clearly then, the growing fragmentation and specialisation of the production process due to changes to the functioning of the world economy have not resulted in the disappearance of flexible processes. Instead, opportunities have been provided for the further transformation and expansion of flexibility in production and labour (Castells, 1989). Labour flexibility is not a new phenomenon, for it may be argued that it has always been essential to capitalist accumulation (Pollert, 1988). In many instances, however, it appears that labour flexibility is now not only becoming increasingly visible and diverse, but is also being incorporated into economic growth tactics to a greater extent than ever before.

Increasingly, small enterprises appear to be situated at the core of flexible production and decentralised networks that are forming the emerging model of industrial management (Castells and Portes, 1989). Flexibility has allowed for the growth of a range of smaller firms and independent divisions that interact with each other in a complex array of supplier and purchaser arrangements. As rigid job descriptions and work rules become more and more obsolete, 'flexibility has remade the firm and redrawn the map of industry' (Graham, 1992: 395) while many developing countries embrace flexibility,

> vis-à-vis their competitors as well as vis-à-vis their own formal laws, so as to obtain a comparative advantage for their production relative to the more regulated areas of the world economy.
>
> (Castells and Portes, 1989: 29)

Amongst the range of flexible labour relations which a small enterprise might adopt, subcontracting is an intermediary industrial process, one situated between firms which solely rely on market transactions and those which internalise all their processes (Storper and Walker, 1989). It covers a wide variety of production strategies from those with 'formal' relationships between the contractor and subcontractor, to those that are based on 'informal', flexible arrangements. Used in this way, subcontracting is broadly defined as:

> A situation where the firm offering the subcontract requests another independent enterprise to undertake the production or carry out the processing of a material, component, part or subassembly for it according to specifications or plans provided by the firm offering the subcontract.
>
> (Holmes, 1986: 84)

There are numerous explanations for the prevalence of subcontracting. Holmes (1986: 87), for instance, argues for three broad explanatory hypotheses based on:

1   the structure and temporal stability of product markets;
2   the fixed capital requirements of the production process and the nature of the production technology used in the labour process;
3   the structure and nature of labour supply conditions and, in particular, the questions of labour cost minimisation and control over the labour process.

Similarly, Holmes (1986) also defines three dominant forms of subcontracting arrangement. First, *capacity subcontracting*, where the production of the subcontracted part is carried out according to the instructions of the parent firm, when the latter wishes to meet fluctuations in demand without increasing its own capital stock. Second, *specialisation subcontracting,* where the subcontractor provides skills or technology usually not available to the parent firm as well, an arrangement also defined as vertical disintegration by Scott (1983). As will be discussed in Chapter 6, such subcontracting occurs in the small enterprise sector in Makassar in gold and silver jewellery and handicraft production, as well as among tailors and wooden furniture enterprises. A third form is *supplier subcontracting,* used in situations where the subcontractor is primarily an 'independent supplier with full control over the development, design and fabrication of its product, but is willing to enter into a subcontracting arrangement to supply a dedicated or proprietary part to the parent firm' (Holmes, 1986: 86). This sometimes occurs when it is more profitable for the larger firm to allow another enterprise to undertake a certain part of the production process (van Diermen, 1997).

Subcontractors often contract entrepreneurs from small enterprises to supply them with intermediate goods. This may occur when certain sections of the production process prove unprofitable for larger enterprises and the activity is transferred wholly or partially to small enterprises. Such arrangements often result in these enterprises remaining small enough to avoid existing regulations concerning workers' protection and minimum wage levels (Hemmer and Mannel, 1989; Wallace, 1990). Such arrangements also allow 'large firms considerable numerical flexibility as it shifts the balance of risk from contractor to subcontractor' (Morris, 1988: 303).

Homeworking occurs when workers undertaking subcontracting processes carry out the tasks in their own homes/outliers (Wah Chu, 1992). Materials are delivered to the outworkers or the materials are collected by the outworkers themselves. They then either add value to the goods or finish and assemble them in their own homes and return the products within a certain time period to the small enterprise, itself often operating as a subcontractor to a larger firm. Outworkers are normally paid by piece-rate and have little control over profit extraction (Wah Chu, 1992). Also important is the fact that the costs of production are met by the outworkers, such as all overhead and running expenses (MacEwen Scott, 1979; Semlinger, 1993). This is very similar to the putting-out system defined by Wallerstein when discussing the urban industry of Europe in the sixteenth century. This, according to Wallerstein (1980: 193), involved a situation where:

> The actual producer worked in his domicile with his own equipment. He used his own tools. Either he was a master for a few apprentices, or he worked alone or in small family groups. He received the necessary raw materials for his transformational task from a merchant-entrepreneur . . . who thereby received the right to 'purchase' the transformed product at a fixed price and who took charge of transporting the product to a market.

Perhaps the most noticeable difference in Makassar was that the outworkers often borrowed tools from the respective small enterprises they were working for, rather than owning all their own tools. In turn, the small enterprises may have borrowed the tools from a larger firm if the two had a subcontracting arrangement. However, as will be discussed in Chapter 5, the other characteristics of the homeworking system were certainly apparent within the small enterprise sector in Makassar.

Networks and trust

The network concept, in industrial production literature, is used to mean an arrangement of units or contacts (including small independent enterprises, subcontracting enterprises, large enterprises, suppliers, purchasers or a mixture of these) interconnected through various types of relationships that enable enterprises to enlarge their spatial potential (Lipietz, 1993). These relationships may include the exchange of commodities, information and services. Networks of small enterprises also often have a mutual reliance on technical specifications or standards, as well as a common labour force, language and location if they are to operate successfully (Pedersen *et al.*, 1994).

Although much has been written about the different possible organisational forms of enterprise networks (see Lorenz, 1992; Lipietz, 1993; Sverrisson, 1994), the network concept itself implies that, whatever the specific terminology used, the boundaries of enterprises are becoming less stable and indeed increasingly fluid. It has been suggested that an enterprise is 'a dense network at the center of a web of relationships' (Badaracco, 1991, in Dicken, 1994: 106), yet not all enterprises within a broader structure of networks have equal roles to play or hold equal power. Nonetheless, such a conceptualisation allows enterprises a great deal of flexibility regarding whether to internalise or externalise different production aspects (Dicken, 1994).

Within networks, transactions occur in a huge variety of market, non-market and hybrid forms. Such transactions range from those which are highly localised, such as household and neighbourhood, to those operating at the regional, national and international level. The complexity of such relations is highlighted by Pedersen (1994a: 23) who observes that:

> In this dynamic network of interacting and interadapting enterprises and organizations, some relations may be pure market relations, others strictly hierarchical power relations, but most are likely to be somewhere in between, implying some degree of trust and reciprocity, because the market is seldom purely anonymous and the powerful seldom almighty.

At the local level, networks – and transactions occurring within them – often depend on 'spur of the moment' contacts which rely to a high degree on mutual confidence between the parties involved (Storper and Scott, 1995). Such economic transactions generally occur within a context of expected reciprocity, implying future obligations and rewards for actions undertaken (Powell, 1991). These norms of obligations and co-operation are often implicit rather than explicit, and suggest the existence of a community of shared values (Bradach and Eccles, 1991; Grabher, 1993). The stability of networks over time also leads to increasing interdependence and 'through mutual adaptations between the exchange partners, relations within the network are consolidated' (Grabher, 1993: 9).

If they are to operate successfully, then, many networks require significant levels of trust among members.[4] Trust-based transactions among local buyers and sellers, as among different enterprises, are a key factor within many industrial networks and districts. Small-scale entrepreneurs frequently rely on local suppliers and specialists 'whom they have learnt to trust and this trust can be a condition for important competitive advantages' (Cox, 1995: 218). These relations are usually facilitated by close spatial proximity and 'the "embedding" of these interfirm relations into a deep local social fabric will be particularly effective in conditions of relative cultural homogeneity' (Gertler, 1992: 264). Relocation elsewhere would involve the loss of significant contacts and time-saving arrangements, as new contacts were found and relationships strengthened. Therefore the necessity of firms working within such relationships to remain situated in one location is considerable (Cox, 1995). Examples of the depth of spatial embeddedness of this kind are visible in small enterprise clusters like those in Makassar where there are often wealthier families, with a range of conspicuous consumption articles, living among poorer families, yet reluctant to move due to the continuing importance of spatial proximity to workers, suppliers and other family members.

These relationships among economic actors are closely related to the socio-cultural context within which such networks are situated. This includes habits, attitudes, customs and local business knowledge. An entrepreneur's past work history will also significantly influence the social and professional networks into which s/he is incorporated (Rasmussen, 1992; Dicken, 1994). The nature of a network reflects the different power structures involved and not all networks will be purely harmonious, as each contact is also a source of potential conflict. Accordingly, network structures may restrict access for newcomers entering into local competition, barring them in intentional or less than subtle ways (Powell, 1991; Grabher, 1993). These concerns re-emphasise the need for an investigation into networks and inter-firm relations using a framework which is context sensitive. These concerns are acknowledged in this book, and the study of small enterprises in Makassar takes into the fullest account possible the 'embeddedness of industrial practices in [a] specific context . . . and region' (Storper and Scott, 1995: 513).

In direct contrast, proponents of neo-classical economic theory state that markets and competition are the sole factors producing economic order and that 'firms engage in cost-rational decision making independent of each other' (Holmes, 1986: 82). Likewise, neo-liberalists propose that there is a current regime of unregulated markets and cut-throat competition, it being argued that neo-liberalism itself is a symptom of the period after Fordism collapsed, representing the politics of the unresolved crisis (Peck and Tickell, 1994a). However, there is growing evidence – in the network arrangements of small enterprises in developing countries – to dispute these paradigms in terms of their all-inclusive claims. Here it is argued that 'innovative behaviour is expected . . . and competition is tempered by co-operation' (Pedersen *et al.*, 1994: 2), and therefore network relationships are central to the social 'embeddedness' of economic actions (Dicken, 1994). Thus 'markets and competition are not socially decontextualized activities' (Storper and Scott, 1995: 509; see also Fukuyama, 1996); rather they are shaped by personal interaction, friendship, trust, reputation and interdependence. In turn, these are often influenced by institutional structures and norms such as educational systems, the law and the structure of labour relations. All are important factors that must be taken into account within a framework to effectively analyse small enterprises in developing countries.

Collective efficiency and clusters

Collective efficiency is based on the premise that competitiveness cannot be achieved by small enterprises acting individually but requires *active collaboration*, supported by *physical agglomeration* and *sectoral specialisation* among enterprises (Smyth, 1992; Pedersen, 1994b). Originally proposed by Schmitz in 1989, the concept of collective efficiency has since found a place in the wider literature on small enterprises in developing countries (Smyth, 1992; Sverrisson, 1992; Pedersen, 1994b). In this, collective efficiency is dependent on a number of basic prerequisites:

- co-existence within a geographical region of enterprises with a common potential product range, input needs, skills required, and a similar level of technological sophistication;
- co-operation between these enterprises and a range of services accessible to them all;
- competition controls and social cohesion expressed in non-economic interaction among the enterprises;
- a certain degree of permanence and stability in business relations within enterprise clusters.

(adapted from Sverrisson, 1992: 28)

Those small enterprises able to obtain collective efficiency operate within an 'enterprise cluster', defined as 'a loose organization competing with other large and small enterprises, governmental and non-governmental organizations, households and other social organizations for resources and markets' (Pedersen, 1994b: 5). Thus, rather than isolated objects, individual enterprises are players in an interrelated system of production and distribution. Such systems or clusters incorporate networks through which member enterprises may obtain raw materials and machinery, thus increasing efficiency and flexibility (Schmitz, 1992). Assisted by forward and backward linkages, other benefits accrued include being able to achieve economies of scale, to diversify and specialise – hence attracting a wider range of customers – and to accelerate innovation (Pedersen, 1994b).

Within such clusters it is customary to have physical agglomeration. Locational proximity facilitates transportation, since small enterprises in developing countries often rely on inexpensive means of transportation using human energy, such as bicycles, handcarts or trishaws to carry raw materials and finished goods (Smyth, 1992). It also facilitates flows of information concerning levels of demand, prices, wages and current government attitudes towards certain enterprises, and so on. Clearly, 'it takes density to cultivate the required contacts not only with other enterprises but also with influential people within the local administration, bank and party, with employees, suppliers and customers' (Aeroe, 1992: 17).

In the reality of the market then, there is a tendency for firms to prefer physical closeness in order to reduce the costs and difficulties of enterprise transactions and 'in order to maximise their access to the cultural and informational context of the production system' (Storper, 1990: 437). Although close proximity itself does not mean that clustering will automatically occur, it is a major facilitating factor and collective efficiency often results from the nearby physical presence of producers of similar commodities (Schmitz, 1992; van Dijk, 1992). While Storper and Scott (1995) argue that there has been a decline in locational constraints due to numerous advances in modern technology, there is increasing evidence that many of the current networks of transactions are highly sensitive to distance due to their complexity and uncertainty. This has led Mingione (1994: 26) to suggest that now, more than ever before, there are 'complicated mixes of old and new reciprocal networks, with associated interest groups emerging'.

Kinship ties also play an important role in supporting collective efficiency in that they make the merging of community and economy even more complete (Smyth, 1992). Indeed, as Mingione (1994: 24) has stated:

> Nowhere can industrial development be fully understood without devoting great attention to the adaptation and change of reciprocity networks and to family and kinship strategies, which have maintained a crucial role as the fundamental socio-organizational background.

Accordingly, Piore and Sabel have argued (1984: 275), 'it is hard to tell where society (in the form of the family and school ties or community celebrations of ethnic and political identity) ends, and where economic organisation begins'. In particular, personal relations diminish the threat of opportunism and the need for elaborate formal structures for governance (Bradach and Eccles, 1991). In addition, Scott and Storper (1992) have recognised a continuum of trust relations, with family at one end of the scale and impersonal market transactions at the other. Indeed, for small enterprises, the realms of the 'social and cultural, including family life, kinship ties and education tend to influence the organisation of small enterprises in a number of fundamental ways' (ibid.: 12). Such ways are expressed geographically in the form of 'a mosaic of distinctive neighbourhoods and communities within which subtle and intricate processes of family life, childrearing, and social interaction take place' (Storper and Scott, 1989: 33).

Not surprisingly, close collaboration within and among small enterprises has resulted in the identification of a broad array of different cluster types:

> A cluster of enterprises may be base[d] on vertically or horizontally specialized enterprises or a mixture of both; it may comprise the whole chain of vertical specializations in a production and distribution chain from raw material to consumer, or it may be specialized in a single or a few links of the chain; and it may be horizontally broad comprising many different sectors or narrowly specialized in a single or a few sectors. The types of collective efficiencies achieved, and the distribution of the benefits resulting from it, depend on the structure of the cluster.
>
> (Pedersen, 1994b: 13)

Due to the complexity of cluster arrangements, Pedersen (1994b) has divided them into two subsectors based on vertical or horizontal specialisation. Clusters organised in terms of *vertical specialisation* are commonly called Marshallian districts (Pedersen *et al.*, 1994). As discussed in Chapter 2, this name was originally given to industrial districts at the end of the nineteenth and beginning of the twentieth century, hence suggesting a strong conceptual link between the 'craft systems' of the past and the collective efficiency strategies of small enterprises today. These clusters involve 'small vertically disintegrated enterprises within the same broad sector and clustering in the same area' (Pedersen, 1994b: 13). There is a flow of goods, services and information, as well as collaboration occurring among small enterprises or within subcontracting relationships between small and large enterprises (Pedersen, 1994b; Hayter, 1997).

Clusters distinguished by their *horizontal specialisation* are commonly interpreted in terms of central place theory. As Pedersen (1994b) points out, such small enterprises do not directly obtain collective efficiency for themselves; rather, the benefits accrue to the customers who have reduced transportation costs and lowered search costs; therefore more customers come to the area than one enterprise alone would be able to attract. Nonetheless, Pedersen (1994b) has also suggested that this greater number of customers does allow small enterprises to exploit economics of scale and thus indirectly obtain collective efficiency. In classical central place theory individual sectors are assumed to be homogeneous, all enterprises within the sector being the same, and competition among them being purely on price, with no collaboration. Market segmentation is therefore based on product differentiation and quality. However, Pedersen (1994b) argues that this is an unrealistic approach for developing countries where market segmentation is more often based on scarcity or availability of products and inputs, sources of labour and capital and on delivery services. Market segmentation is thus seen by Pedersen as being a way of overcoming scarcities and is a sign of collective efficiency. Nonetheless, he also argues that market segmentation is based on a process of competition and mutual adaptation, rather than on direct collaboration, leading Pedersen to the conclusion that for an industrial cluster to be truly successful, it must comprise and control at least some vertical production processes.

Within these two categories of specialisation, both vertical and horizontal, Pedersen (1994b) has further divided the cluster groups, producing the typology of four different enterprise clusters summarised in Figure 3.2. As may be seen, vertical specialisation comprises a *diversified industrial cluster* and a *subcontractor cluster*. The first of these, comprises enterprises producing a range of products for a specific sector, and they compete with large businesses by shifting among production for local, national and international markets. Their production systems are flexible and they are willing to collaborate in the development and purchasing of new resources.

On the other hand, the *subcontractor cluster* is defined by the narrow vertical and horizontal specialisation of individual enterprises within the cluster, with most of the enterprises linked to one or a few large ones located inside or outside the cluster (Pedersen, 1994b). In this category, collective efficiency derives from the reduced transportation costs for the small enterprises, rather than on collaboration among them, with most of the benefits usually accruing to subcontracting firms. However, such a system might allow small enterprises to increase their competitive position in relation to other small enterprises.

Within horizontal specialisation, Pedersen (1994b) distinguishes between the 'market town cluster' and 'specialised petty commodity cluster'. The *market town* (or distribution) cluster includes enterprises which are horizontally specialised among and within sectors. It is dominated by retailers and producers supplying local consumers, who are often in direct competition with large enterprises. In this case, collective efficiency is based on the reduced costs of transactions with suppliers and customers, rather than on collaboration among the small enterprises.

In contrast, the *specialised petty commodity cluster* includes enterprises that specialise horizontally, mainly producing but also retailing directly to low income consumers. Within this cluster, 'collective efficiencies achieved by clustering primarily are due to reduced transaction costs for customers, but

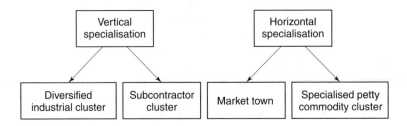

Figure 3.2 A typology of small enterprise clusters.

Source: adapted from Pedersen (1994b: 16)

some collaboration between enterprises may also take place' (Pedersen, 1994b: 17). Such clusters usually have limited resources and operate under unstable conditions, and while the enterprises are closely linked with the household economy, their social networks and patron–client relationships are important (Pedersen, 1994b).

It emerges, then, that clustering is an important dimension of small enterprise development, but recognition of this is relatively recent, 'a *deliberate* focus on clustering in research on small enterprise development in LDCs [less developed countries] . . . going back no further than 1989' (Nadvi and Schmitz, 1994: 5; emphasis in original). Since then, it has been recognised that clusters must be incorporated fully into a framework within which such enterprises are researched (Nadvi and Schmitz, 1994). As discussed in Chapter 6, it appears to be the specialised petty commodity cluster which is most apparent in the context of small enterprise production in Makassar, the main customer base being low income populations surrounding enterprise locations. However, aspects of vertical specialisation also become apparent, the evidence being collaboration among similar-sized small enterprises, supported by some subcontracting arrangements with larger firms. This, in turn, highlights the point that in developing countries these categories are not absolute, but 'ideal types' from which variation will be the norm rather than the exception. The concept of collective efficiency also implies positive benefits for those enterprises involved. Nonetheless, this is not always the case in reality and clusters may exist within which there are conflicts and inequalities (Smyth *et al.*, 1994).

Innovation

The final building block of the small enterprise integrative framework discussed here is innovation; that is, the introduction of something new or previously unknown (an idea or object) into somewhere or something that is known (*Oxford English Dictionary*, 1989). Such innovations might be technological, or be identifying an opportunity in the local market, responding through differentiation and diversification to produce a new product.

To be innovative, a small-scale entrepreneur must first be aware of and have knowledge concerning a possible change; second, be able to carry out the change; and third, have the choice to decide whether or not to implement the change, and when to do so (Yuwono *et al.*, 1994). A number of factors will influence whether an entrepreneur will adopt an innovation, among them:

- Personal factors (age, skills, education, risk attitude, knowledge about innovation, expectations, etc.).
- Firm features (present level of production, skills of workers, profitability, possibility to receive credit contribution to household income, etc.).
- Social networks are important . . . [and] may relate to friends, colleague entrepreneurs, family relationships with village leaders, etc. Social

networks may also be important for mobilizing credit needed for the adoption of an innovation.

- Characteristics of the existing product/technology compared with the new one. Here issues of compatibility, complexity, and availability of inputs play a role.
- Market considerations (expected selling price of new product, marketing channels, expectations about growth or decline of market demand).
- Wider environment, including for example government policies, extension services, infrastructure.

(Yuwono *et al.*, 359–360)

It is possible that after some experimenting with a new innovation the idea will be abandoned because the associated increase in profits is not deemed sufficient. It is also likely that a few small enterprises may produce innovative products at the same time as other small enterprises within the cluster or local region are still producing the old version of the same product. In other words, the adoption process will not be the same for all entrepreneurs (if they decide to adopt the innovation at all). In this respect the clustering of small enterprises can assist the innovation process, for while the individual aspects of the enterprise and the entrepreneur are important, the adoption of innovation is heavily dependant on the small enterprises' geographical and socio-economic environment. If an enterprise is part of a cluster, then knowledge concerning new ideas and opportunities spreads faster, support for innovative behaviour perhaps coming from other members of the cluster, although some might also offer discouragement. Moreover, as pointed out in earlier discussions on clustering, the latter can also reduce the costs of inputs which might otherwise hinder innovation. This aspect has been documented by Sandee (1994) and Yuwono *et al.* (1994), and more recently by Berry *et al.* (1999), and Sandee *et al.* (2000) in research undertaken in Java, Indonesia.

However, there is also a significant risk that small enterprises in developing countries will stagnate technologically (Piore and Sabel, 1984). For example, entrepreneurs in clusters or industrial districts making clothing often limit themselves to continual but very slight changes in the product, while neglecting improvements in design and processing that could lead to greater outputs and growth. Sometimes even this 'limited innovation' disappears, so that the enterprise operations must rely on closely guarded design and production secrets. It is when this strategy also fails that many firms resort instead to sweat-shop-style production, cutting costs by sweating labour or using inferior raw materials. Indeed, 'it is these breakdowns of innovative capacity that often make small firms a symbol of misery, not creativity' (Piore and Sabel, 1984: 263). Innovation may be especially difficult to achieve if a small enterprise has found a certain marketing niche. For these enterprises, it is tempting to remain there rather than try to compete in another market, where profits may not necessarily be any higher. In addition, the flexibility of enterprises and the fluidity of the resources they use may make it difficult to co-ordinate innovative activities (Piore and Sabel, 1984).

CONCLUSION: A MORE APPROPRIATE FRAMEWORK

All of the parameters reviewed above – flexible labour relations, networks and trust, collective efficiency and clusters, and innovation – form the critical essence, the building blocks of the proposed *small enterprise integrative framework* for examining small enterprises in developing countries.

Developed throughout Chapter 3, this framework emerged from an in-depth review and critique, in Chapter 2, of past approaches to the study of small enterprises. It was argued that a more appropriate framework was required with which 'to study small enterprises in relation to their socio-cultural environment and as integral parts of the entire industrial system' (Rasmussen *et al.*, 1992: 4). Such a framework must recognise the importance of diversity in theory, and acknowledge the essential need for issues relating to class, ethnicity, gender and local politics to be incorporated. With these factors in mind, Chapter 4 carries the discussion forward with an examination of the context of production in which my study of the small enterprises in Makassar is set. For this purpose we examine, in Chapter 4, the socio/economic/political/cultural local and regional contextual environment; that is, the contents of the outer ring of Figure 3.1, and an essential part of the small enterprise integrative framework.

4   Setting the scene
The context of production

Amir, the goldsmith whom we first met in Chapter 1, lives and works in Makassar, Sulawesi. To gain a greater comprehension of the structure and operations of his enterprise as well as his future business plans, together with those of other small enterprises in the city, it is necessary to understand the social and economic, as well as the political and cultural local and regional contextual environment – the contents of the outer ring of Figure 3.1 – within which the enterprises are situated. To achieve this, I present a brief analysis of the economic and political context nationwide, then bring the focus to a regional level, discussing the disparities within Indonesia in relation to Eastern Indonesia and specifically Sulawesi. An examination of the economy of South Sulawesi and Makassar precedes consideration of the urban design and local industry, and the introduction of the small enterprise realm. We conclude this chapter with an examination of the ethnic and cultural diversity of the city and gender relations within it.

The events that occurred prior to 1997 remain highly relevant to the current investigation of small enterprises in Indonesia, as they provide the historical context in which these enterprises were formed and functioned for many generations, still strongly influencing their composition and operations. As indicated later (see Chapter 8), the majority of small enterprises in Makassar have remained little changed since the 1997 general election and the beginning of the Southeast Asian economic crisis. Their operating environment has, instead, continued to be strongly influenced by the historical context of production, discussed later in this chapter, while changes that did impact on a minority of small enterprises in Makassar are addressed in Chapter 8.

INDONESIAN ECONOMY SINCE 1980

During the 1980s and early 1990s dynamic economic growth in the Asia-Pacific region made it the focus of world attention. Although poverty remained widespread, as did large disparities in income, the Asian NICs emerged as global players in the new world economy. As a 'second generation' NIC (defined in Chapter 2), Indonesia was 'one of the success stories of the third world over the past three decades' (Hill, 1997a: 256). Since the beginning of Suharto's New Order regime, the economy had grown six-fold and income per capita had increased four-fold (Hill and Mackie, 1994).[1] Moreover, economic reforms that began in 1983 and continued through the 1990s resulted in a more open and export-orientated economy (van Diermen, 1997), which in turn became more diversified as dependency on oil declined and an export-oriented manufacturing base emerged. Paralleling these changes and reinforcing them were large inflows of foreign direct investment and high levels of domestic savings (Government of Indonesia, 1998).

Despite strong macroeconomic performance, throughout the early and mid-1990s a number of underlying weaknesses became evident within the economy. Beginning in 1969, the Suharto Government had outlined national economic objectives in a series of Five Year Plans, the sixth (*Repelita VI*) being for the period 1 April 1994 to 31 March 1999. In this, the Suharto Government outlined policies to bring about greater deregulation, yet these were never fully implemented. The Government retained considerable control over the economy and by 1996/97 the transparency and consistency of its policies were becoming increasingly questioned. Some Indonesian economists even began to contemplate whether there was to be a move away from export orientation back to import substitution policies (Economist Intelligence Unit Limited, 1995; *Far Eastern Economic Review,* 1996; *Guardian,* 27 July 1996). Oligopolistic practices remained common, it being estimated that the ten largest trading houses in Indonesia controlled 82 per cent of the total turnover of the country's commerce in 1996 (*Jakarta Post,* 24 March 1997).

In the 1990s there was also a continuing reluctance by many foreign investors to become involved in Indonesia due to the bureaucratic web of licence laws and permits, not to mention the widespread existence of 'irregular payments' (Forbes, 1986). These *pungli* ('cash payments to make things happen') were collected by 'an army of 4 million underpaid bureaucrats [who] lurk in ambush in thickets of red tape' (*Far Eastern Economic Review,* 1996: 40). The proliferation of arrangements such as these, at once non-market and certainly non-transparent, was rife throughout Indonesia at all levels of business, and was one of the key causes of demonstrations that occurred in 1998 (see Turner and Seymour, 2002). The significance of these matters for small enterprises in Makassar is a dimension documented in Chapter 7.

POLITICAL ENVIRONMENT: CENTRAL CONTROL[2]

> The outstanding features of the New Order regime as it has developed in the past eighteen years, have been: the entrenchment and centralisation of authoritarian rule by the military, the appropriation of the state by its officials, and the exclusion of political parties from effective participation in the decision-making process.
>
> (Robison, 1986: 105)

Throughout the regime, the Suharto Government maintained close control over funding and economic activities in the twenty-seven different provinces of Indonesia. Regional spending policies were determined by the National Planning Agency and other agencies and ministries based in Jakarta (Schwarz, 1999). Indeed, there was such strong central control during the 1980s and early 1990s that according to Ranis and Stewart (1994: 43), 'President Soeharto holds virtually complete authority and other governing bodies generally do little more than "rubber stamp" his initiatives'. Each province in Indonesia has been headed by a Governor, appointed by the Home Affairs Ministry and usually drawn from the military. Each province was then divided into *kabupaten* (administrative districts) headed by a district head, and within these, *kecamatan* (subdistricts), consisting of thirty to forty villages. Nonetheless, although at the provincial and district levels there were elected legislative bodies, there was in general still a high percentage of central Government nominees, often military personnel (Ranis and Stewart, 1994), leading to the view that:

> As a result, local administrations represent the interests of the central government rather than those of local citizens. The dependence of the administration is partly caused by the fact that the appointment of local leaders (governors and regents) is often executed to fit the political preference of the central elite with the effect that merit considerations are put aside.
>
> (Jemadu, 1997: 5)

Despite a declared push towards decentralisation, little progress was made under Suharto's rule against the concentration of power based in the capital city, Jakarta. There was a reluctance to devolve power away from the central bureaucracy, as well as a certain element of 'cultural snobbery' (Schwarz, 1994: 62). As Schwarz explains, 'many Javanese, Indonesia's most numerous ethnic group, see no reason why their political and bureaucratic norms shouldn't be adopted nation-wide' (ibid.).[3] Many officials at the central and regional level also felt threatened by initiatives from local groups who might have wished to bypass their authority. Nevertheless, 'accusations from officials that the money will be "wasted" ring rather hollow, given the obvious signs of extravagant bureaucratic consumption at both central and regional levels everywhere in Indonesia' (Booth, 1994: 37). South Sulawesi was probably typical in this regard, for there,

> neither the indigenous economic or political institutions have been allowed to develop through their own initiative during the past seven decades. . . . The result has been a build-up of pressures and frustrations – of economic underdevelopment and the maldistribution of political power.
>
> (Forbes, 1981b: 146)

URBAN LABOUR FORCE

The economic and political environment in Indonesia strongly influences the regulatory framework within which the labour force operates. In 1971, the 39 million people employed in the country were heavily concentrated in rural areas, while a large proportion of those in urban areas were in the 'informal sector' (Jones, 1994). Since then, the composition of employment opportunities has changed dramatically, a decline in the proportion of people employed in the agricultural sector being accompanied by the diversifying growth of employment in non-agricultural activities, in all the major service industries, manufacturing and construction (Simanjuntak, 1993; Sjahrir, 1993; Manning, 1998). From 1985 to 1990 employment in the manufacturing sector grew by 7.2 per cent, a major contribution coming from growth in labour intensive export industries. Simultaneously, there was a rise in female labour participation rates (Jones, 1994; Wardhana, 1996). A growth in productivity in the manufacturing sector resulted from increased numbers of skilled and capital intensive activities, as well as technological changes within industries, especially those producing textiles, footwear and *kretek* cigarettes (Hill, 1990). In this sector, from 1993 to 1996, wages rose as much as 60 per cent (*Far Eastern Economic Review,* 1996). Whereas in 1990 the Indonesian labour force was near 75.9 million, by 1997 it had reached 85.4 million (aged 15 and above), and had expanded to 87.7 million a year later (Booth, 1994; Feridhanusetyawan, 1999; *Biro Pusat Statistik (BPS)* Republic of Indonesia, 2000).[4]

Despite these encouraging trends, from 1980 to 1990 the level of recorded *unemployment* in Indonesia rose from 1.7 to around 3.2 per cent, and on the eve of the economic crisis in 1997 stood at about 4.7 per cent (Hill, 1999b). Unemployment was especially noticeable in the urban areas where 'according to the 1980 census, the number of urban unemployed was about 275,000 people and this increased almost fivefold to 1.248 million in 1990' (Sukamdi, 1996: 64), with unemployment higher among women than among men (Simanjuntak, 1993). Both trends continued through to 1997, when, in addition, more than half of the unemployed were in the 20- to 29-year age group (Ahmed, 1999). Nonetheless, it has been argued by several authors that overt unemployment was not so high, because a large proportion of the young unemployed were educated, middle-class people looking for the 'right job' and were prepared to wait in the hope that they would find a high-paying urban position sometime in the future (Jones, 1994; Sundrijo, 1997). However, Sukamdi (1996: 64) contends that unemployment among the young should be of serious concern because in his view 'high unemployment among this group is likely to bring about social and political problems in the cities and nationally', a debate brought to the fore with the largely urban-based riots in 1998.

The underutilisation or *underemployment* of labour was much more evident, the economy being unable to absorb people into productive employment with fair wages. This was manifest in the many people who worked short hours in occupations with very low returns, many having to undertake multiple jobs to survive (Simanjuntak, 1993; Jones, 1994). Their plight was confirmed by the 1990 Population Census which reported that approximately 38.7 per cent of people worked fewer than thirty-five hours a week, numbers being at their highest in rural areas. The census also recorded that approximately 34.3 per cent worked more than forty-five hours a week, mainly in urban areas where they earned lower wages, working long hours, often in multiple jobs to gain an adequate income on which to live (Simanjuntak, 1993). By 1996, the total underemployment rate stood at 35 per cent of workers, a circumstance that re-emphasises the continuing importance of small enterprises as a means of survival (Feridhanusetyawan, 1999).

Due to the fact that throughout this period a large proportion of the working population received wages that were exceedingly low, attempts were made to encourage employers to increase wage levels and to develop social security measures. In 1989 to 1990, the Department of Manpower set specific guidelines for the implementation of minimum wage legislation, a minimum wage level being set for each province, as well as legal sanctions for non-compliance (Manning, 1993). Notwithstanding, in 1993 the official minimum wage level set was approximately 76 per cent of the value required to meet minimum physical needs (MPN). Indeed, as recently as 1997 the Suharto Government admitted that the minimum wage levels were still not enough to live on, with estimates that they met 92.5 per cent of minimum physical needs (Simanjuntak, 1993; *New Zealand Herald*, 27 January 1997).[5] For Jakarta, the minimum daily wage was Rp.5750 a day in 1997, and for Makassar Rp.3750 in 1997, an increase from Rp.3400 in 1996 (*Jakarta Post*, 23 January 1997).[6] Nonetheless, payments of wages below these levels remained common, 'especially among illegal and semi-legal "backyard" operators who often employ a high proportion of child and female labour' (Manning, 1993: 73). Workers involved in 'putting-out' or homeworking production were also subjected to very low incomes and had little or no protection under existing labour laws (Manning, 1993). This was commonly the case among small enterprises in Makassar, as we will see in Chapter 5.

Another considerable factor that hindered companies from paying their workers according to government regulations and therefore inhibited a real improvement in labour wages were legal and illegal levies, called 'invisible costs' in the business sector. For instance, a report from the Indonesian Employers' Association's West Java branch showed that companies had to allocate 22 per cent of production costs to bribes and levies, and suggested that in other regions the allocation could be as high as 40 per cent (*Jakarta Post*, 23 February 1997). Other, more conservative research has suggested these cost penalties to be between 5 to 8 per cent of operating costs (Hill, 1997b). Yet, as Wilhelmus Bokha, the chairperson of the All-Indonesia Workers Union Federation observed, 'if we really want to compete in the free market, we have to stop monopolies, collusion and the infamous illegal levies' (quoted in *Jakarta Past*, 23 February 1997). The impact of such 'invisible costs' on the operation of small-scale entrepreneurs in Makassar is discussed in Chapter 7.

SMALL ENTERPRISES IN INDONESIA

Assessments of the numbers of small enterprises in Indonesia, their development and success, are frequently hampered by a lack of consistent data, as discussed by Hill (1996). However, it has been suggested that in the early 1980s the number of small enterprises expanded rapidly, and by the mid-1980s three-quarters of manufacturing was in cottage and small enterprises (Wolf, 1993; Manning, 1998). By the 1990s growth had slowed but was still notable, stimulated by increasing wage employment opportunities, such as homeworking associated with small enterprises (defined in Chapter 3), and later also by a decrease in employment in large labour intensive industries (Manning, 1998).

By 1994 the Central Bureau of Statistics reported that '99.8 per cent or 33.4 million of the 33.5 million businesses in Indonesia were small enterprises, each with a turnover less than Rp.1 billion a year' (*Jakarta Post*, 27 May 1997). The bulk of these (97.6 per cent) were considered 'tiny with turnover less than Rp.50 million each' (Lalkaka, 1996: 1). Of these 'tiny' enterprises, 63 per cent were involved in agriculture; 17 per cent in trade; 7 per cent in industry; 5 per cent in services; and 4 per cent in transportation (Lalkaka, 1996). It is clear, then, that small enterprises had (and continue to have) a substantial role to play in providing a livelihood for a large majority of the Indonesian population.

The Suharto Government's stance on small enterprises fluctuated throughout the New Order regime. It oscillated between strong state intervention on the one hand to, on the other, a reliance on market mechanisms, or a combination of the two. The shifting priorities were due largely to conflicts of interest among different entrepreneurial groups, such as indigenous Indonesians, the Chinese, and foreign companies, in addition to being linked to Indonesia's position in the global economy and Government support for certain enterprises located in particular geographical regions within the country (Smyth *et al.*, 1994).

During the early years of Suharto's Government the focus was on the stimulation of foreign direct investment (FDI), rather than on indigenous enterprises, resulting in many entrepreneurs operating the latter becoming marginalised from important economic sectors (Smyth *et al.*, 1994). Policies introduced to assist small enterprises during the mid-1970s were largely a response to political disturbances caused by the 'Malari affair'.[7] The Government responded by introducing a number of new policy measures designed to promote indigenous businesses, reduce conspicuous consumption and increase controls over foreign capital (Chalmers, 1997a).

The main policy innovation was the *Bimbingan dan Pengembangan Industri Kecil (BIPIK)* (Programme for Guidance and Development of Small Industries) which included technical assistance (focusing on cluster areas) as well as training courses operated by the Department of Industry.[8] Other new programmes included the *Kredit Investasi Kecil (KIK)* (Small Investment Credit) and *Kredit Modal Kerja Permanen (KMKP)* (Working Capital Credit), their purpose being to provide assistance to small industries (Utrecht and Sayogyo, 1994). In a geographical sense, these programmes were concentrated on Java and had limited success, their major outcome being the introduction of some new products and techniques in certain sections of industry that were already well established, such as the rattan furniture sector (Utrecht and Sayogyo, 1994). The majority of the funds were also 'grabbed by middlemen and stashed in high-yielding time deposits in the very banks which issued the credits' (Schwarz, 1999: 119). Continuing problems with the KIK and KMKP programmes, a default rate of approximately 27 per cent, and a decline in Government oil revenues, led to their reduction and gradual elimination (Pangestu, 1996).

In the 1990s, the Suharto Government's position on small enterprises appeared to remain somewhat ambiguous, for 'the promotion of small-scale establishments in Indonesia, as in other developing countries, has always been important in rhetoric if not in practice' (Smyth *et al.*, 1994: 6). Despite recognition that the Suharto Government was generally positive about the importance of small enterprises in economic development, acknowledging that they were highly labour intensive and thus represented an important sector for employment creation (Sandee *et al.*, 1994; *Jakarta Post*, 24 April 1997), government policies have been categorised as 'somewhat muddled' by Hill (1998: 33). More forcibly, Soerjadi argued that: 'Conglomerates are expanding but small business is slowly dying because the government's economic policy only benefits big business' (*PDI* candidate, reported in *Jakarta Post*, 17 May 1997). Likewise, Sandee *et al.* (2000: 185) maintain that 'the growth of small-scale industries during Indonesia's period of rapid economic growth is remarkable given that it occurred at a time when the policy environment tended to be biased towards medium and large-scale industries'.

Indeed, the Government's policies of promoting industrialisation had many adverse effects on small enterprises, and although the policies were paralleled by others designed to support them, the outcome led Joseph (1987: 30) to claim that 'the two sets of policies and programs are inherently contradictory'. Large-scale industries producing goods similar to those manufactured by small enterprises made it difficult for smaller firms to compete successfully, simply because the larger firms were able to produce goods either less expensively or of a higher quality (Poot *et al.*, 1991; Latanro, 1994). In addition, export promotion tended to favour larger firms that had easier access to both duty-free immediate inputs and credit facilities than had small enterprises. Changes in consumption patterns also led to a declining demand for certain small enterprise products which were seen as being of inferior quality to large factory-produced or imported goods (Joseph, 1987; Sandee *et al.*, 1994). Nonetheless, because not everyone benefited from increasing incomes, there was still a demand for small enterprise goods.

Government programmes to assist small enterprises

Several Government departments and ministries have a role in supporting small enterprises. Among these are the Ministry of Co-operatives and Small Enterprises, the Department of Manpower, and the Office of the Minister for the Development of the Role of Women (Joseph, 1987). The Ministry of Co-operatives and Small Enterprises has, as part of its mandate, the role of co-ordinating assistance programmes for small enterprises provided by other Ministries, and is involved in the preparation of new legislation concerning small enterprises (Berry *et al.*, 1999). However, the agency most closely linked with the objective of promoting small-scale and cottage industries remains the *Departemen Perindustrian dan Perdagangan* (Department of Industry and Trade) and within it, in particular, the *Direktorat Jenderal Industri Kecil* (Directorate General of Small Industries). The Directorate seeks, among other aims, to provide guidance for small industries, and to promote links between small industries and larger private and Government enterprises. However, the target group remains very large, based as it is on a broad definition of small-scale and cottage enterprises with assets under Rp.600 million, as mentioned in Chapter 1.

To stimulate small-scale and cottage enterprises, the Department of Industry and Trade operated five main programmes at various times in the 1990s, the details of which are included in Appendix 2.[9] Briefly, these included:

1   *Program Keterkaitan Sistem Bapak Angkat* (Adoptive Father System/Foster-Parent programme).
2   *Pemanfaatan 1–5% Keuntungan BUMN* (Using 1 to 5 per cent of State Enterprise Profits for Small-Scale and Cottage Industry Development).
3   *Kredit Usaha Kecil (KUK)* (Small Business Credit).
4   *Penjualan Saham kepada Koperasi* (Selling Shares to Co-operatives).
5   *Pendidikan dan Latihan bagi Industri Kecil* (Education and Training for Small Industries).

There were a number of problems with these programmes. Concerns were raised about the 'foster-parent' system, adopted as part of the first programme. This has been described as being little more than subcontracting arrangements between large and small firms, often benefiting the larger firm to the greater extent (Smyth *et al.*, 1994). Moreover, as Utrecht and Sayogyo (1994: 51) observe:

There is no question about the fact that implementation of the policy has experienced failures of different kinds, caused in some cases by the technological gap between the giver and the recipient of assistance . . . or by financial delays and manipulations.

For such reasons the 'foster-parent' programme has been deemed to be ineffective. There are a number of examples of mismatched business types, and the Government has been criticised for coercing large enterprises into the programme and expecting them to solve the problems of the small enterprises (*Jakarta Post*, 29 March 1997). More explicitly, Schwarz (1994: 119) argues that: 'The program splutters on but is disliked by leading Chinese-owned firms, who find it vague and confused, as well as by leading *pribumi*-owned companies, who find it patronising and insulting.'

Often small-scale entrepreneurs were uncertain as to how to make a proposal for assistance. Procedures varied among different state enterprises in the case of the second programme, and the amount that could be borrowed was often relatively small (Rp.5–10 million). It could also take between three months to a year to obtain the assistance requested (*PUKTI*, 1995). Regarding the second programme specifically, in a letter to the Editor of the *Jakarta Post* (3 June 1997), one concerned individual observed that: 'We cannot let the programme waste energy and resources, while its impact creates increasingly more collusion and corruption and abuse of authority.'

The third programme too has been relatively unsuccessful, largely because 'banks, especially those which specialize in corporate banking, have trouble identifying feasible small-scale enterprises' (*Far Eastern Economic Review*, 1996: 48). At the same time, small-scale entrepreneurs often do not have the skills required to provide the correct application information, nor fulfil technical banking requirements (*Far Eastern Economic Review*, 1996). The result has often been that banks have complied by creating fictitious borrowers (Schwarz, 1994).

The Department of Manpower also introduced training programmes for small-scale entrepreneurs to learn certain industry skills. These activities were conducted by the *Balai Latihan Kerja* (*BLK*) (Work Training Centre) within the Department. The main objective of the programme was to improve employment opportunities, especially among school 'drop-outs' and young people, with one scheme operating that sent students overseas for work experience (Utrecht and Sayogyo, 1994; KI 2, 22/11/96). Nonetheless, a German volunteer working with the scheme in Makassar commented: 'There's heaps of "kickbacks" involved. The staff subsidise themselves with bribes. You "buy" your way into the scheme, especially if you want to go overseas later' (Interview, confidential personal communication, 2 May 1997). Hill (1998: 33) adds that these schemes are 'rarely customer friendly and are generally supply driven'.

In 1995 the Small Business Act was passed by the Indonesian Government with the aim of strengthening the contribution of small and medium enterprises to the national economy and to help transform some 50,000 small enterprises into more viable medium sized enterprises by the end (1998) of *Repelita VI* (the Sixth Five Year Plan). As mentioned in Chapter 1, definitions used in this Act were different again from those previously used, with small enterprises defined as having below Rp.200 million in assets (excluding land/buildings) or under Rp.1 billion in turnover (*Departemen Koperasi dan Pembinaan Pengusaha Kecil*, 1995; Lalkaka, 1996). Lalkaka (1996: 1; emphasis in original) points out that:

> *This* [Act] *calls for new strategies, skills and structures to overcome the traditional constraints of the small enterprise sector,* that is, limited access to capital, information and marketing together with weaknesses in management, marketing, networking, and applying technology to enhance quality and competitiveness.

The following analysis chapters document that these aspects have remained of considerable concern to the small-scale entrepreneurs interviewed in Makassar, while the Act appears to have done little to reshape actual Government intervention (Competency Based Economies through Formation of Enterprise (CEFE), 1996).

Clustering of small enterprises producing the same or similar goods is a common feature in rural and urban Indonesia (Sandee *et al.*, 1994). Officially sanctioned clusters (*sentra*) were initially established in the 1970s with foreign sponsorship, to be taken over by the Indonesian Government fully in the 1980s (Berry *et al.*, 1999). The *sentra* are now promoted by the Department of Industry and Trade, and Ministry of Co-operatives and Small Enterprises, and defined by these agencies as 'a concentration in one location of at least 20 business units that make the same product' (Utrecht and Sayogyo, 1994: 49). The *sentra* are initially formed by Department of Industry and Trade officials observing which enterprises were spatially near each other, while walking around a specific area (KI 1, 14/4/97; Department of Industry and Trade official, confidential personal communication, 1 May 1997). Thus although entrepreneurs may have been members of different 'informal' clusters in the past, they often suddenly became organised into new *sentra* with previous outsiders/competitors. Assistance is given by the Departments to those *sentra* considered to have the most potential for development and expansion, yet the full implementation of the programme has suffered from a lack of finance and experienced personnel (Utrecht and Sayogyo, 1994; Berry *et al.*, 1999). Such *sentra* in Makassar are discussed in detail in Chapter 7.

Semi-autonomous organisations

Pusat Pengembangan Usaha Kecil Kawasan Timur Indonesia (PUKTI) (Centre for Development of Small Enterprises, East Indonesia) is a semi-autonomous organisation working with small enterprises in Makassar. The

Centre operates under the auspices of *Universitas Hasanuddin*, but gains the majority of its funding from *Konrad Adenauer Stiftung,* a German non-governmental organisation working with small enterprises in Indonesia. This funding was supplemented by further contributions from the Ministry of Co-operatives and Small Enterprises. The Centre provides training on basic business development, primary accounting methods, banking proposals and general money management for small-scale entrepreneurs in Makassar. It also acts as an umbrella organisation for seven universities in East Indonesia, each of which has its own centre for small enterprises. Officials from *PUKTI* travel to these centres to exchange information and provide support for local training schemes (KI 1, 18/1/97).

Another semi-autonomous organisation is the Indonesian *Kamar Dagang dan Industri, (KADIN)* (Chamber of Commerce and Industry), established in 1968 as a means of encouraging business representation at the national level of politics (MacIntyre, 1991). The national headquarters (*KADIN*) are located in Jakarta, with branches in each of the provinces (*KADINIA*). Initially, from 1968 to 1979, *KADIN* as a national organisation was chaired by senior military officials involved in business. Since then, private business people have been the chairs, but the distancing from the Government has been perceived as merely symbolic. In fact, MacIntyre (1991: 43) maintains that, 'put bluntly, the business community has tended to see *KADIN*, or more specifically its leadership, as self-serving and virtually a tool of the government rather than as a representative of industry interests'.

Nevertheless, in stark contrast, the South Sulawesi *KADINIA,* established in 1972, has been described as 'an independent, non-governmental, non-political, non-profit organization' (Business Advisory Indonesia, 1991: 2), which plays an active role in improving business in the region and in particular enhancing export opportunities. Training courses, often jointly run with Government Departments in the city, are offered to members in tax preparation, general accounting, exporting possibilities and preparation of bank loan applications. Business training programmes are also provided for newly graduated high school and university students (McMahon, 1992; KI 19, 12/5/97). The South Sulawesi *KADINIA* (partly funded by European non-government organisations and partly by members' fees) provides liaison support for members requiring assistance with recommendations; help for facilitating contacts with Government officials or other institutions; and supplies information to those requesting it. Members are from private and public companies as well as from co-operatives. They must have a *Surat Izin Tempat Usaha* (licence for a business or work site) and usually a *Surat Izin Untuk Perusahaan* (licence for an enterprise to operate) as well. However, if a prospective member did not have these, *KADINIA* workers could help the entrepreneur obtain them (KI 19, 10/5/97).

The impression given of the South Sulawesi *KADINIA*, during initial field work and a return visit to the office in 1999, was that it was efficient and well organised, although additional funding would have been beneficial. Unlike equivalent branches elsewhere, South Sulawesi *KADINIA* had not been able to gain funding from the local provincial government (Business Advisory Indonesia, 1991; KI 19, 12/5/97). The Secretary-General appeared to have played a major role in the success of the organisation and spent considerable time helping young people in the city, providing them with information about establishing an enterprise. To summarise, then, '*KADIN* [South Sulawesi] is an impressive and vibrant organisation with considerable assets: a general secretary of rare vision and energy, a hard-working and talented staff, a wide and well-established networks of contacts within rural and urban public and private sectors' (McMahon, 1992: 13).

Co-operatives

The first Constitution of the Republic of Indonesia (1945) stated that 'the Indonesian economy was to be based on the principle of all being of one family' (Rahim, 1957: xxv). In this, there were to be three equal partners in development: co-operatives; the private sector; and the Government (Schwarz, 1994). As such, the purpose of economic co-operation, according to Hatta (1957: 2), the Vice-President of Indonesia from 1945 to 1956, was 'to improve the lot of the economically weak by means of their working together'. To this end the Government promoted a variety of different co-operatives including, among others, multi-purpose village co-operatives and credit co-operatives (with credit in kind or money), as well as production co-operatives and consumption co-operatives (Hatta, 1957). In addition, official clusters of small enterprises (*sentra*) could become co-operatives if they registered with the Ministry of Co-operatives and Small Enterprises (Sandee *et al.*, 1994).

Suharto believed that co-operatives were the solution to problems relating to trickle-down-led growth, such as the inability to obtain equity and social justice. By transferring wealth to co-operatives he concluded that this would solve the problems for *pribumi* (indigenous Indonesian) operated small enterprises (Schwarz, 1994). Yet by 1979 criticisms of the co-operative system were already being made by members of the Indonesian Chamber of Commerce and Industry (*KADIN*). They maintained that its development had been too slow (Mubyarto, 1979, translated in Chalmers and Hadiz, 1997), so much so that fifteen years later Schwarz (1994: 100) concluded that

> co-operatives have fallen far short of their constitutionally prescribed place in society. The roughly 34,000 active co-operatives account for less than 5 per cent of gross domestic product, and they are by far the junior partner to private and government-owned companies.

It has often been suggested that co-operatives were under the domination of the Indonesian Government rather than being autonomous, to the extent that Abdurrahman Wahid, the leader of Indonesia's largest Muslim organisation *Nahdlatul Ulama* at the time, and later President of Indonesia, felt compelled to assert that 'we need to develop a new approach to small businesses. Co-operatives are unhealthy for us and a burden on society. They are only killing the real entrepreneurs. Everyone knows the co-operatives are just tools of the government' (Wahid, 1990, reported in Schwarz, 1994: 121). To Seda (1990, translated 1997: 245) the co-operative system needed a radical overhaul:

> What is needed urgently is deregulation and debureaucratisation in promoting co-operatives. Co-operatives can only become one of the mainstays of the national economy and an effective means for realising economic equity and social justice if they are independent!

Access to co-operative assistance was often determined by class, with the more wealthy small-scale entrepreneurs usually being the main beneficiaries of government programmes. Indeed, 'participation in training courses, credit schemes, raw materials acquisition, and marketing projects is usually by pre-selection' (Joseph, 1987: 33). Frequently, too, participation required registration with a certain government department, a step that small-scale entrepreneurs were often reluctant to do due to tax, labour and licensing regulations. There was also little support for workers within industries, most of the advice being directed to the entrepreneurs alone (Joseph, 1987).

In Makassar in 1995 there were 560 *koperasi* (co-operatives) listed as 'legal bodies', or 'not yet legal bodies' by the Ministry of Co-operatives and Small Enterprises. Of these, sixteen were *koperasi industri* (industry co-operatives), fifty-two were *koperasi serba usaha* (general business co-operatives), and thirteen were *koperasi simpan pinjam* (savings and loans co-operatives). Other co-operatives listed included those for the Army, women, consumers, workers, and government workers (*Biro Pusat Statistik (BPS) Kotamadya Ujung Pandang*, 1996: 181). Nonetheless, these statistics did not agree with those available from the Department of Industry and Trade, which stated that in 1995 there were eleven co-operatives operating as *koperasi industri kecil dan kerajinan* (small-scale industry and handicraft co-operatives), including those producing silver handicrafts, car seats, *tahu* and *tempe* (tofu and fermented soya bean cake), children's shoes, rattan handicrafts and embroidery (*Departemen Perindustrian Dan Perdagangan, Kotamadya Ujung Pandang*, 1995: 23). The lack of reliable and comparable information between the two agencies is worrisome when considering the future possible assistance they might guarantee to members of such co-operatives.

Under Suharto's rule numerous Government and non-Government programmes have been put into place since the 1970s to assist small enterprises. In reality, however, it appears that Government policies have generally been unable to improve the circumstances of small enterprises, due to mismanagement in programme organisation, erroneous assumptions on which some of them have been based and an inability to change market structures (Smyth *et al.*, 1994). In reality, then, as Hill (1996: 170) argues, 'these initiatives have frequently failed to address some of the more fundamental impediments to the development of an efficient SSI [small-scale industry] sector'. Likewise a CEFE (1996: 6) report documented:

> Government-sponsored support mechanism[s] have generally lacked the needed flexibility, motivated personnel and political leadership. [C]omprehensive SME [small and medium enterprise] development strategies do not exist, and international technical assistance projects and development loans have been unsuccessful in leaving behind sustainable activities.

In contrast, the semi-autonomous *PUKTI* and South Sulawesi *KADINIA* appeared to have had more success in reaching their target audiences with training and information, although the smallest unlicensed enterprises were still not receiving assistance. These organisations had not been plagued with bureaucracy and corruption to the extent that the Government organisations/programmes had, and during the late 1990s there were a number of enthusiastic and dedicated staff working for them. The range of small-scale entrepreneurs in Makassar able to benefit from such assistance, and the reasons why others were unable to do so, are both examined in more detail in Chapter 7.

DEVELOPMENT DISPARITIES IN EASTERN INDONESIA[10]

> Indonesia's major regional challenge is no longer rural poverty in Java, as it was portrayed in the 1960s, but the increasingly bypassed areas of Eastern Indonesia. It is unlikely that these provinces will attract much industry in the next decade or two, apart from a limited amount of simple resource-based processing, based on timber, fisheries and some food and cash crops.
> (Hill, 1993: 22)

Despite Indonesia's previous rapid economic growth, the country has continued to contain wide regional disparities, Eastern Indonesia being the poorest national region. It has been suggested that this region might be thought of as a 'peripheral economic zone, vis-à-vis, the western major islands of Java and Sumatra' (Japan International Co-operation Agency (JICA), 1996: 3-6). This is largely due to a Java/Outer Island dichotomy that broadly relates to a manufacturing/resource extraction dichotomy. Historically, the development of manufacturing and industry in Indonesia has been concentrated on Java, a trend that continued in the 1980s and 1990s when around 78 per cent of medium- and large-scale firms were located there, the most concentration being that surrounding Jakarta (Forbes, 1986; Drake, 1989; Manning, 1998). Manufacturing has brought benefits to Java, Bali and Sumatra in terms of infrastructure development, and they have tended to receive most of the subsequent new private investment, while Eastern Indonesia has languished (Schwarz, 1994). So much so that according to Azis (1996: 75):

> Eastern Indonesia is, in general, less developed in terms of output and almost all production factors except its vast area and richness in natural resources. The insufficiency of infrastructure and the lack of a critical pool of skilled labour are frequently identified as important factors hindering further growth of the region.

In fact, between 1970 and 1990, Eastern Indonesia received less than 8 per cent of foreign and domestic investment, a much smaller share than one might expect, given that it accounts for 14 per cent of the total Indonesian population (Sondakh, 1996: 153). Clearly, as Forbes (1986: 128) notes, 'the net gains from foreign investment . . . have flowed disproportionately to the Jakarta and West Java core, compounding the spatial unevenness of Indonesian economic development'.

A major constraint to business development in Eastern Indonesia is that due to centralised trade and investment policies imposed by the Government the majority of Eastern Indonesian products exported internationally have to be transferred initially to Surabaya in East Java (Business Advisory Indonesia, 1991; *Jakarta Post*, 28 April 1997). Despite repeated attempts to promote Makassar as Eastern Indonesia's trade port, Surabaya has remained of great importance as a trading centre for the eastern islands (KI 5, 8/9/96). Indeed, Sulawesi's role as

> the commercial capital of eastern Indonesia has not been as pronounced as might have been expected, it has to some extent been bypassed as a trading centre, manufacturing performance has been most indifferent, and the economic slowdown in the 1980s has been sharper than the national average.
>
> (Kristanto *et al.*, 1989: 406)

In addition, there are already a number of large downstream processing plants on Java and Sumatra which can use economies of scale and lower labour costs to undercut new entrants (Babcock, 1990). Similarly, a large share of the value added to products, especially to primary commodities from Eastern Indonesia, occurs in Java (Barlow, 1996b; Sondakh, 1996). The latter still remains the ultimate market for products from Eastern Indonesia, whilst, concurrently, producers in these islands find it difficult to compete against similar commodities imported from Java (Mboi, 1996).

In Suharto's Budget Speech of January 1990, he referred specifically to the importance of developing the eastern region of Indonesia. This was an important departure from the usual Government policy of emphasising the unity of the country and was 'the first time a region had been singled out as a development problem' (Chauvel, 1996: 61). This occurred at the same time that concern over the growing inequality of wealth distribution in the country was beginning to be discussed openly, and it became recognised that Eastern Indonesia had been 'left behind' in the 1980s. Specific concerns singled out included the limited infrastructure; small isolated communities; low and declining levels of domestic and foreign investment; lack of skilled labour; and limited access to markets (Azis, 1996; Chauvel, 1996).

Since then, in his 1995 State Address, Suharto identified five categories of industries which he stated should be developed as key means to improve growth. These included industries which could stimulate economic activities in regions *outside* of Java, especially in the eastern islands (Soesastro, 1996). Nonetheless, a number of large industries already operating in Eastern Indonesia have failed to generate significant spill-over effects for the surrounding populations and the region lacks a dynamic leading sector that can stimulate the local economy (Hill, 1994). This has led to the suggestion that the industrialisation processes underway in other parts of Indonesia are not necessarily appropriate for Eastern Indonesia with its distinct physical, economic and social factors. For Eastern Indonesia, 'activities by private indigenous investors should be promoted, *even* if they are *small-* or medium-scale industries' (Azis, 1996: 117; emphasis added).

SULAWESI, SOUTH SULAWESI AND MAKASSAR

> Local areas are not just in passive receipt of changes handed down from some higher national, or international, level. The vast variety of conditions already existing at local levels also affects how these processes themselves operate.
>
> (Massey, 1983: 75)

Throughout the 1950s and 1960s there was a series of rebellions on Sulawesi (formally named the Celebes). These were initially against the Dutch reconstructing the local colonial government following the Second World War, then in support of demands for an independent East Indonesia state. When the federal state of Sulawesi was brought into the Republic of Indonesia in 1950, further discontent concerning impatience with the weakness of the Government in Jakarta appeared (Reid, 1990b; Pelras, 1996a). The 'South Sulawesi Rebellion' from 1950 to 1965 caused significant upheaval in the region, such that the rebellious forces controlled all but the cities of South Sulawesi by 1965 (Harvey, 1974). It was only when peace was restored after 1965 that economic development could again take place on the island, so that 'Sulawesi got off to a slow start in restoring communications, rebuilding the national infrastructure and opening the country up to tourism and investment' (Reid, 1990b: 37; see also Adams, 1997a).

Sulawesi's population stood at 14.1 million in 2000 (*Biro Pusat Statistik (BPS)* Republic of Indonesia, 2002). As shown in Figure 4.1, the island is

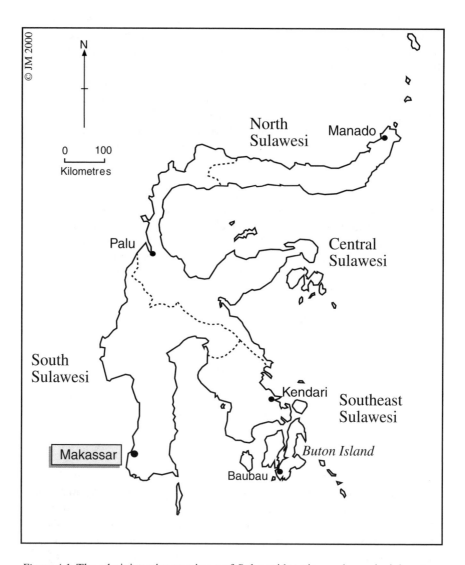

Figure 4.1 The administrative provinces of Sulawesi locating each provincial centre.
Source: adapted from De Koninck (1994: 3)

divided into four administrative provinces. In 1971, the total population of the South Sulawesi province stood at a little more than 5.1 million, a number that had grown to 8.1 million by the time of the 2000 Population Census. On average, each year from 1990 until 2000, the province's population grew by 1.5 per cent (JICA, 1996; *Biro Pusat Statistik (BPS)* Republic of Indonesia, 2002).

The South Sulawesi economy has remained based predominantly on primary resources, the ten main exports in 1994 being, in descending order of monetary value, nickel, as well as cacao, frozen prawns, wood processing, and coffee arabica, followed by cashew nut, cassava, frozen fish, rubber and rattan (Regional Investment Co-ordinating Board, 1995; see also 1996a, 1996b). Despite the island's considerable natural resources, by the late 1990s only nickel had been exploited to any large degree and in general had not had a significant impact on the development of the local economy. Accordingly, the small-scale processing of agricultural products and food manufacturing remained predominant activities. Since the 1980s the Government also focused on the production of secondary food crops in the region, such as cassava, corn and pulses, that were more suitable to the local climate and land conditions than was rice in many districts (Babcock, 1990).

Service industries such as transportation and tourism have become increasingly important to the island's economic performance, yet as Mboi (1996: 130) records: 'There are no policies or concrete efforts at the moment to integrate high-tech, capital intensive industries with local, slow-moving economies, or to involve the local people in the broader economy.' 'Cottage activities' are still commonly found in South Sulawesi, including silk production and weaving in the Soppeng and Wajo areas, and weaving in the Majene district, as shown in Figure 4.2. Traditional crafts are produced in the Tanatoraja area mainly to take advantage of the tourist trade located there, while gold- and silversmithing is undertaken extensively in Makassar (South Sulawesi Chamber of Commerce and Industry, 1996). In 1994 the total number of small enterprises in South Sulawesi was calculated to be 69,835, with 214,608 workers, and in 1993 there were 453 *sentra* (official clusters) (*Permerintah Daerah Tingkat I Sulawesi Selatan*, 1996, 1997: 15).[11]

Political environment

As indicated earlier, South Sulawesi is part of a provincial system and is administrated by a governor, who although 'on paper' is selected from five candidates or fewer by the *Tingkat I* (Provincial Parliament), in reality was more likely to be a Central Government supported appointee (Loveard, 1996). Within the South Sulawesi province there are twenty-five *Tingkat II* (governmental administrative areas): two *Kotamadya* (municipalities), one of which is Makassar (previously Ujung Pandang), and twenty three regencies. Under the Makassar Mayor's jurisdiction are a number of departments which include various *Dinas* (regional/local Departments) such as the

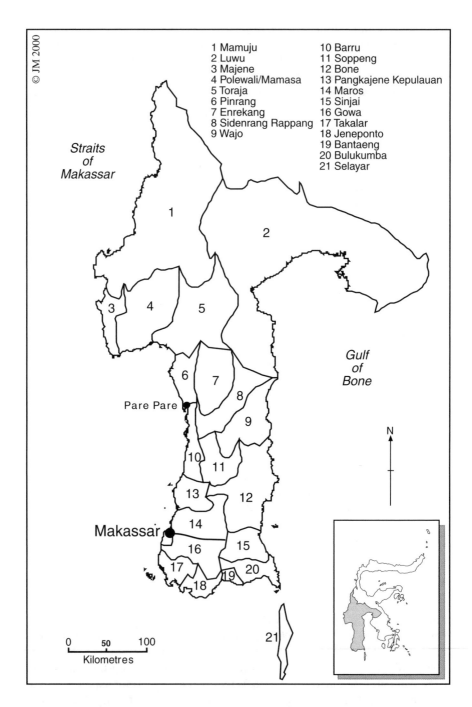

© JM 2000

1 Mamuju
2 Luwu
3 Majene
4 Polewali/Mamasa
5 Toraja
6 Pinrang
7 Enrekang
8 Sidenrang Rappang
9 Wajo

10 Barru
11 Soppeng
12 Bone
13 Pangkajene Kepulauan
14 Maros
15 Sinjai
16 Gowa
17 Takalar
18 Jeneponto
19 Bantaeng
20 Bulukumba
21 Selayar

Straits
of
Makassar

Gulf
of
Bone

Pare Pare

Makassar

N

0   50   100
Kilometres

Figure 4.2 South Sulawesi, showing *kabupaten* (administrative districts).

Source: adapted from Forbes (1981b: 144)

Regional Revenue Department, the Urban Management Department, the Public Works Department, together with the Health Department, Market Department, Tourism Department, and so on. *Badan Perencanaan Pembangunan Daerah (BAPPEDA)* (local planning development agencies) operate at the provincial and municipal levels. *BAPPEDA I* operates as the provincial planning board, generating its own plans, albeit following those set out by the Government. *BAPPEDA II* operates in a similar manner at the municipal level, formulating plans to guide city development (JICA, 1996).

As mentioned above, municipal governments in Indonesia have been heavily dependent on external funding in the form of central and provincial grants and loans for the greater proportion of their revenue. Central government regulations under Suharto meant that the Makassar municipal government was tightly constrained in terms of the efforts it could make to raise funds and had to rely heavily on Government transfers, so further restricting its autonomous decision-making capacity (JICA, 1996).

At the same time, however, there are a variety of complex 'informal politics' operating within the city. At the time of field work, for example, six very wealthy families in South Sulawesi (based mainly in Makassar) tended to control most of the decision-making concerning who received certain municipal contracts, specific trading licences, and so on (KI 14, 4/9/96). Two of these (Bugis families that owned the *BOSOWA* and the *Hadji Kalla Group* businesses) had formed an alliance through marriage, and in turn amassed considerable local power. Furthermore, three of the most wealthy people in Indonesia in 1996 originally came from Sulawesi, and had significant influence at both local and national level (KI 14, 24/11/96).[12] What appeared to be an astute comment concerning the manner in which such business people operated and interacted in the local political sphere was made by a local small-scale operator who claimed that 'it's better to know what is going on, but stay out of it' (KI 7, 19/12/96).

Urban design and local economy

Makassar is the capital city of the South Sulawesi province and the principal growth centre of Eastern Indonesia (Reid, 1990c).[13] At the end of the Second World War, Makassar had a population of over 100,000, which had increased to 1,019,948 by the time of the 1993 Census, and to an estimated 1.3 million by 1999 (KI 1, 12/1/99). By 1996 it was the largest Indonesian city and communications centre to the east of Surabaya, and there were estimates that the population would increase to 2.2 million by the year 2015 (Forbes, 1981a; JICA, 1996). Population growth in the city has been especially rapid since 1980, being the result of natural increase as well as migration (Forbes, 1981b). The central city area has the heaviest concentration of population, the seven central *Kecamatan* (subdistricts), shown in Figure 4.3, having a density of 225 persons per hectare, well above the city's average density of fifty-nine persons per hectare (JICA, 1996: 1-1).

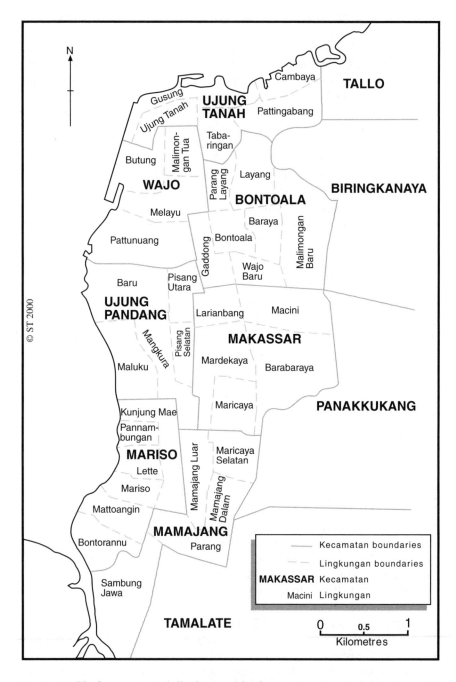

Figure 4.3 The *kecamatan* (subdistricts) and *lingkungan* (smaller administrative units) of Makassar.

Source: adapted from Forbes (1979: 4)

Makassar has been described as a 'compact city with a complex of land-use' (Forbes, 1979: 13), some of which, with other features of the city, are shown in Figure 4.4. The 1990 Census recorded 160,000 'housing units' in the city, with 'slum' areas (defined as 'a congested area with temporary housing that lacks basic sanitary facilities' (JICA, 1996: 5-2)), being found throughout the city, especially on the fringes of the central area. These areas, often home to small-scale entrepreneurs, contained approximately 19,000 households with an estimated population of 114,000 people and accounted for 11 per cent of the city's total population. Housing, sanitary and related conditions in many slum areas were very marginal (JICA, 1996) and were among a number of major urban development problems which challenged the city. These included:

- very rapid growth and uneven distribution of the population
- large slum areas
- lack of urban infrastructure such as roads, bridge, transportation facilities, water supply, sanitation, solid waste, education, medical, cultural facilities
- lack of regional revenue as financial source of development
- poor co-ordination in development implementation with overlap between sector/area projects and other projects
- insufficient manpower [sic] of regional government to manage the city development.

(JICA, 1996: 1–3)

BAPPEDA, the local development planning agency, has attempted to alleviate some of these problems. There have been programmes of new road construction and widening, improvements in drainage and primary channels, programmes to install sanitation systems, construction of a new dam nearby to improve water supply and management of flood control undertaken on local rivers (JICA, 1996).

With regard to industry, a major focus of *BAPPEDA*'s plans for the period of *REPELITA VI* (Sixth Five Year Plan 1994/1995 to 1998/1999) was the expansion of *Kawasan Industri Makassar (KIMA)* (Makassar Industrial Zone) owned and managed by *PT Kawasan Industri Makassar*, a *Badan Usaha Milik Negara (BUMN)* (state-owned enterprise).[14] The realisation of a number of these programmes has not been without problems, while the construction of a toll road to link the airport, port area and the industrial estate has resulted in a large number of people living in 'slums' and poorer housing areas – many of whom operate or are associated with small enterprises – being forced to relocate with limited compensation (*Panjatapda TK. I Prop. Sulawesi Selatan,* 1988; *Jakarta Post*, 7 June 1997).[15] Policies of these kinds connected with 'modernisation' in Makassar concerned Forbes (1979: 6), who observed that not all people benefit from such programmes:

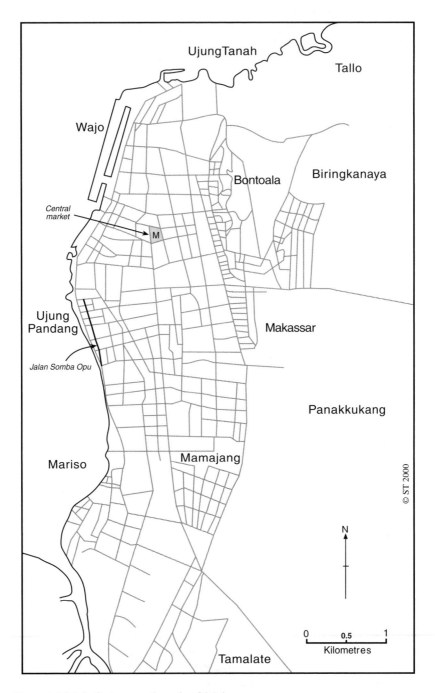

UjungTanah

Tallo

Wajo

Bontoala

Biringkanaya

Central
market

M

Ujung
Pandang

Makassar

Jalan Somba Opu

Panakkukang

Mariso

Mamajang

© ST 2000

N

0   0.5   1
Kilometres

Tamalate

Figure 4.4 Main features and roads of Makassar.

Source: adapted from Forbes (1979: 5)

Such a policy appears to overlook several crucial features of the informal sector. For a start it overlooks the extent to which the informal sector has become an integral part of the urban landscape. More importantly, per-haps, it overlooks the needs of the people who work in the informal sector.

During 1996/1997 the local environment was increasingly 'modernised' by considerable large-scale investment. Two new four-star hotels opened in late 1996, and redevelopment of the container wharf was completed in May 1997. Directly controlled by Jakarta-based conglomerates, these investments appeared to have no notable positive impact on the city's small enterprises. Although local casual labourers were employed on the construction sites, the majority of workers were brought from Java and no local small enterprise products such as furniture and fittings were used in the construction of the hotels. Many of the large-scale enterprises in Makassar were also owned by Java-based conglomerates that, again, generated little interaction with local small enterprises (KI 6, 24/2/97). Similarly, other large enterprises controlled by South Sulawesi business people, for example the *Hadji Kalla Group*, tended to operate vehicle dealerships, or be import and/or construction com-panies, again with very weak linkages to the small enterprise sector (Kalla, 1995). It is thus not surprising that such investment in the city's economy failed to filter down to benefit the small enterprise sector to any significant extent.

Labour force

In 1971 the workforce of Makassar stood at 107,694 but with few employed in the industrial sector, whereas the tertiary service sector, which included small-scale traders, accounted for 75.1 per cent of the workforce (Forbes, 1979). In 1979, Forbes estimated that 30 to 44 per cent of the urban work-force was 'informal sector' workers, most of them either being *becak* (trishaw) drivers or traders, with the remainder providing other services or working in informal manufacturing. Industries which had, in 1975, an above-average proportion of workers working over sixty hours a week comprised those employed in communications, transport and storage (this included *becak* dri-vers and dock workers), as well as a high proportion in wholesale and retail trade (including hawkers and street vendors) (Jones and Supraptilah, 1976). In one survey, by Jones and Supraptilah (1975, cited in Forbes, 1979), it was found that 38.6 per cent or over one-third of the city's workforce was either without work or employed in jobs which gave them insufficient resources to meet their needs.[16]

In 1995, it was calculated that 219,877 people over the age of 10 were eco-nomically active in Makassar (*Biro Pusat Statistik (BPS) Sulawesi Selatan,* 1996). Of these, nearly one-third were private workers (31.9 per cent), a quarter were government employees (25.6 per cent), and nearly one-fifth operated a business alone (19.0 per cent). A further 15.3 per cent operated a business with workers irregularly employed by them, 5.9 per cent worked for their family, and the remaining 2.3 per cent operated businesses that had a regular workforce (*BPS Kotamadya Ujung Pandang,* 1996: 30). This latter percentage, for businesses with regular workers, appears to be rather low, but perhaps it indicated the large number of unregistered enterprises in the city. Certainly, the high number of civil servants, and low number of entrepreneurs able to provide regular employment to workers, attested to some of the employment biases in the city that hindered growth and productivity. In 1995 some 42,263 people were recorded as looking for work in Makassar (ibid.).

Small enterprises in Makassar

Published articles based on Dean Forbes' doctoral thesis on petty commodity producers in Makassar (1978, 1979, 1981a, 1981b, 1988) provide both useful background information for this work, and baseline insight into the role and position of petty producers in the city in the late 1970s. The overriding impression gained from Forbes' work was that a significant proportion of the urban economy suffered from chronic stagnation. There was an oversupply of labour, too little capital, intense competition and considerable market uncertainty. This led Forbes to the conclusion that 'Ujung Pandang [Makassar] is faced with insignificant satisfactory employment opportunities for its population. It is manifest in the widespread problem of underemployment or a high degree of labour under-utilisation' (1979: 1). Survivalism, then, was very much the common feature in this sector of the urban economy. There were, however, a number of petty capitalists (along with mainstream capitalists) who had enhanced their economic power and influence considerably, for example, by lending capital, providing materials on credit and controlling markets. These things were at the expense of weaker and more vulnerable petty producers whose livelihoods typically depended almost entirely upon their continued access to their stronger neighbours. In effect, the arrangements that underpinned economic mobility for some, perpetuated disadvantages for others.

Forbes' research revealed that although this situation was driven by the prevailing economic system, there being a significant transfer of wealth from labour to capital, the situation was constantly reinforced and appeared to be sustained by the local socio-political context. He believed that there was 'unrealised potential', claiming that the socio-political organisation of the production system prevented advancement for a significant proportion of producers and traders, who played an 'involuntary role' in the perpetuation of underdevelopment (Forbes, 1979). The dynamics of the petty component of the market were therefore 'involutionary' rather than 'evolutionary'. At the same time the Government was seen more as a hindrance than a help, with a predominantly negative attitude towards petty and informal producers and traders. The city authorities did not regard the 'informal sector' highly and while there were no policies to eliminate the sector altogether, there appeared to be attempts to maintain it at an 'optimal' size (Forbes, 1981a). Accordingly, the authorities' attitude towards the sector was ambivalent. People involved with informal sector activities in Makassar were associated with a traditional 'past' and thus not part of the modernisation plan that the city government wanted to achieve. Consequently, a series of minor laws were introduced to restrict the spatial extent of the petty producers and trishaw operators (Forbes, 1981b).

Forbes (1979) divided the informal traders in Makassar into three categories, namely *punggawa* (wholesalers), larger retailers and smaller retailers. The *punggawa* (the term is used in this context only in South Sulawesi) referred to 'the partner with the greater reserves or control of capital in an economic relationship', or to the entrepreneur who organised and financed the distribution of goods (Forbes, 1979: 7). The *punggawa* had two interrelated roles in relation to the petty commodity producers in Makassar. First, they provided fixed or working capital for a large proportion of the petty producers, and second, their position in the production structure meant that their 'organizational skill and power are critical to petty producers' ability to participate in petty commodity production' (Forbes, 1981b: 135). Hence the *punggawa* wielded significant power over the petty commodity producers who often relied on them for capital, contacts, accommodation, financial skills and knowledge of marketing strategies, with patron–client relationships frequently becoming established (Forbes, 1981b; Pelras, 1996a).

Retailers who operated a small shop or *warung* (stall), or who were market traders, were included in Forbes' 'larger retailer' category. The location of these trading sites was permanent, in that the structure remained from one day to the next, although tenure may have been less certain. Other large traders operated from *gerobak* (handcarts) which they walked around the city with their goods. These operators were basically autonomous small business people, although they might be reliant on *punggawa* for credit or act as *punggawa* for other traders. 'Smaller retailers' paid nothing or very little for their sites and were often located on the fringe of larger markets. As traders they frequently operated illegally and had no security of tenure over their location. Other small traders were peddlers, including those using bicycles and those walking with goods in baskets attached to shoulder-poles (Forbes, 1979).

As Forbes (1981b) ascertained, many small retailers and traders in Makassar survived within an economic system that was straining to cope, yet they often still believed themselves to be better off than back in the villages from which they came. In comparison, in some circumstances, the *punggawa* and larger traders prospered. Nonetheless, in general, income levels showed the petty commodity producers to be very poor, 59.7 per cent of them earning under Rp.600 a day and only 10.9 per cent more than Rp.1,000 (Forbes,

1981b).[17] This situation led Forbes (1979: 13) to the view that 'the urban economy . . . has clearly expanded beyond its ability to support significant parts of its workforce at anything other than a subsistence level'.

By the late 1990s not a great deal seemed to have changed. A number of small enterprises appeared to be still struggling to make a living, and although there appeared to be more optimism about the city than in Forbes' time (albeit perhaps because of the theoretical approach he used), the over-riding impression was still one of small-scale entrepreneurs 'treading water' rather than 'swimming'. The evidence on which this impression is based is analysed in chapters 5, 6 and 7.

Statistics collected in 1995 by the Department of Industry from licensing information indicated that 2372 small enterprises were licensed (see Table 4.1) (*BPS Kotamadya Ujung Pandang*, 1996). Most commonly, between 1992 and 1995, small enterprises produced chemical and building material-related commodities, while the numbers in handicraft production were constantly the least common. However, it is known that a large proportion of small enter-prises were unlicensed, and therefore did not appear in Department of Industry statistics. Forbes (1981b: 126) endorses this conclusion, observing that 'it is impossible to accurately estimate the number of petty commodity producers in Ujung Pandang [Makassar]'. This is of much concern if such data are used for policy development in the future by Government agencies, for instance, to decide the level of assistance required by this segment of the economy.

Details of the number of people in Makassar *working in* small indus-tries/enterprises during the 1990s have been published by the Department of Industry and Trade (Table 4.2). These data are in agreement with details of total small enterprises discussed above. They show that most workers were involved in chemical and building materials-related employment. Again, how-ever, such figures must be considered as a 'rough guide' only, due to irregularities in the city's licensing procedures, from which the data were obtained.

Table 4.1 'Total' numbers of *industri kecil* (small industries/enterprises) in Makassar by product type, from 1992 to 1995, as recorded by the Department of Industry and Trade

Industry type	1992	1993	1994	1995
Food	513	519	544	548
Fabric and leather	285	312	327	348
Chemicals and building materials	519	594	596	617
Handicraft and general	260	282	289	292
Metal	534	537	550	567
Total	2111	2244	2306	2372

Source: *BPS Kotamadya Ujung Pandang* (1996: 157)

Table 4.2 'Total' numbers of workers employed in *industri kecil* (small industries/enterprises) in Makassar, from 1992 to 1995, as recorded by the Department of Industry and Trade

Small industry type	1992	1993	1994	1995
Food	4295	4192	4249	4278
Fabric and leather	3939	4546	4681	4953
Chemicals and building materials	6601	6868	6838	6973
Handicraft and general	1171	1558	1599	1611
Metal	2885	2437	2589	2632
Total	18891	19601	19956	20497

Source: *BPS Kotamadya Ujung Pandang* (1996: 161)

When asked specifically about the role of *punggawa* in Makassar in 1997, a key informant confirmed that it was still a common way in which certain small enterprises were organised. The example given involved the *punggawa ikan* (*punggawa* working with fish) who would give a certain amount of capital to fishermen who would then work for them. Relationships were informal, but unwavering loyalty was expected from the workers (KI 6, 24/1/97; see also Pelras, 1996a). A similar form of work organisation found in Makassar during my research, and one which is indeed common throughout Indonesia, was the *pondok* system. 'These are dwellings where the petty traders live and from where they obtain their equipment and raw materials. But they are not employees. Each trader is an independent businessman working for his own profit' (Jellinek, 1978: 135). As documented in Chapter 5, *bakso* (meat ball soup) and soya bean milk enterprises in Makassar were operated in this fashion.

Ethnicity and social relations[18]

> The persisting strength of ethnicity in urban settings, even among the 'modern' urban middle class, reflects the continuing importance of a local focus for ever-changing expressions of identity [in Indonesia].
> (Guinness, 1994: 300)

South Sulawesi is home to four major ethnic groups: the Bugis, the Makassar, the Mandar and the Toraja, as illustrated in Figure 4.5 (following Pelras, 1996a). Unfortunately very few statistics regarding these groups in the South Sulawesi region are available. In 1989 there were reported to be approximately 3.2 million Bugis, 1.5 million Makassar, 400,000 Mandar and 550,000 Tanatoraja people in the region (Millar, 1989). However, there were also Chinese and immigrants from other areas of Indonesia. Information regarding the ethnic composition of Makassar's population was unavailable from accessible Census data, a reflection of the political sensitivity surrounding such questions (Drake, 1989).[19] The population was considered only in terms of Indonesians and 'foreign citizens', the latter including 16,312 Chinese in 1995 (*BPS Sulawesi Selatan*, 1996). Nevertheless, an official at *PUKTI* estimated that in Makassar city in 1997, 30 per cent of the population were Bugis, 40 per cent were Makassar, with the remainder consisting of Mandar (5 per cent), Toraja (5 per cent), Chinese (3 per cent), and 17 per cent 'others', among whom were Javanese and those from the other Outer Islands (KI 1, 14/4/97). Reid (1990c: 68) details the complexities of the Makassar population further:

> At latest count, in addition to the large proportions of Indonesian, Makassarese, and Bugis speakers, there were 2000 speakers of Javanese, 300 of Sudanese, 380 of Batak, 130 of Minangkabau, and 100 of Banjarese, but tens of thousands in the 'others' category which comprises most of eastern Indonesia's myriad languages.

Cultural boundaries between different groups were a vital element in the formation and modification of social changes in Makassar city. They directly affected the daily lives of the small entrepreneurs who worked in the urban realm. Among them, as among others in the city, there was a clear awareness of its ethnic heterogeneity (Antweiler, 1994). An integral feature of the local cultures was *adat* (customs or traditions), each ethnic group being said to have its own *adat* (Kahn, 1980).[20] *Adat* was instrumental in forming the everyday socio-economic life of the small-scale entrepreneurs in Makassar, as it controlled relationships between people in networks of social relations, and provided a model of acceptable behaviour within local cultural boundaries (Kahn, 1980).

Bugis

The Bugis and Makassar people share many cultural features. These include 'the adoption of Islam and its institutions; a strongly developed market orientation and a mix of economic activities; a bilateral kinship system; [and] a flourishing literary tradition' (Lineton, 1975: 10). Through the kinship system neither partner in a marriage loses membership in his/her previous family, and land is inherited according to Islamic rules, with all the children inheriting, yet with males obtaining two parts and females one part (Millar, 1983).

In the past, the Bugis were known throughout Indonesia and its neighbouring countries as traders, seafarers, pirates and settlers. At the same time their society was divided into groups of nobles, commoners and slaves and was characterised by a high level of formality. Bugis people are generally competitive and status conscious in a system of strongly hierarchical relations. Within their society, individuals compete to achieve higher social status, while at the same time guarding the privileges they have gained from ascribed status (Millar, 1989). The point is well made by Pelras (1996a: 4):

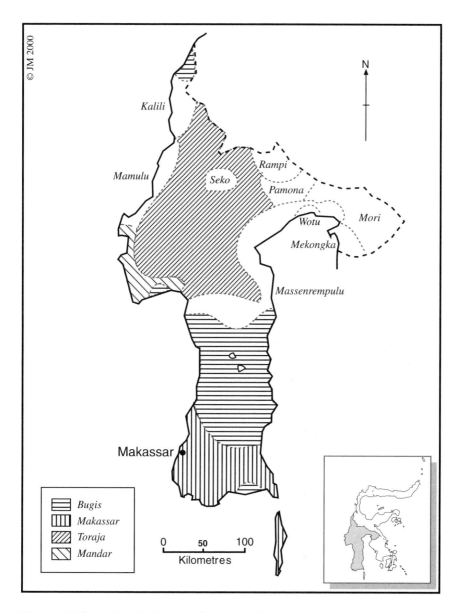

Figure 4.5 The major ethnic groups in South Sulawesi.

Source: adapted from Volkman and Muller (1990: 43), and De Koninck (1994: 3)

The cohesion of their society is based largely on the existence of a system of pervasive and interlocking clienteles; and yet most of them have a strong sense of their individuality. Bugis society is one of the most complex and apparently rigidly hierarchical of any in Insulindia; and yet competition for office or wealth ranks high among their motivations.

The Bugis have maintained a reputation of being aggressively competitive, perhaps due to the struggle for political hegemony, rivalry for social status and to avoid *siri,* commonly a loss of honour and dignity, but historically more complex, embodying 'social solidarity, social identity, prestige and self respect' (Mattulada, 1982, cited in Morrell, 1998: 161). Amongst key informants, *siri* was used to portray the loss of self-respect or dignity, and consequently the loss of one's place in society. If this had been caused by another's actions, then it was commonly believed among Bugis that the offended person had the right to defend and restore their respect, even if this meant killing the perceived offender (KI 13, 28/1/97; KI 6, 23/2/97; see also Morrell, 1998). Competition, including that in business, did not result in the destruction of the social order, but rather connected with 'the need to establish or maintain one's rightful place in that order, or to address the necessity to restore one's *siri*', a point discussed further in Chapter 5 (Morrell, 1998: 162). Competition is an essential part of Bugis society because of its strongly hierarchical nature, Bugis finding it difficult to co-exist as equals. This is certainly the case during social interaction when it is necessary to know who should defer to whom. Due to this, the Bugis compete to resolve the matter and create new social hierarchies (Millar, 1989).

Since Independence it has been suggested that the most desirable occupation for many Indonesians is a government office position as a *pegawai negeri* (government employee), with its attached social and financial security (Guinness, 1986). Nonetheless, unlike many Javanese, Bugis people do not consider trading and business to be low-status occupations (Millar, 1989). As Pelras (1996a: 334) suggests:

> Leadership, however, remains in the hands of those four categories which the Bugis have honoured since ancient times: the *to-sugi* (nowadays, the successful entrepreneurs); the *to-warani* (the military); the *to-acca* (the holders of academic diplomas); and the *to-panrita* (the Islamic masters).

In terms of employment, the status of an occupation among the Bugis is defined more in terms of whether someone else is controlling a person's decision-making and activities, rather than the actual occupation. However, despite the status and honour that comes with having a successful enterprise, it has also been commented upon by key informants that Bugis entrepreneurs are not as successful in business as they could be, or as many Chinese have been, due to high levels of conspicuous consumption (KI 3, 11/12/96; *PUKTI* researcher, confidential personal communication, 22 February 1997). This is because achievement and public presentation are inherently linked as means by which one's social status is indicated. Social status for Bugis depends as much on what other people 'make of them' as it does on their own self-esteem, as well as strong ties to their descent history (Lineton, 1975; Millar 1989). Nonetheless, it has been suggested by Sutton (1995) that the Bugis still comprise the wealthiest group when compared with the Makassar, Mandar and Torajan, a relationship explored further below in the case of the Makassar.

Makassar

'Cultural, political, and kinship ties extending deep into the past bind the Bugis with the other ethnic groups that inhabit the south-western penin-sula . . . [of] South Sulawesi' (Millar, 1989: 13). Thus, as indicated earlier, the Makassar people have much in common with the Bugis, sharing 'their basic cosmologies and some of their most important myths and they partially per-form the same rituals' (Antweiler, 1994: 18). While the Makassar are located predominantly on the southern coast of South Sulawesi, they also intermix with the Bugis population as far north as Maros (Millar, 1989). Moreover, the Makassar and Bugis languages have a common origin and 'there has been considerable intermarriage among their upper classes' (Harvey, 1974: 12). Nevertheless, Antweiler (1994) has maintained that while *adat* often serves to merge the Bugis and Makassar ethnic groups, it can also differentiate them.

Due to the fact that the southern region, especially Jeneponto, is dry and infertile, the Makassar depend on the sea for their livelihood to a greater extent than the Bugis (Millar, 1989). Many also migrate, temporarily or per-manently, to Makassar city in search of work (KI 4, 3/11/96), and it is not uncommon for Bugis to erroneously regard the Makassar people as 'inferior farmers who are content to undertake lower status employment' (KI 6, 2/3/97; see also Antweiler, 1994).

More generally, for a number of centuries, Makassar people have been very successful in business. Due to this tradition, however, it has been sug-gested by key informants that in recent years such success has come to be 'taken for granted', so that in the 1990s the performance of Bugis business people was actually superior (KI 4, 11/11/96). The Bugis knew they had to work hard to compete with the historical image of the Makassar people, and although since 1999, as in the distant past the city is known as 'Makassar', political power in the 1990s was actually in the hands of Bugis families and politicians (KI 14, 24/11/96; Sutton, 1995).

Mandar

Also culturally closely linked to the Bugis people are the less numerous Mandar. For the most part, they occupy the northwestern area of the south-ern peninsula as far north as Mamuju. Traditionally, due to the fact that the land is somewhat inhospitable, the Mandar people, rather than organise in extensive kingdoms like the Bugis and Makassar, have maintained relatively autonomous villages that co-operate informally with each other (Millar, 1989). Although a small number have migrated to Makassar city, their impact on the city's economy has remained fairly limited, quite unlike the also numerically small Chinese population.

Torajan

Culturally, the Torajan people share only a few affinities with the Bugis, Makassar or Mandar people (Millar, 1989). The Torajan population of approximately 350,000 come from Sa'dan Toraja, a mountainous interior region in the north of the South Sulawesi province. Traditionally, most Torajan were wet rice cultivators, although more recently they have diversified into cash crops such as coffee and nutmeg (Adams, 1997b). Historically they lived in scattered households, social ties being maintained through elaborate ritual exchanges. They were brought under a single political authority only in 1906 to 1907 when Dutch forces overcame local resistance (Reid, 1990a). When compared with their closest neighbours, the Bugis and Makassar, the Torajan are 'marginalized by geography, religion, and a diffuse power structure' (Adams, 1997b: 311).

In the 1990s, over 80 per cent of the Torajan people were Christian (Adams, 1997b). Introduced to the Torajan by Dutch missionaries in the early 1900s, Christianity became more important during the 1950s and 1960s. This trend, according to Yamashita (1994), was a counterbalance to the Islamic movements of the 1950s and 1960s in which the Bugis were dominant. Hence, 'the mountain Toraja accepted Christianity in reaction to a movement among the coastal Muslim peoples' (Yamashita, 1994: 76). However, others have maintained that this growth in Christianity derived from the success of mission schools and the Government's policy of encouraging those practising indigenous religions to convert to one of the Government's five recognised 'world religions' (Adams, 1997b). Torajan society is hierarchical, being based on descent, wealth, age and occupation, and 'in precolonial times Torajan society was roughly divided into three social strata: the aristocracy, commoners and slaves. Status was determined by birth, although economic aptitude or failure permitted some degree of mobility' (Adams, 1997b: 311).

While the traditional Torajan religion has declined in strength, it has recently been revived in a new form, as 'ethnic tourism' spectacles in Tanatoraja (Yamashita, 1994: 78). This began on a significant scale in the mid-1970s during the second Government Five Year Plan, when the Outer Islands were promoted as tourist destinations. Since then, tourism has continued to grow rapidly, and at times proceeds have become important family sources of capital for the establishment of new small enterprises in Makassar city (Adams, 1997b).

Torajan people, especially the younger generations, have also been involved in rural to urban migration since the late 1960s. This is largely because Tanatoraja has no major university or any major industry except for a coffee plantation company. In fact 'it is estimated that more than 230,000 Toraja have migrated to various parts of Indonesia, which is approximately two-thirds of the current population of the Regency of Tana Toraja' (Yamashita, 1994: 76). Such migrants usually retain contact with their families in Tanatoraja, remain attached to their traditions and remit much of their income back to family still in Tanatoraja (Sandarupa, 1984). Indeed, it has been suggested that while the Bugis, Makassar and Mandar cultures may be seen as 'centrifugal', with members motivated to seek their fortunes outside their home area, the Toraja are instead 'centripetal', with migrants generally wishing to return to Tanatoraja (Antweiler, 1994).

Chinese

The Chinese community makes up less than 4 per cent of Indonesia's population, yet businesses owned and operated by Chinese families are an integral part of Indonesia's economy (Schwarz, 1999). Indeed, they are 'responsible for perhaps as much as 70 per cent of all private economic activity' (Schwarz, 1999: 99; *Guardian Weekly*, 1 February 1998), a situation that has been traced back to:

> the fact that the minority Chinese were treated as a distinct group, privileged under colonial regimes, contained under independent governments, led them to consolidate business and community links exclusive to Chinese and to concentrate on commerce when other avenues of employment, such as the public service, were denied them.
>
> (Guinness, 1993: 317)

However, while they might be considered an economic asset to the country, Schwarz (1999: 99) maintains that 'they are also – and always have been – a political liability'. Perhaps because of their political vulnerability, the Chinese tend to 'save much of their money, distrust strangers and depend to a great extent on personal relationships and family networks, all of which are conducive to the rapid growth of family-run businesses' (Schwarz, 1999: 107).[21]

Among the Chinese in Makassar, estimated to number just over 16,000, there was a division between the longer established *peranakan* Chinese and the more recent *totok* immigrants. Many of the *peranakan* Chinese had intermarried with local ethnic groups, and had hence become more integrated culturally. They tended to be employed in a variety of occupations and were less conspicuous than the *totok*. The latter were 'pure' Chinese, generally living in culturally distinct communities and often in commercial occupations, a division found throughout Indonesia (Robison, 1986; Drake, 1989;

Schwarz, conference discussion, 9 September 1998).[22] In Makassar, the majority of Chinese entrepreneurs were *totok,* and although the longer established *peranakan* sometimes viewed the *totok* as 'crass and unscrupulous', such divisions were less important to the other ethnic groups in the region, who still tended to doubt the Chinese population's sense of nationalism and resent their wealth (Schwarz, 1999: 103; KI 14, 24/11/96).

Relations among ethnic groups

In the 1990s, there was continuing inter-ethnic competition among the different cultural groups in South Sulawesi. Bugis interviewees were quick to mention how, historically, the Torajan people were a source of slaves and, in the 1990s, were willing to be servants in Makassar city (KI 17, 3/5/97). Many Bugis believed this indicated that the Torajan people, despite greater educational achievements, were of lower descent rank. At the same time, many Torajan people, believing that their historical circumstances were due to physical domination by other groups, were less preoccupied with descent rank (Millar, 1989). In contrast, 'according to the Bugis, the Makassar people are more hotheaded, inferior farmers, and less devout Muslims' (Millar, 1989: 17).

More obvious, however, were the tensions between the Bugis and Makassar on the one hand and the Chinese on the other. Many non-Chinese residents believed that the Chinese, who maintained significant control over wholesale and retailing in the city, dominated the entire local economy. A symptom of the considerable resentment towards Chinese in the city were the 'Makassar riots' which lasted for three days, from the night of 15 September 1997. The riots, initially following the murder of a Muslim girl by a mentally ill Chinese man, escalated into widespread violence against Chinese homes, shops and businesses throughout the city, and left six dead. Further ethnic linked riots occurred in the city from 1998 to 2000 (*Jakarta Post,* 18 September 1997, 19 September 1997, 19 January 2000; *The Straits Times,* 23 September 1997; Cohen, 1998b; *Institut Studi Arus Informasi* [Study Institute for the Flow of Information], 1998). The distrust that exists among these different groups is further explored in chapters 5 and 6.

Social relations[23]

In Indonesia in general, there are vast differences between rural producers and small-scale entrepreneurs on the one hand, and the upper levels of the bureaucracy, armed forces and those involved with the large-scale industrial sector on the other, in terms of their wealth and social relations (Kahn, 1980). Consequently, all small-scale entrepreneurs and enterprise subcontractors in Makassar tended to be 'seen' as one distinct group by other members of the city's population, although there were complex systems of social and cultural relationships and stratification among the entrepreneurs (KI 3, 29/8/96; KI 5, 21/9/96). Such patterns of 'social relations' were determined by the broad social and cultural structures of the different ethnic communities in Makassar, their changing patterns of consumption, the shifting national ideological and political environment, and local reactions to these.

The continuing importance of social status in Makassar was very evident in the 1990s. For Bugis and Makassar social status was initially linked to birth, but social mobility was possible through marriage, or through 'self-enterprise' (Pelras, 1996b: 8). In recent times, 'self-enterprise' has come to include being a successful small-scale entrepreneur (Pelras, 1996b). Amongst those interviewed, social status appeared to be attributed to age, whether one owned land and occupation. In terms of neighbourhood relations, employment type was seen as highly significant and gave one prestige among neighbours (KI 2, 12/9/96; KI 6, 18/2/97; see also Guinness, 1986; Antweiler, 1994). As the city continued to modernise, *status economi* (economic status) and *jabatan* (duty, occupation) were increasingly seen as means by which an individual could gain status (KI 6, 26/2/97).

Gender

As a social construct, gender also impacts on small enterprise organisation by influencing the roles that men and women carry out within them. This point is well captured by Heyzer (1986: 121) who, when discussing gender relations in Indonesia, maintains that 'traditionally women have been fixed within the existing social structure as supportive and secondary personnel whose directions in life are dictated by the job and social requirements of their husband'. Such ideology, it has been argued, tends 'to confine women to traditionally female occupations. That is, domestic production, child care and socialization responsibilities are placed solely on the shoulders of women' (Joseph, 1987: 34; see also Guinness, 1994; Silvey, 2000).

Yet while women are encouraged to see themselves as a repository for traditional and family values, the major development programmes for women supported by the Indonesian Government tend to be efficiency orientated; that is, they aim to increase women's economic participation, or welfare orientated. This leads to somewhat contradictory messages for women. On the one hand, they are encouraged to participate in economic development, and on the other, they must not neglect their roles as wives and mothers (Heyzer, 1986; Kindon, 1995; see also Blackwood, 1995). The *peran ganda* (dual role) ideology of women in Indonesia as economic producers and domestic reproducers is reflected in the Government's promotion of *Panca Dharma Wanita* (Five Duties of Women), defining women's gender roles and relationships with others in society. These five duties require women to be:

- Loyal companions of their husbands
- Managers of their households
- Educators and guiders of their children
- Supplementary wage earners for their families
- Useful members of their community.

(Suryakusuma, 1991: 52)

Although the Government does also define men's roles, these are fewer, namely 'to be the family's primary earner ("to the best of their ability") and the family's public representative in all political, social and religious affairs' (Kindon, 1995: 62).

The defined role of women as 'secondary wage earners' often means that those with a central role in a small enterprise are not recognised. Likewise, if working as family members, their economic roles are often 'invisible', and as a consequence they are often excluded from decision-making processes involving other enterprise/family members or co-operative members. This is evidentially because, at least in part, there are 'deeply embedded patriarchal values which did not consider the possibility of a woman becoming the family breadwinner' (*Jakarta Post,* 27 December 1996).

Nevertheless, since 1971 the share of female workers in the Indonesian work-force has risen, reflecting in part changing attitudes to women's work (Jones, 1994). Of the total workforce of 7.99 million in 1996, 35.3 per cent (2.82 million) were women (*Jakarta Post,* 21 April 1997). However, there is still significant regional divergence in the female workforce participation rates. In Jakarta, and on Java in general, new opportunities for wage employment in export-orientated manufacturing have resulted in an over-representation of new young, female labour force entrants (see Wolf, 1992, 1993; Manning, 1993; Hancock, 1996). Yet this has not been the case in other regions, as much of the growth in manufacturing has been concentrated on Java (Hill, 1990). In direct contrast to Javanese and Balinese women who tend to be very active in the labour market, this is not apparent in Sulawesi (KI 10, KI 11, 6/9/96). Such differences confirm the importance of taking regional social and cultural diversity into account when examining how women are situated within the labour force (Oey-Gardiner, 1993). While Oey-Gardiner (1993: 210) argues that 'low work force participation across all age categories is difficult to explain among women in South Sulawesi. Female education is low and average incomes are substantially below the national average', it also seems that '[c]onservative social values regarding female work outside the home, especially in . . . South Sulawesi, probably influenced this outcome' (Manning, 1998: 239).

In Bugis as well as Makassar societies, the position of women within small enterprises and the family is made more difficult to determine by the significance of hierarchical family systems and social status. The importance of social status can blur gender hierarchies, as women may hold positions of power within society. In Bugis society according to Millar (1983: 477), for example, 'gender relations . . . are almost entirely subordinate to a cultural preoccupation with hierarchical social location', and the work roles of Bugis men and women are considered distinctly different, albeit complementary. Yet despite such views (see also Errington, 1990), it has been argued that throughout Southeast Asia, the overall prestige and power of men typically exceeds that of women (Ong and Peletz, 1995). With reference to small enterprises in Makassar, I would argue that the women entrepreneurs and workers remain embedded within a strong patriarchal system, a topic taken further in Chapter 5 (KI 12, KI 16, 19/2/97).

The types of small enterprises that women were involved in in Makassar in 1996 to 1997 reflected both the gendered division of labour found within the household, and the activities deemed culturally and socially appropriate for women. Tasks undertaken by the majority of women were those traditionally related to domestic labour, such as cooking and sewing, while customarily it was men who learned 'new skills' like machine repairing, welding and aluminium joinery (see also Heyzer, 1986). Cultural norms therefore shaped women's experiences within small enterprises, confirming that the local dynamics of gender and social life must be seen as producing overlapping webs of power (Ong and Peletz, 1995).

CONCLUSION: THE SCENE

Political, social and economic circumstances in Makassar reflect forces promoting change as a whole in Indonesia, but also at work are significant locational variations and dynamics. The Indonesian economy has been increasingly brought into the global economic sphere yet, at the same time, small enterprises appear to have been left behind as large-scale industry has expanded. Even a range of programmes specifically introduced to improve the position of small enterprises across the country have not been very successful, the corruption and collusion involved in many such programmes significantly diminishing their potential for improvement.

The Eastern Indonesian provinces have been largely excluded from the economic development that has focused predominantly on Java and the more central islands. The regional disparities perpetuated by this polarisation have meant that not only is the local economy of Makassar a peripheral one, but also that the local political sphere has been controlled largely by those outside of the island. Not surprisingly, local development has been slow, with a high incidence of poverty and un/underemployment remaining. The small enterprises studied in this book were thus operating in circumstances that did not appear particularly conducive to their growth. This difficulty was accentuated by the local ethnic and gender relations in the city as well as social relations that for some acted as barriers, and for others acted as a source of support for the growth of their enterprises. It is to these that I now turn, in an analysis of small enterprise structures and operations in Makassar.

5   Small enterprises in Makassar
Internal dynamics

Small enterprises in Makassar, like those elsewhere in developing countries, are distinguished by their distinctive combination of internal dynamics and organisational features. These aspects are explored in this chapter while we also gain an initial understanding of their interactions with other enterprises and actors, analysed more fully in Chapter 6. For both of these chapters we adopt the *small enterprise integrative framework* outlined in Chapter 3. By doing so, we are able to determine whether or not the enterprises were exhibiting features of growth and 'success', as emic, locally defined objectives, or whether 'survivalism' was closer to their reality.

In this chapter, information appertaining to the internal dynamics of the enterprises in the study area is divided into three general but closely related sections, namely the history and organisation of the enterprises, the production process, and labour relations. In the second section of the analysis, presented in Chapter 6, inter-firm dynamics operationalised through networks and trust are investigated, as is the question of innovation, and clusters and collective efficiency. The focus then turns to an analysis of the future attitudes and expectations of those interviewed. It must be stressed at the outset, however, that the *small enterprise integrative framework* can only be accurately applied by considering the combined effect of all the aspects which for ease of presentation are mostly discussed, at least initially, one at a time.

Our discussion here draws on information from the initial 100 questionnaires (Group A) completed during field work. These provide detailed quantitative data on organisational aspects of small enterprises,[1] evidence which is complemented by more qualitative information gathered from a further 200 interviews with small-scale entrepreneurs (Group B).[2] The product categories used are shown by ethnicity of the entrepreneur for Groups A and B in Table 5.1.

At this point it should be reiterated that the fifty 'formal' businesses in Group A held at least a *Surat Izin Tempat Usaha (SITU)* (licence for a business place). In contrast, the fifty 'informal' businesses were members of *sentra*, that is, 'official' clusters of small enterprises, often without licences, but being promoted by the local Department of Industry and Trade, and Department of Co-operatives and Small Enterprises. Within Group B,

Table 5.1 Product categories by ethnicity of entrepreneur for Groups A and B
combined

Ethnicity	Food	Clothes	Building materials	Handicrafts	Metal	Total
Chinese	5	1	5	1	12	24
Bugis	9	45	22	40	18	134
Makassar	14	10	20	11	23	78
Bugis and Makassar mix	3		2	2	3	10
Kalimantan		2	1	2		5
Irian Jaya	1					1
Torajan	3	1	5	2	3	14
Java	24		2		1	27
Mandar		1	2	1		4
Sumatra	1		1			2
Nusa Tenggara			1			1
	60	60	61	59	60	300

Note: Sampling was undertaken to gain as close to sixty questionnaires from each category as
possible.

approximately three-quarters of the small enterprises did not hold *SITU*
licences nor were they members of officially sanctioned clusters. Instead,
these enterprises operated mainly by paying bribes to officials when necessary,
or else they were 'hidden' behind entrepeneurs' houses.

ENTERPRISE HISTORY AND ORGANISATION

The history and organisation of the enterprises surveyed were examined to
establish a general understanding of their origins and evolution. Also pertinent is an understanding of the extent to which they were operating with
flexible and informal management, the types of machinery in use, and
whether the enterprises could respond to an increasingly specialised and fragmented market.

Within Group A, nearly three in every four (72 per cent) of the enterprises
had been established by the present owner, another 7 per cent by the parents
of the present owner, and 12 per cent by other relatives. Begun in 1918, the
oldest business, a Bugis goldsmith enterprise, had been operating for seventy-
nine years. However, the average life span was only thirteen years, 58 per
cent being younger than ten years. Those longest established were run by
Bugis, Makassar or Chinese entrepreneurs, and next came those of Torajan
and Javanese entrepreneurs. Most recent were Mandar entrepreneurs, along
with those from Kalimantan, Sumatra and Irian Jaya, as shown in Table 5.2.
For Group B, one entrepreneur, a Bugis wooden chair-maker, had established his business in 1957. However, the average length of ownership was ten
years, with 106 (53 per cent) under a decade old. In other words, not many

Table 5.2 Approximate times of initial establishment of different ethnic groups operating small enterprises in Makassar

Time period in Makassar	Group A	Group B
Circa 1955–1965: most established groups	Bugis, Makassar, Chinese	Bugis, Makassar
Circa 1970s: second wave	Torajan, Javanese, Bugis and Makassar 'rural refugees'	Torajan, Javanese, Chinese
Circa 1980s and 1990s: relative newcomers	Mandar, Sumatran and from Kalimantan and Irian Jaya	Sumatran and from Irian Jaya

enterprises had been passed down through several generations, reflecting in part a continuous migration to the city from nearby rural areas over the past decade (Forbes, 1981b). As with Group A, the longest established enterprises in Group B were again run by Bugis or Makassar entrepreneurs, whereas those owned by Chinese, Torajan and Javanese had been founded within the past twenty years, and those owned by entrepreneurs from Sumatra and Irian Jaya were the newest.[3]

The fact that Bugis and Makassar entrepreneurs were the longest established reflected the area's past, in that historically, Makassar city was controlled by the Makassar people, yet since the eighteenth century had also become home to many Bugis (Pelras, 1996a). The only other ethnic group to have a significant presence in the city as small-scale entrepreneurs before 1965 were the Chinese, many of whom had been traders when Indonesia was under Dutch control, and who had subsequently shifted to operate their own small enterprises (Forbes, 1981b; Schwarz, 1994).

The lack of involvement of other ethnic groups in small enterprises before the late 1960s may be accounted for by the 'South Sulawesi Rebellion'. Led by Kahar Muzakar from 1950 to 1965, this caused significant upheaval in the region, and deterred entrepreneurs from other islands migrating to Makassar (Lineton, 1975). During this time too, there was a notable migration of rural South Sulawesi inhabitants to the city, motivated by severe economic hardship because of factional fighting and through being cut off from urban areas and commodities for personal consumption (Harvey, 1974; Forbes, 1981b; Pelras, 1996a). Yet while a number of the Bugis and Makassar entrepreneurs interviewed stated that they had moved to the city during that time, most had been unable to establish an enterprise immediately. This was simply because many of the newcomers were 'refugees' lacking sufficient funds, and indeed, it was not until later in the 1970s that these migrants had accumulated sufficient reserves to enable them to establish enterprises (KI 14, 23/1/97).

It was only after the local rebellions had ceased that entrepreneurs from other ethnic groups such as Torajans, and those from Sumatra, Irian Jaya and Java began to migrate to Makassar city, a second-wave movement *circa* the

1970s (Table 5.2) that could also be related to the increased push towards national integration and unity at that time (Hill, 1994). More specifically, the movement of Torajan people into small enterprises in Makassar reflected a growing affluence among this group. In the first place this was due to tourism, and in the second, the increasing migration of workers to other parts of Indonesia or overseas. Typically, these workers sent home remittances which could be used as the source of capital for establishing an enterprise (Yamashita, 1994; Adams, 1997a; Cohen, 1998a).

In order to clarify the structure of the small enterprises, they were divided into categories depending on the level of family labour used.[4] As shown in Table 5.3, large numbers of the enterprises had only family members particiipating as workers. For both Groups A and B there were 'significant' negative correlations between the total number of workers in an enterprise and the number of family workers involved, family labour being of far greater importance to those enterprises with fewer workers in total. For enterprises in Group B, there was a 'very significant' relationship between the enterprise product type and the level of family labour involved. Predominantly, gold and silver handicraft producers used family labour, as did those undertaking other metalwork, whereas the rest of the enterprise types had a more even distribution of family and non-family workers. This demonstrated a preference for family labour within certain product types, especially those involving expensive raw materials, a finding that highlighted the importance of trust between enterprise owners and workers. For Group A the result was rather mixed, perhaps because the enterprises tended to be those more 'recognised' in the city and consisted of a broader range of production organisation.

A number of the small enterprises in Group B were operating as subcontracting units, rather than as autonomous enterprises. Within this group, as seen in Table 5.4, 33 per cent had some such linkages, whereas in Group A it was as few as ten enterprises, all of them operated by male Bugis goldsmiths subcontracting for Chinese-operated gold shops in the city.

Table 5.3 Percentage of family workers within small enterprises in Groups A and B[5]

Percentage of family workers	Group A enterprises (100 in total)	Group B enterprises (200 in total)	
100	35	116	(58.0%)
81 to 99	2	4	(2.0%)
61 to 80	7	8	(4.0%)
41 to 60	12	17	(8.5%)
21 to 40	13	4	(2.0%)
20 to 1	14	4	(2.0%)
Work alone	1	17	(8.5%)
All non-family workers	16	30	(15.0%)

Table 5.4 Percentage of subcontracting and independent small enterprises in
Groups A and B

Enterprise type	Group A (%)	Group B (%)
All subcontracting work	10	23
Some subcontracting, some independent	–	10
All independent work	90	67

The owners of subcontracting enterprises had different relationships with
their suppliers and retailers of goods from those undertaking independent
work. The former were effectively paid a 'wage' from a larger subcontractor
firm, usually in the form of piece-rate payments. Such subcontractors (for
example, a number of furniture-makers, general tailors and goldsmiths in
Group B) had very little control over their own management decisions and
operated with fairly formal and inflexible management styles. They could
not be considered 'true entrepreneurs' because 'they work in a subcontracting
system that does not allow them to make decisions about styles, materials,
capital or marketing' (Thamrin, 1993: 150).[6]

Enterprises using only non-family labour tended to be involved with independent work instead of subcontracting work, in which family labour
predominated. In addition, those operating in a subcontracting fashion
tended to be smaller enterprises, comprising only two enterprises with over six
workers involved solely in subcontracting, a relationship discussed in more
detail in Chapter 6.

Males overwhelmingly dominated enterprise ownership in both Groups A
and B. Of the 100 respondents in Group A, only fourteen were women operating as independent entrepreneurs and none were enterprise subcontractors.
This was similar for Group B. Here, 133 men and twenty-two women made
up the 155 operating independent enterprises, but women did represent a
much larger proportion of the subcontracting entrepreneurs, being thirteen of
the forty-five (29 per cent), as detailed in Table 5.5. Nevertheless, the number
of women operating enterprises in collaboration with their husbands could
well have been higher but not recorded as such because the husband took the
role of 'spokesperson' when the two were interviewed. In other words, women
with a decision-making role within an enterprise may have been hidden from
this analysis, although an attempt was always made to identify and include
such women in discussions (see also Heyzer, 1986).

The ethnic distribution of independent entrepreneurs and enterprise subcontractors in Groups A and B, as recorded in Table 5.6, is consistent with
the pattern of population composition discussed in Chapter 4. As one would
anticipate, Bugis and Makassar independent entrepreneurs and subcontractors were the predominant groups in the sample. The fact that Group A
included more Chinese than Group B probably reflected the success Chinese
entrepreneurs have had in establishing small enterprises that were larger and
more prosperous, and registered with the Department of Industry and Trade.

Table 5.5 Gender division of enterprise subcontractors and independent
entrepreneurs in Groups A and B

Gender of the enterprise owner/operator	Independent enterprises	Enterprise subcontractors	Total
Group A:			
Women	14	–	14
Men	76	10	86
Total	90	10	100
Group B:			
Women	22	13	35 (17.5%)
Men	133	32	165 (82.5%)
Total	155	45	200

This may also have reflected the influence of another dimension of ethnicity too, in that Government officials, very few of whom were Chinese, were more likely to 'pick' on Chinese, rather than on Bugis or Makassar entrepreneurs, due to negative feelings towards the Chinese among the local Bugis and Makassar communities. Hence, the Chinese entrepreneurs had less opportunity to operate without the formal licences required. The fact that the figures in Table 5.6 also included a higher percentage of Javanese than that of the total city population was perhaps not surprising, since Javanese migrants to Makassar city were known for their entrepreneurial spirit (KI 6, 21/3/97).

The evolution of independent enterprises represented in Group A over the past ten to fifteen years (or, if less, over the length of time the enterprise had

Table 5.6 Ethnicity of the 300 independent entrepreneurs and enterprise
subcontractors interviewed

Ethnic groups	Group A (100 total)		Group B (200 total)	
	Independent entrepreneurs	Enterprise subcontractors	Independent entrepreneurs	Enterprise subcontractors
Bugis	17	10	67 (33.5%)	40 (20.0%)
Makassar	30	–	46 (23.0%)	2 (1.0%)
Bugis/Makassar mixed blood	–	–	10 (5.0%)	–
Torajan	11	–	1 (0.5%)	2 (1.0%)
Mandar	4	–	–	–
Chinese	16	–	7 (3.5%)	1 (0.5%)
Java	10	–	17 (8.5%)	–
Sumatra	1	–	1 (0.5%)	–
Kalimantan	–	–	5 (2.5%)	–
Irian Jaya	–	–	1 (0.5%)	–
Nusa Tenggara	1	–	–	–

Table 5.7 Most significant problems entrepreneurs stated their enterprises faced

Most significant problems	Rank
Constraints to marketing	1
Difficulties gaining suitable basic materials	2
Problems concerning the production process	3 =
Formation of capital	3 =
Acquisition of capital	4
Labour aspects	5
Business organisation	6

been established) was examined in terms of technology and methods of production. This analysis sought to gain further insight into ways in which the enterprises may have changed over time. Over half (52 per cent) of the independent entrepreneurs reported 'no change' in the technology they used over this period, 2 per cent reported a deterioration, while the remaining 46 per cent recorded improved technology. Given these findings, it is perhaps not surprising that two in every three entrepreneurs (65 per cent) reported no change in the methods of production, while 35 per cent announced an improvement. These figures suggest that the production operations of a large number of entrepreneurs had been static over a relatively long time period. The data also revealed that ethnicity was more important than product types in determining whether improvements had occurred. In particular, Torajan and Mandar entrepreneurs as well as those migrating from other islands were more likely to have made improvements than were Bugis, Makassar or local Chinese.[7]

Overall, entrepreneurs interviewed reported that the most difficult problems faced by their enterprises were a range of constraints to marketing, ranked first ahead of other problems represented in Table 5.7. Entry of small enterprises into the relevant production sectors was relatively easy, enabling a large number of them to make the same product, and thus create high levels of competition. The entrepreneurs' ability to improve their circumstances was further constrained by the prevailing economic conditions and the influence of the bureaucracy. Together, such factors acted as barriers that kept the majority of entrepreneurs in a defensive, weak position which inhibited their ability to advance their enterprises in a hostile operating environment.[8]

From this brief review of the historical emergence and organisation of the enterprises, then, patterns already begin to emerge regarding their operations, as well as some of their constraints.

PRODUCTION

Another aspect of small enterprise activity explored related to the production process. Issues arising from this were examined to gain an understanding of the types of machinery used and whether these were general purpose or specialised. Also considered, and a closely related issue, was the ability of the entrepreneurs (independent and subcontracting) to change production rapidly in response to shifts in demand, beneficial in an unstable operating environment. Products were summarised into sixty-six different types for Group A.[9] Thirty-five (53 per cent) of these were 'simple'; that is, they needed limited technology, the tools and equipment used being general purpose and capable of producing only low value-added goods (such as simple wood carpentry, and sewing cushions and headscarves). For this reason the production process was uncomplicated, repetitive, and required only that workers had general, basic skill levels.

The remaining thirty-one (47 per cent) product types incorporated more significant levels of complexity in the production process, such as welding, making stoves and ovens, gold and silver jewellery production and more complex tailoring, such as trousers and hats. A variety of these enterprises is shown in Plates 5.1 to 5.4. The tools and equipment used (for example, welding equipment and sewing machines) still tended to be multi-purpose, being used to manufacture a number of different products.

Indeed, for both Groups A and B, the machinery or equipment used was overwhelmingly general or multi-purpose. At the same time, however, because the production process was often relatively easy and repetitive, craftspersonship was not encouraged so that the skill levels among workers remained limited, an aspect discussed more fully in the next section on Labour.

Plate 5.1 A Bugis entrepreneur, making stoves and *bakso* cooking pots, who worked by himself at a small site, in a disused marketplace.

Plate 5.2 A typical scene in a Bugis goldsmith's home, with work carried out on small work-benches, often in workers' bedrooms.

Plate 5.3 A small silversmith enterprise producing silver-filigree jewellery for local shops.

Plate 5.4 A Makassar worker constructing a chair with raw materials obtained from a number of suppliers around the city and wood from a nearby village.

The information collected in the field indicated notable ethnic specialisation in the production of a number of goods. Thus, Bugis and Makassar entrepreneurs tended to produce wooden furniture and stoves, Chinese were involved in welding, and the Bugis with gold jewellery and sewing, both general clothing and tailored garments. In addition, the Javanese made *tempe* (deep-fried fermented soya beans) and *bakso* (meat ball soup), the Makassar traditional ice-cream, and the Torajan were shoemakers and repairers. For other goods there was more heterogeneity. This was especially so in the case of metal window frames, metal car parts and drinks, all of which were not only commonly made by the most recently established in the city, but were also among the least 'traditional' for local ethnic groups to undertake. This suggests greater ease of entry into such enterprise types for those without historical, ethnic or family connections in the city.

While there was a notable range of complexities among production processes used by the small enterprises, 44 per cent of Group A entrepreneurs were producing only one product, while the others (56 per cent) were producing goods that were very similar, with little evidence of product diversification. Such enterprises would find it difficult to produce varied products quickly in response to changing market demand, as this would require workers with a broad range of skills.

A lack of product diversification meant that competition was an important concern for the small-scale entrepreneurs. Indeed, 96 per cent of independent entrepreneurs in Group A admitted that they faced competition from sellers of the same goods in the city, with larger enterprises or importers being seen as specific rivals. Often, entrepreneurs appeared to respond with a somewhat 'survivalist' attitude to the high levels of competition, rather than attempting to meet it by undertaking diversification and innovation in designs. As one tailor reported when asked about his profits, 'they are declining 100 per cent. Five years ago I could buy a car, now I can't even buy a motorcycle. Now there are too many people sewing, in competition, so I have to reduce my prices' (15b, 23/1/97). This particular entrepreneur either could not or would not alter his production methods in response to an increasingly intense competitive situation.

When asked what were the most significant production problems facing their enterprise, the independent entrepreneurs in Group A responded with thirty-seven different concerns. For 44 per cent of them, the most serious was their continuous reliance on simple, basic equipment or technology. Many argued that if they had access to more modern and advanced technology their enterprise would develop rapidly, because then they would be able to produce higher quality products for which there would be greater demand. Nonetheless, this objective is likely to be frustrated by a number of related factors. First, access to more advanced technology alone would not solve production problems and, second, the connected issues of affordability, equipment maintenance and training must also be considered. In addition, if new machinery was not multi-purpose it would also restrain entrepreneurs from responding rapidly to changes in market demand.

Another notable implication drawn from the field work data was that, by itself, access to new equipment might not change the competitive position of entrepreneurs unless they could diversify production and gain access to a wider and more profitable market. In this context marketing becomes a crucial factor. It highlights the interrelatedness between production and marketing processes, suggesting that entrepreneurs could not hope to solve their enterprise difficulties by focusing on one isolated factor alone.

Other production problems mentioned by entrepreneurs were numerous and varied. Shown in Table 5.8, they ranged from concerns about raw materials, to specific details of production, the quality of workers and limited capital.

Over half (52 per cent) of the entrepreneurs in Group A complained that either individually or in combination, such problems caused low productivity, resulting in an inability to fulfil orders, a factor which was crucial to the ongoing viability of their enterprises. Not surprisingly, many entrepreneurs experienced difficulties purchasing basic materials due to a lack of cash flow, fluctuating incomes, and problems arising from being late completing and delivering products. Thus many entrepreneurs faced declining trust and confidence from their customers, so further inhibiting the growth of their enterprises.

Table 5.8 Production problems mentioned by entrepreneurs

Raw materials
• unreliable sources or limited availability of raw materials
• poor quality of raw materials.
Details of production
• many errors in production
• equipment breaks down frequently
• site of production is too small, restricting production
• production is too slow
• product is perishable
• volume of production fluctuates because it is directly dependent on orders.
Quality of workers
• workers have low skills
• entrepreneur cannot find regular workers/had inadequate numbers of workers
• poor quality of the finished products.
Capital
• inability to expand production due to limited capital.

When asked how they would hope to overcome the production difficulties they faced, 37 per cent of the replies were somewhat pessimistic, in that the entrepreneurs themselves were at a loss to know any means by which their problems might be solved. Some thought they would have to give up the business and return to their *kampung* (village), others that they would 'just let it happen', or that they could not change production as they were committed to making certain (souvenir) designs, and still others, in response to errors in production, said that they would simply redo the order. Their inability or reluctance to improve production techniques indicated that a number of the entrepreneurs were not prepared or able to improve their business or expand their production through innovation, but were trying to 'get by' instead, as they struggled to survive on, what was for some, a daily basis. This attitude is reflected in further responses that ranged from asking customers for more time to complete the orders, to trying to explain to customers why there were production problems, to working longer hours.

Confronted by their difficulties, a range of respondents appeared to adopt defensive coping mechanisms, rather than attempt innovative means by which to overcome production problems. Such answers also began to suggest that the *kampung* was seen by some as a 'safety net', one on which entrepreneurs operating in the city could rely if difficulties arose, in preference to making innovative production decisions. Nonetheless, for other entrepreneurs, returning to their *kampung* was not considered a viable option, either because they were 'too proud' to return or were avoiding a family dispute, suggesting that cultural and social relations often influenced their decisions.

Nevertheless, other entrepreneurs – providing 63 per cent of the total suggestions – nominated a wide range of positive solutions. The most common of these included purchasing new, more advanced technology or machinery; increasing the size of the workforce; getting other people to help through subcontracting arrangements; and providing better training for workers. A small group of respondents wanted to establish or join existing clusters and co-operatives, and saw them as a means by which to acquire raw materials and market finished products, as well as being sources of new credit and a channel for borrowing equipment. Such linkages point to a production strategy with forms of interaction and mutual interdependence which, in time, could lead to collective efficiency. However, this group represented only 10 per cent of the total entrepreneurs.

In terms of production, therefore, it was found that the vast majority of entrepreneurs were using multi-purpose machinery and yet, as production methods tended to be relatively simple, workers' skills remained limited. Competition was a serious problem for virtually all the entrepreneurs, many of them taking a 'survivalist' rather than an innovative or aggressive approach to this challenge. Strategies for overcoming the wide range of production problems varied, but few entrepreneurs appeared to have found innovative solutions.

LABOUR FLEXIBILITY

Turning to a closely related building block of the *small enterprise integrative framework*, as detailed in Chapter 3, labour flexibility may refer to either functional or numerical flexibility. For functional flexibility, the qualities needed by workers relate to a 'core labour force with broader and more general qualifications' (Pedersen *et al.*, 1994: 4). In contrast, numerical flexibility often distinguishes enterprises that follow a more 'survivalist', sweat-shop strategy offering 'poor working conditions, low wages and unstable employment' (ibid.). The 'survivalist' approach includes, among other factors, high levels of worker turnover, part-time or short-term work and homeworking. The employment offered in such enterprises is usually 'casual' or marginal, with little or no security (Dos Santos, 1979; Storper and Scott, 1989). In developing countries there is the potential for small enterprises showing signs of functional flexibility to operate side by side with those practising a more 'survivalist' production strategy.

The situation in Makassar appeared to mirror this. A limited number of the small enterprises had workers who were broadly skilled and paid reasonable wages, the entrepreneurs providing accommodation and food calculated to entice employees to remain with the enterprise. Other entrepreneurs however, offered only short-term work with low pay and poor conditions. All the 300 entrepreneurs interviewed employed casual labour, in that none of their workers had employment contracts nor any form of security. If they wished, entrepreneurs could lay off workers any time there was no work, but because many were family and/or paid on a piece-rate system the tendency was instead for workers to produce less and take a reduction in piece-rate earnings during that period.

A wide range of data on labour was gathered. Questions on this topic were to gain insight into whether there was a broadly trained workforce that exhibited evidence of craftspersonship, or alternatively whether skills were limited. They also sought information about how informal and flexible the management was in terms of relations with workers, or whether it was hierarchical and formalised. In addition, the questionnaires were designed to ascertain the degree of integration achieved in the processes of conception and execution of production.

In total, the 100 enterprises in Group A employed 628 workers, of whom two-thirds were men (65 per cent) and the balance were women (35 per cent). While the average age of all workers was 29 years, their ages ranged from 18 to 63 years, half being between 24 and 31 years old. A similar average age for workers was reported by Jones and Supraptilah (1976) in their survey of labour force participation rates in Makassar as a whole, while the petty commodity producers whom Forbes (1981b) interviewed in Makassar also had an age profile much the same as that of the overall urban labour force. These findings, then, contradict Mazumdar's (1976: 655) argument that a 'disproportionately large number of informal-sector workers are . . . very young or very old', and thereby confirm the importance of small enterprises in providing employment opportunities in the city.

Yet another unexpected finding was yielded by data for Group B on the gender distribution of workers and operators (Table 5.9). Contrary to traditional gender norms in the city (see Chapter 4), five female entrepreneurs employed only male workers. Four of them operated wooden furniture enterprises, two having inherited the enterprise from their parents, with younger male siblings working for them, and two worked with their husbands, yet said the enterprise was their own. The fifth woman had also inherited from her parents, in this case a goldsmith enterprise, further discussed later in this chapter. Nevertheless, compared with male entrepreneurs, proportionately more women operated as subcontractors, a difference which suggests that it was not easy for women to establish an independent enterprise in the city.

Forbes (1981b) noted that a substantial proportion of the women whom he interviewed in the petty commodity production sector were widowed or divorced. However, this did not appear to be the case among the women entrepreneurs whom I interviewed. The majority were married with a small enterprise that operated separately from their husband's work; for example, many of the men in business as goldsmiths had wives who operated tailor enterprises, or else women were operating enterprises within their parents' home.

In Group A over half (53 per cent) of the workers had been born outside Makassar, suggesting that a relatively high number of migrants worked in small enterprises in the city. On average, two-thirds of each enterprise's workforce were Bugis and/or Makassar people from Makassar city or surrounding areas, yet there were also employees from other parts of South Sulawesi, such as the Tanatoraja and Mandar regions. Others, however, came from different Eastern Indonesian islands, Java and Sumatra. In comparison, just

Table 5.9 Gender of enterprise entrepreneurs or enterprise subcontractors and their workers, Group B[10]

Gender of workers	Subcontracting enterprises, with examples of products		Independent enterprises, with examples of products	
	Woman operator	Man operator	Woman entrepreneur	Man entrepreneur
All women workers	12 songkok, general clothing	–	6 general clothing	5 food, general clothing
All men workers	–	32 goldsmithery, chair frames	5 wooden furniture, goldsmithery	93 wooden furniture, ice-cream, stoves welding
Mix of women and men workers	1 general clothing	– –	7 savoury food, general clothing	23 drinks, general clothing
No workers	–	–	4 personal tailoring	12 metal pots, spray-painting, goldsmithery, personal tailoring

under half (46 per cent) of the entrepreneurs were themselves migrants to the city.

An even higher frequency of migration occurred among Group B entrepreneurs, in total, 88 per cent of them having migrated to the city at some stage in their lives. Interestingly, 22 per cent of these migrants were from Sidenreng Rappang province in the north of South Sulawesi (known as 'Sidrap'),[11] a traditional source of Bugis goldsmiths, with a further 14 per cent coming from much further afield, from other Indonesian islands. Conversely, 22 per cent of the entrepreneurs had been born in Makassar.

Here it is relevant to recall that the entrepreneurs interviewed in Group B represented the more 'flexible', unorganised and unrecognised of the small enterprises, whereas most in Group A had some form of recognition by the Department of Industry and Trade. This in turn suggests that the difference between Groups A and B in their relative proportions of migrant entrepreneurs may have arisen because of the greater ease with which migrants could establish a smaller, more 'invisible' enterprise in the city.

In addition, a number of the goldsmiths interviewed stated that one had to move to Makassar city in order to operate as a goldsmith, simply because there were no such employment opportunities in 'Sidrap' or elsewhere in South Sulawesi. There was thus a strong 'pull' factor for such persons to relocate to Makassar. Nonetheless, despite the presence of a substantial migrant population, the entrepreneurs were not necessarily 'new' migrants to the city. Of the 200 entrepreneurs in Group B, well over half (113 or 56.5 per cent) had been in Makassar for twenty years or more, compared with 53 or a little more than a quarter, who had arrived in the past ten years.

Many of the factors that took entrepreneurs and workers in Groups A and B to Makassar from other parts of Indonesia are embedded in the region's history as well as in its socio-cultural context. Historically, many Bugis and Makassar who later became entrepreneurs or urban workers moved to Makassar city during the period of regional rebellions from 1950 to 1965, as discussed earlier in this chapter. Since that time a number of social pressures have encouraged the migration of South Sulawesi inhabitants to the city. Chain migration through family ties has been highly influential as a pull factor, with women tending to follow male household members to the city, the elderly tending to follow their children. Social networks have also meant that new migrants can often rely on relatives already in the city to gain access to employment (Lomnitz, 1997). In addition, the hierarchical and formalised social stratification in Bugis, Makassar and Torajan *kampung* in South Sulawesi acts as a migration push factor, since movement to the city is a means by which to escape such restrictive structures and find new avenues for social mobility (Harvey, 1974; Forbes, 1981b; Grieco, 1995).

The labour force characteristics of the small enterprises were distinctive. In Group A, the number of workers within an enterprise varied from none (8 per cent) to fifteen (2 per cent), the average being four. Moreover, as many as thirty-five of the small enterprises employed only family labour, but, as Table 5.3 showed, sixteen had none from this source.

When asked if they had enough workers, 4 per cent of the entrepreneurs in Group A replied that they had 'more than enough', suggesting perhaps that their responsibility to provide employment for family members was a cause of inefficiencies within the enterprise, while another 68 per cent said they had 'enough' workers. Yet labour supply was problematic for a considerable proportion of the entrepreneurs, with 26 per cent replying they 'did not have enough' workers. Some replied that labour shortages could be overcome by using family members and that there were nearly always extended family members who could be called upon when necessary to increase the size of the workforce temporarily. Nevertheless, it is most unlikely that such an unstable workforce would be able to build up skill levels and craftspersonship.

Sometimes fluctuations in labour demand were met by using an outlier system, while this was a more permanent arrangement for others. Indeed, for Group A, twenty per cent had regular outlier arrangements whereby individuals worked in their own homes (21 per cent for Group B independent entrepreneurs), the payment usually being through a piece-rate system.

Goldsmith outliers, however, were usually paid in a certain percentage of gold, rather than in cash.

While there was some variation in length of working week, all workers spent long hours on the job. Within enterprises, non-family labour tended to work six days a week for seven or eight hours a day, while family labour worked even longer hours, commonly eight hours a day, seven days a week. There was a tendency for outlier workers to put in long hours too, doing so for nine hours a day for the whole week if they had a large order to fulfil. However, there was much flexibility within enterprises, the hours worked by many being directly dependent on demand for goods and the supply of raw materials. Work availability was highly uncertain, such that few workers had a guaranteed income. When asked how regular was the work that they provided, an overwhelming 76 per cent of the independent entrepreneurs in Group A replied that they could offer only irregular and variable work. The main reason for this situation was the direct dependency on customer orders (46 per cent). Problems relating to the availability of raw materials were also significant (17 per cent), as were seasonal variations in demand (11 per cent), the availability of capital, and a dependence on daily sales. Such problems showed once again that many of the enterprises were functioning purely on a day to day, order to order routine, no savings or stocks of raw materials being held.

Additional information requested from independent entrepreneurs in Group B concerning their outlier arrangements further highlighted the level of flexibility required from workers. Of the twenty-one enterprises that had outliers, four had over ten people in this category, all at different locations. One entrepreneur had had outliers for over twenty years, with the average relationship lasting five years. In terms of commodities produced, ten of the enterprises had outliers sewing general clothing and bedspreads, the others employing workers who produced all or part of goods for a variety of employers. These included a goldsmith, a traditional musical instrument entrepreneur, wooden framed chair entrepreneurs and a *songkok* (velvet hat for men) entrepreneur. For twenty of the outlier groups, payment was received in cash on a piece rate basis, while the goldsmith operated a piece-rate system with payment in gold.

Such indicators of a highly adaptable workforce with little security and a high labour turnover raise questions about 'whose flexibility' is being discussed when looking at such work arrangements (Schmitz, 1989: 15). Outlier systems like those found among Group B enterprises forced the burden of maintenance and welfare on to the workers and at the same time often took advantage of relatively 'weak' new entrants to the labour market. Outliers faced with a range of costs in terms of job security, real wage rates, support and so on were clearly in a tenuous situation in the Makassar context.

Payment systems

Flexibility of labour was also expressed in the form of the payment systems used. For Group A, whereas half of all workers were paid on a piece-rate system, another 11 per cent were paid daily. A further 10 per cent were on a 'contract' system, whereby the worker received a certain percentage of the final value of the finished product. On the other hand, a small minority (4 per cent), all family members, received no payment, the entrepreneur covering their 'basic needs' instead, while the amount which other entrepreneurs gave their workers depended on the profits made. In effect, no workers in any of the small enterprises had any formal job security. Perhaps most secure were the few (5 per cent) paid on a monthly basis, depending on the number of days they worked. The frequent use of piece-rate systems, in which workers merely undertook tasks assigned to them as quickly as possible, their payment being dependent on completion of the work, meant it was not surprising that there was no evidence to support flexible and informal management systems. In fact, there was very little delegation of management tasks to workers, and because entrepreneurs remained in control of all aspects of production, few workers had any input into managerial decision-making processes.[12]

Payment practices in Group B were not dissimilar. Within the independent enterprises, 40 per cent of workers were paid on a piece-rate basis, 19 per cent were immediate family who received no cash payments, and almost one-third (31 per cent) were paid weekly or monthly depending on the numbers of days they worked. Other workers were paid a certain percentage of sales. In contrast, all enterprise subcontractors rewarded their workers on a piece-rate basis, either in cash or in goods, such as gold for those working for goldsmiths. By paying workers according to days worked or on a piece-rate system, the benefits accrued to the employer who could increase or decrease the number of workers according to demand. Workers were clearly disadvantaged by such a numerically flexible system which meant that they could be hired and fired at will. As a consequence they emerged as the 'flexible casualties' of such an arrangement. This is in contrast to the ideal of functional flexibility, where worker flexibility is thought of in terms of workers with broad skills, who can move rapidly from one task to another (Galhardi, 1995).

The piece-rate systems used by entrepreneurs were diverse across enterprise types, yet all highlighted the numerical flexibility incorporated in such a payment strategy. Payment by piece-rate was especially common among goldsmiths, their workers being remunerated in gold. This resulted in a totally cashless system of transactions between the goldshops, goldsmith enterprise subcontractors and their workers. The payment rate for gold workers varied, but the norm was between 0.2 and 0.4 grams of gold for every 10 grams of gold product produced.[13] Sometimes when the workers toiled in their own homes, rather than at the subcontractor's workplace, they were employed in an outlier-style arrangement. For these workers the gold was weighed before it was given to them, then weighed again on its return to ensure the workers did not steal any (16a, 28/8/96).

For workers in subcontracting or independent small enterprises upholstering wooden chair frames, the payment was also piece-rate. For a good-quality, upholstered chair a worker received Rp.10,000, and Rp.12,500 for larger sofa-like chairs. It usually took a worker two to three days to complete an item, and to keep track of production a few entrepreneurs had blackboards at the entrance to their workshops where workers noted the goods they had completed (25b, 26b, 28/1/97; 36b, 29/1/97). For each of the poorer quality chairs, made of cheaper fabric and lower quality padding, the workers were paid Rp.2000–3000 a chair (31b, 32b, 33b, 29/1/97).

Many tailors operated as enterprise subcontractors. Their retailers supplied the raw materials, while the workers acted as outliers by working in their own homes. They were paid using a variety of methods. In one subcontracting enterprise, they received Rp.500 for each blouse produced (55b, 4/2/97), while in another, they gained Rp.250 of each Rp.750 the subcontractor received from the final retailer (56b, 5/2/97). From the retailers, who usually had a stall in a local indoor/covered market, the subcontractors were paid approximately Rp.8500 for a pair of trousers and Rp.3000–5000 for a shirt, giving them an average monthly wage/profit of Rp.200,000 (58b, 5/2/97).

Workers who sewed general clothes parts, such as collars (not individually tailored garments) in outlier arrangements in their own homes appeared to have one of the most numerically flexible labour arrangements. These outliers were often contacted by the enterprise subcontractor or entrepreneur (by telephone or in person) and asked to finish a certain number of pieces of work when there was the demand, resulting in highly uneven work levels. Commonly, outliers worked for more than one employer as a means of overcoming such fluctuations in their incomes.

A different labour pattern, yet again highlighting numerical flexibility, involved people who travelled daily to the city from local *kampung* (villages). They rented a *gerobak* (handcart) from an urban entrepreneur, who also often supplied the food or drink they were to sell. At the end of each day the entrepreneur gave the worker between 30 and 50 per cent of the profits, the worker making on average Rp.1000–2000 a day (KI 8, 11/12/96). While this was one of the city's employment opportunities that had the easiest entry, it nevertheless offered the lowest wages along with trishaw riders and building site workers (KI 9, 14/11/96).

Workers employed by entrepreneurs producing *es putah* (traditional ice-cream) walked around the city with a *gerobak* (owned by the entrepreneur) carrying their ice-cream in large aluminium vats/containers. These had a double lining, the space between being filled with a mixture of ice and salt, the inner container holding the ice-cream. *Es putah* vendors received Rp.5000 if they sold the contents of the container. If they sold half they received Rp.2500 and the container was 'topped up' for the next day (128b, 26/2/97). However, it was on average only once a week that a worker could not sell the contents in a day (130b, 26/2/97).

A somewhat different employment arrangement was practised by an entrepreneur who recycled reinforcing iron from demolition sites. He employed a core group of five people, but explained that when he found a large demolition job, he would hire friends on a daily basis to help. Prior to *Idul Fitri* (feast/celebration at the end of the fasting month), however, family members sought work from him so that they could earn extra cash. Because they were family, he felt obliged to provide work for them, again confirming the role of social obligations as a factor affecting the operation of the enterprises (44b, 3/2/97).

All of the entrepreneurs or enterprise subcontractors discussed above paid their workers on a piece-rate basis. In other situations, however, workers bought products to sell from their employer, but remained under the latter's control through other ties such as borrowing the equipment needed to sell the goods or having accommodation and food provided. Many workers sold *bakso* (meat ball soup) from a *gerobak* (handcart) located on the roadside or on the waterfront. They bought the prepared food from the entrepreneur, who, in turn, usually had his wife or a female relative prepare the food. *Bakso* workers often lived and ate at the entrepreneur's home and used/borrowed the entrepreneur's *gerobak* (42b, 30/1/97; 45b, 3/2/97). This was an example of the *pondok* (boarding-house) system that operated for workers involved with some of the small enterprises, but which was more common for trishaw operators in Indonesia, an aspect already discussed in Chapter 4 (KI 9, 20/12/96). One such entrepreneur had fifteen workers living at his house, compared with a norm of ten among the others interviewed. It was usual for the workers to buy the meat balls from the entrepreneur for Rp.65 each and sell them at Rp.100 each, customers paying Rp.500 for a bowl of *bakso* consisting of five meatballs and soup (60b, 5/2/97).

The case studies detailed above provide evidence of a wide variety of flexible labour relationships among small enterprises in Makassar.[14] Predominantly, workers were paid using some form of piece-rate system, or bought goods to sell per piece, often yielding highly variable earnings for the workers involved and providing little job security. In contrast, one of the few types of enterprise to give a regular wage was spray painting, in one case providing a wage of Rp.20,000 a week for workers, all of them non-family (80b, 11/2/97). Likewise, entrepreneurs making iron fences and providing a welding service paid their workers a flat rate of Rp.25,000 a week in one case, and in another Rp.20,000 (102b, 19/2/97; 110b, 20/2/97). Wages paid by other entrepreneurs depended on the skill levels of their workers. This was especially the case for employees in enterprises making screen-printed signs, name cards and wedding invitations from cardboard, wood, plastic, fabric or aluminium. Workers within these enterprises were usually remunerated according to the tasks performed and their skill level. For one such enterprise this resulted in workers receiving wages ranging from between Rp.25,000 and Rp.75,000 a month (120b, 25/2/97). Nonetheless, despite their more regular wages, these workers could still be hired and fired at the will of the entrepreneur in times of fluctuating demand.

The use of unpaid family labour was the easiest way to maintain an enterprise in which the entrepreneur was unable to cover production costs (Sjaifudian, 1992). Family workers commonly worked seven days a week, receiving food and accommodation and their 'livelihood needs' in return. There were numerous examples of children, spouses, parents, older and younger siblings, cousins and extended family members working irregular hours for an entrepreneur and receiving no direct wages. For instance, one entrepreneur, a fruit juice-maker, maintained that 'I don't have to pay them [his workers] as they are my brothers, I buy all their basic needs instead' (90b, 17/2/97), while a second, a tailor, claimed that 'they don't get paid, they are my wife and children so I must supply their basic livelihood needs' (92b, 17/2/97). Likewise, a male entrepreneur making metal cake trays and moulds, explained that 'the payment system for my workers isn't constant as they are my children, they live here so I provide food and things that they need. Maybe sometimes I give them money for small things' (127b, 26/2/97).

These examples identified some of the most flexible labour arrangements in the small enterprises examined, at least in terms of their payment/compensation systems. Nevertheless, at the same time there was a strong bond of loyalty that existed between entrepreneur and workers because they were family members. When demand was low, the entrepreneurs still felt obliged to provide for the workers, leading to a decline in their profits at times, yet this served to guarantee the workers' loyalty at other times when their labour might also have been in demand elsewhere. Hence labour mobility was reduced.

Children as young as 5 or 6 years old commonly worked in the small enterprises, often after school, on Sundays and during holidays. On the other hand, women in the family often undertook certain tasks for the enterprise in between their 'domestic responsibilities'. As Sjaifudian (1992: 182) has explained, these arrangements were advantageous from the entrepreneur's perspective, 'because it is difficult for entrepreneurs to obtain wage workers who are willing to work irregular, broken and often excessively long hours (frequently in the evening), they prefer to use family workers'. One implication to be drawn from such arrangements is that in a number of small enterprises using totally family labour in Makassar, there existed, yet again, 'flexible casualties'. This situation is strongly reminiscent of Chayanov's (1966) description of unpaid family labour as 'self-exploitation'. This concept was central to his model of smallholder agriculture and household organisation in which the costs of unpaid family labour were not taken into consideration by the family when calculating the profits and losses, an omission which explained why a family enterprise could exist in conditions that a capitalist enterprise could not.[15]

Returns to labour

As was established in Chapter 4, the minimum daily wage for Makassar in 1997 was Rp.3750, indicating a monthly wage of approximately Rp.97,500, based on a six-day working week (*Jakarta Post*, 23 January 1997).[16] On the other hand, when the entrepreneurs in Makassar were asked to indicate their average monthly profits, it became clear that a number were able to make as much as, or more, operating their own small enterprise, than if they had been working for another employer. Indeed, in Group B, only fourteen (7 per cent) of the entrepreneurs had profits less than the average monthly wage, while producing goods ranging from traditional cookies, stoves and cooking pots, to *bakso* and bedspreads, as well as candles, knives and, in four cases, gold jewellery. All the other entrepreneurs (186) interviewed in Group B were able to make monthly profits higher than the average monthly wage. Of these, the highest returns were obtained by those producing metal car parts, the backs of small trucks, *durian* cakes and cookies, cupboards and beds, and aquariums. Nevertheless, whether the official minimum wage is enough to cover the minimum physical needs of individuals continues to be contested in the Indonesian context (KI 3, 6/11/96; van Diermen, 1997; *Jakarta Post,* 30 May 1997).

Table 5.10 sets out details of daily earnings for various workers employed on piece-rate in small enterprises in which half the workers or more were non-family labour. This reveals considerable variation above and below the minimum daily wage for Makassar. For instance, tailors, goldsmith-workers, chair-workers and ice-cream sellers were able to obtain more, in some cases much more, than the average daily wage while working on piece-rate. At the other extreme, those making candles and embroidering blouses received only 53 and 64 per cent of the average daily wage respectively. That there were small-scale entrepreneurs obtaining more than the average daily wage contradicts the findings of Guinness (1994), but supports those of van Diermen (1997) for small enterprises in Jakarta.

Such information suggests that, for some, it was more profitable to remain in the small enterprise sector than to seek an alternative livelihood. There are various reasons why this was so. First, joining the public sector in Indonesia was difficult because of the (unofficial) need to pay an 'entry fee' and often to have existing contacts in the sector. A second reason was that a number of entrepreneurs or workers in small enterprises spent long hours to obtain such wages, so 'self-exploitation' was a significant factor in being able to gain reasonable returns for work undertaken.

Acquiring new workers

The entrepreneurs in Group B were asked how they recruited new workers. The most common response was that they gained them (usually family) from their *kampung* (village) (31 per cent). As one tailor entrepreneur explained, 'I

Table 5.10 Approximate daily earnings of workers in small enterprises with below 50 per cent of family labour

Work undertaken	Piece-rate	Approximate daily earnings	Minimum daily wage for Makassar (%)
Padding and upholstering wooden chairs – high quality	Rp.10,000. More than a day's work	Approx. Rp.5000 a day	133
Padding and upholstering wooden chairs – low quality	Rp.2000–3000. Could complete two or more a day	Rp.4000–6000 a day	106–160
Sewing blouses	Rp.500. Could complete 7–8 a day	Rp.3500–4000 a day	93–106
Sewing embroidery on blouses	Rp.300. Could complete 8–10 a day	Rp.2400–3000 a day	64–80
Sewing collars	Rp.50. Could complete up to 60–80 a day	Rp.3000–4000 a day	80–106
Making candles	Rp.1000 for 100 candles. Takes four hours to make 100	Rp.2000 a day	53
Selling ice-cream		Rp.5000 a day	133
Spray-painters		Rp.3333 a day (paid weekly)	89
Drink-makers and sellers		Rp.3333 a day (paid weekly)	89

go back to the *kampung* if I need new workers, then I teach them in my home here in Makassar, so they can work for me' (1b, 21/1/97), while another claimed that 'my outliers are friends of people I already have working for me, or else I go to the *kampung*' (15b, 23/1/97).

Some of the entrepreneurs who originated from Java maintained that they would return to their *kampung* on Java to recruit new workers, a claim indicating that linkages of some strength were maintained with the *kampung* even if it was a considerable distance away and expensive for the entrepreneurs to return to. The linkages were especially strong for Javanese entrepreneurs involved with food production. They believed that Javanese people from their *kampung* were the only workers who could produce certain food in the proper manner and to the correct standards (KI 14, 4/12/96). One entrepreneur who produced *bakso*, and his wife *jamu* (traditional herbal medicines), claimed he would still continue to recruit new workers in this manner, even after having lived in Makassar for seventeen years (53b, 4/2/97). Likewise, a Javanese man making *kerupuk udung* and *kerupuk ikan* (prawn and fish crackers), and a resident of Makassar for nine years, also claimed he would still return to his *kampung* to recruit new workers (111b, 20/2/97).

Javanese migrants were also preferred to make *tempe, tahu* and *martabak* (folded, fried crêpe filled with spices and pieces of meat and/or vegetables) because it was believed that they produced the most appetising products.[17] Similarly, the often expressed view that only Makassar people could be employed to produce *es putah* (traditional Makassar ice-cream) served to confirm the strong influence of cultural factors on the small enterprises associated with food production. Indeed, it has often been observed that among small enterprises in Indonesia 'particular foods are marketed by different ethnic groups, while members of a particular village or area often monopolise trade in a particular item' (Guinness, 1994: 293).

For other entrepreneurs and also enterprise subcontractors requiring workers, the need was often too immediate to return to the *kampung*. Therefore, in addition to *kampung* links, 16 per cent of the Group B entrepreneurs took on new workers from among family already in Makassar and 13 per cent employed workers from people who approached the entrepreneur asking for work. Other entrepreneurs answered that they went looking for workers themselves in the surrounding district, or gained information about possible employees from existing workers or friends in Makassar.

Neighbours were sometimes asked to work for a short period. As one woman tailor explained, 'yes, I have people that help me finish my goods. Sometimes these are my family, sometimes I ask women in the same street. I pay them money for each piece' (23b, 27/1/97). Others used informal networking to gain new labour, asking current workers to get friends and family to work as well (109b, 20/21997). Such networking was important for new migrant workers who usually obtained employment through family and friends who had already moved to Makassar from the *kampung* and would 'guarantee' a new arrival to the entrepreneur (Guinness, 1993). If a worker misbehaved, the other workers would quickly rebuke the newcomer or force him/her to stop working for the enterprise, because this reflected badly on themselves due to their social connections. In this way there was an informal 'code of ethics/behaviour' among the workers. This self-regulating workforce was yet another reason why it was advantageous for entrepreneurs to recruit workers who were connected to each other through such networks.

Nonetheless, these labour networks could only go so far in advancing the enterprise before other constraints became apparent. These included limited training (inhibiting the possibility for craftspersonship characteristics among workers), willingness to undertake certain tasks, other family commitments, and so on. Women entrepreneurs tended to rely on family and *kampung* connections to a greater extent than men to find new workers, very few of them employing people who had come directly to the enterprise looking for work, a factor that at times prevented these enterprises from recruiting skilled workers.

Thus small enterprises in the city adopted a wide variety of labour patterns. These reflected cultural and family linkages involved in production, the varying ease of entry into different types of work, the different relationships entrepreneurs had with their workers, and fluctuations in demand for the goods produced. Many of the enterprises had people working for them in outlier-style arrangements so that the costs of production could be lowered. Nevertheless, while wages were good for many workers, they were still often in a tenuous position regarding work security, especially if not related to the entrepreneur for whom they worked.

Worker skills

A further dimension of small enterprise activity was documented by a comparison between the number of workers wanted by the entrepreneurs in Group A and the skill levels of the workers. This revealed a significant relationship between entrepreneurs who did not have enough workers and the high skill levels required of them. Entrepreneurs who had more than enough workers also reported low skill levels among their employees. This relationship implies an extreme disparity between supply of and demand for skilled labour employed by small enterprises. In turn, this meant that a substantial number of enterprises had a distinct lack of workers with high levels of craftspersonship. From this evidence it appeared that only rarely were workers learning new techniques and skills, and putting them into practice, as having a high degree of craftspersonship would imply. While many workers seemed to quite readily adapt to the tasks required of them, this frequently involved relatively simple production methods so that the degree of craft skills utilised remained limited.

The vast number of workers considered by entrepreneurs in Group A to have less than 'high' levels of work skills (86 per cent) was not surprising when one examines the training provided. In particular, while 38 per cent of the workers in Group A were provided with on-the-job training either by their employer or by other workers in the enterprise, half of the entrepreneurs indicated that they offered no training whatsoever. Workers in this situation had to know how to undertake the task already, or to 'pick it up' – a type of informal training – from copying other employees.

Not surprisingly too, levels of formal training were very low with only 6 per cent of Group A workers having received any prior to employment. Then, after workers had gained their position, 84 per cent of entrepreneurs provided no formal training or paid for or encouraged workers to join training schemes. That all the workers who had received formal training were men perhaps suggests the existence of some formidable barriers to women entrepreneurs and their workers in accessing formal training courses and apprenticeships run by government and non-government departments and institutions in Makassar. Indeed, many of the courses offered were not relevant to the work women were undertaking in small enterprises.

On the other hand, when asked whether they preferred to employ trained or non-trained workers, most (78 per cent) Group A entrepreneurs replied that they wanted trained workers, while the remainder sought non-trained (13 per cent) or had no preference (9 per cent). The pattern was similar for both men and women entrepreneurs. Those who wanted trained workers explained that this would enable them to begin production immediately. Not only that, but such workers were preferred because they did not require a great deal of supervision, their productivity was higher, and for some (such as goldsmiths) they already possessed the level of precision required for the production process.

In contrast, entrepreneurs who wanted non-trained workers professed a different rationale to explain their preference. One dimension of this was that if they provided training the workers would remain tied to the business, so instilling in them a 'loyalty factor'. In addition, non-trained workers were easier to find and would work for lower wages. Nonetheless, many entrepreneurs in both categories mentioned difficulties in matching needs with reality. Specialisation was thus constrained by the fact that there were often many workers able to undertake basic tasks, but few who could carry out the more specialised ones. This tended to concentrate workers into the low-skill end of the production process and therefore to discourage innovation.

There was also quite strong competition for labour among entrepreneurs. As many as one in four (26 per cent) of Group A admitted that this was the case. Once again, because too few people were available who had the skills for the tasks required, they had to 'pinch' workers from other enterprises, and were in competition on a wage-level basis as well as for workers who could be trusted. Competition for workers was also seasonal, labour being scarce during *Puasa* (fasting month) when many enterprises were at their busiest in anticipation of *Idul Fitri*. During other seasons, some entrepreneurs reported that it was difficult to retain their workers, who tended to 'drift' to other enterprises that had more work available. This generated frequent worker turnover, 16 per cent of the enterprises having lost one worker within the year prior to interviewing, and a further 28 per cent having lost two or more workers within the same period. The most often cited reasons why workers left an enterprise were to return to their *kampung* (15 per cent), because the enterprise had no more regular work or orders (10 per cent), that they wanted to work for another enterprise, or to marry. There were also those who left to set up their own business after having learned the skills from a former entrepreneur (8 per cent), their departure depriving the latter of skilled workers.

The competition for labour and high labour turnover presented entrepreneurs with a quandary. This was whether or not to provide training for workers who might then 'jump ship', taking their expertise with them when prospects appeared to be brighter elsewhere. This was a strong disincentive for entrepreneurs to invest time, energy and resources into training workers, a dilemma reflected in the low levels of formal and informal training that the workers had acquired. The continuous ebb and flow of workers from one enterprise to another meant that the more successful producers could draw the better workers from the less successful, leading over time to a widening of differences between enterprises and a continuing cycle of survivalism for the less competitive producers. It was only if workers subsequently 'drifted back' to their previous employer after completing work elsewhere that a 'balance' could be said to be occurring among the enterprises involved. Although this sometimes happened within clusters of enterprises it was not the norm, workers tending to move continuously from one enterprise to another throughout a district in response to changing demand (KI 2, 4/3/97).

Entrepreneurs adopted a variety of strategies in seeking to remain competitive for labour. Eighty per cent provided what could be seen as incentives for workers to stay with a particular enterprise. These included lending money to workers, matching the wages of competitors, maintaining good relations with workers, providing bonuses for work carried out on time or in advance of deadlines, guaranteeing employees their jobs if they became sick, and paying them on time. By offering fairly inexpensive 'gestures' such as these, entrepreneurs sought to give themselves an advantage over their competitors in attempting to retain workers. Nevertheless, 20 per cent of the employers in Group A had no means of competing for labour, implying that the success or failure of their enterprise was very dependent on changes in the labour market as a whole.

Entrepreneurs also provided a range of welfare support for their workers. Indeed, a large majority (71 per cent) of those in Group A provided at least one meal daily for their workers. In addition, the vast majority provided accommodation to at least some workers, with as many as 37 per cent having all their workers living on site, and only 19 per cent providing no accommodation at all. Not surprisingly, there was a 'very significant' correlation between the number of family workers and the level of accommodation provided, entrepreneurs in general feeling it their duty to do so.

Yet such welfare support had other advantages shared among both the entrepreneurs and their employees. Among the former it was recognised not only as a way of increasing loyalty among non-family workers, but also productivity, time efficiency and motivation, hence it was a means by which workers could be 'held on to'. To employees, on the other hand, such welfare support was a strong incentive to work at a certain enterprise. Compared to those prepared to offer such benefits, entrepreneurs who did not do so were severely disadvantaged in gaining and maintaining workers and their loyalty.

As well as direct incentives and welfare support, entrepreneurs felt socially obliged to provide a range of other measures, not only for workers, but frequently for extended family and neighbours as well. In extreme cases, the number of people supported regularly reached fourteen for one entrepreneur in Group A. The kinds of support given in groups A and B ranged from gifts, loans and social contributions for festivals and religious ceremonies to neighbours and friends, to education and training costs for some family members and workers. In general, entrepreneurs in Group A had a positive perception of the provision of such support, 34 per cent of them believing that this did not have any negative effect on their enterprise. A further 28 per cent believed it made the workers they supported more diligent and motivated, and thus assisted the growth of the enterprise. Others talked about a 'responsibility towards Allah' to provide such support (29a, 6/9/96), that it was 'my duty' (31a, 20/8/96; 37, 2/9/96) or that it was 'for the prosperity of the family, workers and community' (70a, 1/9/96; 91a, 30/10/96). Very few (only one Mandar, one Makassar and one Bugis entrepreneur) were of the opinion that the provision of such support had a negative effect on the general operation of their enterprise.

Such support was seen by the many entrepreneurs who provided it as not only essential to the operations of their enterprises but also as an important element of social responsibility. The mounting evidence for Makassar city, then, confirms that for entrepreneurs there, 'success' was a multi-faceted concept that included other factors in addition to economic growth alone. In other words, 'success' for these entrepreneurs often included the ability to provide support for workers, family and members of the community, as well as to undertake philanthropic actions. Using entrepreneurial resources for these purposes, in effect directly draining profits from the enterprise or limiting growth, was in no way looked upon as a negative factor.

However, entrepreneurs were well aware that skill levels and productivity were weakened by a number of factors. Nearly two-fifths (38 per cent) indicated that their most serious labour problems were a lack of skills and limited competency among their workers, some commenting that many workers were not careful and often made mistakes. For a smaller group of entrepreneurs, employees who were 'lazy' and lacked motivation were a problem (10 per cent), as was frequent truancy for a further 7 per cent. The major impacts of such difficulties for the enterprises were a decline in productivity and in the quality of finished products (57 per cent), difficulties in matching the quality of the goods demanded with that of those produced, a decline in profits, the pedestrian pace at which work was undertaken and the slow development of the enterprise as a whole. Such observations confirm once more that many of the entrepreneurs themselves did not regard their workers as having significant levels of craftspersonship.

Nevertheless, information gathered from entrepreneurs implied that a sizeable group were not perturbed by the impact of labour factors that reduced the productivity of their businesses. For example, 35 per cent of the Group A entrepreneurs indicated that they had not thought about what general changes they would like to see in the future in regard to their workforce. The vast majority of them (90 per cent) employed 50 per cent or more family labour, and were mainly Bugis goldsmiths, Makassar tailors or Javanese *tempe* entrepreneurs. The entrepreneurs did not see the necessity to expand their enterprise, since they perceived themselves as being already 'successful' in providing for family needs. Again, this situation confirms the wisdom of using emic definitions of success as understood by the entrepreneurs of Makassar.

Worker movement

Worker movement was a critical concern for a number of the entrepreneurs as innovative ideas could be gained or lost by workers moving in or out of their enterprise, as well as production difficulties arising from workers disappearing to take up a different employment opportunity.

As previously mentioned, non-family workers often moved among small-scale or subcontracting enterprises when orders were limited at their present place of employment and there were better prospects elsewhere. Over time the more successful enterprises tended to attract the more skilled workers, leaving other enterprises in a disadvantaged position. By this means too, the more successful enterprises gained a broadly trained workforce, while less successful enterprises were severely disadvantaged in this respect. Nonetheless, even among the more successful enterprises, there was still a considerable turnover of workers which, in turn, reduced the ability of entrepreneurs to build up the skilled workforce many wanted.

A number of the interviewees complained of fluctuations in the size of their workforce. The point was well made by one independent entrepreneur making wooden cupboards and sideboards who protested: 'my workers aren't constant, they change daily. It depends on if they want to work that day and if they want some money, or already have enough money for a while. Sometimes they go elsewhere if they hear about a better job, they just leave, maybe they return a week later' (95b, 18/2/97). When asked how he found new workers, another entrepreneur manufacturing wooden tables, sideboards and chairs explained: 'sometimes I find that friends who are carpenters want to move jobs, it's common for them to move locations, so then they come to work for me, and other times there are often people coming here looking for work' (153b, 4/3/97).

Labour mobility was one way in which new enterprises entered the market. Workers sometimes left enterprises to establish their own after initially learning the requisite skills from their original employer, in anticipation that they could obtain greater earnings in their own enterprise. Thus the new entrepreneur would often compete directly with a former employer. This was common among goldsmiths who would save a small amount of working capital and buy the tools required to begin a business, often then competing with their past employer to gain orders from the same Chinese retailers in the city. Another example was provided by a man who made flour sieves, a skill developed when working at another such enterprise in Makassar, before he decided to establish his own (79b, 11/2/97). In another case, the entrepreneur had worked for a large electrical goods company in Makassar until June 1996, when he left to establish his own business making dynamos for fridges, fans and radios, an enterprise which he maintained was developing well (115b, 24/2/97).

As discussed in Chapter 4, social status is of particular importance for Bugis and Makassar people. To them, in modern-day society, owning one's own business, even if a small enterprise with only family members as workers, is seen as a potential way to climb up the social ladder. This was a significant reason why workers aimed to save enough to begin their own small enterprise (KI 4, 15/4/97). Not surprisingly, such worker mobility helps to explain why entrepreneurs were often reluctant to provide training to a level that would make it possible for workers to set up their own enterprise in direct competition. Nonetheless, as Pedersen *et al.* (1994: 4) contend, 'the high mobility of labour is important for rapid innovation diffusion among the enterprises', and on occasion ideas were incorporated into the newly established enterprises which had been rejected by a past employer, a point made by both a newly established entrepreneur making screen-printed signs and another making fences (10b, 22/1/97; 137b, 26/2/97). Such innovation was often limited within established enterprises, hence the process of new enterprise formation was one of the few potential avenues for such innovation to occur, a topic addressed further in Chapter 7. Again, however, this situation highlights the complexities involved concerning worker mobility, as the positive results brought by innovation made possible by such mobility might so easily be negated by the lack of skills and training such movement also imposed.

By providing accommodation and food for workers, as well as other welfare provisions such as loans and social contributions for festivals and religious ceremonies, entrepreneurs often assiduously cultivated a patron–client relationship with their workers. Workers did not usually have the economic means to return favours in kind, and hence returns were in labour, as well as loyalty and dependability. For their part, entrepreneurs expected workers to be diligent and remain in their employment for some time, and hence feel 'bound' to an enterprise (Grieco, 1995; Arghiros, 1996). Such strategies reduced the fluidity of workers by curtailing their movement among enterprises, and engendered a more stable relationship between entrepreneurs and workers than might otherwise occur. Moreover, the strength of the patron–client relationship meant that the provision of training for workers did not always result in the workers moving away to establish their own enterprises.

Nevertheless, because of the social status related to having one's own enterprise, there were a number of cases of previous workers who had begun new enterprises while maintaining close connections with their previous employer. This often occurred when a worker got married which led, in turn, to the creation of production networks and inter-firm linkages. One silversmith had trained a worker for two years at his enterprise, the worker living on site. The latter had then married and started to work with his wife in their own home, under an outlier arrangement with his previous employer who provided the tools and 'raw' silver. The worker brought back the finished products to be sold through the initial enterprise. In such cases, therefore, there appeared to be a reciprocal social/moral 'obligation' between the worker and employer, who called the worker 'my friend . . . my student' (183b, 12/3/97).

This was not the only way in which new enterprises were established, however. Another variant involved a shoemaking entrepreneur. He had set up a small enterprise in 1965 and had twelve people working directly for him, eight cutting and sewing the basic shoes and four finishing, cleaning and inspecting the product. Such workers usually remained with the entrepreneur for a year as trainees. Then, if they wished, and had saved enough capital, they could open their own enterprise. The entrepreneur explained that there were five shoemaking enterprises in Makassar, four of which were operated by former workers. Yet none of the four was operating as a subcontractor because raw materials had been gained directly from other sources. In reality, then, a complementary rather than competitive relationship had evolved. The four were able to use their previous employer as a retailing channel because he had diversified his operations to include a showroom and shop, run by his wife and son, while also having connections with a number of retailers in Makassar through whom the shoes of the linked enterprises were sold (122b, 25/2/97).

Thus it appeared that while a worker might have wished to establish his/her own enterprise, a lack of capital and being part of an existing patron-client relationship often meant that new enterprises became integrated instead into complex inter-firm linkages and networks with previous employers. This may be construed as an embryonic form of collective efficiency, in that there appeared to be a balance between competition and co-operation among the small enterprises involved, as well as economies of agglomeration in terms of marketing channels. A critical factor lacking, it seemed, was the just-in-time delivery system of inputs, new enterprises drawing their raw materials from a variety of suppliers, and often with delays in obtaining goods. One cause of this was that raw materials, such as rubber soles for shoes, came from Surabaya, Java, and delays in shipping were common (123b, 25/2/97). Hence, once again, contextual factors such as the physical location as well as the political environment influenced the operation of such enterprises considerably.[18]

Gender divisions

As noted in Chapter 4, considerable regional diversity in women's workforce participation has existed for some time in Indonesia, a noticeably lower workforce participation rate being recorded for women in South Sulawesi when compared to other areas of Indonesia (Oey-Gardiner, 1993). Perhaps this reflected the influence of the *peran ganda* (dual role) ideology regarding women's participation in development, whereby 'home-based income-generating activities are meant to supplement women's primary role of homemaker', an ideology that has retained greater significance in South Sulawesi than in some other areas of Indonesia in which manufacturing industries employing large numbers of women workers away from home have become numerous (Joseph, 1987: vi).

Certainly, clear gender divisions existed in a number of the small enterprises studied in Makassar, plenty of them being 'closed' to women, a point also noted by Forbes (1981b). Gold- silver- copper- and blacksmithing, cement-making, as well as welding, door and window carpentry, and rattan furniture-making were all exclusively male occupations. In contrast, it was usual for women to prepare any food that was produced on private premises for use by enterprises. Nonetheless, gender divisions in other small enterprises were more blurred, such as in tailoring where there were men and women entrepreneurs as well as workers, although a single enterprise would usually have workers of only one gender.

From evidence gathered during field work it also appeared that gender stereotypes were used to limit women's access to certain employment opportunities. So-called 'innate' female characteristics such as concentration, patience, agility and so on were given by entrepreneurs as reasons why women were more suited to some specific types of work rather than to others. In seeking further insight into the gender division of labour, entrepreneurs were asked specifically whether they preferred men or women workers and why they did so. Of those who preferred men, the most common answer was because of their strength and endurance, that men worked faster, or that the job was 'more appropriate for men' such as in welding and construction, gold and silver handicraft production, blacksmithing, making ovens, and producing building materials. In contrast, entrepreneurs who preferred women maintained that they were more careful, could be paid less, and were more nimble, skilful and agile. It was also considered that women were easier to control, that they wanted to stay at home (where outlier work could be undertaken), and that the work was 'more appropriate for women'. Such 'appropriate' work included the production of certain foods and sewing clothes. Hence, to provide a deeper insight into the gendering of labour in small enterprises, it is appropriate to explore in some detail the work of goldsmiths, tailors and food enterprises. These demonstrate a range of gendered employment patterns within Makassar.

Goldsmithing was an exclusively male domain. When goldsmiths who were interviewed were asked if they preferred men or women workers, all expressed a preference for men, for a variety of reasons. These ranged from simple statements like 'but this is men's work' (2b, male, 21/1/97), to 'you don't have women working as goldsmiths' (5b, male, 21/1/97), while others maintained that it was 'heavy work', although this did not appear to be the case in reality. Another goldsmith believed that it was because men were stronger, but he also added that 'there aren't women working as goldsmiths here, but there are women that own goldsmith businesses' (8b, male, 22/1/97). The goldsmith enterprise in which this man was working had been inherited by his employer, a Bugis woman entrepreneur, from her parents and she had continued to manage the enterprise. When pressed further to elaborate on their replies, 'tradition' was offered as the key factor that explained why women did not work as goldsmiths, a point that emphasises the role of culture and social relations in the organisation of production in Makassar (5b, male, 21/1/97;

8b, male, 22/1/97).

Unlike goldsmithing, the tailoring enterprises showed a range of gender combinations. The independent and subcontracting tailoring enterprises studied usually employed only men or only women workers. When there was a mixture of genders, the enterprises tended to be family operated. Personal tailors, producing specific 'one-off' clothes for customers, tended to be male and to have male workers, while general tailor enterprises committed to filling bulk orders tended to be owned by women, and to employ women workers and outliers. One such entrepreneur responded that she employed women as tailors because they were 'more diligent than men' (9b, 22/1/97). Clearly then, the preference of female entrepreneurs for workers of their own gender were shaped as much by culture and social relations as were those of their male counterparts. This was evidently so for one female tailor who claimed that she preferred to employ single women because they could then stay at her house, not least because 'sewing and embroidering is women's work' (58a, 11/9/96).

Other examples of explicit gender divisions in employment were readily apparent. They included a male entrepreneur producing *songkok* using four women outliers, sewing in their own homes. To him, this was an appropriate arrangement: 'I choose women, because women prefer to stay at home' (55a, 9/9/96). Also interviewed was an entrepreneur producing traditional Mandar weaving who maintained that he preferred women from his extended family because 'women like to weave' (87a, 19/9/97).

The number of women who worked for tailoring enterprises was far greater than the number of women owning them. The chairperson of a co-operative for tailors which had fifty members reported as few as nine women entrepreneurs among its members, even though females accounted for 90 per cent of the workers in the enterprises involved. It was 'normal', he said, for men to own the business and have control, and then went on to make a series of disparaging jokes about women in general, and in particular their inability to invest money wisely in a business enterprise (Co-operative Chairperson, confidential personal communication, 27/8/96). On occasion during field work, officials from the Department of Industry and Trade were observed talking to different small-scale entrepreneurs in an officially recognised cluster. When the officials talked with male entrepreneurs they were visibly relaxed and informal, yet when they visited small enterprises operated by women they ignored them and talked to their husbands instead. This provides further confirmation of a point made earlier in this chapter, namely that when women were operating an enterprise in collaboration with their husbands, the husband often took the role of 'spokesperson' in public. However, by these actions, women were excluded from decision-making discussions within co-operatives in regard to the clusters. The same actions also prevented women entrepreneurs from gaining direct information concerning a number of aspects such as credit availability, training opportunities, new technology and so on. These gendered experiences substantiated similar findings reported by

Utrecht and Sayogyo (1994) in their research on the impact of different government interventions on women's non-agricultural production in West Java.

Even more complex were the gender divisions in enterprises connected with food preparation and marketing. Within the home in South Sulawesi cooking was traditionally seen as a woman's task and it was very rare for a man to cook. Nonetheless, there was some blurring of gender divisions when it came to cooking for small enterprises. In this context one found men cooking *bakso* (meat ball soup) in the home, before it was sold by workers using *gerobak* (handcarts), or at a stall. Yet such entrepreneurs were usually from Java and had migrated to Makassar in search of work, often leaving their wife and family in Java. Only when the entrepreneur had established an enterprise would the rest of the family follow. As soon as this occurred the cooking of the *bakso,* as well as family meals, reverted back to being a woman's task (KI 12, 19/2/97; KI 6, 26/2/97).

The only other situation in which men cooked was when the task occurred outside the home. This was the case for men preparing *coto Makassar* (local traditional soup) at stalls on the side of the road. This was regarded as an acceptable task for men because it was a productive, rather than a reproductive one, which provided the family with income. As one male key informant explained, 'it's OK for men to cook in public if it's for the family income'. When I commented that it seemed that cooking was regarded as women's work in Sulawesi he gestured that we were standing in the street as he replied, 'but this is in a different place' (KI 4, 2/3/97). The distinctions between public and private spaces were thus clearly reflected in the activities perceived as suitable for women or men.

Nonetheless, there were a few notable exceptions to these gender divisions that placed women in the public sphere as well as men. Two such sites involved the sale of *bakso* from a stationary stall located on the streetside but close to the home, or from a *gerobak.* In one case, the wife, often accompanied by her children or a female relative, operated the stationary stall, while the husband walked around the city selling *bakso* from a *gerobak* (59b, male, 5/2/97). This division of labour seemed to suggest a belief that a woman was 'safe' and behaving in a culturally appropriate manner when operating an immobile stall within her immediate neighbourhood.

Nevertheless, a woman could and sometimes did work on a stall or from a stationary *gerobak* away from her neighbourhood. In such situations, however, other arrangements to ensure that she was 'safe' were applied, like always working with other male family members or having male relatives operating another stall/*gerobak* nearby. Historically, it has been unacceptable for women to work on such stalls as it was considered 'unsafe', especially if the stalls were operating at night. Nevertheless, women have worked on such stalls since the mid-1980s for several different reasons (KI 6, male, 26/2/97). While one key informant believed it was due to changes in people's perceptions of what was acceptable for women to do for employment (KI 4, male, 3/3/97), another believed it was because many of the women were Javanese and that gender roles were 'less divided in Java for things like this' (KI 15, female, 2/3/97).

Although a number of interviewed women who worked on such stalls were indeed from Java, there were also some from Makassar and Tanatoraja, so perhaps the comments from both key informants were valid. Perhaps, too, social norms had been relaxed as a matter of necessity because such work had become an economic imperative for the households concerned. Yet, despite such evidence of merging gender roles, at no time did it appear acceptable for a woman to walk around the city with a handcart (*gerobak*). As one entrepreneur maintained, 'men sell the bakso from the *gerobak*, women can only help in the home' (42b, male, 30/1/97), while another saw such a division of labour in terms of physical capability. To him, 'women don't work on *gerobak* because they are not strong enough to walk it around' (186b, male, 13/3/97).

The gendered division of labour was further differentiated by ethnic group. A number of Javanese women sold *jamu* (medicinal herbal tonic), while their husbands traded food such as *bakso* from a stall or *gerobak*. The women walked or rode a bicycle around the streets of Makassar during the day selling their goods from large baskets (53b, female, 4/2/97; see also Forbes, 1981b). In essence, although it was not considered appropriate for women to walk around the city with a *gerobak*, it was acceptable for them to walk or cycle with a heavy load of full bottles, again suggesting the strong importance of cultural norms and traditions among a proportion of small enterprises in the city. It was also clear that female *jamu* sellers made a considerable contribution to the family income. Of four such couples interviewed, while the husbands in each case earned approximately Rp.100,000–120,000 a month selling *bakso*, the wives made, on average, about Rp.90,000 during the same period (45b, male, 3/2/97; 53b, female, 4/2/97; 64b, male, 6/2/97; 75b, male, 10/2/97).

Chair production was another strongly gendered small enterprise type. Here the norm was that men rather than women sawed the wood to make the chair frames they also created, a gender preference that became clear in the responses of entrepreneurs. One of these, a male frame-maker, when asked if he employed men or women, exclaimed 'men of course, look at the type of work they are doing, women can't hammer, men are faster' (26b, 28/1/97). A second entrepreneur, a male, gave a similar reply, pointing out that it was 'men, well it's sawing wood isn't it?' (29b, 28/1/97). Once assembled, the rough frame of the chair was padded and covered with fabric which had already been sewn into the required shapes. This task was less gender specific insofar as both men and women undertook the sewing, but the actual application of the padding and fabric to the frame was again seen as men's work, perhaps because it consisted largely of tacking the fabric to the wood frame with a hammer, an activity considered to be 'using a man's tool' (32b, male, 29/1/97).

Entrepreneurs who had wives helping them in their enterprises all declared that their spouse was not paid. In theory, this would seem to imply that the wife shared the ownership of the enterprise and hence was obliged to share responsibility for enterprise development as well. In reality, however, women rarely shared equal decision-making rights, such as would have been given to a male business partner (Sjaifudian, 1992). In summary, 'flexibility' appeared to be nearly invisible in terms of gender roles. This situation reflected certain cultural and traditional 'norms', based on a mixture of the different cultural traditions and Islamic influences, having a bearing on which work was considered suitable for women and which for men in the city, where, in general, women's work was linked with lower earnings (International Labour Office, 1995). As an entrepreneur producing fruit drinks reasoned, it was better to employ women because 'you can pay women a lower daily wage and they're easier to give instructions to' (12a, male, 16/8/96).

In the case of the small enterprises in Makassar, then, it is clear that social and cultural norms limited women to specific roles within, or excluded them altogether, from individual enterprises. Although recent changes occurring in some spheres increased profit-making opportunities available to women, this appeared to be a slow process. At the time of my field work women usually had less direct control than men over the way a family enterprise was organised. In addition, women entrepreneurs were often excluded from decision-making processes in clusters and co-operatives, a situation that limited the ability of women-led enterprises to become integrated into clusters supported by government policies. In effect, the situation in Makassar appeared to be strikingly similar to that described by Azis (1996: 120) for Eastern Indonesia in general:

> It is not unusual for women to be more involved in small trading activities than men. Their trading activities may already contribute significantly to the marketing system for a number of locally produced products. Hence they provide one of the most important services for the production sector in Eastern Indonesia. Unfortunately, the funding needed to enhance their activities is often difficult to obtain, since financial lending practices are usually less favourable in that they furnish smaller access to women than to men.

Whose flexibility?

The evidence, therefore, indicates that while entrepreneurs in Makassar required a flexible supply of labour, this was accompanied by a number of negative consequences for workers. There was very little job security and, for those operating as subcontracting enterprises or as outliers, the costs of production had to be borne by themselves, not by their 'employer'. Nevertheless, one senses that the situation in Makassar was somewhat different in several ways from that enshrined in the traditional critique of flexibility in small enterprises, as discussed by Morris (1988), Wilson (1992) and Curry (1993). First, in Makassar, strong cultural and family influences contributed to the system of hiring and firing workers, so that decisions regarding who to employ and when were not clear-cut rational economic decisions but were dependent on a number of contextual factors as well. Second, remuneration levels for some workers were reasonably good compared with the average wage in the city and were often supplemented with other support such as accommodation and meals. Furthermore, family, neighbourhood and worker obligations – including the provision of a range of benefits to retain labour – often meant reduced profits for the entrepreneurs. They also often had to pay for the costs of flexibility in the labour force. Patron–client-style relationships improved non-economic loyalty, reduced the mobility of workers and created a more complex pattern of flexibility – with positive and negative results for both employers and workers – than has often been suggested in past examinations of labour flexibility. In summary, then, it appears that among the Makassar enterprises surveyed, a broad range of social and cultural factors considerably influenced the pattern of labour flexibility. In Chapter 6 we look at how small enterprise production and labour flexibility was further enhanced by the operations of networks and clusters.

6   Small enterprises in Makassar
Inter-firm dynamics

We now move beyond the internal dynamics of Makassar's small enterprises, to ascertain the degree to which they were embedded in a range of linkages and networks, and the levels of trust involved. The networks are analysed in terms of two levels of relationships, namely within extended families, as well as between enterprises and their suppliers and distributors. After this we consider the innovative behaviour apparent in a number of small enterprises, often supported by networking structures, before turning to an examination of enterprises operating within clusters. The chapter concludes with an examination of attitudes to, and expectations held by entrepreneurs concerning the future, before we turn, in Chapter 7, to examine the constraints they faced in reaching whatever future goals they had in mind.

NETWORKS AND TRUST

For small enterprises in Makassar, 'socio-cultural factors, such as the existence of ethnic, religious or kin groups, have a major influence on how business relations develop' (Rasmussen *et al.*, 1992: 4). The strongest network systems among enterprises studied in this field were within such kin groups. As mentioned in Chapter 5, there was often a conflict between the provision of training for workers who might then set up their own business in competition, or alternatively having to rely on less skilled workers producing lower quality products. One way that entrepreneurs avoided this was by using family labour because such workers tended to be more loyal and less likely to enter into direct competition. Family training was especially strong among goldsmiths, silversmiths and tailors. Thus, not only were skills and techniques kept within the enterprise; the family links were also important for goldsmiths and silversmiths because of the high value of the raw materials.

Networking among family members was also important as an avenue through which to obtain capital. Few entrepreneurs were able to borrow from banks or other institutional sources (as will be detailed more in Chapter 7), and hence depended to a large extent on more informal channels, including family. For the most part those interviewed had clear reasons why they would prefer a loan from such a source, rather than through formal channels, such as a bank. Many believed that small entrepreneurs did not have the security required by banks, which were said to apply too many rules. They also believed that small entrepreneurs did not have the trust of those bank workers, and doubted they could meet the time requirements for loan repayments. Their position was well expressed by a chair-maker who maintained that 'I'd have to borrow from family members. If I go to the bank I have to take all my certificates and it takes too long, there are too many rules. No one trusts us to borrow capital so it's difficult' (26b, 28/1/97). A *bakso* entrepreneur offered a similar assessment: 'I have to go to family or friends because it's easier to borrow and I can return it when it's possible' (62b, 5/2/97). Likewise, an entrepreneur making oil stoves pointed out that in his case 'the basic materials I need aren't always ready so my sales aren't constant. I'd go to family. It's easier and there aren't lots of procedures, it's quicker' (136b, 26/2/97).

One of the big advantages of borrowing from family was that there was no interest to be paid on the loan. Clearly, this was well understood by an entrepreneur making *martabak* and *terang bulan* (thick pancakes) who remarked that 'I have borrowed capital from my parents before, it was Rp.150,000 and there was no interest. I don't have a name for my business and I don't know the procedure at the bank' (161b, 6/3/97). This assessment was shared by a goldsmith who observed that 'if I borrow from family there isn't any procedure and if I return the money a little late there's no problem and also no interest' (70b, 10/2/97).

Statements like these highlight the role played by family capital resources in supporting small-scale entrepreneurs while attesting to the extensive barriers faced by those among them who wished to gain loans from formal lending institutions. Generally, entrepreneurs talked of it being 'safer' to borrow money from family and friends, due to the lack of complicated procedures and bureaucracy (48b, 3/2/97). A variant of such family-based arrangements was provided by entrepreneurs who talked of borrowing money using the *sistem kekeluargaan* (family-like system). Used by many of them, this had evolved to become an informal, flexible system of obtaining a loan of money or goods from family, friends or neighbours. No or very little interest was demanded, while there were flexible repayment times.[1]

The operation of the system was described by a Javanese food producer who explained that 'I would go to my friend in the city to get capital, because my friend is already like my brother, so it would be like borrowing in the *sistem kekeluargaan* manner' (78b, 11/2/97). Similarly, a *tahu* and *bakso* entrepreneur from Java 'borrowed Rp.300,000 from a friend near here. I have to pay it back Rp.50,000 a month, but there's no interest. If I need to borrow more capital I would go to friends . . . I don't have family in Makassar and can't borrow from the bank' (131b, 26/2/97). Thus, such a system was especially important for entrepreneurs who had migrated from elsewhere in Sulawesi or from other islands without close family in Makassar on whom to rely for support.

Another means used by some entrepreneurs to gain or save their money was through belonging to an *arisan*. This was an informal rotating savings and credit association, in which members had regular social gatherings at which they contributed to and took turns at 'winning' an aggregate sum of money (International Labour Office, 1995). One such *arisan* operated among members of a *tempe* cluster in Makassar. A member who was interviewed explained that it was preferable to save through the *arisan* rather than the bank, as one could obtain a loan at short notice if it was necessary for the enterprise or for social obligations if they arose (86a, 2/10/97).

Friendship linkages were another form of informal support. These some-times helped entrepreneurs gain favourable trading sites, as they did for a woman entrepreneur selling *nasi kuning* (yellow, flavoured rice), which she sold from a stall outside one of Makassar's military bases. She had a friend stationed at the base, and consequently occupied a privileged position in being the only food seller allowed to have a stall at that location, a clear competitive advantage that had enabled her to increase her profits markedly (47b, 3/2/97).

The loans and general support that entrepreneurs gained from family and friends pointed towards a flexible interdependent and interactive system which could operate only in a cultural environment of high trust and co-oper-ation. There was strong local embeddedness of skills and social networks, which helped form a climate of trust among the various local economic actors. This contributed to the attainment of elevated levels of enterprise co-operation. Yet as will become clear in later discussion, factors that promoted such interdependent systems were not always positive and, as a result, the growth of the enterprises was still not necessarily assured even by operating within such networks.

A number of the small enterprises produced goods for which the demands were highly varied due to seasonal fluctuations or associations with specific religious and cultural festivals. *Idul Fitri*, the festival at the end of the fasting month, is traditionally a time for purchasing new items such as clothes, jew-ellery, furniture and, for some, even cars and houses. Consequently, for a woman interviewee who was a tailor producing *songkok*, *Bulan Puasa/Ramadan*, the fasting month, was the busiest time of the year, it being usual for Muslim men to buy new *songkok* for *Idul Fitri* at this time. Thus for that month the tailor concerned had profits in excess of Rp.3 million, whereas for each of the other eleven months she made between Rp.100,000 and Rp.200,000. Part of her seasonal profits were used as a source of working capital, while the majority went on gifts for extended family members for *Idul Fitri*. Such uneven demand and subsequent profits, including a lack of a long-term saving plan, added to the difficulties such entrepreneurs had in securing loans and working capital from formal institutions, not least in terms of requirements for regular repayments. Not surprisingly, when the same tailor was asked if she would borrow from a bank she replied 'I don't want to borrow, I'm scared to borrow from a bank, this is all my own [working capital] money, in the future I might go to family for help' (27b, 28/1/97). Similarly, a chair-maker interviewed was confronted by an equally difficult cash flow problem and when asked where he would go for working capital replied: 'This type of work is seasonal, so I don't have a regular income to go to the bank. My family understands this, but the bank doesn't' (28b, 28/1/97).

The pilgrimage to Mecca also imposed a large seasonal fluctuation in demand for clothing, and consequently in cash flow for general tailors. A number of the latter sewed clothing worn when one was on the *Haj*, the Islamic pilgrimage to Mecca (*pakaian umroh*), white prayer veils specifically worn during *Puasa* (*mukenah*), and veils for daily use (*jilbab*). Due to the great demand for these before and during the month of *Puasa* (fasting month), and before the month in which people performed the *Haj*, both demand for raw materials and for finished items was highly irregular. Not surprisingly, such tailors specified they would go to family for loans. As one of them, a woman, explained: 'If I go to my family I don't have to pay interest and there is no risk if I'm late with my repayments. I can't use a bank as they don't understand I can't always pay on time' (52b, 4/2/97).

Likewise, the demand for traditional wedding dresses and traditional clothes for members of wedding parties was highly seasonal. For example, the majority of Bugis and Makassar weddings took place after the rice harvest when families had assessed their incomes for the year. Due to this seasonal demand, one entrepreneur affected maintained that it was impossible for him to try to get a bank loan and so relied on his extended family to help out with a short-term loan when it was necessary (97b, 18/2/97).

Thus local cultural and religious factors were highly influential in making it necessary for many entrepreneurs to turn to family and friends for support rather than to formal institutions. Such networks, linkages and trust-based relationships were often primarily used as coping mechanisms, simply because the many barriers erected by formal institutions made it difficult, if not impossible, for entrepreneurs to contemplate using formal credit facilities, no less because the institutions were not prepared to operate in tune with local seasonal variations. Hence while there was certainly evidence of networks, they differed markedly in terms of whether they supported the advancement of the enterprises, or whether they functioned as a day-to-day survival mechanism.

Enterprise subcontractors' networks

Enterprise subcontractors operated the most complex networking systems among the enterprises studied. In essence they demonstrated a just-in-time delivery system of inputs based on the close links they had with their larger supplier firms.

The production of furniture among those enterprises sampled in Makassar was a complex interactive process, as detailed in Figure 6.1. This involved a number of enterprises carrying out different parts of the production process, as well as sawmills, those providing transportation and retailers. Chair-makers showed signs of specialisation and networking, with one group producing the rough wooden frames of the chairs, others sewing the covers and upholstering the frames. Sewing was often given to workers operating as outliers, so that production was undertaken in at least three spatially different locations. The wooden frames were usually ordered by the subcontracting enterprises overseeing the sewing of covers, on a weekly basis and paid for on a piece-rate with cash. The sewing, undertaken as an outlier function, was also paid for on a piece-rate basis. The subcontracting enterprises then fin-ished the production line by upholstering the covers on to the chairs. They often worked for retailers located nearby. The latter had initially lent the fabric to the enterprises, again paying for the final product on piece-rate. Many of these retailers then acted as suppliers for other shops in and around Makassar and in South Sulawesi.

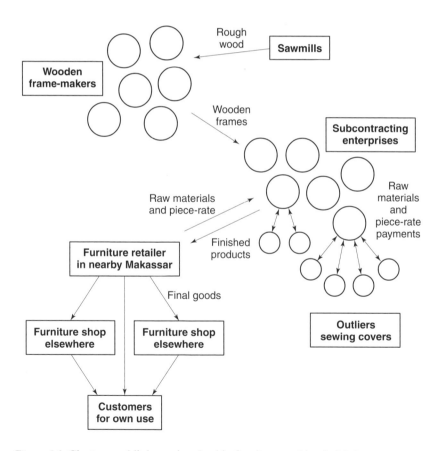

Figure 6.1 Clusters and linkages involved in furniture-making in Makassar.

When interviewed, furniture subcontractors referred to a number of positive aspects relating to working in this style of arrangement with Chinese retailers. There was a guarantee of more or less regular work, raw materials were easily obtainable, and the retailers provided a channel through which to gain informal loans (31b, 33b, 29/1/97). This was the case for one chair-maker who maintained, when discussing his Chinese retailer, that 'I've borrowed small amounts from him, for about one week when I've needed it, about Rp.100,000' (36b, 29/1/97). However, such trust was not always apparent among other entrepreneurs, such as one cupboard-maker who worked in a subcontracting arrangement for a Chinese retailer. He lamented that 'I've already worked for the Chinese for a long time, but the Chinese still don't trust us 100 per cent, they're still suspicious' (95b, 18/2/97). A chair-maker originally from Sumatra who worked for a Chinese supplier/retailer in a similar manner reported that it had taken three years to build a trust relationship with the retailer to enable transactions to occur in a subcontracting form (32b, 29/1/97). Thus, while such linkages with Chinese retailers were valued, they took time to build a sufficient degree of trust.

Yet, due to the cultural characteristics of enterprise subcontractors, such relationships were usually only seen as positive in the short term. This was because of the increased social status that came with owning one's own autonomous enterprise, and because of continuing ethnic tensions in the city involving the Chinese population (36b, 29/1/97). Therefore both social relations and cultural dimensions entered into the decision-making processes of the entrepreneurs and influenced their opinions as to whether or not the networking systems with the Chinese retailers were positive. For this reason, networking decisions were not necessarily made on the basis of purely 'rational' economic thought.

Many general tailors operating as enterprise subcontractors in Makassar displayed characteristics similar to the furniture subcontractors, with complex linkages, involving trust relationships that had not always been established rapidly. The tailors, however, appeared to have more geographically dispersed retailer linkages than the furniture-makers. For the tailor subcontractors, the general pattern was that retailers provided them with cloth and sometimes also loaned them sewing machines. In turn, the subcontractors had a number of workers at their enterprise site and/or outliers tailoring in their own homes, sewing all or part of the goods made. However, many such workers undertook only part of the production process, such as sewing collars or hemming garments, the latter being passed among many workers or outliers to complete the final product. The finished goods would then be returned to the retailer.

The cloth was usually delivered to the enterprise subcontractors by their suppliers/retailers, who were often Chinese. It was to these 'bosses', a number of subcontractors explained, that they would turn if they required help with a loan for working capital, or for a family emergency, such as money to meet wedding, funeral or hospital expenses (57a, 30/1/97). Thus, as well as maintaining supply and marketing links, good relationships with retailers were also important due to the range of support that they could supply.[2]

Some retailers had relationships with a number of small enterprises, often to compensate for irregular production. One such retailer, with a stall in the city's Central Market (shown in Figure 4.4), had three subcontracting enterprises operating for him. He received women's clothes from one enterprise, children's clothes and Muslim veils from a second, and other women's clothes from yet another. The retailer supplied the subcontracting enterprises with the fabric and paid them per finished piece. In addition, the same retailer had connections with other retailers in Maros, Pangkep, Pinrang, Pare Pare, Kendari and Palu. These travelled to Makassar and bought goods from him, paying half the price up front and the rest when they were sold (4c, 28/4/97). This division of production and retailing processes surrounding small enterprises required a number of complex linkages and networks to operate effectively, many of which were supported by family, friendship and neighbourhood relationships, strengthening the trust involved.

Far more ethnically segregated and reliant on trust relations were the goldsmiths like Amir. Many such Bugis goldsmiths were part of subcontracting networks incorporating Chinese retailers who owned goldshops on Jalan Somba Opu, in the city centre (shown in Figure 4.4). Retailers would supply gold in small amounts and subcontractors would fashion it to the styles requested (although Amir was also able to experiment with his own designs when customer demand was slow for his Chinese retailer). Many goldsmiths also relied on the retailers for support with loans for new equipment and working capital if necessary. When asked if there were other channels of support for goldsmiths, one replied, 'no, they don't exist for goldsmiths, we depend on our suppliers' (5b, 21/1/97). He explained that if someone required help with working capital, he would go to his Chinese gold shop supplier/retailer.

For goldsmiths, ethnicity was highly significant for networking arrangements and the degree of trust incorporated within these networks. In the past it was Bugis people who were known to be goldsmiths in South Sulawesi and, as Pelras (1996a: 252) contends, 'there is a long-standing tradition of gold working in the Bugis area'. As discussed in Chapter 5, many goldsmiths, like Amir, had originally migrated from the Sidenreng Rappang district ('Sidrap'), or had been trained by other Bugis goldsmiths in Makassar city. Generally the Chinese trusted Bugis goldsmiths with their raw materials, whereas the Makassar goldsmiths did not have this historically based trust relationship. If the Bugis goldsmiths employed non-family workers at all, they employed other Bugis workers only, hence there was a high degree of ethnic homogeneity within the goldsmith community. Although three Makassar entrepreneurs working with silver and gold were interviewed, they had links with tourist handicraft shops rather than gold shops, while all of the entrepreneurs interviewed who worked specifically as goldsmiths were Bugis.

Within Group B, 39 per cent of the Bugis goldsmiths who were operating as enterprise subcontractors obtained their gold through a longer established Bugis goldsmith acting as a 'middleperson'. That they did not deal directly with Chinese merchants pointed to the importance of ethnicity and trust in business relationships. Such linkages through another member of the same ethnic group were often positive in that they allowed enterprise subcontractors access to raw materials that they would otherwise have been denied due to cost, distance or social/cultural barriers. The linkages often involved expected reciprocity and future obligations such as gifts during cultural or religious festivals. The result was often myriad complex networks of patronage and support, implying that the production process was deeply embedded socially. Moreover, while such a pattern of supply was, in a socio-cultural sense, inclusionary for some, it was exclusionary for others.

Trust was usually gained through the length of time the 'middleperson' had worked for the supplier/retailer, a relationship that was particularly important because of the high value of the raw materials. Due to this, new migrants to the city from the 'Sidrap' region usually began working as outliers or subcontractors for other Bugis goldsmiths in their neighbourhood, often through family networks, rather than directly for Chinese retailers. As one goldsmith replied, 'I have a trust system with my supplier, he's another goldsmith here, there are always goldsmiths that don't go direct to the Chinese' (6b, 21/1/97).

Interviews during field work revealed that networking among goldsmiths was arranged in layers – one such system is depicted in Figure 6.2. This

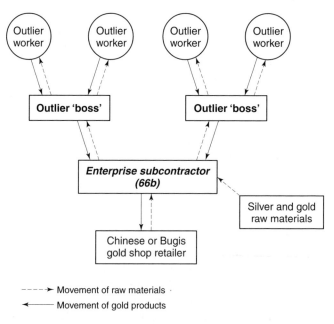

Figure 6.2 Networking arrangements of a Bugis goldsmith interviewed (66b, 6/2/97).

small-scale goldsmith gained some of his raw materials (gold) from retailers from whom he had worked, but bought other raw materials (silver and copper) himself. He had ten people in his immediate workforce, each at a different location in a subcontracting arrangement, and each of these, in turn, had between five and ten people working for them as outliers in their own homes. There were thus four layers of interaction, from retailer through entrepreneur to outlier 'boss' and outlier worker (66b, 6/2/97).

The networks throughout the small-scale goldsmith neighbourhoods were vast and complex, a very strong demonstration of the argument that 'markets and competition are not socially decontextualized activities' (Storper and Scott, 1995: 509). To add to the complexity, there appeared to be two levels of gold jewellery production, one of higher quality products for Chinese retailers owning gold shops in the centre of the city, the other of lower quality products and matching prices. These were produced for the local Bugis gold shops supplying Bugis and Makassar customers. One Bugis goldsmith explained that it was usual for the Chinese retailers to order from the goldsmiths products that were twenty-two-carat gold, whereas many Bugis retailers ordered goods that were eighteen-carat gold (21c, 7/5/97).

Gold jewellery had a double function for many Bugis and Makassar people. First, it had an economic function, often being used as savings, being considered a more stable investment than the *Rupiah* and safer than a bank account (Hutagalung *et al.*, 1994). It was also used as security for loans, or pawned for working capital. Second, it was an important status symbol, a point well made by Lineton (1975: 202) who has claimed that, 'it is said that if a Bugis makes some money, he [sic] first buys gold; when his wealth increases still further, he goes to Mecca'. One goldsmith believed that his business would continue to develop in the future because of this dual role, asserting that 'we can compete and increase our orders as requests for gold products from consumers are increasing, because gold jewellery can have a double function' (82a, 16/9/96).

There is strong evidence, then, that among the small-scale tailors, furniture makers and goldsmiths in the city, subcontracting arrangements were very important for the continuing existence of many enterprises. For many subcontracting enterprises, these linkages were the sole channel through which they could gain the raw materials required to undertake production, as they did not have direct trust relationships with suppliers of raw materials. Workers within such enterprises were reasonably broadly skilled because they had to respond rapidly to changes in demand by retailers, and the machinery used was usually general or multi-purpose in nature. Nonetheless, in such arrangements the enterprise subcontractors neither had the freedom to choose the methods of production nor the final goods to be made, and had little opportunity themselves to introduce innovative ideas into their enterprises. Thus, although the subcontracting enterprises did share tools, equipment and sometimes workers as well, it did not appear that collective efficiency was occurring among them. Evidently, this was because the linkages with the retailers that were by far the most important to them, largely inhibited both innovation and informal management structures from occurring within the enterprises themselves.

Networks of independent entrepreneurs

The subcontracting enterprises discussed above did not have informal management structures, and were thus unable to enjoy the freedom to choose their production methods and the goods made, as well as being stifled in innovativeness. As such, it is now important to examine whether the outcomes for *independent* small enterprises involved in networking relationships were any more positive. We turn first to examine the many supply networks in place for gaining raw materials, and then the diverse marketing and distribution links used to extend their spheres of operation.

Sample data revealed that 59 per cent of small entrepreneurs in Group A reported regular, reliable sources of raw materials. Nonetheless, this still left 41 per cent of them with erratic supplies, largely because of an irregular supply of working capital and/or fluctuating raw material prices. Indeed, two of the greatest anxieties among these entrepreneurs were the quality of the raw materials they could acquire and the dependability of supplies.

Not surprisingly, the ability of the entrepreneurs to gain adequate raw materials was often closely related to the relationships they had with suppliers. Only rarely were such linkages just economically based; usually they were more complex, involving social and ethnic linkages. Nearly half of the entrepreneurs stated they had a 'strong relationship' with their regular supplier of goods, a connection often based on the latter being close acquaintances, family, friends, or members of the same co-operative.

Trust relationships with suppliers of their raw materials had greatly benefited a number of independent entrepreneurs. They brought good prices, an increased likelihood of constant supplies, and sometimes led to the opportunity to pay for raw materials on credit. Trust was often gained and strengthened by constantly using the same retailer over a number of years or, if the enterprise had been inherited, by continuing to use the same retailer as had the entrepreneur's parents. One tailor who regularly returned to the same retailer explained that by doing so she always received her raw materials at a good price, something she was unable to do elsewhere (18b, 27/1/97). Likewise, an entrepreneur making a number of savoury dishes sold from a *gerobak* on the city's waterfront, a popular eating area at night, explained that he always went back to the same stall in the local market to purchase his goods, and as a consequence consistently obtained good-quality produce for a fair price (144b, 3/3/97). Due to the trust relationships established, entrepreneurs could usually depend on their suppliers. However, such links were rather fragile because suppliers might move location, or lose confidence in the ability of the entrepreneur to pay on credit if repayments were continuously late.

The Bugis entrepreneurs had the greatest percentage of trust-based relationships. These were dependent primarily either on the length of time they had known the supplier or that their parents had used the same supplier. Amongst those who did not have such trust relationships, Chinese entrepreneurs and those from Sumatra and Irian Jaya were most noticeable, reflecting the lack of trust that the predominantly Bugis and Makassar local population had of the Chinese, as well as the difficulties confronting migrants from other islands in building up trust-based relationships (KI 6, 18/9/96). Such variation, dependent as it was on the cultural affinity of the entrepreneurs, once again stresses the importance of considering contextual elements when evaluating small enterprise operations in Makassar.

An examination of what networks the entrepreneurs had established with suppliers in other regions of Indonesia, and how these networks were maintained, revealed that a range of entrepreneurs had looked far afield to secure raw material supplies. Such inter-regional networks were often based on historical connections, many established and developed by Bugis traders since 'a high propensity to emigrate from the homeland to other regions is seen as one of the characteristic attributes of Bugis society' (Lineton, 1975: 11; see also Andaya, 1995). Many Bugis have migrated to other regions of Indonesia, as well as Malaysia, the Indonesian census reporting as early as 1930 that 10 per cent of Bugis and 2 per cent of Makassar people were living outside South Sulawesi, with large Bugis settlements in Pontianak and Balikpapan on Kalimantan which continued throughout the 1990s (Harvey, 1974; KI 3, 26/9/96). The bulk of worker movements between Indonesia and Malaysia have remained undetected by official sources, one of the major routes used being from South Sulawesi to East Malaysia (Hugo, 1993). This migration has occurred via Pare Pare, to the north of Makassar, and is an extension of the long tradition of Bugis migrants moving from South Sulawesi to Borneo and Singapore (Lineton, 1975; Andaya, 1995; Tirtosudarmo, 1996). Many of these migrants maintain strong connections with family and friends in South Sulawesi.

Family links between migrants to Makassar and their place of origin were very important in the successful operation of other enterprises. This was the case for a woman entrepreneur who made traditional Bugis cakes and who obtained some of her ingredients from family in her *kampung* in the 'Sidrap' region. A family member of hers worked as a bus company driver, who travelled between Makassar and her *kampung* area. She would visit the bus terminal in Makassar, tell the driver what raw materials she required (usually rice flour) from her family, and pick it up when the driver returned to Makassar (46b, 3/2/97). Likewise, a woman who produced cream soda and lemonade drinks relied on family for raw materials. She was supplied with the majority of these (such as carbon dioxide, colouring and citrus flavouring) from Jakarta, where she had family who organised and shipped the raw materials to her. Her male cousin worked for her as a distributor and travelled around the South Sulawesi province in a truck supplying shops with her drinks (106b, 19/2/97).

Trust-based relationships were important for the vast majority of entrepreneurs dependent on raw materials purchased from outside Makassar. One such case was a drink entrepreneur who purchased his fruit from farmers in nearby rural areas. Bugis and Makassar farmers travelled to Makassar city with an unspoken understanding that they would go to this entrepreneur first to sell their fruit, and if they had any remaining they would then offer it for sale at a local market. This entrepreneur was buying *srikaya* (a tropical fruit, sweetsop) from farmers from Jeneponto, and pineapples from growers on the outskirts of Makassar. The farmers would often bicycle to the city, then either return to their *kampung* the same day or the following one. This same entrepreneur also had links with retailers in Bone and Palopo, servicing them using workers who took the bottled drinks to these shops on public transport (81b, 11/2/97).

Independent entrepreneurs in Group B were asked about the physical origins of the raw materials they purchased, in an attempt to further clarify connections with other regions of Indonesia. This enquiry showed that such origins were rather varied, with forty-seven locations in all being recorded. Moreover, there was a close connection between location and the nature of the goods, the production processes involved and the resource endowments of Sulawesi. However, as much as 44 per cent of raw materials originated from Java, 15 per cent from Makassar city, with a further 10 per cent of entrepreneurs obtaining their goods from both Makassar and Java. In addition, 3 per cent came from either Sumatra, Irian Jaya or Kalimantan.

While many raw materials were purchased from shops in Makassar, the local districts around South Sulawesi were also prominent source areas for raw materials, especially basic ingredients for food production and wood for furniture. Many food entrepreneurs gained their raw materials from farmers who travelled to Makassar daily from Takalar to sell goods directly to their regular customers, or at markets. Many farmers selling wood transported truckloads to clusters of enterprises in Makassar from nearby districts.

For many entrepreneurs the continuing reliance on Java for a range of raw materials was problematic due to the considerable shipping costs and irregular supplies. There were also significant time delays concerning goods coming from other Outer Islands, especially during the monsoon season, reducing the ability of the entrepreneurs to complete orders on time and thus satisfy and retain customers. This indicated that there were often significant environmental constraints to the smooth operation of the enterprises.

When asked about the impact of raw material supply problems on their enterprises, nearly half (48 per cent) of the entrepreneurs in Group A pointed to disrupted production, reduced orders, increased costs of production, an inability to fulfil orders and a general decrease in profits. These factors in turn impacted negatively on the quality of finished goods. The entrepreneurs commented that, in combination these problems placed small enterprises at a competitive disadvantage compared with other enterprises in the city, as well as with retailers selling imported goods.

When the entrepreneurs were asked how they overcame such supply problems, 15 per cent replied that there were no solutions, or that the solution was either to reduce the volume of production or buy lower quality raw materials. This, in consequence, led to the production of lower quality products, and the need to have a range of defensive survival mechanisms. More optimistically though, a number of entrepreneurs did have ideas – in total, fifty-two different ways – that they might overcome their supply problems. Among the most popular were to diversify the sources of raw materials, purchase goods on credit or order stocks from outside Sulawesi. Also listed were going directly to the suppliers of raw materials and avoiding middlepeople, taking more care in the production process and asking for down payments from the customers as well as building up stocks of raw materials when their prices were low.

When suggestions were subdivided by ethnicity, all groups nominated more positive than negative ones, yet saying so is clearly quite different from being prepared to put them into practice.[3] In the different product categories, the highest percentage of positive answers came from those making metal doors, window frames and gates on the one hand and, on the other, those making building materials and goods from cement. Such groups tended to comprise larger enterprises operated by Bugis, Makassar or Chinese entrepreneurs, to include larger numbers of non-family workers, and return higher profits. This suggests that, compared with more 'traditional' enterprises, those producing 'newer' products tended to have the more innovative outlook regarding changes that could be made to improve supply channels.

Successful marketing and distributing links were vital for the entrepreneurs who wished to expand their customer base, and respond to changes in market demand rapidly. Yet the entrepreneurs interviewed ranked 'constraints to marketing' as the greatest problem their enterprise faced, as shown in Chapter 5, Table 5.7. Key marketing concerns, among others, included the geographical barriers faced by enterprises operating in Makassar, interacting with middlepeople with greater power in the business relationship, and a declining customer base.

Limited product marketing was believed to be inhibiting the growth of most of the independent enterprises. Some 46 per cent of those in Group A marketed all their goods in Makassar, and 69 per cent did so within South Sulawesi, unable to expand to reach new customers. Among those who also marketed to other areas (31 per cent), 19 per cent sent goods to other provinces in Sulawesi, 9 per cent shipped products to another island in Indonesia and 3 per cent had international links, being entrepreneurs producing Torajan carved wooden souvenirs, silver handicrafts and Muslim clothes.

The geographical constraints were even greater for the majority of enterprises in Group B. Of these, 78 per cent of the owners sold goods within Makassar, operating in a strongly competitive environment often saturated with similar goods. Nonetheless, some had managed to expand their marketing sphere to cover thirty-six locations outside of Makassar. These included outlets within South Sulawesi (14 per cent) (such as Maros, Pare Pare, Sidrap, Takalar, Bone, Enrekang, Gowa, Palopo and Sengkang), and locations in other parts of Sulawesi including Palu and Kendari. They also sent goods to the Indonesian islands of Irian Jaya, Kalimantan, Bali and Java. Only two small enterprises, one producing Bugis traditional musical instruments, and the other – connected through family with the former – producing traditional Bugis and Makassar ceremonial clothing, had managed to establish international marketing links with Malaysia, Australia and Egypt.

Entrepreneurs that had the more geographically restricted marketing spheres were mainly food producers – limited by a lack of technological infrastructure such as refrigeration – as many of their products were non-durables, with a short 'shelf life', especially those based on soya beans. The limited marketing area reached by many of the small-scale entrepreneurs restricted their ability to expand output, as competition remained intense in the sphere of production within which they were operating, resulting in continuous market uncertainty. The local market locations are shown in Figure 6.3, while the limited marketing spheres for Group B entrepreneurs compared with those of Group A are illustrated in Table 6.1, especially in the final row.

The limited *control* many entrepreneurs had over product marketing was perhaps even more important than the geographical sphere covered. In Group A only half of the entrepreneurs marketed over half of their goods directly to the public. They did so through their own street stall, by having workers or themselves take the products around the streets of Makassar using a *gerobak* (handcart), by having a stationary *gerobak* site or *warung* (stall), or by using a bicycle to take products around markets. A further 30 per cent marketed at least half of their products through a retailer (including the 10 per cent who were enterprise subcontractors), and a further 14 per cent used a wholesaler or middleperson to distribute at least half of their products. In total, two thirds of the entrepreneurs in Group A used retailers to some

Table 6.1 Marketing spheres for finished products of 300 Makassar small enterprises

Destination of finished products	Group A (100)	Group B (200)
Enterprises that sold goods overseas as well as within Indonesia	3	2
Enterprises that sold goods to other islands in Indonesia, as well as in Sulawesi	9	14
Enterprises that sold goods within Sulawesi only	19	7
Enterprises that sold goods in South Sulawesi only	69	28
Enterprises that sold *some* of their goods in Makassar	100	200
Enterprises that sold their goods *only* in Makassar	46	156

Note: Some enterprises had more than one destination for their goods.

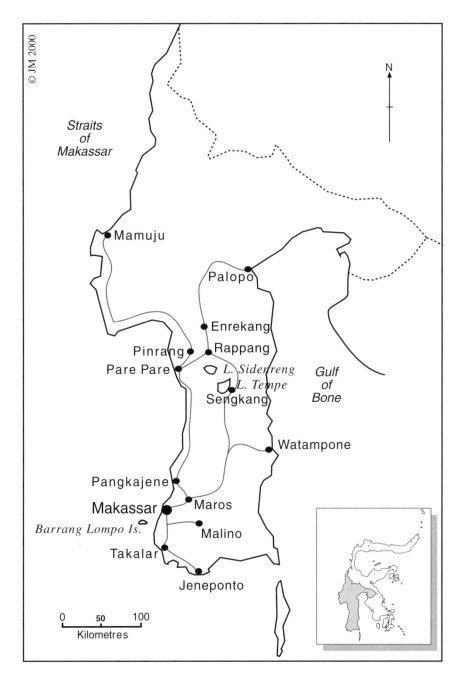

Figure 6.3 Locations in South Sulawesi with which small-scale entrepreneurs in Makassar have marketing connections.

Source: adapted from De Koninck (1994: 3)

extent to market a proportion of their goods, while another 17 per cent employed wholesalers and middlepeople. The entrepreneurs generally complained about their dependence on middlepeople or retailers who were often extremely powerful in business relationships, maintaining as they did significant control over market access. Yet this appeared to be a 'double-edged sword', in that the middlepeople/retailers not only provided the entrepreneurs with a means of accessing markets, but also sometimes capital and equipment to which they might otherwise have had difficulty gaining access.

In addition to the role of middlepeople and retailers, Group A entrepreneurs cited a wide range of further problems they regarded as important impediments to marketing their goods. Most frequently mentioned were a declining number of customers and intense competition. Amongst other common problems identified were the lower prices of competitors' goods, having to provide credit terms for sales, and the narrowness of the marketing range. Also mentioned were the lack of promotion of the enterprise as well as customers who were late with credit payments and not being able to control the price of the product due to reliance on raw materials being supplied by middlepeople or retailers. The major impact these problems had on marketing was a reduction in sales and a restricted market, resulting in declining profits. Only 3 per cent of the entrepreneurs (a car seat-, a handicraft- and a drink-maker) reported that they faced no competition. Perhaps this was because relatively few entrepreneurs were producing car seats or cheap locally-produced drinks in Makassar, while the silver entrepreneur had received help from the Department of Industry and Trade in management training and had friends in Jogyakarta who were selling his goods there (85a, 18/9/96).

Despite the diversity of marketing problems encountered by entrepreneurs in Group A, some of which impacted severely on cash flows, a substantial proportion felt compelled to offer credit terms to customers. In fact, 42 per cent declared that they provided at least some credit – from between one week to four months – for their customers. This reflected the low incomes of those who constituted the majority of their customers, and also appeared to be a response to the fact that because of the large number of small enterprises producing similar goods, entrepreneurs were faced with a 'buyers' market'. Customers could demand favourable terms for themselves, which meant that those enterprises able to offer credit terms were therefore in the better position to gain orders. However, nearly one-third of the entrepreneurs then complained that customers were frequently late with credit payments, resulting in unpredictable levels of working capital. Such problems, they argued, hindered the continuous operations of their enterprises and were an added constraint to business growth. Entrepreneurs were hesitant to be innovative in production methods when they were in such an unstable position, leading them instead towards more 'survivalist' approaches in an environment of intense competition and market saturation.

Their situation in this respect was exacerbated by an inability to pursue a market development strategy. Lack of knowledge was clearly a very important hindrance. For instance, when asked about their *current* plans for market development or expansion for their goods, 19 per cent of the entrepreneurs, spread throughout the range of product types and ethnicities, replied that they did not know how to do so. Among those who were attempting to develop their market, a number of means were commonly used. These included promoting the enterprise product using 'word of mouth', producing brochures and business cards and trying to expand the market for the goods into new districts. They also sought to increase the volume of orders and/or product quality, to keep prices low compared with imported goods and to improve customer service by taking the product to the customer. Other methods employed included offering discounts for those who purchased large quantities, providing a discount if people bought with cash and developing personal relationships with purchasers.

When asked a similar question about how they *intended* to extend the market for their goods in the future, the reaction was more positive. In reply, 38 per cent of the entrepreneurs in Group A declared that they wanted to increase the geographical range covered by the enterprise, while others had thought about strategies such as opening a showroom in a strategic location, perhaps increasing the volume of sales, or employing specialist marketing staff, or making a more durable product. Two other possibilities were to look for new sources of raw materials and reducing dependence on middlepeople.

A small minority (10 per cent) of Group A entrepreneurs did not have suggestions concerning how they might extend their market. Nonetheless, while members of this group were spread among product types as well as ethnicities, they all used only family workers, a finding strikingly similar to the cohort discussed previously in the Labour section of Chapter 5, whose members had not thought about future workforce improvements. There appear to be several reasons for this. Either such entrepreneurs could not expand the market for their goods because the pressures to provide for their family were too intense and their enterprises were operating in a fairly critical 'survival' mode; or alternatively, being able to provide for one's family's livelihood means was the overall aim of the entrepreneurs, with expansion of the enterprise not necessarily considered to be crucial.

At the same time it was clear that many of the entrepreneurs who said they wanted to develop their enterprises were continuously constrained from doing so by the contextual environment in which they operated. This was undeniably expressed in their responses to questions about general changes they believed necessary to overcome market constraints. Amongst factors believed important were guidance with technology and equipment, access to new information and help from banks in gaining capital. Furthermore, the entrepreneurs stressed the need for training to increase competitiveness and improve skills, the formation of associations to improve marketing and exhibitions to promote products. A decline in the bureaucracy and the stabilisation of the economy were also seen as key necessities, as was increased government support to help make competition fairer. Such responses suggest that there could be considerable latent potential for the advancement of these small enterprises if such barriers to marketing were removed.

Retailers involved with independent small enterprises were usually operating a *toko* (shop) or *warung* (stall).[4] A common characteristic of these retailers was the rapid turnover of stock and its swift replenishment by the small enterprises. This reflected the consumption patterns of many of the households in the surrounding neighbourhoods, where it was common to find day-to-day purchasing of goods, especially food, in line with incomes which were often received daily. Frequently, the retailers were also not equipped to store perishable food, so accelerating the required turnover of stock.

A case in point was one retailer, who had been selling *kerupuk* (flavoured fried crackers) made by a small enterprise for the past four years, supplied with new stock every four days. The retailer then paid the entrepreneur for what was sold and returned the remaining supply after four days, as the goods were perishable. At that point the entrepreneur replenished the stocks, and the retailer paid only for goods that had been sold. As this retailer explained: 'I only pay as much as necessary, so I only pay for what I sell' (1c, 24/4/97). Another retailer had a similar relationship with a small enterprise supplying him with cakes, the unsold goods being replaced every two days (17c, 6 /5/97).

Many of the links between small enterprises and retailers had been established by the entrepreneur visiting a potential retailer with examples of products. Links established in this way were often enduring, as they were for one entrepreneur producing large cooking knives, whose relationship had lasted since 1987, while another entrepreneur had supplied the same retailer with cake moulds since 1990 (6c, 29/4/97). The retailer involved in these transactions had connections with other retailers in Maros and Pangkep who wished to buy the products, and hence the first retailer acted as a middleperson between the local small enterprises and retailers elsewhere. The retailers in Maros and Pangkep visited his shop in Makassar to buy the goods, paying 50 per cent up front and the remainder on credit, repaid when they had sold all the goods (3c, 24/4/97).[5]

Alternatively, another common way in which initial links had been established was for the retailer to gain information concerning an entrepreneur making a product that the retailer wished to market, and then establish contact. For some, this was because the retailer had heard positive reports about the product through friends or family. Occasionally, retailers visited the small enterprise premises to check whether the conditions of production were satisfactory for their needs. This was the case for a Chinese retailer wishing to retail cream soda drinks produced by a small enterprise. He had initially inspected the enterprise to see if the hygiene standards were acceptable (1c, 24/4/97). In other cases a visit was to establish a trust relationship between entrepreneur and retailer. In one instance an entrepreneur making knives had taken samples of his work to a retailer who, after visiting the location of the small enterprise, had asked the entrepreneur to supply his shop and had given him a Rp.100,000 loan for working capital (18c, 6/5/97). Such relationships appeared to be positive for the entrepreneurs, in that they were assured of fairly constant marketing channels for their products.

Products made by small enterprises, such as wood and metal products, and clothes were often sold through middlepeople to shops in other areas of South Sulawesi. The links were sometimes purely trade relationships, but more frequently were through extended family connections or *kampung*-based relationships. Some metal products were exported as far as Irian Jaya and Kalimantan, the links often being family who had migrated, since Bugis from South Sulawesi often established small enterprises if they moved to other areas of Eastern Indonesia, such as Maluku and Irian Jaya (Tirtosudarmo, 1996). Other links were through Bugis traders in other islands who travelled to and from Makassar to gain products.

Since the linkages between the small-scale entrepreneurs in Makassar and the retailers in other locations had often been established through family and friends, payment for goods was often on a credit system. Again, the retailer paid half up front and the remainder when all the goods were sold, hence the requirement for a strong trust relationship.[6] A varied array of products were sold in this way, among them small cooking ovens and stoves (to Maros and Palopo) (48b, 3/2/97), candles (to *kampung* around Makassar city) (49b, 3/2/97), wood wall decorations (Maros, Pare Pare) (85b, 12/2/97), cake trays and cake moulds (*kampung* around Makassar) (87b, 12/2/97), oil stoves (Takalar, Maros, Gowa) (136b, 26/2/97), clothes (Maros) (141b, 3/3/97), and school uniforms (Sengkang, Bone) (171b, 10/3/97).

A further example of small enterprise networking involving other regions is provided by an independent Makassar silversmith in the city. Thirty people worked for him as outliers on a piece-rate basis on the nearby island of Barrang Lompo, traditionally known as a home of silversmiths. He also had another eleven people working in his enterprise, paid on a daily basis at a rate of Rp.15,000 for silver craftspeople and Rp.5000 a day for helpers. Retailers in the city, as well as Jakarta, Jogyakarta and Surabaya, ordered his silver products specifically because he was making models of items which traditionally represented Sulawesi, such as *prahu pinisi* (traditional Bugis cargo boat) and Tanatoraja rice barns (popular souvenirs with overseas and local tourists) (85a, 18/9/96). Another silversmith had a shop in Legian, a coastal tourist resort area on Bali, where one person worked for him on commission. Although there were many silversmiths operating in Bali, their designs were different from those traditional on Sulawesi which incorporated more filigree work; hence, he explained, the reason why there was still a demand for his products (26a, 13/8/96).[7]

Tradition also had a role to play in strengthening retailing links for an entrepreneur who produced Bugis and Makassar wedding dresses, which were being purchased by Sulawesi migrants who had moved to new locations but still wished to have a traditional wedding (103b, 19/2/97). This entrepreneur had connections with retailers in Irian Jaya and Kalimantan, through whom she sold her products. These retailers, who were friends and family of the entrepreneur, bought the costumes from her and then operated their own rental services.

Other Bugis migrants now living elsewhere in Eastern Indonesia desired to establish and/or maintain connections with clothing retailers in South Sulawesi, as Makassar was known throughout the region as a cheaper source of clothes than Java due to lower labour and transportation costs. Thus clothing retailers in Makassar did not usually go to other islands to market their goods, people from those islands travelling instead to Makassar to find suppliers. As discussed below, this was seen as an important reason why small enterprises clustered so that retailers from outside the city needed to visit only one neighbourhood to obtain supplies of finished products (9c, 30/4/97).

Marketing linkages with other regions appeared to be successful only if they were filling a certain market niche. For instance, this was so for silversmiths who were supplying a specific design not produced elsewhere, wedding dress enterprises catering for the demands of particular cultural groups, and clothes entrepreneurs who had become recognised as providers of cheap clothing. Nonetheless, in many circumstances this response to specific demands did not appear to have been paralleled by an increase in innovation. Indeed, many of the goods supplied to other regions were 'traditional', such as certain styles of silver jewellery, traditional wedding dresses and *songkok*, and were not being extensively modified. In other cases the goods were simple cooking ovens, candles and cooking utensils, produced at very low cost, for poorer sections of the communities. Thus while these producers were expanding their marketing spheres and being responsive to specialised demands, this did not appear to encourage innovation in the technology adopted or in the nature of the final product (Spath, 1992).

INNOVATION

We will now consider the building block of innovation in more detail and examine which small enterprises were able to be innovative in the production methods they used, as well as in the designs of goods they made.

Innovation through imitation

Pedersen *et al.* (1994) suggest that innovation in networks of small enterprises is possible because an entrepreneur operating within such a network can experiment, launch a new product, introduce new machinery and so on without risking the network itself. Then, if the experiment works, other entrepreneurs within the network are likely to imitate it in a diffusion-like spread. If the experiment is not a success, the network should still remain intact. Pedersen *et al.* (1994: 11) contend that such processes are especially relevant to small enterprises in developing countries where 'experimentation usually means being the first to introduce a technique, which is mature in and of itself, and make it work in the local social context'. They also argue, however, that such potential development can be realised only if the innovation is divisible – in that it can be introduced into an existing production process – as well as being multi-purpose in character (yet have a single function), such as the introduction of a drill, which can accomplish one function, but on many different materials (Pedersen *et al.*, 1994).

Innovation of this kind occurred among small enterprises producing embroidered cloth in Makassar. In 1997 a number of small enterprises were producing broderie anglaise, made by using a soldering iron to burn holes in the fabric after its border had been machine-hemmed, demonstrated in Plate 6.1 (13b, 14b, 23/1/97; 18b, 27/1/97). This idea was initially introduced to small enterprises in 1925 when the daughter of a *kampung* headman in Tasikmalaya district, West Java learned the process in the Dutch-owned *Singer* sewing company factory in Jakarta. After marriage she returned to her *kampung* and passed on the skills to her friends. More recently, the skills had been spread from her *kampung* by migrants settling in other islands where they established their own small-scale embroidery enterprises, including those

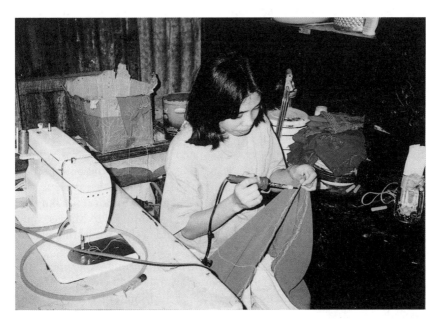

Plate 6.1 Innovation through imitation: a soldering iron being used to burn holes in cloth for broderie anglaise.

in Makassar (Grijns *et al.*, 1994). Here then is a clear example of innovation occurring through imitation, and the introduction of a technique from one geographical location to a new one.

Small enterprises in Makassar also produced many items that previously had been made in Java and imported to Sulawesi, such as aquariums, candles and machinery parts. Although this could be classified as a diffusion process at work, in that the original articles were introduced from outside Makassar, it was common that the entrepreneurs in the city had no outside training in how to produce the goods and were being innovative in the design and manufacturing process. One such Bugis entrepreneur had been designing aquariums for three years. He had taught himself from looking at designs available in shops in the city, and had calculated through experimentation how to build the aquariums and how much water an aquarium of a certain size could hold, in relation to the strength of the glue that he was using (104b, 10/3/97).

Other examples of diffusion processes at work, showing considerable individual ingenuity, were apparent among the entrepreneurs interviewed. One Javanese entrepreneur making *bakso* (meat ball soup) and *tahu goreng* (fried tofu) had learned the skill himself by watching others in his home town of Solo, Java. After moving to Makassar in 1977, he and his wife had continued to cook and sell the products (59b, 5/2/97). This man was seen locally as an innovator, introducing to Sulawesi, as he did, a 'new' production method based upon Javanese traditions (although there had probably been earlier migrants who also took Javanese food production methods with them to Sulawesi). In 1997, people still talked of Javanese and Bugis styles of *bakso*, the two remaining quite separate over the years. Yet another Javanese *bakso* entrepreneur had learned the trade by reading the recipe for *bakso* in an Indonesian cooking magazine, and had experimented with his own style, adding different spices from those normally used. This had proved to be popular, and thus represented direct innovation in his recipes (62b, 5/2/97).

Expatriates had also influenced the designs of goods produced by the small-scale entrepreneurs in the city. One had begun to make tables fashioned from black wrought-iron curved bars topped with sheets of glass, after an expatriate woman had drawn the design she wanted for the entrepreneur. The Makassar entrepreneur had then experimented with other designs using the iron and glass combination and had built a number for local retailing outlets (KI 17, 2/5/97). Thus, while the initial idea had diffused to Makassar city from elsewhere, the entrepreneur had later extended this by creating his own designs.

Other examples of innovation through imitation and experimentation included a Javanese entrepreneur, a printer, who gained new ideas from the 'electronic media' (9a, 19/8/96). By watching television, especially advertisements, he had developed novel designs of book presentation and advertising material for his customers. Another variant was provided by a Chinese entrepreneur who made tomato and chilli sauces. He explained that he had gained information for new recipes by visiting supermarkets in the city to examine the ingredients listed on sauce bottles, and had then experimented with new recipes (54a, 12/9/96).

These cases provide evidence that there were entrepreneurs in the city who were being directly responsive to changes in market demand. Each of the entrepreneurs discussed above was operating an independent enterprise, had no subcontracting linkages to larger firms, and mostly employed non-family workers. Such a pattern again implies that strong networking relationships and linkages may occur more often as survival mechanisms among small enterprises, and not necessarily, as suggested by Pedersen *et al.* (1994), as progressive means of encouraging innovation, co-operation or interdependence among enterprises.

Innovation *in situ*

Taking a narrower approach to the definition of innovation, it was also possible to find examples of entrepreneurs creating new ideas *within* small enterprises in Makassar. This was the case for one entrepreneur producing traditional Mandar weaving. In 1995 he began to experiment with producing new products, such as table cloths and bathrobes. Before these were woven, cotton threads were dyed using traditional sources including chillies, ginger, indigo plants, and the roots (*akar bengkudu*) and fruit/spice (*keluak*) from the *kepayang* tree which he obtained from markets around the city. The products were sold through tourist shops in the city, the retailers continuing to return with more orders so that the entrepreneur was able to maintain a stable production (87a, 19/9/96).

Although the majority of the goldsmiths were working for suppliers/retailers or other goldsmiths in outlier-style relationships, there were some who had managed to save enough working capital to buy their own small gold supplies. At the time of field work, these entrepreneurs were experimenting with new designs, attempting to produce their own range of jewellery (3b, 21/1/97). If the new designs did not sell well the goldsmiths melted the gold and developed other designs (KI 2, 8/5/97). Since the mid-1990s there had been a resurgence of interest in gold jewellery designs from the 1960s and 1970s. Goldsmiths learned these from drawings given to them by retailers, or else hired older men who had been in the trade in the past to teach new workers the designs (66b, 6/2/97).

A few goldsmiths, with broadly skilled workers, were able to respond to changes in market demand with new designs. These goldsmiths had broken away from the traditional subcontracting arrangements typical among the goldsmiths to become more independent. However, the trade-off had been an increase in the numbers of hours worked, and a reduction in spending power, as profits had to be saved for working capital instead. One such goldsmith interviewed had individual customers who visited him with basic materials, such as gold and stones (usually semi-precious). They asked him to sketch a suitable design for different pieces of jewellery, and when interviewed he was experimenting with a range of intricate ring designs for a Chinese customer (108b, 20/2/97).

Another entrepreneur was experimenting with new designs of tables (35b, 29/1/97). He had examined products available in shops in Makassar and in magazines, and had then tried to design similar goods while also experimenting with his own designs. He had personally invented a new style of 'coffee table' made of plywood which was painted a bright colour, covered with a picture poster and then covered again with glass. Through family and friends to whom he had given sample tables, orders for these had been gained from Pare Pare, Soppeng, Pinrang, Kendari and Palu.

As well as innovation in terms of the products produced, entrepreneurs were also sometimes innovative in the use of basic materials and equipment as well as enterprise organisation and marketing. This was true of one entrepreneur who made boat propellers. He used second-hand goods as basic materials, including empty drink cans, broken cooking pans, second-hand woks, pistons from motorbikes, and broken aluminium machine parts. He explained that his brother and he had constructed propellers from old woks as new sheet metal was too expensive. They bought the used woks, from an itinerant second-hand dealer who saved any he found for them (62a, 11/9/96).

From the cases discussed in detail above, it is evident that the majority of innovation among the sample of small enterprises in Makassar had originated through a process of diffusion and experimentation. New technologies and product ideas had been brought to Makassar by migrants, by travellers passing on ideas, by the media, and by customers and retailers coming to entrepreneurs with new designs. Entrepreneurs had then attempted to integrate new designs and ideas into their production systems. *In-situ* innovation had also occurred in the form of small-scale entrepreneurs experimenting in their own time with their own designs, although it seemed rare that these were not influenced by outside ideas to some extent.

In the course of this analysis, it has become clear that the *small enterprise integrative framework* truly allows the diversity among small enterprises operating in Makassar to be recognised. Through the use of this framework, three notable sets of inter-firm dynamics emerged. First, there were enterprises in subcontracting relationships with larger firms. These enterprise subcontractors usually had just-in-time delivery systems of inputs, a broadly trained workforce and craftspersonship; however, the enterprise subcontractors often remarked that these very same relationships constrained product innovation and enterprise development. Second, there were independent enterprises involved in strong networking arrangements, yet complaining of limited marketing channels and high levels of competition. Frequently, these entrepreneurs operated on a day-to-day basis with little evidence of innovation and product diversification.

Third, other enterprises showed a high degree of innovation, and the ability to change product designs rapidly in tune with shifts in customer demands, an ability made possible by the highly skilled craftspeople in the enterprises. Mainly non-family-operated, these enterprises undertook predominantly independent production and acted outside strong networking systems. However, to complete a thorough investigation of small enterprises in Makassar adopting the *small enterprise integrative framework*, we need to move on from examining networks, trust and innovation in this chapter, and flexibility in labour and production processes in Chapter 5, to the two remaining building blocks of the framework: clusters and collective efficiency.

CLUSTERS AND COLLECTIVE EFFICIENCY

A number of different horizontally or vertically specialised cluster types were discussed in Chapter 3. It was argued that the specialised petty commodity cluster might well be the most relevant in the context of small enterprises in Makassar, within which 'collective efficiencies achieved by clustering primarily are due to reduced transaction costs for customers, but some collaboration between enterprises may also take place' (Pedersen, 1994b: 17). The purpose of this section then, is to establish whether or not such clusters existed in Makassar. Here, the big question is the extent to which small enterprises comprised a grouping distinguished by a common product range, co-existing within a limited geographical area, with common input needs and skills requirements, while also exhibiting a balance between co-operation and competition among enterprises, and a certain level of permanence and stability in terms of business relationships.

Reduced transaction costs[8]

Physical clustering of the small enterprises was most apparent among those involved in furniture production, metalworking, tailoring and goldsmithing. For the furniture enterprises the clusters tended to be a mix of independent entrepreneurs and enterprise subcontractors, who together through their various networking relationships supplied finished products mainly to local retailers and some direct consumers. Transactions which occurred on a frequent basis among the independent entrepreneurs and enterprise subcontractors required a certain proximity, as many of the individuals concerned did not have access to reliable communication or transportation infrastructure. Cheap, small-capacity transportation modes were often relied upon, such as *becak* (trishaws), handcarts and bicycles.

Likewise, the transportation of other goods such as small stoves, bundles of clothing and a variety of raw materials was undertaken by *becak*. Due to the transportation methods used, small and subcontracting enterprises as well as retailers were frequently located in the same vicinity in the city, often within a kilometre of each other. For a number of furniture clusters studied, the wooden frame-makers were concentrated along one road, which was less than half a kilometre from where subcontracting enterprises sewing and upholstering the furniture were clustered. Near to both groupings was a main road on which the retailers they supplied had their shops.

For one of the clusters of chair-makers manufacturing the wooden frames in *kecamatan* Tallo (Tallo subdistrict), members obtained their wood from a supplier in a *kampung* in Gowa. Together, the chair-makers placed an order for a number of trees to be cut and purchased. The farmer then cut the wood at a sawmill in the *kampung* and delivered the wood to the small enterprises. The cluster members had developed a high degree of trust with the farmer, he in turn valuing such a large order, all from one neighbourhood. The wood was taken to the individual small enterprise sites once a fortnight, making delivery from the *kampung* more cost-efficient (29b, 28/1/97). Another supplier to this cluster was a man who collected used cardboard boxes, which the entrepreneurs making low-quality chairs and sofas used as part of the padding/stuffing material. This supplier visited the enterprises weekly, each entrepreneur placing an order during the previous visit the week before. Enterprise clustering in this case meant that the costs of transportation were kept low and the delivery could be completed quickly (36b, 29/1/97).

When asked directly why they were clustered, a wide range of entrepreneurs reported that this was because customers would know where to come. Many retailers visited Makassar from other regions or islands with prior knowledge about where to find products such as chairs and sofas, clothes, cooking pots, small stoves, demolition iron, concrete pots and pillars, machinery parts, and aluminium cupboards and shelves. Certain locations within the city had gained a reputation for containing small enterprises which made these products.

It is of note that the soya bean drink and *bakso* entrepreneurs interviewed, while often living in close proximity to each other, did not function within clusters. Instead they operated the individual *pondok* systems discussed in Chapter 4 (Context). The fact that they lived so close to each other appeared to owe little to networking considerations and to be more a function of their standard of living, and proximity to neighbourhoods in which the majority of their customers could be found. These entrepreneurs did not borrow equipment or raw materials from each other and were in competition for customers and workers (see also Jellinek, 1978; 1997).

Collaboration

Clustering has been described as a means of facilitating collaboration among small enterprises, as a means of increasing the possibility that they would share tools, workers, raw materials and general information. Members of the chair-making clusters, for instance, frequently borrowed expensive tools from one another, one entrepreneur explaining that a 30cm plane would cost Rp.75,000 to buy. Different chisels were also borrowed from each other regularly. Indeed, it was usual to have only a few of the more expensive tools in the cluster, individual members owning different tools. As explained by one member, 'we borrow lots of things from each other, it's normal. That's why we all work in the same area, like the same place, because it's like that' (25b, 28/1/97).

Clustering among goldsmiths bestowed certain economic advantages. It enabled them to sometimes gain new ideas for designs from their neighbours and other goldsmiths in the same cluster (16a, 28/8/97). They also relied on being able to borrow tools and equipment from other members of clusters, including rasps, files and threading machines used for making gold thread from thick gold strips. A threading machine cost approximately Rp.300,000 and thus many goldsmiths were not able to afford their own (KI 2, 8/5/97). As documented in the network section of this chapter, most of the goldsmiths were from the 'Sidrap' region, so among them there were strong family and friendship ties going back a number of generations, the basis of their mutual trust when borrowing tools and equipment. They also shared information regarding the characteristics of the Chinese gold retailers in the city, including information on which had orders available at a certain time, who paid the best rates, who would provide small loans, and who was less critical concerning the quality of finished goods (KI 2, 8/5/97).

Tailors (18b, 27/1/97), goldsmiths (19b, 27/1/97), metalworkers (89a, 26/9/96) and wooden furniture-makers (32b, 29/1/97) also talked about the possibility of 'borrowing' workers from nearby enterprises if they received a large order, or if a specific skill was required. Workers were borrowed periodically within some of the goldsmith clusters, and as pointed out in the earlier discussion on innovation, certain entrepreneurs were 'borrowing' older goldsmiths who knew how to make designs from the 1970s (KI 2, 30/1/97).

It was usual that the clustering of small enterprises in Makassar was closely related to family and neighbourhood ties, and people who had participated in a certain enterprise as a worker or family labourer were sometimes able to establish a similar enterprise if they saved enough capital. Successful established entrepreneurs occasionally lent tools and capital to relatives or neighbours so that they could set up their own enterprise. It did not appear to be a concern to restrict entry because more enterprises would increase competition although, because they were unknown, entry was certainly restricted in the case of those outside family and neighbourhood networks. Instead, there appeared to be a general belief that having many entrepreneurs producing the same or similar goods in a neighbourhood was positive in that it would increase their profile and thus the size of their general market. Although this appeared to be something of a paradox, it is explained by the nature of the market. As discussed above, advertising was usually by word of mouth and hence enterprises were grouped together so that buyers would know where to search for a certain product, compare prices and have a range of goods to choose from (van Dijk, 1993; see also Alexander, 1987, for similar findings in central Java).

At this point in the discussion it is appropriate to respond to the critical question, 'is the cluster merely a multiplication of producers making similar products or has specialisation and inter-firm divisions of labour developed?' (Schmitz, 1989: 66; see also Nadvi and Schmitz, 1994). The evidence from field work reviewed above indicates that a number of the small enterprises in Makassar were operating within clusters. In the case of the furniture enterprises it was clear that a significant inter-firm division of labour and specialisation had occurred. Some of the tailors were also operating in this style, different enterprises undertaking particular parts of the production process, although it appeared more usual for the specialisation to occur between enterprises and their connected outliers. Turning to the goldsmiths, numerous complex networks were found among them and their retailers, yet at the same time there did not appear to be notable levels of inter-firm division of labour or specialisation occurring. Thus what physical clustering existed seemed primarily motivated by a desire to reduce transportation costs for the entrepreneurs, as well as for the customers and retailers they supplied. There were also cases of interaction and interdependence among enterprises in terms of sharing both tools and workers. It has to be concluded, however, that only among the furniture enterprises did there appear to be elements of specialisation and inter-firm division, which had a potential to achieve collective efficiency.

THE FUTURE: ATTITUDES AND EXPECTATIONS

One of the objectives of the questionnaire survey of small enterprises in Makassar was to establish a more informed perspective on, and deeper appreciation of, barriers to the realisation of the entrepreneurs' wishes for their enterprises in the future. Accordingly, the entrepreneurs in Group A were asked how they *expected* their enterprise to be functioning in terms of development in five to ten years time and how, within the same time frame, they would *like* their enterprise to be functioning. Where there was a difference between the two responses, the entrepreneurs were asked what were the most significant perceived constraints to the achievement of their aspirations.

The most common impediments mentioned, reflecting responses to questions previously analysed, were marketing problems, the difficulties in gaining access to adequate funding/capital, and cost and access problems linked to raw materials.[9] Relating to marketing, there were a range of noted difficulties including uneven seasonal demand, competition and a continuous dependence on middlepeople for marketing, as well as for raw materials. Other constraints included low productivity and, in turn, the limited skills of workers, inadequate technology and the constrained business development of the enterprise. External to the enterprises, a general uncertainty regarding the future of the economy and the Government was seen as problematic.

These impediments and difficulties confirmed the concerns of many small-scale entrepreneurs discussed above. They were operating, almost without exception, with elementary technologies and a basic organisation of production, intermittent investment of capital and a limited ability to be innovative in design and technology. Such entrepreneurs faced a highly competitive market which was limited in scope and often a continued reliance on middlepeople and retailers.

The entrepreneurs were asked how willing they would be to respond to certain initiatives and activities that would change aspects of their enterprise. This was in part an attempt to obtain insight into which of these were along the lines of the entrepreneurs' aspirations themselves, as the list was a range of changes commonly supported through small enterprise support programmes (Tambunan, 2000). The responses, summarised in Table 6.2, show that the entrepreneurs were 'willing' or 'very willing' to consider making a broad range of changes to their enterprises in the future. The most frequently cited change was to improve product quality, followed (in descending order) by improving working conditions, exploring a wider market, improving worker welfare, increased borrowing of capital and expanding the use of technology. These were followed by raising the number of workers and improving management training for the owner, changing both the product design and type, entering into a co-operative system, and increasing general risk. The only change that less than 50 per cent of the entrepreneurs were willing to undertake was the location of the enterprise. This reluctance highlighted the importance of family and neighbourhood networks, a familiar environment and the embeddedness of production in the local neighbourhood.

As cultural groups, the Bugis, Makassar and Torajan entrepreneurs gave first priority to investing more capital into their enterprises or to borrowing capital, whereas for the Chinese and Javanese entrepreneurs exploring a wider market was the most important decision. There thus appeared to be a clear relation between entrepreneurs who belonged to cultures not 'indigenous' to South Sulawesi and a willingness to look outside normal marketing spheres for new opportunities.

The data in Table 6.2 strongly suggest that, other things being equal, small-scale entrepreneurs in Makassar were willing to consider making a range of changes to the structure and everyday operations of their enterprises, changes that might well place them in a potentially more successful position in the local economy. Given the opportunity, a number of entrepreneurs were willing to innovate with new and varied technology, and in the design of their products. They were keen to explore new markets as a means of reducing the competition they faced in narrow marketing spheres, and they were open to considering new ideas relating to management and co-operation, for instance, by undertaking management training schemes and entering into co-operative arrangements.

Nevertheless, on reflection, one must remember that while it was easy for

Table 6.2 Willingness of entrepreneurs in Group A to change certain aspects of their enterprises (%)

	Very unwilling	Unwilling	Neutral	Willing	Very willing	**Total: willing or very willing**	Rank: most willing to change
Improve product quality	–	1	8	63	28	**91**	1st
Improve working conditions	–	1	10	69	20	**89**	2nd
Explore a wider market	–	3	9	50	38	**88**	3rd
Improve workers' welfare	1	2	11	74	12	**86**	4th
Increase borrowing of capital	2	4	10	50	34	**84**	5th
Increase use of technology	–	6	14	51	29	**80**	6th
Increase number of workers	–	9	13	62	16	**78**	7th=
Management training for owner	0	4	18	62	16	**78**	7th=
Change product type	1	12	22	56	9	**65**	8th
Change product design	2	14	22	42	20	**62**	9th
Enter into co-operative system	1	13	26	54	6	**60**	10th
Increase risk	4	21	16	55	4	**59**	11th
Change location of enterprise	4	28	31	28	9	**37**	12th

the entrepreneurs to *say* they would like to make such changes given the opportunity and/or incentives, assuming that such opportunities were actually offered, the entrepreneurs could easily reject them or change their minds for myriad reasons, many influenced by culture, gender and/or social relations.

CONCLUSION: DIVERSITY IN DYNAMICS

Conceivably, perhaps the strongest conclusion to emerge from the whole overview of evidence is that there is an enormous diversity in the range of enterprise organisation structures among the small enterprises in Makassar. The latter ranged from those operated single-handedly by an entrepreneur working with purely economic-based transactions to gain access to raw materials and the market, through to those embedded in dense webs of inter-firm linkages, either as independent or subcontracting enterprises.

While analysing the building blocks of the *small enterprise integrative framework* it was found that the majority of the small enterprises had a broadly trained workforce, yet not necessarily one that reflected high levels of craftspersonship expressed through an ability to learn a range of new tasks and improve skills. Due to the transient nature of some of the workers, entrepreneurs were often reluctant to provide skilled training, as workers could easily move to more appealing enterprises offering better returns to labour.

Similarly, for enterprises operating on a subcontractual basis, it was possible to discern a just-in-time delivery system of inputs and the ability of the enterprise subcontractors to respond rapidly to changes in demand. Yet the same enterprises were limited in their ability to have an informal management structure and to have control over production decisions, and to be innovative in design or technology.

Interactions among the independent small enterprises spanned a complicated array of linkages and networks, which at times incorporated other islands in Indonesia. Enterprises that operated within cluster formations appeared to have gained benefits in obtaining access to raw materials, workers and new technology, but this appeared to be the case only for entrepreneurs producing certain product types in the city. On the other hand, other entrepreneurs had retained a degree of independence in the production of their goods. In their case, family, friendship and cultural links remained key aspects in terms of support and marketing channels, often critical for informal loans and capital, important if not vital functions in a corrupt bureaucratic environment in which many of the entrepreneurs were scared to approach formal institutions for loans.

In summary, it appears that a range of barriers prevented the entrepreneurs and subcontractors from reaching a full realisation of their personal goals concerning their enterprises. These barriers originated both from within the enterprises, as well as from the broader contextual environment in which they were operating, important among these being cultural tensions, constraints due to gender, the local political environment, as well as the local economic situation and bureaucracy. In the next chapter I investigate these barriers in more detail, and examine how they prevented the small-scale entrepreneurs and subcontractors from reaching their objectives.

7   Constraints to small enterprise growth

Evidence presented in Chapter 6 confirms that small enterprises examined in Makassar did not, in general, enjoy the business success hoped for by their owners, but were instead trading on the margins. That success was denied due to a range of constraints, some internal to the enterprises, others external to them. Of importance in the first category were factors such as a lack of innovation within many enterprises, inferior product quality and poor accounting records. The negative impact of these was compounded by numerous influences outside the control of the small-scale entrepreneurs upon which their shifting fortunes depended. Among such external factors were high levels of competition faced by many entrepreneurs, corruption within relevant Government agencies in the city, the complex structure and operations of the bureaucracy, difficulties in gaining access to credit, and ever present ethnic divisions and tensions within the city. This chapter, then, explores the constellation of internal and external constraints which diminished the ability of small enterprises in Makassar to achieve their full potential.

GROWTH LEVELS

A key concern of many small-scale entrepreneurs was the ability of their enterprises to grow. To clarify this issue, information on income, expenditure and profits in their enterprises over the past ten to fifteen years was gathered from entrepreneurs in Group A and summarised in Table 7.1. In regard to *income*, just over half (56 per cent) had experienced more than a slight increase (over 4 per cent change), while a further 13 per cent had experienced only a 'very slight' expansion. A further 19 per cent recorded fluctuating or constant incomes, leaving 12 per cent who had recorded an actual decline. Turning to the *expenditure* side of the cash flow equation, the large majority of entrepreneurs had experienced some escalation in costs. Ninety per cent had expressed an increase in expenditure, with only 2 per cent recording a decline.

For 58 per cent of the entrepreneurs in Group A however, the shifts in income and expenditure had resulted in a positive outcome in regard to *prof-*

Table 7.1 Income, expenditure and profit levels for Group A enterprises over the previous ten to fifteen years

Income	Per cent
Significant increase (over 70% change)	2
Reasonable increase (5–69% change)	54
Very slight increase (1–4% change)	13
Fluctuating or constant	19
Decline	12
Expenditure	
Costs rising by over 10%	55
Slight increase in expenditure (1–9%)	35
Fluctuating or constant	8
Decline in costs	2
Profits	
Significant increase (over 25% change)	14
Increase (between 5–24% change)	44
Minimal/'survival'	24
Decline	18

its. However, another 24 per cent declared that their profits had been minimal or defined them as 'survival' rates, while an additional 18 per cent recorded a decline. Those with the greatest profit increase were metal window frame and door entrepreneurs, goldsmiths, tailors and general sewing enterprises, while those enterprises with the largest decline were blacksmiths and small oven entrepreneurs.

Classified by ethnicity, there were clearly large differences among entrepreneurs. As a group, the eleven entrepreneurs interviewed from Tana Toraja had the highest median profits. They operated enterprises employing no family labour, were among the larger of the enterprises in terms of worker numbers, and five had received help from a formal institution such as a bank or the Department of Industry and Trade. Six of these enterprises had been established by Torajans using money remitted from family members working outside of Sulawesi, and in some cases outside of Indonesia, who had sent remittances home (10a, 15/8/96; 17a, 28/8/96; 31a, 20/8/96; 34a, 28/8/96; 63a, 19/9/96; 78a, 9/9/96). In other words, these entrepreneurs had independent sources of capital in the form of gifts, not loans, with which to establish their enterprises, an advantage reflected in their higher profits (see also Cohen, 1998a).

The history of intense ethnic and religious tensions between the Torajan highlanders and the Bugis and Makassar lowlanders (Adams, 1997a) also appears to be an influential factor in their success. It was suggested, for instance, as a reason why the Torajan entrepreneurs in the sample had initially established large enterprises, as there were few networks and linkages for supporting smaller Torajan-owned enterprises in the city because they were largely excluded from those involving Bugis or Makassar entrepreneurs (KI 7, 21/2/97). Accordingly, it appeared that the Torajan entrepreneurs had stronger linkages with distant *kampung* members than with other entrepreneurs in the city.

Capital sources

Sources of capital available to the small enterprises were examined to gain an understanding of the ease by which entrepreneurs could expand and develop their enterprises if they wished. The *fixed* capital of the enterprises in Group A was overwhelmingly provided by the entrepreneurs themselves. On average, they relied almost entirely on their own money to purchase premises (94 per cent), machinery (96 per cent), equipment (99 per cent) and vehicles (93 per cent).

In regard to *working* capital, the greatest dependency was on income from capital rotation including daily sales rather than, for instance, savings or loans. Income from sales was the sole source of working capital for 35 per cent of the entrepreneurs in Group A with almost two-thirds (62 per cent) indicating that at least some came from sales. 'Own savings', or a mixture of proceeds from sales and savings contributed working capital for 26 per cent. The extensive use of sale proceeds to act as working capital hindered those who wished to invest more in the development of their enterprises, restricting their ability to gain new technology and equipment, and hindering long-term growth.[1]

For Group A, 'personal' family and informal channels had also been used to gain working capital, a source chosen by over half (55 per cent) for at least some such capital. Nevertheless, the degree to which such channels were adopted did not correlate with the level of family labour involved in the enterprise, suggesting that family support was important for many of them. For Group B, the most prominent source of working capital was 'personal sources', including own savings, as well as family (26 per cent) and friends (6 per cent). Rather unexpectedly, however, a further 61 per cent had never borrowed to cover their needs for working capital and had thus relied solely on capital rotation. This indicated a higher level of self-reliance, which was perhaps attributable to the environment in which they were operating. In this, there appeared to be constant uncertainty regarding the reciprocal actions that might be expected in the future from a variety of informal and formal lending sources (KI 2, 4/3/97). Conceivably, the need of those operating as enterprise subcontractors to gain working capital was also less urgent because raw materials were supplied as part of the production arrangements.

Neither formal nor informal means were adequate to satisfy the actual capital needs of the enterprises. Indeed, the formation of capital or the acquisition of working capital was cited as their major problem by 29 per cent of the entrepreneurs. When asked specifically about the types of problems they

Table 7.2 Common problems faced by entrepreneurs trying to raise capital

---

Corruption/bias in formal lending procedures
- difficulties in obtaining a loan if one was Chinese
- the need to pay the bank staff a 'commission' or bribe.

Problems with bureaucracy
- bureaucracy was 'too complicated and difficult'
- numerous 'rules and regulations in getting a loan'
- uncertainty over how and when the loan was to be repaid
- inadequate amounts that were available from banks or BUMN.
- no sources were quick

Problems internal to the enterprises themselves
- lack of collateral or security for obtaining a loan
- not knowing how to apply to formal institutions for loans
- small enterprise premises had to be tidy and clean to be approved when applying for a loan
- inadequate accounting system within the enterprise.

---

faced when trying to gain adequate capital, two thirds (66 per cent) indicated common factors which are shown in Table 7.2, and ranged from problems with corruption/bias in formal lending procedures and other problems with the bureaucracy, to problems internal to the enterprises themselves.

Nearly all the problems listed in Table 7.2 related to formal lending channels, so it was not surprising that only a fraction of the entrepreneurs had actually successfully gained assistance from a variety of such channels. Amongst the formal sources that had been approached to obtain capital by the entrepreneurs in Group A, ten had secured bank loans, of which Chinese and Makassar entrepreneurs were the most common. A further two, both Makassar entrepreneurs, had gained working capital in the form of a loan from industry co-operatives, while one had secured a loan from a Government pawn trader (Bugis), another had done so from the Department of Industry and Trade (Javanese) and five from BUMN (Bugis, Torajan and Makassar). In total, Makassar entrepreneurs had received the most support, those from Java and other islands receiving the least, perhaps reflecting a bias based on ethnicity.

Similarly, a variety of loan sources was tapped by Group B entrepreneurs. In this case, thirteen had used 'formal' methods to borrow working capital, while banks provided money for ten (Bugis and Makassar entrepreneurs being the most common), and one had borrowed from *BUMN* (Bugis) and two from co-operatives (Makassar). Again Makassar entrepreneurs had gained the most support, while none from Java in either Group A or B had gained a bank loan. Indeed, only one Javanese entrepreneur had gained any type of support. Once more, such contrasts stress the importance of taking ethnicity into account as a factor influencing the level of institutional support available to entrepreneurs.

Government-sponsored co-operatives offered an alternative way of organising entrepreneurial activity in Makassar. To develop an understanding of these, Group B entrepreneurs were asked if they had been or were presently members of a co-operative. Only six of the 200 entrepreneurs sampled had had such a connection, four being present members (two Bugis goldsmiths and two Makassar metalwork entrepreneurs), and two having been affiliated in the past (Bugis entrepreneurs making *bakso* (meat ball soup) cooking pots). One of the entrepreneurs who made *bakso* pots said he was no longer a member because 'it wasn't any help to me' (39b, 30/1/97). Another *bakso* pot entrepreneur at the adjacent site had also been a member of the same co-operative. He too was no longer a member, explaining that 'they never gave me any help, but you had to pay a fee, so I stopped being a member' (41b, 30/1/97). The same entrepreneur had subsequently borrowed an interest-free loan of Rp.100,000 from his family, hence the disincentive to be a member of a co-operative which charged fees (usually between Rp.1000 and 5000 a month), but often with no tangible benefits (KI 1, 14/4/97).

Many entrepreneurs talked about being 'scared' to approach lending institutions. It was often commented that '*BUMN* doesn't play fair', that they were 'afraid' to go to sources outside the family, and that people providing loans 'want bribes and tips'. Few of the entrepreneurs had formal qualifications and they frequently lacked the 'connections' that many knew were necessary to succeed in gaining formal loans in Indonesia. For the entrepreneurs, this inability to utilise formal channels for capital formation was a serious barrier to being able to gain significant capital funds to expand their enterprise premises, introduce new technology or change products.

Group B entrepreneurs were also asked where they would source funds if they needed to borrow in the future. In reply, about half (53 per cent) said that they would turn to family members, 8 per cent to friends and 3 per cent to their raw materials supplier, a distribution that re-emphasises the importance of personal relationships and networks. Of the 'formal' methods available, 23 per cent (most commonly Bugis and Makassar entrepreneurs) said they would approach a bank and just 1 per cent (two entrepreneurs, both Bugis) nominated a co-operative instead. However, a few (4 per cent) Bugis and Torajan entrepreneurs claimed that 'I just wouldn't do it' when discussing borrowing from formal channels, again reflecting the fear entrepreneurs often commented upon regarding any approach to formal banking mechanisms and the bureaucracy. Nonetheless, the relatively high number of entrepreneurs willing to seek a loan from a bank in the future was unexpected, given that those who had already approached such institutions had made negative comments about the payments of bribes and the informal connections required. Perhaps this showed a naivety on behalf of some of the entrepreneurs concerning a banking system that they had not yet had contact with, although a few Makassar and Bugis entrepreneurs hinted that they had friends working in banks who would help them.

Not surprisingly, sources of funding for enterprise development differed between those staffed entirely by family workers and those that employed only non-family workers. Those in the first category indicated that, in the future, they would tend to go to relatives for funds, whereas most of those in the second category would go either to the bank or to friends. Yet responses were mixed. Take, for example, the individual entrepreneur who recorded the highest profits in Group B. A Chinese man producing aquariums, he did not use family labour, and said he would go to the bank or friends if he required funds in the future. In contrast, the second most profitable enterprise was owned by a Bugis/Makassar (mixed-blood) man who sold or rented traditional wedding ceremony dresses and accessories. He indicated that he would never go to a bank but would continue to rely on family support, as he did not trust the bank staff (97b, 18/2/97). Thus family was an important source of support even for high profit-making entrepreneurs, while a distrust of bank officials and also a lack of understanding of banking procedures remained a barrier to many in obtaining formal funds.

Restricted access to working capital affected the long-term growth of the enterprises in a variety of ways. For Group A entrepreneurs, it not only generally slowed development (67 per cent), but also limited the capital available for marketing, and reduced the funds available for improving equipment, while also causing financial instability for particular enterprises. Many of the entrepreneurs were faced with a continuous juggling act because of their limited access to loan capital. They reported that they often had little opportunity to accumulate capital because of the constant need to either repay credit themselves, or 'chase up' credit payments from customers, many of whom were in the same plight. This situation again focuses attention on the importance of the prevailing, wider economic context. The interest burden accrued from borrowing on credit, from either non-institutional or institutional sources, tended to erode the entrepreneurs' real earning potential, leading to the repeated complaint that this factor hindered their advancement.

When the entrepreneurs were asked how they thought their problems of gaining access to capital could be overcome, 30 per cent said they would 'just let it be'. Of these, the majority were Makassar using an all-family labour force, with the lowest number being Torajan and Chinese entrepreneurs. Some, who claimed they would 'let it be', were content to operate at a level that provided for family and social obligations, again pointing to the need to use emic definitions of success.

Yet there was also a number (17 per cent) of entrepreneurs who were prepared to take defensive action when barriers to advancement were encountered. Those in this group claimed they would scale down production, work only when they had raw materials available, 'look for other work to survive', or use their savings as working capital.

One in four respondents (26 per cent) indicated that their response would be a proactive one. This included a range of initiatives, from increasing the volume of sales, looking for alternative sources of working capital, perhaps asking for cash advances from customers, or improving their savings techniques and accounting records in order to increase their stocks of raw materials. This pro-active perspective was held most often by Torajan, Chinese and Javanese entrepreneurs, which in turn may imply that they were more 'profit orientated' in terms of the development of their enterprises than those from other cultural groups. Alternatively, perhaps this was because the small size of the Chinese and Torajan populations in the city meant that they had fewer supporting 'social nets' to fall back on in the city, and hence had to be more rigorous and active than other ethnic groups in finding solutions to such problems. Key informants agreed that both hypotheses were possible (KI 1, 30/1/97; KI 3, 5/2/97).

The evidence gathered from small-scale entrepreneurs in Makassar demonstrated that, without exception, social relations and culture were important influences in shaping the ability of entrepreneurs to gain support from official institutions, as well as influencing their decision-making processes that determined how they responded to difficulties. These factors all impacted upon the production organisation of the small enterprises and in turn, the levels of growth they achieved. The limited support derived from formal institutions suggested that the growth entrepreneurs strove for was continuously hindered by numerous barriers in the bureaucratic environment and strongly influenced by local socio-cultural relations.

Enterprise support

The local business environment in which they operated and the support mechanisms available to them also influenced the level of profitability achieved by the entrepreneurs. Of those in Group A, only sixteen enterprises had gained support other than for working capital from the Department of Industry and Trade, seven from co-operatives, six from *PPPK* and *KAS*, and two each from the local government and a non-government organisation. Funds or training from the Department of Industry and Trade were received only by Bugis, Makassar and Mandar entrepreneurs, a situation that again suggests an ethnic bias in support provided by Government institutions. Women entrepreneurs had far less success than men in gaining formal support for their enterprises, only five having done so. Two of these had received 'start-up' loans from banks (Bugis and Torajan), another had support from *PPPK* (Bugis), a fourth gained advice from the Department of Industry and Trade (Mandar), and the fifth secured a loan and advice from *BUMN* (Bugis).

The weak record of women in this regard reflected the barriers they faced when attempting to access formal support. Those interviewed not only often lacked knowledge of the support available but how to apply for it. Often, too, an assumption was made by officials from lending institutions that a male was the head of the enterprise – and hence a male family member should attend training sessions. Moreover, there were religious constraints to Muslim women attending courses far from their homes. Also evident was an apparent reluctance on behalf of institutions to provide support to women (KI 22, 26/11/96; for similar findings elsewhere in Indonesia see Machfud *et al.*, 1994; and Berry *et al.*, 1999).

Support secured from organisations and individuals was provided for a variety of purposes other than working capital. Management training was funded, as was the purchase of raw materials, equipment and tools, enterprise promotion and transportation as well as information regarding the production process, help with marketing strategies, technical training and on-the-job training. Generally, it was felt by respondents that these types of support had been effective in the past, for instance, in raising skills and productivity and increasing levels of raw materials, equipment and profits. It was not necessarily the non-family labour enterprises that had benefited from such support. Indeed, as many as twenty nine enterprises using all-family labour had been granted support from formal institutions, a number comprising 60 per cent of the total group of entrepreneurs that had been given non-working capital support. Most commonly this was from a co-operative or the Department of Industry and Trade. In other words, at least some government initiatives appear to have reached the targeted audience of small enterprises, yet they were still heavily biased in terms of the cultural groups and gender advantaged.

Entrepreneurs who had successfully elicited institutional support were usually positive about the level and type received. This suggests that if more of the barriers to small-scale entrepreneurs seeking support were removed, there should be a significant improvement in their ability not only to improve enterprise production and marketing ability, but also to be innovative in product construction and design. In turn, if implemented, these changes may well lead the way towards more co-operative networking and cluster arrangements. Indeed, three-quarters of the Group A entrepreneurs identified a number of Government reforms and initiatives that would help their enterprises, the most prominent being to improve access to and provision of capital (38 per cent of the suggested ways). Other initiatives the Government might take (detailed in Table 7.3) ranged from improving marketing channels, and reducing bureaucratic hurdles, to increasing enterprise competitiveness, as well as improving enterprise development.

If nothing else, the number and range of such responses confirm that far-reaching changes affecting the operation of enterprises are still necessary to enhance the prospect that they could succeed in a supportive environment. It is also clear that much opportunity exists for local government and institutions to assume a leading role in the growth of small enterprises in Makassar. Nonetheless, whether or not this eventuates will depend to a large degree on the autonomy such institutions are granted, because local initiatives can often be stifled by centralised decision-making processes. Unfortunately, as discussed in Chapter 4 and again in Chapter 8, such barriers remain strong in the case of Indonesia.

Table 7.3 Potential government initiatives identified by Group A entrepreneurs to help their enterprises

---

Improve marketing channels
- provide more information regarding marketing
- increase promotion and exposure of products.

Reduce bureaucratic hurdles
- improve co-ordination among Government agencies
- help with overcoming the bureaucracy regarding BUMN
- provide faster access to loans with lower interest rates
- reduce the number of taxes levied.

Increase enterprise competitiveness
- create a number of industry clusters – with consultation
- stop temporary businesses that destroy the prevailing prices
- increase cohesiveness among small enterprises.

Improve enterprise development
- help with management and designs
- provide training regarding the production process
- standardise commissions and wages received by workers
- generally help with business development for small enterprises.

ORGANISATION

Although there were small enterprises in the city that had seen an increase in profits over the past ten to fifteen years (as documented in Table 7.1), the barriers they faced when wishing to expand production remained immense. When trying to gain additional capital they faced difficulties with bureaucracy, biases in lending institutions and problems due to the structure of their enterprises. When it came to enterprise support, the entrepreneurs produced a long list (Table 7.3) of the assistance they would like to see come from the government and lending institutions in the city, to help them overcome a range of obstacles. Furthermore, an additional four key constraints linked to internal enterprise organisation were found to be inhibiting the development of many small enterprises: a lack of innovation, limited accounting records, low product quality and high levels of conspicuous consumption.

Innovation among Bugis or Makassar workers within small enterprises was considered culturally inappropriate by a number of key informants interviewed due to social relations being strongly hierarchical (KI's 8, 12, 14, 18, and 21; Millar, 1989). As one key informant explained, 'there's a major stumbling point to innovation, it's that most of the time it's considered culturally inappropriate for workers to show more initiative or intelligence than their employer' (KI 21, 11/5/97).[2] For this reason, the decision-making process regarding technology, marketing and working conditions was nearly always executed by the entrepreneur. As a consequence worker initiative was stifled and they usually just followed instructions issued by their employer (see also Sjaifudian, 1992). A number of entrepreneurs explained that it was not the 'job' of workers or younger family members to suggest improvements or innovations in the small enterprises, which leads once again to the under-standing that social and cultural influences were prominent in economic decision making processes in the enterprises (57a, 30/1/97; 68a, 16/9/96).

This situation is well illustrated by one Bugis, a small-scale entrepreneur and also a key informant. He had been able to make innovative changes to his enterprise only because he had become the owner at a relatively young age (20 in 1991), after his father had died. He explained that in the past he had not been able to suggest new ideas to his father, as this would have been seen as impertinent. While the younger man had to 'know his position' within the family, cultural constraints had been removed by his father's death. Subsequently, the son had introduced new technology, labour structures and marketing links to the enterprise (KI 6, 3/2/97).

Another key informant, a Bugis man who worked in a local organisation operating to improve small enterprise productivity in the city, had a rather different perspective on the lack of innovation in some small enterprises. In his view 'people here like to use the activities they already know, they don't want to try new things, this is a problem here'. He added: 'People don't think about innovation, they don't use their brains . . . people here aren't necessar-ily lazy, but they have lazy brains. You have to teach them to use their brains…people will just follow what their *bapak* [employer] says, it makes life easier' (KI 19, 10/5/97). In other words, the contextual environment, and not least cultural norms as well as the levels of education and training available to entrepreneurs and their workers, appear to have a major influence on deci-sion making processes and innovativeness within the sample of small enterprises.

Nevertheless, a difference in cultural perspective on the nature of innova-tion may add further insight into this part of the enquiry. According to one Javanese key informant, I was being too impatient in my hunt for evidence of innovation among the small enterprises in my study. He argued that local Bugis and Makassar people were innovative, but that changes took place more slowly in their cultural context than might be expected in the West. For this reason, it would often be very difficult to recognise the occurrence of innovation, simply because it was likely to be realised over several generations (KI 14, 16/5/97). In some ways this supported the experience of the young entrepreneur, discussed above, who had been able to introduce new ideas into the enterprise only after his father had died. Therefore, for many of the small enterprises, innovation should be perceived as a long-term process that required 'generational change'.[3] Yet the fact that innovation often straddled a change in ownership from one generation to another led to long delays in the implementation of changes enabling the small enterprises to respond to the increasingly specialised and fragmented market.

At a macro level, Schwarz (1999: 47) approached the issue of innovation in a somewhat different manner. He suggested that 'in social terms, a [Suharto-led] government obsessed with control squashes initiative and makes individuals afraid to speak their minds'. The levels of corruption and bureaucracy discussed in this chapter may well have been highly detrimental to the spirit of entrepreneurship in general, including that found among small-scale entrepreneurs and their workers, again emphasising the considerable influence of the local political environment on small enterprise operations.

Another internal organisational problem that hindered the growth of the small enterprises was that very few of their owners kept accounts.[4] This often made it difficult for the latter to estimate requirements for raw materials and other supplies on more than a day-to-day or week-to-week basis, and stocks of raw materials were commonly kept for only short periods. Correspondingly, few entrepreneurs attempted to overcome fluctuations in raw material prices by maintaining stocks on a long-term basis.

One consequence of poor accounting was that often when asked, the entrepreneurs could not estimate the monthly profits made by their enterprise, as they were operating on a piece-rate system. This in turn hindered their ability to save for more expensive items such as new technology or equipment. It also greatly constrained the ability of an entrepreneur to secure a bank loan because the feasibility assessments of the latter were complex and rigid, requiring 'a proper system of accounts, business permits and an easily examined cash flow' (Thamrin, 1993: 151; 30b, 29/1/97).

Reducing product quality was a means by which some entrepreneurs, sharing a certain 'survivalist' attitude, attempted to overcome declining profits. They lowered the quality of their goods and reduced prices, rather than try to make improvements to their products or marketing spheres. This was exemplified by three separate Javanese *tempe* and *tahu* entrepreneurs. They would mix corn, they explained, with soya beans, their main ingredient, to 'bulk out' the *tempe* and thereby produce 'an inferior product' (17a, 19a, 28/8/96; 69a, 16/9/96). Another alternative, but one with a similar outcome, was offered by a Makassar entrepreneur producing traditional ice-cream. Because the raw materials used were not of good quality, he sold his product at a price lower than the norm, a response governed by a lack of the working capital required to buy the quality of materials used by other entrepreneurs (184b, 12/3/97). Such a continuous cycle of low levels of rotation capital and poor-quality goods perpetually impeded enterprise development.

Being status orientated posed yet another barrier to 'growth'. Many Bugis and Makassar people were very sensitive to this issue, one that emanated from within the enterprises themselves. The pressure to conform often ensured that a significant portion of the enterprise profits were devoted to conspicuous consumption, rather than reinvested in the enterprise as capital (as discussed in Chapter 4). Pelras (1996a: 172) helps to explain this pressure:

Economic success, too, can contribute to a rise in status: when a person is wealthy, owns a lot of land and has a large and beautiful house, it is easily assumed that he has some – perhaps forgotten – traces of noble blood in his veins.

A variety of status symbols were valued by the entrepreneurs. Housing and ornamentation were two. Of the entrepreneurs interviewed, many had externally decorated their houses by adding accessories, while gold jewellery was frequently used as a show of wealth linked closely to social status (KI 12, 19/2/97). Intangible rather than physical symbols of status were also projected. A Muslim key informant remarked, for example, that he believed many small enterprises owned by Muslim people did not improve because of the significant prestige that their owners connected with going many times on the *Haj* to Mecca. Thus, if such entrepreneurs accumulated extra capital, sometimes even through a loan for enterprise development specifically, they would use it for the pilgrimage instead (KI 5, 25/8/96).[5] In addition, a researcher working at *PUKTI* reported that the effectiveness of loans given to small enterprises was linked to numerous problems associated with the high levels of conspicuous consumption among entrepreneurs. Instead of being invested into enterprises, loan money was often being used to buy cars, refrigerators, stereos and so on (confidential personal communication, 28/1/97).[6] Here it is important to note that although there were individuals in the city who saw such consumption as hindering the growth of small enterprises because of the limited reinvestment, such consumption was within many of the entrepreneurs' *own* definitions of 'success'.

BROADER ENVIRONMENTAL CONSTRAINTS

Whilst internal organisation of enterprises, production decisions and consumption patterns were argued by a range of entrepreneurs to hinder their ability to operate enterprises at full potential, even more barriers were evident in the broader contextual environment. This environment was highly competitive, as well as being shaped by a range of bureaucratic and often corrupt practices manipulated by a range of local actors.

The small enterprises studied in Makassar were operating in an intensively competitive environment. Competition came from other small enterprises, from larger firms producing similar goods in the city, and from shops importing products from elsewhere in Indonesia or from overseas. Part of the reason for this, as far as it involved Bugis people, might well have been related to the competitive nature of their society. In this, achievement leads to tension and competition as new hierarchies are formed, a process discussed in Chapter 4. In turn, this situation probably inhibited close co-operation among Bugis entrepreneurs, as each competed with their fellows to find their rightful place in society (see Millar, 1989).

Competition

Although there did not appear to be strong competition among members of clusters that had formed gradually over time, there certainly was among members of the *sentra* (officially sanctioned clusters) promoted by the local Department of Industry and Trade, and the Department of Co-operatives and Small Enterprises. As explained by one entrepreneur (127b, 26/2/97), this was because Department officials decided who was to be a member of the different *sentra* by walking around an area and observing which enterprises were located near each other, rather than discussing the potential clusters with entrepreneurs in the area, a point confirmed later by a Department official (confidential personal communication 1/5/97). Thus while in the past entrepreneurs might have been members of different 'informal' clusters, suddenly they were required by an external agency to join outsiders or previous competitors in a *sentra*. A blacksmith in this situation said that his main competition was from other members of the same *sentra*, which he had been made to join in 1995 (43a, 12/9/96). A second blacksmith operating in another *sentra* in the city had faced the same problem, his main competitors being the other members of his *sentra*, which had been organised in 1994 (44a, 10/9/96). Similar problems with official clusters were also found by Berry *et al.* (1999) among small enterprises making press tiles in Java.

Competition within different production sectors disadvantaged a number of other entrepreneurs. These, producing a range of products, complained of the levels of competition they faced from other small enterprises in the city, evidently because of the ease of entry into their particular sector of production. This was confirmed by an entrepreneur making floor tiles, pillars and pots from cement. He reported a decline in profits because there were too many competitors, especially in the area in which he was located (124b, 25/2/97). Similarly, a woman *songkok* entrepreneur claimed that her profits had also declined over the past five years. As she explained, 'there are now too many businesses like this. I have big problems with capital and because I have to send all my children to school', hence losing a source of free labour, as well as having to pay for school equipment (27b, 28/1/97). Another example was of a Javanese man making *bakso*. In his case competition had continued to increase as Bugis and Makassar people began to produce *bakso*, whereas in the past it had been the exclusive domain of Javanese people (53b, 4/2/97). Perhaps a pertinent point in this regard is that these small entrepreneurs faced direct competition from others of their kind because they did not enjoy the more protected or 'sheltered' position attained when operating as a subcontracting enterprise.

As well as competition among themselves, small enterprises also faced competition from larger enterprises and from imports to the city, most of which came from Java, via Surabaya. Such competition had a negative impact on the viability of small enterprises in Makassar. This point was well made by one small subcontracting goldsmith who believed that the future of his enterprise was threatened because, increasingly, the Chinese gold shops had their own goldsmiths working on the premises, thus reducing the number of orders available for subcontracting Bugis goldsmiths in the city. He was concerned that in future the traditional linkages between Bugis goldsmiths and the Chinese suppliers/retailers would disappear, perhaps because only the larger goldsmithing enterprises or those with specific skills would be able to maintain subcontracting relationships with the shops (26a, 27/8/96).[7]

Small-scale entrepreneurs producing other goods were also affected. For instance, a woman tailor reported that the increasing range of clothes and new fashions being imported from outside the city had resulted in declining profits for her enterprise (18b, 27/1/97), while a blacksmith maintained that it had become increasingly difficult to compete with larger businesses in the city that imported bolts from Java (168b, 10/3/97). Yet another entrepreneur, in this case making *songkok* (the national hat for men), lamented that she had problems importing regular supplies of blue velvet, her primary raw material, from Jakarta or Surabaya because of demand for the same materials on Java (55a, 9/9/96).

Bureaucracy and corruption[8]

Competition from other small enterprises and also larger enterprises was only one of the barriers that affected the performance of many entrepreneurs. Their difficulties were accentuated by bureaucratic influences and corruption. These made the immediate institutional environment for the small enterprises in Makassar a difficult one in which to operate. It was shaped by a range of authorities responsible for city by-laws, health and environmental regulations, as well as control of the provision of infrastructure, education and training. Their effect was to impose a maze of procedures to be followed for registration and taxation, such that obtaining formal credit was beyond the capabilities of most small-scale entrepreneurs in the city (Spath, 1992). Indeed, procedures to be met in order to become a recognised business activity in Makassar were complex, expensive and time-consuming, strong confirmation of Spath's (1992: 10) argument that 'what still prevails in many developing countries is a legal and regulatory environment which is badly distorted, and an administrative and institutional setting which is hardly supportive and often discriminatory'.

As a result of the bureaucratic impediments they faced, many small enterprises in Makassar were operating without a *Surat Izin Tempat Usaha-SITU* (licence for a business or work site) or a *Surat Izin Untuk Perusahaan-SIUP* (licence for a business or enterprise to operate; one must have a *SITU* before acquiring a *SIUP*). These had to be obtained every five years from different locations in the city,[9] and were expensive documents for small-scale entrepreneurs. For many of them there were no perceived immediate (or delayed) benefits in having such documents. Indeed, one entrepreneur, who had attempted to gain a licence, but gave up trying because of the financial costs involved, observed that 'there's lots of corruption if you want a *SITU*. You have to pay at the office an amount depending on what the official there decides for that day' (175b, 11/3/97). When this issue of licensing procedures was discussed with another entrepreneur, he simply joked '*Indonesia, negara korupsi*' (Indonesia, a corrupt country) (79b, 11/2/97), a point substantiated by Hill (1996: 116) who asserts that 'the operation of the licensing regime is sometimes quite different from official objectives and intentions. And the costs to the business sector are not insubstantial, in compliance, uncertainty and illegal extractions.'

Not being officially recognised meant increased insecurity for such enterprises. As many were operating 'illegally', it was common for officials from the Department of Industry and Trade or the City Council to walk around districts known to house many small enterprises and ask to see licences. These requests were met by a denial that a small enterprise existed on the site, many being hidden at the rear of the premises, or bribes of cigarettes or money were given to the officials. Only when the hassles became too frequent did many entrepreneurs decide they must try to obtain a *SITU* (KI 2, 26/11/96). An additional pressure to register derived from the fact that enterprises without a licence were denied access to technical assistance or training, formal credit institutions and positive government assistance.

Hidden 'extra costs', such as bribes, under-the-table payments, 'enforced' promises of services which must be upheld at a later date and so on, were expected at all levels within government and many non-government institutions. To meet them cost time and money for small-scale entrepreneurs as well as larger industry operators. But the 'extra costs' confronting small-scale entrepreneurs in Makassar when applying for licences did not end there. Those who gained such a licence faced yet more 'hidden costs' if they wanted to undertake training or apply for credit from banks or non-banking institutions. One successful small-scale entrepreneur producing bottled drinks reported that many people from Government departments with whom he had previously dealt visited his enterprise throughout the year requesting money. This happened especially before *Idul Fitri* and Christmas, the entrepreneur being a Christian from Manado (KI 23, 6/5/97).[10] Other entrepreneurs also reported similar requests, calling such corruption '*penyakit*' (a disease), one silversmith entrepreneur claiming that 'it's a disease, the whole country's got it' (130b, 26/2/97). However, such requests usually occurred only in the case of the more 'visible' small enterprises, suggesting another reason why smaller enterprises did not wish to innovate and expand because, as they became more 'visible', such demands could rapidly increase operating costs (KI 7, 8/2/97).

Schwarz (1999: 135) has identified two levels of corruption in Indonesia. The first consists of the small bribes, pay-offs and other inducements that 'grease the wheels of the bureaucracy', while the second is the 'big corruption' that has 'profound implications for Indonesia's economic and political future' (Schwarz, 1999: 137).[11] The first category is generally regarded as fairly inescapable, in a country where civil servants are paid very low salaries.[12] In fact Schwarz (1999: 135) contends that the relationship between civil servants and the general public is like a 'quasi-feudal culture', in which 'it would be more accurate to say that government employees are the "owners" of the nation and the general public their servants'. Whilst such attitudes may be slowly changing, most government employees still see their salaries as a retainer, extra payments from the public making up the rest of their legitimate portion of income. Indeed, challenging the idea that the corruption is solely linked to salary levels, a *Jakarta Post* editorial (3 March 2000) argued that after the Government proposed to raise civil servant salaries in 2000, the 'experience has taught this nation that breaches of public trust by bureaucrats are not so much to do with the size of their wage packets but mainly with their mentality'.

'Big corruption' also impacts on the small enterprises in Makassar. It not only hinders the growth of the economy, but also adds to political uncertainty. Cronyism in business actions impact on all levels of society, providing examples of how one gets ahead in business. Indeed, as Schwarz (1999: 149) points out, 'examples abound of ministers, provincial governors, regional military commanders, district chiefs and others operating miniature patronage networks based on the model used by Soeharto' (see also Kingsbury, 1998). Moreover, as was asserted in another earlier *Jakarta Post* editorial, 'corruption is not only rife and deeply rooted in Indonesia, but it has become accepted by many people as a fact of life' (*Jakarta Post*, 1 April 1997). Thus 'corruption has remained an endemic problem' (Mackie and MacIntyre, 1994: 21) and not surprisingly it has often been reported that Indonesia is the most corrupt country in the Southeast Asian region.[13] More globally, Transparency International, an 'anti-corruption watchdog', rated Indonesia ninety-sixth out of ninety-nine countries on its *Corruption Perception Index 1999* with a score of 1.7 (zero indicating a country indexed as 'highly corrupt'), a deterioration from 2.0 in 1998 (*New Zealand Herald*, 24 September 1998; Transparency International, 2000).

There is much evidence that, without doubt, the contextual environment created a range of barriers which impeded the operations of small enterprises in the city. Delving even deeper into this predicament it was found that while there were public and private sector institutional arrangements designed, one might say, to assist small enterprises in gaining credit, developing new marketing schemes and providing training, the potential recipients were continually thwarted in their efforts to do so by the constraints and norms of the bureaucratic environment which permeated local Indonesian society. The reality for the small-scale entrepreneurs was one of having to give pay-backs, bribes, and to deal with an impenetrable bureaucracy.

When field work for this book was undertaken there were a number of institutional arrangements for the provision of credit already established or being initiated to help small enterprises in Indonesia, but these were predominantly concentrated in the Western Islands, or on rural development.[14]

Those that targeted urban small enterprises appeared to have complex lending procedures, and were focused on well-established small enterprises. Earlier in this chapter it was observed that very few entrepreneurs in the Makassar sample had gained access to formal credit facilities and that many more were 'too scared' to attempt to gain such access or did not have any understanding of the procedures involved. Moreover, it was clear from the many discouraging reports from those entrepreneurs who had actually attempted to gain access to such credit that the bureaucratic nature of the banking sector was hindering the development of many small enterprises. Clearly, 'an attempt to eliminate these extra costs would help our entrepreneurs improve operating efficiency' (*Bisnis Indonesia*, reported in *Jakarta Post*, 25 January 1997).

Impediments erected by banks took various forms. That small-scale entrepreneurs were usually requested by the bank to produce a proposal setting out why they wished to borrow funds was a significant hurdle for the many who did not understand what was required (64a, 6/9/96). The time delays between applying for a loan and actually receiving the money were also far too long to meet the more immediate needs of a number of the entrepreneurs. One such *songkok* entrepreneur declared that he had waited for sixteen months before finally obtaining his loan, but even then he had had to pay the bank official 5 per cent of the total amount as a 'tip' (73a, 5/9/96). Such procedures led another entrepreneur who made aluminium cupboards and window frames to the conclusion that the corruption involved in gaining support for his enterprise negated any possible positive results. He added that 'any process with officials takes a long time, it's very difficult to obtain credit and you have to give a tip to the staff' (88a, 24/9/96). Likewise, a goldsmith poignantly described this 'catch-22' situation in which many small-scale entrepreneurs found themselves because 'the bureaucracy is too complicated and long. The bank staff keep a commission from the total amount they say they'll lend you. This can be about 5 to 10 per cent. Because I can't get working capital, my volume of production has declined by 30 per cent' (50a, 11/9/96).

Yet another difficulty for small-scale entrepreneurs was that often they wanted only a small amount of capital, perhaps less than the minimum banks would lend (95b, 18/2/97). This was the case with one making cement-based flowerpots and ornamental pillars who, when asked where he would seek capital, replied, 'I don't know really, I haven't yet and if I did I'd only want a small loan or I'd be in too much debt, it would cause too many problems later' (165b, 6/3/97). Adding to their difficulties was a lack of the necessary collateral to set against a loan from a bank, the situation for one furniture entrepreneur who explained: 'I can't get a loan, I haven't got any security and the interest is too high' (24a, 29/8/96).

High interest rates charged by banks for loans of capital presented a further significant barrier to entrepreneurs, the average 20 per cent per annum interest rate charged by banks being well beyond the means of most small-scale entrepreneurs (KI 1, 17/1/97; *Jakarta Post*, 20 January 1997). In this regard the experience of one entrepreneur, a welder, was certainly far from atypical in that while one such barrier was often crucial, it was not the only one. In his case the effect of high interest rates was exacerbated by 'too much bureaucracy' (11a, 22/8/96). In turn, the inability to secure a loan impacted negatively on the welder's business insofar as 'I can only be known through my previous customers, I can't advertise, it affects the capacity of my firm to develop a lot and makes business more difficult'.

As well as the numerous barriers preventing entrepreneurs from securing loans, there were also many who were unaware of the different types of assistance in theory available to them in the city. Their ignorance appeared to be related to a lack of understanding among the entrepreneurs concerning the roles of the different government departments. None of those relevant to the entrepreneurs' needs had offices near areas with high densities of enterprises, so it was physically difficult for entrepreneurs to gain access to information and training. Their difficulties in this regard were compounded by a general reluctance to approach official channels for assistance, especially when details were disseminated among entrepreneurs about the numerous obstacles to be faced.[15]

Expressing an awareness of the loan-raising difficulties confronting small enterprises, the Government had established a scheme specifically to help them to apply for low interest rate loans through *Badan Usaha Milik Negara (BUMN)*, or state-owned enterprises, introduced in Chapter 4. Nonetheless, one Makassar entrepreneur producing wooden tables said that the process of securing such a loan had been confusing and time-consuming (35b, 29/1/97). His first visit was to the *Kanwil Koperasi* (local level office of the Department of Co-operatives and Small Enterprises), from where, after his loan application had been approved, it was passed to the *BUMN* office in Makassar. In 1997 this was managed by the state-owned enterprise *P.T. Semen Tonasa*, a local cement producer. A number of entrepreneurs interviewed had been confused about this stage of the process, believing erroneously that they had to travel to the actual *Tonasa* factory, situated approximately 60 kilometres to the north of the city, to negotiate their loan. Even after the entrepreneur involved had obtained his loan, a process taking as long as five months, he had been required to pay 6 per cent interest per year. However, he had heard informally that if one approached the actual *BUMN* industry directly, bypassing the Department of Co-operatives and Small Enterprises, one could gain the loan for 2 per cent. Nevertheless, because of the time and energy involved, this entrepreneur for one was not prepared to apply for another loan from the same source in the future. Rather, he would go to a bank or ask family members to help him.

Clearly, then, there is much evidence that the excessive bureaucracy involved was a major deterrent to small-scale entrepreneurs even contemplating an application for loan assistance initially promoted in their interests by the Government. Furthermore, it was argued by a Chinese entrepreneur who produced drinks that the assistance was not available equally to all ethnic groups. He believed that it was easier for *Bumiputra* (ethnic Indonesians) to gain loans from the Government-controlled *BUMN* than it was for Chinese, and that the high level of bureaucracy made it far too difficult for him to gain such a loan (12a, 16/8/96).

Koperasi (co-operatives) were yet another government initiative set up to support small enterprises. Controlled by the Department of Co-operatives and Small Enterprises, their role was to assist small enterprises in obtaining access to credit facilities, technology and training. Nevertheless, as established earlier in this chapter, few of the enterprises studied belonged to them. This was largely because members had first to establish a co-operative themselves and then, before assistance was made available, write a report outlining its structure and membership. In effect, there appeared to be no initial grassroots support to encourage and guide the growth of such groups (Department of Co-operatives and Small Enterprises official, confidential personal communication, 18 February 1997). A few of the entrepreneurs interviewed were aware that such co-operatives covering their enterprise type existed locally, but they had little understanding of their functions, a situation which again emphasises the lack of effective assistance from the Department in publicising and marketing such support systems (7b, 22/1/97).

In theory, once enterprises belonged to such a co-operative, they could attempt to gain loans either through the co-operative itself, or directly through the Department of Co-operatives and Small Enterprises. Although the latter had a section to help small enterprises with credit, achieving such an outcome was fraught with difficulties. Again, and perhaps predictably, bureaucratic practice impeded the process. This was exemplified by one small entrepreneur in the Makassar sample, a tailor, who maintained that he had had continual problems with the Department. In particular, the section dealing with credit for co-operative members had a number of staff who demanded tips or percentages of the total credit received by the entrepreneur. In this case, the tailor had finally given up trying to arrange such a loan (68a, 16/9/96).

There appeared to be very little co-ordination or co-operation among the different Government departments assisting small enterprises in the city, such as between the Department of Co-operatives and Small Enterprises, and the Department of Industry and Trade. There was also a significant lack of current data concerning small enterprises within either department, and a fragmented approach to supporting different initiatives to help small enterprises, leading to the conclusion that there is a notable waste of financial resources due to the differing bureaucratic agendas within institutions. Intervention by the Government to help small enterprises with training and credit programmes, as well as appearing to be biased in terms of ethnicity and gender, had been concentrated largely on specific *sentra* (officially recognised clusters), with entrepreneurs operating outside such clusters often ignored.

A number of key informants were critical of the local government's role in supporting small enterprises. As one informant commented rather cynically, 'the Mayor, he's not really any use at all. He shuts his eyes and ears to such difficulties' (KI 19, 6/11/96). Another informant maintained that there was a lack of support to start up businesses or improve existing ones in Makassar because the Government was so centrally controlled by mainly Javanese officials who concentrated on development only in Jakarta or Java. He lamented that it was difficult to get highly skilled city planners to work in the outer islands because the most talented civil servants always stayed in Jakarta (KI 6, 12/5/97).

Corruption at various levels of government also limited small enterprises from being able to gain overseas financial assistance. A comment made by an Overseas Trade Office official highlighted their predicament: 'our country in general is hesitant to become directly involved with [helping] small enterprises in Indonesia because it believes the Government Departments in Indonesia would screw [sic] any programme to make money out of it' (KI 20, 12/5/1997). Instead he believed that it was more beneficial to small enterprises if support was provided to local non-governmental organisations (NGOs), or semi-autonomous institutions partly funded by the Government, but with private donor support as well.

Nonetheless, apart from the Chamber of Commerce and *Pusat Pengembangan Usaha Kecil Kawasan Timur Indonesia (PUKTI)* (Centre for Development of Small Enterprises, East Indonesia), the role of semi-autonomous institutions involved with small enterprises in the city was very limited. Whilst officials at both of these organisations knew of other such groups working with small enterprises in the city, there appeared to be little or no collaboration between them. This seemed to be because of mutual distrust and a reluctance to share information, perhaps due to political reasons, such as local patron–client relationships that had become instrumental in the operations of different groups (KI 14, 5/3/97). The lack of collaboration was made clear when a *PUKTI* official had to guess that there were four or five NGOs operating with small enterprises in the city (but could only name two) and stated that they usually focused on one specific type of product or cluster to work with. He believed that NGOs with an agenda to help small enterprises tended to prefer to focus on agriculture and fisheries in rural areas, also categorised by the Indonesian Government as small enterprises (KI 1, 14/4/97).

CONCLUSION: A PLETHORA OF BARRIERS

The small enterprises of Makassar sampled during field work were operating in an environment featuring a plethora of internal and external barriers to their advancement. Many entrepreneurs displayed a lack of basic production organisation, some resorting to the production of poor-quality goods to 'survive' in a highly competitive environment. Such competition, from external sources, came from other enterprises and larger businesses making commodities within Makassar, as well as from those importing goods from outside the region.

The difficulties of small enterprises studied were compounded by a number of other external factors. Foremost were the bureaucratic practices among a range of officials within the city who demanded tips and under-the-counter payments from many of the entrepreneurs and offered little in return. Indeed, the tangled web of Government institutions supposedly charged with helping small enterprises had little co-ordination and was riddled with corruption. This not only hindered access to credit and training for many of the entrepreneurs, but also made the position of small enterprises even more tenuous in the local economy.

There is much compelling evidence, then, that small enterprises in Makassar operated in a very difficult environment indeed. This realisation provides strong endorsement of the wisdom of adopting the *small enterprise integrative framework* approach. In particular it has become evident that the contextual environment – which the approach emphasises the importance of – comprising complex social relations and culture and gender bias, the obstructive political environment, a corrupt bureaucracy and a highly competitive local economic environment, influenced or impacted on the organisation of the small enterprises in a variety of strategic and usually negative ways. For the small enterprises it was seldom a single factor but rather a constellation of factors that prevented them from achieving the economic growth and development identified by many – although not all – small-scale entrepreneurs in the Makassar sample as their preferred goals.

Building on the broad understanding of the way in which small enterprises in Makassar operate, and especially of the constraints to growth which many faced, the *small enterprise integrative framework* is further utilised in Chapter 8 to explore the way in which, since mid-1997, the economic crisis has impacted on the small enterprises in the sample.

8 Shifting fortunes of small enterprises

> From afar it can sometimes seem that the effects of the crisis are homogeneous and all-pervasive . . . And yet it is clear that not only are the differences between countries highly significant in mapping out the effects of the crisis but that even within regions of countries there are some industries and some people who have been much more severely affected than others. Indeed, there are people who are doing very well. While some unevenness of impact is predictable, there have also been some surprises.
>
> (Rigg, 1998: 12)

The analysis of small enterprises in Makassar has shown with certainty that a web of local socio-economic and political interactions influenced their daily decision-making processes. It follows that events occurring within the broader economic scene contain the potential to have a range of impacts upon these enterprises, as did the economic crisis that hit Southeast Asia in 1997.[1]

The economic crisis was blamed on a number of different factors, including: 'Overvalued currencies. Speculators. Hot Money. Cronyism. Excessive investments in property and stocks. Financial liberalization without safeguards. Take your pick' (*Asiaweek*, 17 July 1998: 38). Initially, in early 1997, the Thai Government failed to deliver on a promise to buy the bad property loans of financial institutions, prompting foreign creditors to call in loans to Thai banks and businesses. The financial meltdown accelerated with a rush to gain hard currency and the *baht* was devalued (*Asiaweek*, 17 July 1998; see also Hill, 1999a).

In comparison to Thailand, the initial effects of the economic crisis on Indonesia appeared to be quite mild. It was argued that Indonesia's political system was more stable, its financial sector had been liberalised earlier, and its current account deficit was lower (Hill, 1998). Nonetheless, as speculation rose the financial meltdown worsened, and Indonesia, like Thailand and South Korea, was forced to approach the International Monetary Fund (IMF) for loans and recovery programmes (*The Economist*, 7 March 1998; *Asiaweek*, 17 July 1998).

By August 1997 the Indonesian *Rupiah,* beset by speculators, had fallen to a then historic low of Rp.2682 to US$1. In October 1997 the Indonesian Government signed a US$23 billion rescue package with the IMF. On 5 December Suharto began a ten-day rest period and rumours about his health led to the currency falling below Rp.4000 to US$1. One week later Suharto decided not to attend an Association of South East Asian Nations (ASEAN) meeting in Kuala Lumpur and the *Rupiah* fell to Rp.5000 to US$1 because of continuing concerns regarding Suharto's health (*Asiaweek*, 17 July 1998).

By the beginning of 1998 the Indonesian economy was in a dire situation, and people began to talk increasingly of a *krismon* (abbreviated from *krisis moneter*: monetary crisis). On 6 January, President Suharto announced the 1998 Budget, which reneged on IMF pledges and contained unrealistic targets for growth, inflation and the exchange rate (Hill, 1998). The *Rupiah* then fell to Rp.10,000 to US$1 during the following week. On 21 January, Suharto confirmed he would stand for President for a seventh five-year term and on 10 March he was re-elected President, with Habibie as his Vice-President.

On 12 May, riots erupted in Jakarta after *Angkatan Bersenjata Republik Indonesia (ABRI)* (former name of the Indonesian Armed Forces) troops shot six students, instantly killing four, who were protesting Suharto's re-election and corrupt Government practices (Schwarz, 1999). Initially politically motivated, the protests then turned into a devastating looting and raping spree, described by Schwarz (personal communication, 9 September 1998) as a 'humanitarian disaster'. Ethnic Chinese in particular were targeted, due to their perceived high relative wealth (see also Kingsbury 1998; *New Zealand Herald*, 4 June 1998). While debate continues as to whether or not the riots were masterminded, the destruction they wrought – economic, social and psychological – was phenomenal. On 21 May, bowing to pressure and advice from a number of Members of Parliament and past vice-presidents, Suharto resigned. Habibie was sworn in as his successor on the same day (*Asiaweek*, 17 July 1998; 24 July 1998; Kingsbury, 1998).

During 1998 the Indonesian economy collapsed. The *Rupiah* sank to Rp.16,000 to the US dollar before returning to Rp.13,000 in August (Sadli, 1999). As a result, foreign and domestic investors left the market and bankruptcy struck hundreds of corporations. The banking system virtually ground to a halt, there was little lending, and dozens of banks became insolvent. Inflation rose by 78 per cent in 1998, but dropped back to between zero and 2 per cent in 1999, according to different sources (Dodd, 2000; *Jakarta Post*, 22 February 2000). Then, 'the country reshape[d] its political landscape ahead of general elections set for mid-1999 – the first genuinely competitive polls since 1955' (McBeth, 1998: 20).

Accordingly, the newly elected People's Consultative Assembly (MPR) elected Abdurrahman Wahid President on 20 October and Megawati Sukarnoputri was appointed Vice-President the following day (see Cameron (1999) and the United States Department of State's *Country Reports on Human Rights* (2000) for details of the restructuring process).[2]

Although the severe effects of the economic crisis eased to some extent during 1999, the negative impacts were still apparent, the country's annual per capita gross domestic product standing at only US$690, after falling by 18 per cent through 1998 (Rudiyanto, 2000). This statistic hides the highly uneven distribution of wealth and power within the population however, a factor which continues to exacerbate tensions, and unemployment in particular (United States Department of State, 2000). Early in 2000, for example, it was reported by the Manpower Minister, Bomer Pasaribu, that unemployment had reached 36 million (*South China Morning Post*, 24 February 2000).

Early in 2000 too, although the measure was of no help to the unemployed, the Government announced that the minimum daily wage rates would rise across the country. This resulted in the minimum daily wage in Jakarta rising from Rp.5750 a day in 1997, to Rp.9533 a day from 1 April 2000 (*Jakarta Post*, 22 February 2000), whereas that for Makassar rose to Rp.6667 a day in 2000, from Rp.3750 in 1997. However, this occurred at the same time as the purchasing power of the *Rupiah* had fallen dramatically. Indeed, it was estimated that of all the Indonesian regions, the new minimum wage would cover only the living expenses of a single person in onshore Riau and parts of East Java. It would not cover the cost of living of a worker in Makassar, while only covering 81 per cent of such costs in Jakarta (*Jakarta Post*, 23 February 2000).[3]

While the long-term impact of the *krismon* on small enterprises in Indonesia has yet to be determined, there appear to be four broad interpretations emerging in the literature concerning the short-term impact. First, there has been a dramatic increase in the numbers of small enterprises, with new opportunities for entrepreneurship having become available. Second, because small enterprises were doing well before the crisis this enabled them to respond quickly to changing demands, maintaining their record of good performance (Sandee *et al.*, 2000). Third, small enterprises have been on balance more negatively than positively affected by the crisis (Tambunan, 2000). Fourth, there have been differential impacts depending on whether the small enterprises imported their raw materials or sourced them locally (van Diermen *et al.*, 2000). Nevertheless, in the context of small enterprises in Makassar, I would propose an even more complex interpretation outlined below.

First, however, it is important to acknowledge the changing context within which these enterprises were operating. The World Bank estimates that approximately 14.1 per cent of the population were living below the official poverty line in 1998, up significantly from 1996 when the figure reported was 11.3 per cent (World Bank, 1998; Booth, 1999).[4] Nevertheless, such figures must be read with caution simply because Indonesian poverty levels are notoriously difficult to estimate. In July and August 1998 three different documents estimating poverty levels were published by the World Bank, the International Labour Organisation (ILO) and the Indonesian Central Board of Statistics (CBS). These institutions used different methodologies to calculate the numbers of people living below the poverty line, thus arriving at radically different estimates of 14.1 per cent, 48 per cent and 39.9 per cent respectively (Booth, 1999: 132). Then, the Central Board of Statistics estimated an increase to 96 million, or 47 per cent of the population living below the poverty line by the end of 1998 (Healy and Tesoro, 1998). Vigorous debate focuses on these figures in pursuit of which if any of these estimates is closest to the truth. Cameron (1999) for one contends that the World Bank estimates may be more accurate than those of the ILO and CBS, while Breman (1999) argues that the World Bank manipulated its figures, and that poverty increased to between 30 to 35 per cent. Even so, it remains that 'headcount poverty rates are not sensitive to the degree of poverty, and so do not tell us whether those who were already poor are now poorer' (Cameron, 1999: 12).

Nevertheless, no matter which of the poverty estimates is the most reliable, it is clear that the economically vulnerable section of Indonesian society includes numerous small-scale entrepreneurs, many of whom were close to the official poverty line before the *krismon* (Healy and Tesoro, 1998; Booth, 1999). Despite these circumstances, in late July 1998 President Habibie was of the view that 'the experience of developed nations shows that in a depression, small and medium-sized companies become the backbone of the economy' (quoted in *The Straits Times*, 29 July 1998).

Habibie also admitted that the economic strategies pursued by Suharto had contained failings and even that the biggest business people had enjoyed unfair advantages. He declared that official efforts to encourage small businesses had been hampered by the disproportionate power of large enterprises, and efforts to partner small and large enterprises had failed because of a lack of legal certainty necessary to give small enterprises protection. Habibie then announced that his Government would work to ensure that small enterprises gained the attention they deserved (*The Straits Times*, 29 July 1998). However, few programmes putting this into practice were actioned during his time in office. As policies to help small enterprises under Suharto had often failed because of poor organisation and the bureaucracy involved, it was feared that the same would happen under Habibie and that, similarly, his Government would find scapegoats for its failures (Wanandi, 1999).

Nevertheless, the Government maintained that Law No. 5/1999 on the 'Prohibition of Monopolistic Practices and Unhealthy Competition' would benefit small enterprises, which are exempt from the law, largely because 'the law was designed to protect small and medium-sized companies from monopoly practices' (Pfletschinger, quoted in *Jakarta Post*, 21 September 1999; *Asia Pulse*, 21 September 1999; Lindsey, 2000). Yet it was also argued by the *Jakarta Post* (21 September 1999) that as this the law alone would not be effective in bolstering small enterprise development, the Government should help with concessional loan financing and the establishment of an organisational forum as a political lobby. In July 1999, the Ministry of Industry and Trade also launched a 'Technical Assistance and Training

Programme' to help small and medium-scale companies (*Jakarta Post*, 31 July 1999), while a newly established financial institution, '*PT Permodalan Nasional Madani*'(*PNM*) began operations in August 1999 with initial funds of Rp.300 million for small enterprise credit schemes. The latter has been criticised as a further example of the inconsistencies of the Suharto and Habibie Governments regarding credit for small enterprises, namely that they start new schemes rather than supporting and developing similar ones already in operation (*Indonesian Observer*, 20 July 1999).

After Abdurrahman Wahid was elected President in October 1999 a handful of plans and policy statements concerning small enterprises, as part of wider Government economic initiatives, were announced. Following the 'National Workshop on Small and Medium Enterprise Development' held in Jakarta in December 1999, an Inter-Ministerial Task Force was established to prepare a strategy to assist small and medium enterprises (SMEs). The Workshop recommended:

> that the strategy include greater co-ordination in SME support schemes; further deregulation to reduce SME business costs; more effective financial intermediation; improved business and technical services; and more informed policy-making through improved consultation with stakeholders.
> (Asian Development Bank, 1999: online)

The next month, in January 2000 the Indonesian Government and the International Monetary Fund (IMF) signed a new 'Letter of Intent', one among the many that had been drafted. This one included, in Clause 95, a Government commitment to small and medium-sized enterprises which read that:

> 95. The government is committed to empowering small and medium enterprises (SMEs). However, we recognise that many current SME support programmes have failed to meet the needs of the SME community. We are thus committed to re-evaluate government interventions so as to increase private sector involvement in SME support programmes.
> (cited in *Jakarta Post*, 22 January 2000; see Cameron (1999) for details of other IMF agreements)

It was also stated that the Inter-Ministerial Task Force was preparing a strategy for small and medium enterprises with the help of the Asian Development Bank and the World Bank (*Jakarta Post*, 22 January 2000). In a related move, the Asian Development Bank reported in March 2000 that it was granting a loan worth US$200 million to Indonesia for a programme aimed at liberalising and deregulating industry, while also increasing opportunities for small and medium-sized enterprises (McIndoe, 2000). Since that time, under both the Wahid and Sukarnoputri governments (Megawati Sukarnoputri became President in July 2001) other similar schemes have been introduced, such as those of Bank Indonesia and the Asian Development Bank (Asian Development Bank, 2002; *Jakarta Post*, 22 June 2002). In theory, 'the policy context for many of Indonesia's [small and medium enterprises] has been radically altered by the recent and ongoing crisis' (Berry *et al.*, 1999: 22). However, full implementation of the Government's programmes and the IMF agreements cannot be taken for granted.

UNEVEN IMPACTS OF THE *KRISMON*

The impacts of the crisis were unevenly felt across Indonesia, Java evidently 'suffering the overwhelming impact of job losses and rising poverty' (Forrester, 1999: 4), with small enterprises there affected more than those in other islands (Berry *et al.*, 1999). Newspaper reports recorded political and economic unrest in Java with dramatic and immediate impact on the daily lives of small-scale entrepreneurs. Furthermore, ethnic tensions and direct conflict destroyed thousands of such enterprises physically and/or economically, while many of the psychological impacts have yet to be recognised (*Guardian*, 14 May 1998; 18 May 1998).

In Java it was found that small enterprises with export links had fared better during the crisis than those producing for the domestic market, which either remained as before or became worse off. Most affected in a negative sense were those enterprises that were highly dependent on imported inputs. It was also found that small enterprises in urban areas faired worse than those in rural areas. In an attempt to survive, various coping mechanisms were adapted including the use of cheaper inputs than in the past, and reducing the size of the labour force (Berry *et al.*, 1999; Tambunan, 2000; van Diermen *et al.*, 2000).

Given that the majority of Indonesian manufacturing was located on Java, many workers displaced from companies there because of the economic crisis entered the small enterprise sector in an attempt to eke out an existence. This led, in turn, to a decline in incomes, and increased competition for existing small enterprises (Hill, 1998; Ahmed, 1999). Compounding these problems, whereas in previous economic downturns a common response for urban workers and small-scale entrepreneurs alike would have been to return to the countryside, in this situation the rural sector too was hit by the *krismon*, as well as by widespread drought. Thus, a traditional 'shock absorber' of urban economic downturn was not as absorbent as in the past (Nasution, personal communication, 9 September 1998; Forrester, 1999). Indeed, it was reported in *The Economist* (25 April 1998) that although in early 1998 the Government cut train fares from Jakarta for those making the annual trip back to their home villages for *Idul Fitri*, and then raised them for the return journey, many still returned to the capital due to food shortages in their villages. Yet, while such impacts have been recorded on Java, have the outcomes for small enterprises elsewhere in the Indonesian archipelago been similar in kind and severity?

In my search for an answer to that question, a return visit was made to Makassar in January 1999 to ascertain whether the widely reported negative consequences of the economic crisis on small enterprises throughout Indonesia accurately conveyed what was happening in Makassar too. At this point, while making an initial attempt to assess the situation there, the story becomes increasingly complex.

SMALL ENTERPRISES IN MAKASSAR

Despite the economic crisis, the majority of small-scale entrepreneurs interviewed in Makassar in 1999 had not experienced a significant change in their operations or the profit levels of their enterprises. Instead, it was stated repeatedly that the barriers to growth that entrepreneurs faced remained those found in initial interviews in 1996/1997, as discussed in Chapter 7 (KI 19, 14/1/99; various small-scale entrepreneurs, personal communication, 14–20 January 1999).

One explanation for the continuing importance of these barriers, rather than new ones specifically related to the economic crisis, was that in the Outer Islands of Indonesia there were far fewer direct impacts from the economic crisis than in Java, with its strong links to the global economy through production and financial flows. As discussed in Chapter 4, although Indonesia has experienced rapid economic growth in the past, the pattern of large regional disparities within the country remains little changed.

Yet in the aftermath of the economic crisis, the fact that Sulawesi had been largely bypassed by industrialisation meant that the island had also been sheltered from many of the effects of the economic crisis that had hit Java's modern economy sectors, such as construction, manufacturing and financial services. Certainly on Sulawesi there was not the rapid growth in unemployment relating to the closure of factories and retailers that was reported for Java (Forrester, 1999; Turner, 2000).

This assessment was supported by an official at the South Sulawesi Chamber of Commerce (KI 19, 14/1/99). He pointed out that the economic situation in Makassar was not as 'bad' as elsewhere in Indonesia, and that small enterprises in Makassar had not been affected as much as those in Java. Other key informants in the city confirmed his statement. They believed that Sulawesi as a whole had not been affected as much as Java by the *krismon* (KI 3, 14/1/99; KI 2, 13/1/99).

The story for the minority

Small enterprises in the city had a range of experiences triggered by the economic crisis. As detailed below, for some the struggle to survive had intensified, as it had in the case of goldsmiths and food enterprises. For others, in sharp contrast, there was an improvement in economic status due to new demands by local people.

Goldsmiths were directly and negatively affected by the economic crisis due to the massive devaluation of the *Rupiah*, simply because the price of gold was dependent upon the value of the US dollar. Small-scale goldsmiths interviewed in January 1999 complained that it was difficult to estimate profits and hence to make plans for their enterprises because the price of gold had not only risen so much, but also fluctuated daily (goldsmiths, personal communication, 18 January 1999). Nonetheless, although some entrepreneurs had laid off workers, others had been able to retain them, often by drawing on capital savings to keep their enterprises in operation (goldsmith, personal communication, 19 January 1999).

Some Bugis goldsmith workers had, however, returned to their *kampung* if they owned land there. When asked what then happened to people working the land for them, as usually absent landowners, it was frequently reported that such workers would be made redundant but would continue to stay in the *kampung* where the *sistem kekeluargaan* (family system) would mean that no one went hungry (KI 2, 11/1/99; KI 6, 14/1/99; see Turner, 1998). In effect, there was a 'safety net' for workers in the villages – not a new phenomenon due to the economic crisis – but a traditional coping system, and one that in South Sulawesi had yet to be fractured significantly by modernisation (cf. Rigg, 1998). Yet at the same time, this lack of modernisation meant that the proportion of people returning to their villages was not nearly as large as on Java, or indeed as had been recorded in Thailand (Rigg, 1998).

Rising prices for numerous staple goods throughout Indonesia resulted in many raw materials for small enterprises – such as cotton, wheat flour, cooking oil and sugar – becoming too expensive for entrepreneurs to purchase. For example, it was reported in the *Jakarta Post* (18 August 1998) that 'the 300 per cent price increase of wheat flour since early this year has left most small and medium bakers on the brink of collapse'. Not only that; it was predicted in the same edition that 'the recent increase in the wheat flour price would force most medium and small-scale noodle producers to shut their business because they could not afford to buy raw materials anymore' (ibid.).

Perhaps not surprisingly, then, the price of noodles in the local markets in Makassar had risen from Rp.3000/kg to Rp.8000/kg, while *daging bakso* (meat ball soup) had escalated from Rp.6000/kg to Rp.15,000/kg. In addition, because farmers had faced increased prices for inputs such as imported fertilisers, the price of local produce in markets throughout the city and local *kampung* had moved upwards in consequence. Nonetheless, an important survival strategy put in place among many small-scale food enterprises in Makassar was not to pass on increased costs to customers, and hence avoid the possibility of reduced demand. To do this many small-scale entrepreneurs simply reduced the quantity of a dish of prepared food such as *bakso* rather than increase the price. Thus whereas *bakso* (meat ball soup) usually had four or five meat balls in it, after the crisis this was reduced to two or three (small-scale entrepreneur, personal communication, 9 January 1999; Setiawan, 1999).

Some surprises

Not all small enterprises affected by the economic crisis recorded negative outcomes, however. It was a surprise to find that a major consequence of the economic crisis for several enterprises in Makassar had been an increase in demand for their goods from Central Sulawesi farmers involved in export crop production. For the farmers, the devaluation of the *Rupiah* had meant that many export crops became more competitive on the world market (Dicken and Yeung, 1999). Cocoa, coffee and clove farmers linked into exporting chains all saw dramatic price increases for their goods during 1998 as the *Rupiah* continued to weaken against the US dollar. The impact reverberated throughout the local economy for, as Booth (1999: 133) has pointed out, 'while it is true that not everyone, even in those regions where export production predominates, will benefit from these higher prices, many millions will do so, and many more [including some small enterprises in Makassar] will benefit indirectly from the expenditure effects of the export boom'. More specifically, Robinson (1999: online) noted that 'South Sulawesi's reliance on export crops cushioned it generally from the effects of the monetary crisis', while Cohen and Murphy (1999: 27) concluded that 'South Sulawesi's economy is relatively vibrant compared with Java's'.

Central, Southeast and South Sulawesi comprise the centre of Indonesia's cacao bean production and it was farmers from these provinces, with increased purchasing power, who began to buy more goods from Makassar small enterprises (Potter, 2000). Before the economic crisis, in the Donggala Regency, Central Sulawesi, one kilogram of cacao sold for Rp.3000, whereas when the Rupiah was at its lowest, farmers were receiving more than Rp.20,000 per kilogram from middlepeople in Makassar. This had settled back to an average price of Rp.16,000 at the start of 1999 (small-scale entrepreneur, personal communication, 9 January 1999; Ibrahim, 1999). The increase in farmers' spending was so dramatic that at one stage the Toyota car dealership in Makassar ran out of stock, as did two motorbike showrooms in the Central Sulawesi town of Parigi (KI 6, 11/1/99; Hill, 1999b; Ibrahim, 1999).

The increased purchasing power for this section of the population had a direct impact upon small enterprises in Makassar from whom farmers bought goods. Of the small enterprises, furniture-makers and tailors were two groups which benefited greatly from the increased demand for their products. Central Sulawesi farmers, with increased profits and more discretionary income, wanted such 'luxury' items as upholstered sofas and dining-table sets made by the small enterprises in Makassar. Likewise, Central Market, a major clothes and accessories retailing site with stalls linked through middlepeople to small enterprises, looked as busy as ever in January 1999, with many items of clothing being bundled into large parcels to be sent north to Central Sulawesi.

There was however concern that just as some small-scale entrepreneurs tend to put profits into conspicuous consumption rather than savings in good times, farmers were also spending on consumer goods rather than investing in the improvement of their farms (KI 6, 11/1/99). Indeed it was reported in the *Jakarta Post* in January (Ibrahim, 1999) that 'the villagers have been in constant party mode, making the circuit of wedding, circumcision and housewarming parties'.

The demand coin had a flip side, however. Local people who had bought imported products in the past, partly due to the associated social status this ensured, began to look elsewhere for goods following the devaluation of the *Rupiah* and subsequent rises in the price of imported commodities. Small-scale furniture producers, for one, did not appear to have been greatly exposed to the negative impact flowing from the economic crisis, due largely to the changes to the Central Sulawesi farmers' incomes discussed earlier, as well as because of increased demand for their products from local consumers. Local middle-class residents who in the past had bought imported goods had, in 1999, changed consumption patterns and were buying from small enterprises instead (small-scale furniture entrepreneurs, personal communication, 15–20 January 1999).

Due to the increased costs of imports to Indonesia following the devaluation of the *Rupiah*, many small enterprises based on recycling also experienced a boom. Prices for new goods such as auto supplies and components had risen dramatically because they were imported and the demand for recycled components had, in response, increased (Sarwono, 1999). Similarly, an enterprise making window seals and mats from used tyres had experienced rising demand (small-scale entrepreneur, personal communication, 8 January 1999).

One factor behind the increase in demand by Central Sulawesi farmers and local city residents for small enterprise products in Makassar was, as explored earlier in this book, the importance of social status and the closely linked issue of conspicuous consumption among the Bugis and Makassar middle class. Although these groups used small enterprises increasingly as a source of essential goods, there were many goods they bought from small enterprises that did not meet immediate needs, but were regarded locally as 'luxury' items. Among these were furniture, such as sofas, dining-tables, as well as new clothes and *songkok* (KI 6, 18/1/99).

Despite the economic crisis, the desire to maintain social status remained strong throughout the Bugis and Makassar communities (KI 3, 20/1/99). As a result, a significant proportion of Central Sulawesi farmers' profits was also channelled into conspicuous consumption, rather than reinvested in their farms as capital. Within Makassar city too, consumers who had previously purchased imported luxury goods turned to small enterprises for substitutes. In effect, local cultural practices appeared to have modified the impact of the economic crisis on production and profitability for some small enterprises in the city.

CONCLUSION: THE LOCAL DOMAIN

In his analysis of the impacts of the Indonesian economic crisis on small enterprises, Tambunan (2000) suggested negative demand and supply-side impacts. On the demand side, he suggested a weakened domestic demand for small enterprise goods from individual consumers with reduced purchasing power, combined with a decline in output from medium and large-scale industries with production linkages to small enterprises. Compounding this effect on the supply side, Tambunan (2000) maintained that bank credit was increasingly scarce along with rising interest rates and a steep expansion in input costs. Yet, in the local context of Makassar, these effects were not always apparent. Demand from certain individuals was still strong due to the consumption of small enterprise products by Central Sulawesi farmers and the local middle class. The production linkages between small and larger enterprises that Tambunan (2000) discussed above had never been important to more than a few of the entrepreneurs interviewed in Makassar, and hence there were not the negative impacts experienced elsewhere. On the supply side, as reported in Chapter 7, only twenty of the 300 entrepreneurs originally interviewed in Makassar had secured bank loans. In turn, this meant that during the economic crisis the small enterprise sector was largely insulated against the increased scarcity of bank credit, even though poor access to bank credit remained a negative factor, as it had in the past. In net effect, per-haps the only impact detailed by Tambunan (2000), one clearly relevant in the Makassar context, was that in some cases input prices had increased.

Overall, then, the *krismon* had made little impact on the operations of the *majority* of small enterprises in my Makassar sample of entrepreneurs. On the contrary, most continued to survive on what for many was a day-to-day basis, much as they had in the past. In other words, they had not suffered *additional* negative effects emerging from the crisis. Of more immediate con-cern were the continuing constraints internal to their enterprises yet linked to the local context, including a basic production organisation and a limited capacity for innovation. The local socio-political environment in which small enterprises operated was little changed from Suharto's time. It included bureaucratic structures riddled with corruption and hindering access to credit and training that persistently restricted their growth.

It should be acknowledged, however, that while this accurately portrays the situation of the majority of the enterprises, two impacts of the economic crisis on other small enterprises in the city had flowed from the devaluation of the *Rupiah*. One was that, for the first time, some Makassar small enter-prises were linked into the global economy through increased demand for products from nearby primary commodity farmers who had benefited from rising export prices for their output. The second impact on small enterprises was through increased demand from local consumers who had turned to small enterprises for goods and services, whereas in the past they had preferred imported commodities because of their association with increased social status. Demand arising from conspicuous consumption, an important factor for Bugis and Makassar cultures, had therefore come from two contrasting sources, the Central Sulawesi farmers and the local middle class.

Two important conclusions arise from the survey of the experiences of small enterprises in Makassar during the *krismon*. The first points to the value of incorporating local processes into the equation when considering the implications of broader economic and political events. This, in turn, leads to the second point, namely that, from the evidence in this study, it is clear that the impacts of the economic crisis on small enterprises in Makassar city did not mirror those occurring elsewhere in the archipelago.

Attempts to examine the impacts of the crisis without undertaking a serious rather than cursory examination of local economic change, ethnic formations, culture and social relations will result in a picture devoid of the daily reality for millions of people. While much of the literature currently being published on the impacts of the *krismon* gives us an understanding of the macro-economic and macro-political processes at work, it is also necessary if not critical to gain a fuller understanding of the impacts of the crisis on everyday life; in other words, an imperative is that a detailed examination of the local domain be incorporated. For small enterprises in Makassar a way forward in this arena is through the adoption of the *small enterprise integrative framework* detailed in Chapter 3.

9　Retrospect and prospect

> Looking into the future is fraught with difficulty, and there is no place more certain to disappoint the soothsayer than Indonesia.
>
> (Kingsbury, 1998: 241)

As we have moved through the evidence presented earlier it has become clear that Amir's story, introduced at the start of Chapter 1, mirrored not only the experience of many other goldsmiths but, indeed, also that of a wider range of small entrepreneurs operating in Makassar. They, just like Amir, relied heavily on family networks, operated in subcontracting arrangements, and had faced the pernicious obstacle of corruption when attempting to gain a bank loan. Even so, Amir was also part of that group of entrepreneurs in Makassar whose interpretations of enterprise success incorporated a number of non-economic aspects, such as being able to provide donations for festivals and religious ceremonies. Although Amir was concerned about the future of his enterprise in relation to the heightened ethnic tensions in the city and, as gold prices continued to rise, the potential long-term impacts of the economic crisis, he explained that his business was currently doing well because he was still able to provide his extended family with gifts at birthdays and *Idul Fitri* (Amir, interview notes, 16 January 1999).

Through gaining a greater understanding of the internal dynamics and contextualised interactions of small enterprises such as Amir's, this book has been able to advance our understanding of small enterprises in Indonesia. In the process a new conceptual framework has been formulated, one which allows for a heightened awareness of local cultural values, a greater understanding of micro-level activities involving small enterprises, and a detailed appreciation of enterprise interactions at a range of scales.

While there exists extensive literature on small enterprises in developing countries, past theoretical approaches critically examined in this book have been found deficient in ways that necessitate their rejection in the light of more recent theoretical debates. In seeking to overcome this deficiency some theorists have turned to industrial production approaches, three variants of which were recognised as giving more agency to all the players involved than previous approaches.

Of these three, it was the flexible specialisation paradigm which, from the early 1980s, attracted growing support as a way of overcoming the inadequacies of past small enterprise theories. Yet while it is true that the flexible specialisation paradigm did give greater attention to the internal structures of small enterprises, as well as to interactions among them, its utility was diminished by a number of inherent weaknesses. It remained somewhat fixed within a broader dualism, disregarded internal contradictions, and gave only limited attention to the position of casual labour. Amongst many proponents of flexible specialisation there was also a tendency to neglect issues of ethnicity, gender and local politics. Also raised were serious concerns about the wholesale transfer of a paradigm from developed countries, where it was first proposed, to developing countries. Similarly, too, the use of a Western definition of 'success' was problematised. With a view to eliminating these deficiencies, a new conceptual structure, the *small enterprise integrative framework,* has been developed here. Revisited in Figure 9.1, it is conceptualised as a tool with which to examine the organisation and operations of small enterprises in developing countries, and as a means by which we might overcome many of the limitations of previous approaches.

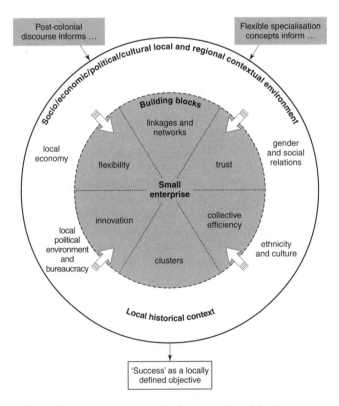

Figure 9.1 The small enterprise integrative framework revisited.

Of factors highlighted by this new approach, in the first instance among small enterprises in Makassar is the role of government with its excessive bureaucratic regulations and corruption. These were major factors impeding the ability of many small enterprises to advance beyond a position of mere survival. Wherever the government's approach to small enterprises in a specific developing country has been examined in previous work, it has been shown that it usually has a crucial impact and influence – be it positive or negative – on the ability of small-scale entrepreneurs to carry out their daily operations. This is because such entrepreneurs nearly always occupy marginal political-economic spaces (see Dos Santos, 1979; Gertler, 1992; Galhardi, 1995; Lomnitz, 1997), a point re-emphasised by Upadhya and Rutten (1997: 26) who observe that, 'while the state may play a positive role, it may also inhibit entrepreneurial development through excessive regulation, harassment by officials, and so on'. Thus the political and institutional environment in which small-scale entrepreneurs operate must be taken into account when determining the factors that act to support or discourage them from achieving their goals.

Regional economic disparities are common in developing countries and, at any one time, impact significantly on the industrial organisation of any specific place (Drake, 1989; Gugler, 1997). Accordingly, a framework for examining small enterprises must discuss trends in regional inequality, while also giving close consideration to both local and broader national economic environments. Indeed, as revealed in the earlier analysis, the influence of the local economic environment on small enterprises in Makassar was strong. This was because the market was saturated with goods made from similar small enterprises, a clear expression of a problem that confronted many entrepreneurs in a very competitive marketplace. Their difficulties in this respect were exacerbated by a number of raw material supply and marketing problems which arose from the comparatively remote physical location of Makassar in Eastern Indonesia, where it is often bypassed in favour of Surabaya on Java as an entry port to the Eastern Islands.

The question of gender relations is also of considerable relevance. In this regard, in a number of developing countries undergoing rapid economic, political and social change 'there has been increasing concern regarding the position of women in society in general, the relations between men and women, and among women from different social groups' (Heyzer, 1986: i). Not surprisingly, gender relations are highly significant in determining the roles that women undertake in small enterprises. Frequently, women find themselves in a marginalised position when they attempt to operate and develop small enterprises in Southeast Asian countries, a situation well documented by Heyzer (1986), Sjaifudian (1992), Machfud *et al.* (1994), and the International Labour Office (1995). The dominant cultural and religious belief systems in a certain location will have important influences on the decision-making abilities of women in small enterprises. This was clearly so in Makassar. There, local cultures and the strong Islamic presence in the city, as well as the Government ideology, were all highly influential in determining women's economic and social roles. To ignore these influences on women and their impact on women's ability to participate effectively in small enterprises is to contribute to the 'invisibility' of the roles of a large proportion of the population within developing countries.

Indeed, in much small enterprise research gender has been given either a negligible role or ignored completely. The position held by many women in small enterprises in developing countries is as unpaid family labour, unaccounted for in official censuses and often even 'forgotten' in studies utilising interviews with male/husband entrepreneurs (van Diermen, 1997). Nonetheless, the success of a small enterprise will often rely heavily on their input which, in turn, once again emphasises why women cannot be ignored within an integrative framework for examining the structure and success of small enterprises.

In sum, one cannot examine small enterprises in developing countries without undertaking a serious rather than cursory examination of ethnic formations, culture and social relations. Not to do so will inevitably result in a picture devoid of the daily reality encountered by those involved in small enterprise activity. Rather, local ethnic tensions and social formations have a key role to play in the daily functioning of entrepreneurs in specific locations within developing countries. Culture is never static but is constantly being re-created and negotiated by conscious actors. Accordingly, a framework designed to examine small enterprises must incorporate the cultural context as a dynamic dimension of human agency (Upadhya and Rutten, 1997). Here a very clear indicator of this, in the Makassar realm, was the heightened sensitivity among local ethnic communities to the position of the city's Chinese during the *krismon*.

In applying the *small enterprise integrative framework*, which incorporates the dimensions of ethnic formations, culture and social relations to small enterprises operating in Makassar, we turned first to the local and regional contextual environment (Figure 9.1). An Outer Island of the Indonesian archipelago, Sulawesi has tended to be on the margins politically and economically in regard to the country's industrialisation and associated economic growth, the bulk of which has remained focused on the Inner Islands, and especially on Java. Makassar city, with its distinctive mix of local ethnic groups, as well as many migrants from nearby islands, has remained a comparatively poor urban centre, but also home to a wide range of small enterprises.

Also of interest to the *small enterprise integrative framework* were the internal dynamics of organisation, management and production within the enterprises themselves. Of the 300 small enterprises in the Makassar sample, it was found that those which used expensive raw materials such as gold tended to be family enterprises. A range of enterprises were found operating in subcontracting arrangements, which had the advantage of a greater degree of security in terms of raw material supplies, but with less control over management decisions and product design than those that were independent. Generally, it was found that production methods remained relatively simple, the skill level of workers limited. Small enterprises faced many production problems too. They ranged from unreliable sources of raw materials to errors in the production process as well as the poor quality of workers and limited access to capital. Yet while strategies for overcoming production problems like these varied, few entrepreneurs appeared to have found innovative solutions.

Labour patterns also showed wide variation among Makassar's small enterprises. For some, the pattern included aspects of functional flexibility, while for others the production strategy was more 'survivalist'. The diverse labour patterns also reflected the range of ethnic and family linkages involved in production, the varying ease of entry into different types of work, and the different relationships entrepreneurs had with their workers; it also reflected fluctuations in demand for goods produced and how these were dealt with. Many of the enterprises had people working for them in outlier-style arrangements in an effort to keep the costs of production low. Nevertheless, while wages were good for many workers, they were often still in a tenuous position regarding work security, especially if not a relative of the entrepreneur for whom they worked.

The advantages offered by such flexibility in labour patterns has not gone unnoticed by larger enterprises operating in the city, and indeed in Indonesia as a whole. Multinational companies in particular have been quick to appreciate the benefits of employment practices like these. As detailed in Appendix 3, Walls Ice Cream, one such multinational company operating in Makassar, has effectively adopted a labour pattern similar to those found among the city's small enterprises as a means of reducing overhead costs and concerns with worker welfare. The *small enterprise integrative framework* can therefore be utilised, in a purposeful extension, to compare small enterprise labour patterns with others operating in the city.

Turning to the inter-firm dynamics of the small enterprises as a means to examine the *small enterprise integrative framework* building blocks of linkages and networks, clusters, and collective efficiency, many of the enterprises were found to be embedded within complex networking arrangements (Figure 9.1). The importance of contextualised social and cultural interactions was clear, especially among certain groups of enterprises, including goldsmiths, tailors and furniture-makers. The *sistem kekeluargaan* (family-like system) was frequently discussed, especially as a means by which money could be borrowed, and hence the complicated procedures of formal lending institutions avoided. The former also provided a more tolerant lending system if there were seasonal fluctuations in enterprise profits.

The marketing connections of the enterprises were also problematic. In general these links were being restricted by environmental constraints such as transportation difficulties during monsoons, and the limited market which producers of non-durables could reach due to a lack of technological infrastructure like refrigeration. In total, less than 8 per cent of the 300 enterprises had marketing links outside of Sulawesi. Likewise, innovation through imitation or *in situ* was apparent in only a small number of the enterprises, ones which tended to operate independently. In comparison, enterprise subcontractors did not appear to be able to use their networks to increase innovation, but rather seemed to operate more in survival mode.

Clusters of small enterprises existed in a number of the locations where interviews were undertaken. In many cases physical clustering was a strategy adopted in order to reduce transaction costs, since small capacity transportation modes were often relied upon. Clustering was also advantageous for customers to know where a certain product could be purchased in the city. Collaboration was also advanced through clustering, with tools, workers and information being shared among cluster members. Nevertheless, what had not happened within such clusters, except in the case of some furniture-makers, was an increase in specialisation or advanced inter-firm division of labour. For most of the small enterprises, however, clustering was not used to enhance collective efficiencies, which could have increased the competitiveness of the enterprises in their wider environment. That this was not being achieved was due to a lack of active collaboration supported by sectoral specialisation.

EMIC DEFINITIONS OF SUCCESS

The mounting evidence for Makassar city confirms that for entrepreneurs there, 'success', as an emic, locally defined objective, was a multi-faceted concept. 'Success', in addition to relating to the ability of an enterprise to achieve economic growth – which certainly remained an important objective to some extent for all the entrepreneurs – often also included the ability to provide support for workers, family and members of the community, as well as to undertake philanthropic actions. Many small-scale entrepreneurs provided a range of assistance, not only for workers, but frequently for extended family and neighbours as well. The support given ranged from daily needs (common for the nuclear family), through to gifts, loans and social contributions for neighbours and friends, as well as education and training costs for some family members and workers. In general, the entrepreneurs had a positive perception of the provision of such support. While some believed it made workers more diligent and motivated, and thus assisted the growth of the enterprise, others detailed religious, social and community responsibilities. In effect, using entrepreneurial resources for these purposes directly drained profits from the enterprise or limited growth, yet this process was not looked upon as a negative factor.

Another key feature of 'success' was economic advancement. Entrepreneurs frequently complained about the constraints that inhibited them from attaining this goal. Discussed throughout this book, they ranged from constraints to marketing and difficulties gaining raw materials, to problems in the production process as well as the inability to obtain capital together with labour concerns and general difficulties associated with business organisation. Also highlighting the economic dimension of their 'success' definition, the entrepreneurs stated their willingness, if given the opportunity, to make a range of changes to the organisation of production in their enterprises, changes that would potentially place them in a more positive position in the local economy. Such alterations included improvements to product quality and working conditions, exploration of a wider market and an increase in the amount of capital borrowed.

In sum, discussions with a sample of 300 small-scale entrepreneurs in Makassar city found that trying to get by, or 'tread water', often literally on a day-to-day basis, was a primary preoccupation of the majority of them. Simultaneously, family and friendship, as well as *kampung* relationships, not only remained critical to the continuing operations of many, but constituted essential support mechanisms in terms of labour supply, informal loans and capital, in an environment containing numerous barriers that hindered the small enterprises in realising their objectives. These barriers included some that were internal, that is, relating to the organisation of the enterprises themselves, such as a widespread lack of innovation, inferior product quality and poor accounting records. Barriers in the broader external contextual environment also impinged on their operations. Not least among those were high levels of competition and corruption within relevant Government agencies in the city, but also important were the structure and operations of the bureaucracy – and the corresponding difficulties in gaining access to credit – rigid gender and social roles as well as ethnic divisions and tensions within the city.

THE WAY AHEAD[1]

> Private sector small enterprises will have a major impact on the overall development and growth potential of the economy during the latter stages of the present economic crisis, and during the postcrisis period. The sectors ability to create employment will make a valuable contribution in stabilizing social structures, which should help to ensure social stability.
>
> (Kingsley, 2000: online)

If one accepts the views of authors such as Kingsley (2000) that small enterprises offer a way forward for the Indonesian economy, then this prospect would be greatly enhanced by the development of a fairer and more equitable 'playing field' for small-scale entrepreneurs. Indeed, this issue is one of fundamental importance because it profoundly influences the country's ability to meet the most pressing basic needs of the millions of people who are directly or indirectly dependent on small enterprises for their livelihoods.

The plight of small enterprises, and of the individuals supported by them, was exacerbated under Suharto's leadership when there was a growing sense of isolation of the general population from those in control, the few who were reaping the benefits of power. Little was done to develop the political and judicial institutions desperately needed by the country. Even after the fall from power of Suharto and Habibie, 'the cost of doing business in Indonesia is still bogged down by government agencies at almost every level' (*Jakarta Post*, 23 February 2000). As Sri Mulyani and Winoto (1999: 67) report:

> In short, the main problem of enhancing small enterprises seems to lie in its implementation. This indicates that solving the problem of small enterprises cannot be separated from macro policies nor from the institutional setting, especially as related to the role of the government institutions and officials.

This view of the situation of small enterprises in Indonesia, and in Makassar in particular, epitomises the principal findings reported in this book, namely that the local political and economic environment in which they operate in the city has a very strong influence on their daily work. If effective change is to be achieved, four issues of fundamental concern will have to be addressed: the need for a more transparent legal system; an independent judiciary; economic development that reaches those in greatest need; and a 'crack-down' on government corruption and nepotism, as well as on widespread bureaucratic incompetence. Only when these nationwide but also highly localised factors are resolved will it be possible to implement the reforms required to create a more supportive environment for small enterprises such as those of Amir and his neighbours.

Appendix 1
Key informants

To maintain the anonymity of my key informants I have been vague concerning their position within an institution or government department if necessary.

The list is by date of first major discussion:

KI no.	Gender	Age	Ethnicity	Education	Employment
1	male	40	Bugis	Master of Arts (MA) Agriculture	Involved with research on small enterprises at *Universitas Hasanuddin (UNHAS)*, Makassar
2	male	26	Bugis	SMA	Small enterprise entrepreneur
3	male	32	Bugis	*S1* Sociology (near equivalent to a British Bachelors degree, normally 5 years)	Travel agent, Makassar
4	male	31	Bugis	*S1* Mineral Extraction	Tourist guide, South Sulawesi
5	male	55	Java	Professor	Professor at *UNHAS*
6	male	34	Enrekang	*S1* Sociology, *UNHAS*	Previously worked for the multinational company *Unilever*. Currently unemployed
7	male	37	Torajan	*Sekolah Menengah Atas (SMA)*, upper secondary school	*Loseman* (guesthouse) owner, Makassar

KI no.	Gender	Age	Ethnicity	Education	Employment
8	female	25	Dutch	MA student, Holland	Studying Makassar 'informal sector'
9	male	25	Dutch	MA student, Holland	Studying Makassar 'informal sector'
10	female	26	Makassar	*SMA*	Insurance salesperson, Makassar
11	female	24	Madura	SMA	Cosmetics sales supervisor, Makassar
12	male	29	English	Bachelors student	Studying Bugis language and pre-sixteenth-century South Sulawesi history
13	male	22	Flores	*S1* student, Makassar	Guesthouse employee
14	male	35	Java	Ph.D. student, USA	Lecturer *UNHAS*, Makassar
15	female	31	Bugis	*S1 UNHAS* Social Science	Lecturer *UNHAS*, Makassar
16	female	22	English	Bachelors student, England	Undertaking research concerning Sengkang silk
17	female	39	English	MA, England	Non-governmental organisation aid worker
18	male	42	English	Veterinary degree, England	Overseas Development Assistance, UK
19	male	50 approx	Bugis?	Not known	South Sulawesi Chamber of Commerce
20	male	40 approx	European	Not known	Trade Official
21	male	40 approx	British	MA, Economic Geography	Consultant for NGO, USA
22	male	60 approx	Enrekang	Not known	Resigned from Army, now retired
23	male	38	Christian Manado	*SMA*	Small-scale entrepreneur producing passion-fruit juice

Appendix 2

Government programmes to assist small enterprises

1 *Program Keterkaitan Sistem Bapak Angkat* (Adoptive father system/foster-parent programme).

This was initially introduced during the Government's *Repelita III* (Five Year Plan for 1979/84) following the deregulation of the economy, as a means of strengthening the links between small and large enterprises, whilst rejuvenating the industrial sector. The programme was revived again in 1990 by the Minister of Industry, the aim being to motivate large enterprises to increase subcontracting links with smaller enterprises, and for large enterprises to buy domestically produced inputs from small enterprises (Schwarz, 1994; Utrecht and Sayogyo, 1994; Chalmers, 1997b). The programme was subsequently extended to require large enterprises to help smaller ones by acting as 'foster-parents' (ESCAP, 1993: 8). Large firms were encouraged to help smaller firms in production, especially with marketing (both domestically and for export), management, technical processes (including design and diversification of products), and financing for equipment. Large firms were also supposed to help in guaranteeing small enterprise bank loans, and were instructed to allocate between 1 and 5 per cent of their profits to this objective (Smyth *et al.*, 1994). By 1993, 9344 'foster-parents' and 76,000 small industries had participated in the programme (ESCAP, 1993). During 1995/1996 the 'Jimbaran group', consisting initially of forty-eight 'business tycoons', launched its programme to support small enterprises largely through such partnerships (*Jakarta Post*, 15 May 1997). A similar programme was established in 1997 involving seventy-nine large companies which formed the 'Co-ordinating Agency for the Implementation of National Business Strategic Alliances' (BKPK-Kunas) (Sri Mulyani and Winoto, 1999).

2 *Pemanfaatan 1–5% Keuntungan BUMN* (Using 1–5 per cent of state enterprise profits for small-scale and cottage industry development).

In this programme state enterprises were ascribed a role as 'activators' of development and had an obligation to help small enterprises with management, production, working capital, marketing and bank credit (ESCAP,

1993). Since November 1989 *Badan Usaha Milik Negara (BUMN)* (state-owned enterprises) have been required by law to spend between 1 and 5 per cent of their profits on assistance to small-scale and cottage industries, and co-operatives. This could include activities such as training programmes and technical assistance (Sandee *et al.*, 1994; *PUKTI*, 1995). In 1995, 146 small enterprises in Makassar had received assistance from *BUMN* companies. Of these, fifty-five were producing clothes, twenty-three building materials, forty-five farming equipment, fifteen metal and construction goods and eight were welding workshops (*PUKTI*, 1995). Thirteen *BUMN* enterprises were involved in the programme in South Sulawesi in 1995, and eleven in 1997 (*PUKTI*, 1995; *Departemen Koperasi dan Pembinaan Pengusaha Kecil, Sulawesi Selatan*, 1997).

3 *Kredit Usaha Kecil, KUK* (Small business credit).

Introduced in January 1990, this programme required banks to allocate 20 per cent of their total credit funds to small businesses, defined as those with total assets of under Rp.600 million (Sandee *et al.*, 1994; Utrecht and Sayogyo, 1994). This programme was introduced to replace the previous *Kredit Investasi Kecil* (Small Investment Credit) and *Kredit Modal Kerja Permanen* (Working Capital Credit) programmes (Utrecht and Sayogyo, 1994; Hill, 2001).

The Small Business Credit programme was extended in 1997 to joint venture and foreign banks operating in the country. These initially had to lend 12.5 per cent of their total credit funds, increasing to 17.5 per cent in 1998 and 22.5 per cent in 1999. The extension of the programme to include foreign banks brought much criticism from directors of such banks, as many of the small enterprises were considered too small for their viability to be easily assessed (*Jakarta Post*, 8 April 1997; 10 April 1997).

4 *Penjualan Saham kepada Koperasi* (Selling shares to co-operatives).

In 1990, to strengthen small enterprises and promote the social welfare of the low income community, Suharto 'appealed' to large private companies to transfer part of their equity to co-operatives to improve their capital base (ESCAP, 1993; Schwarz, 1994). Although Suharto initially 'suggested' that 25 per cent of a company's equity be transferred to the co-operatives, it was later decided by Government ministers that this could be reduced to 1 per cent. The programme was essentially seen as yet another additional tax by the large companies affected (Schwarz, 1994).

5 *Pendidikan dan Latihan bagi Industri Kecil* (Education and training for small industries).

This initiative involved the Department of Industry and Trade, with state and private enterprises providing training, often linked to the provision of working capital. This was the only programme to have a fixed Government budget (Sandee *et al.*, 1994). The training was organised by the Government, *BUMN* (see above) or 'foster-parent' industries and included business and technical skills 'through formal and non-formal courses and apprenticeships, organized on a national scale' (ESCAP, 1993: 11). However, on occasions there have been significant problems relating to this training, as Thamrin (1993: 152) explains:

> [T]here is a scientific bias that tends to transfer the standard knowledge of universities to participants who are not familiar with the terminology; a bureaucratic class that tends to treat participants as inferiors; a middle-class and 'missionary' zeal bias whereby participants are often regarded as stupid; and a modernism bias that tends to encourage participants to adopt techniques that require expensive equipment.

Appendix 3
Imitating small enterprise flexibility: Walls Ice Cream

Such flexibility as that found in the labour practices of a number of small enterprises in Makassar has not gone unnoticed by larger enterprises operating in the city, and indeed in Indonesia as a whole. Multinational companies in particular have been quick to appreciate the benefits of employment practices like these. One such company, Walls Ice Cream, operates in Makassar where it replicates such labour arrangements.

Owned by Unilever, Walls Ice Cream is a popular brand sold throughout Indonesia. In 1997 there were three distributors in South Sulawesi, one of whom lived in Makassar where he had five people operating stock-points under his authority. In turn, each stock point had between eight and fifteen cyclists who travelled around Makassar on tricycles with small freezers attached from which they sold ice-cream, and carried a loudspeaker playing a distinctive 'Walls Ice Cream' tune. The ice-cream arrived by boat from Unilever's factory in Jakarta once a week. The stock point operators in Makassar were one 'outsider' and the three brothers and one sister of the South Sulawesi distributor. Although the cyclists were supposed to keep to specific routes around the city, they did not necessarily do so because of these family connections.

A series of interviews with the 'outsider' stock point operator revealed that Unilever had, at the beginning of operations in Makassar, supplied dry ice (solid carbon dioxide) shipped from Surabaya for the mobile ice cream freezers. However, since July 1996 Unilever had changed to using battery-operated freezers that required recharging on a nightly basis, a cost that had been transferred to the stock point operators. Due to this change, the profits of the stock point operators had declined dramatically, the one interviewed having lost money continuously for the six months preceding the interview and predicting more losses throughout the rainy season (KI 6, 6/3/97).

This 'outsider' stock point operator had initially found one worker, who in turn recruited others from his town Takalar, to the south of Makassar, yet again confirming the use of informal networks to gain workers. There were no fixed wages for the workers, who were paid a 10 per cent commission instead. On a 'good day' this meant they received approximately Rp.10,000. Walls Ice Cream was not seen as a profitable company for which to work as a cyclist because of low sales during the rainy season. This was in contrast to small scale entrepreneurs selling products such as *bakso* from a *gerobak* who could make more money as demand was not as seasonal. The stock point operators gained 10 per cent of all the proceeds of the cyclists who worked for them. During the dry season this could be as high as Rp.200,000 a day, perhaps rising to Rp.400,000 around *Idul Fitri* and Christmas. However, during the rainy season, usually from October to April, profits were considerably less.

Because the stock point operators were working on a commission basis they had no employment security with *Unilever*. Thus, they had no health cover, pension scheme, or any assurance of employment. When interviewed, the stock point operator reflected that 'Unilever is clever working in a developing country like this, it's a good way to exploit the system' (KI 6, 15/3/97). Stock point operators usually covered the social security aspects of their cyclist workers, the workers sometimes living at the operator's house but cooking their own food. There was thus a *pondok* system in operation for the cyclists. The stock point operator would also supply the cyclists with loans if they did not make enough sales to cover costs, such as the bus fares for the workers to return to their *kampung* on their day off each week. In terms of provisions for workers, then, stock point operators played a role similar to that of a small enterprise entrepreneur or enterprise subcontractor, but they had minimal freedom to negotiate their position within the system operated by Unilever.

Commercially made ice-cream sold by cyclists or from shops with small freezers cost between Rp.250 and Rp.2000 an ice-cream, whilst that sold by the traditional *es putah* sellers was Rp.300–500 a cup (which was returned). In discussing the entrance of large ice-cream manufacturers into the Makassar market, Forbes (1981b: 158) forecast that 'we might perhaps anticipate its entrance into the cheaper range of ice-cream products, if only to force petty producers out of business and maximise the market for the more expensive product'. By 1997, in fact, this had occurred to some degree with the cheaper ice creams available from the stores. Nonetheless, traditional ice cream appeared to have maintained its appeal, especially amongst *kampung* residents in the city. There it had a competitive edge in terms of cost for quantity, a full cup being significantly larger than the small ice-cream sold by the larger manufacturers.

Glossary

adat customs or traditions

akar bengkudu root of the *kepayang* tree, used as a dye

arisan an informal rotating savings and credit association, whose members contribute to and take turns at winning an aggregate sum of money

Badan Usaha Milik Negara state-owned enterprises

Baht (Thai word) unit of Thai currency

bakso soup containing meatballs

Balai Latihan Kerja work training centre

bapak (1) used to mean employer; (2) respectful title or form of address for an older man

becak trishaw/rickshaw

Bim Bingandan Pengembangan Industri Kecil Programme for Guidance and Development of Small Industries

Biro Pusat Statistik Indonesian Central Bureau of Statistics

broderie anglaise 'English embroidery': embroidery with holes in the fabric and stitching.

Bumiputra 'sons of the soil': indigenous Indonesians

coto makassar local speciality stew with meat (traditionally buffalo) entrails, flavoured with lime and chilli

Departemen Perindustri Department of Industry; merged with the Department of Trade to become the *Departemen Perindustrian dan Perdagangan,* Department/Ministry of Industry and Trade in 1996/1997

Departemen Perindustrian dan Perdagangan Department/Ministry of Industry and Trade

Departemen Koperasi dan Pembinaan Pengusaha Kecil Department/Ministry of Co-operatives and Small Enterprises

Dinas regional/local department

Direktorat Jenderal Industri Kecil Directorate General of Small Industries

durian a tropical fruit, which is a favourite amongst many Southeast Asian people and has a very distinctive smell as well as being fairly expensive

es putah traditional Makassar ice cream

gerobak handcart

Haj Muslim pilgrimage to Mecca

hati panas 'hot liver', quick-tempered

Idul Fitri *or* **Hari Raya Idul Fitri** feast/celebration at the end of the fasting month

jabatan position, duty (occupation)

jamu traditional herbal medicines and tonics

jilbab female veil for daily use, covers the head and ears, but not the face

kabupaten large administrative district. Sulawesi consists of 21 *kabupaten* and two city areas: Makassar and Pare Pare.

kaca word used amongst goldsmiths as a measurement for gold: one *kaca* is the equivalent of one-tenth of a gram of gold; also means glass

Kamar Dagang dan Industri Chamber of Commerce and Industry

kampung village, neighbourhood

Kanwil Koperasi local-level office of the Department of Co-operatives and Small Enterprise

Kawasan Timor Indonesia the eastern region of Indonesia; includes the islands of Sulawesi, the Nusa Tenggaras, Maluku and Irian Jaya

kecamatan subdistrict

keluak/keluwak fruit of the *kepayang* tree, used as a spice

kepala desa village headperson

kepayang large tree, the fruit of which is used as a spice, as well as the fruit and roots being used as natural dyes

kerang bulan thick pancakes

kerupuk crisp dried crackers made from a variety of ingredients including cassava and rice flour and flavoured with fish (*kerupuk ikan*) or shrimp (*kerupuk udung*), and fried before eating

keuntungan profit

koperasi co-operative

koperasi industri industry co-operatives

koperasi industri kecil dan kerajinan small-scale industry and handicraft co-operative

koperasi serba usaha general business co-operative

koperasi simpan pinjam savings and loans co-operatives

kotamadya municipality

Kredit Investasi Kecil small investment credit (Government programme)

Kredit Modal Kerja Permanen working capital credit (Government programme)

Kredit Usaha Kecil small business credit (Government programme)

kretek clove cigarettes

krismon economic crisis

lingkungan administrative unit smaller than a *kecamatan*

losmen guesthouse, cheap hotel

martabak folded, fried crepe filled with spices and pieces of meat and/or vegetables

mukenah white prayer veils worn especially during *Puasa*

Nahdlatul Ulama 'Revival of the Religious Scholars': Indonesia's largest Muslim organisation

nasi kuning   yellow rice, sometimes flavoured with coconut milk

'negara korupsi'   a corrupt country

Pak (abbreviation of Bapak)   respectful title or form of address for an older man

pakaian umroh   clothes to be worn whilst one is on the Islamic pilgrimage to Mecca

Panca Dharma Wanita   Indonesian Government's stipulated 'Five Duties of Women'

pasar   market

pegawai negeri   government employee/civil servant

Pemanfaatan 1–5% Keuntungan BUMN   Using 1–5 per cent of state enterprise profits for small-scale and cottage industry development (Government programme)

Pendidikan dan Latihanbagi Industri Kecil   Education and training for small industries (Government programme)

Pengembangan Usaha Kecil Kawasan Timur Indonesia   Centre for Development of Small Enterprises in East Indonesia

pengusaha   business owner

Penjualan Saham Kepada Koperasi   Selling shares to co-operatives (Government programme)

penyakit   a disease

peran ganda   'dual role' ideology, identifying women as economic producers and domestic reproducers

peranakan   Chinese longer established than *totok*; many *peranakan* Chinese had intermarried with local ethnic groups, becoming more integrated culturally

pete pete   small minibuses used for local public transport

pisang epe   banana dessert

pondok   dwellings where traders live and from whose operators they obtain their equipment and raw materials, whilst still being independent businesspeople working for personal profits; some operators provide shelter and food, whilst others provide only shelter

prahu pinisi   Bugis cargo boat used for trading

pribumi   indigenous Indonesian

Program Keterkaitan Sistem Bapak Angkat   Adoptive father system/ foster-parent programme (Government programme)

puasa   to fast, also used locally to refer to *bulan puasa*, the Muslim fasting month, also known as *Ramadan*

punggawa   wholesalers

punggawa ikan   wholesalers working with fish

pungli   cash payments that make things happen

Pusat Pembinaan Pengusaha Kecil   Centre for the Establishment of Small Entrepreneurs

Ramadan   ninth month of the Arabic calendar, the fasting month

reformasi   reformation

Rupiah   unit of Indonesian currency

sentra   clusters of certain economic activities, such as small-scale enterprises or traders

sentra industri kecil   clusters of small-scale enterprises, usually referring to those that are officially acknowledged by the Department of Industry and Trade

siri   loss of honour and dignity

sistem kekeluargaan   family-like system. Amongst small-scale enterprises this refers to sharing tools, raw materials, workers and/or information and so on, as family members would. On a broader scale it refers to part of the Indonesian Government's ideology of economic collectivism and co-operation.

songkok   hat for men, usually made of velvet, which is considered the 'Indonesian national hat'

srikaya   a tropical fruit that has a soft edible pulp, also known as sweetsop

status economi   economic status

Surat Izin Tempat Usaha   licence for a business place/site

Surat Izin Untuk Perusahaan   licence for a business or enterprise to operate

tahu   tofu, soya bean curd

tahu goreng   fried tofu

tempe   deep-fried fermented soya bean 'patty'

terang bulan   thick pancakes filled with chopped peanuts and sugar, chocolate syrup or cheese

tingkat   level, storey

toko   shop

tokok   'pure' Chinese, generally more recent migrants with culturally distinct communities

tukang kayu   wood craftsperson

tukang mas   goldsmith

usahawan   industrialist

usahawan industri kecil   small-scale industrialist

warung   small stall usually selling food products or household necessities

Notes

1 Introduction

1 Makassar was named Ujung Pandang from 1971 until October 1999, when the name reverted back to Makassar again. This reversion was granted by Habibie, President at the time, in an effort to marshal support for himself and his troubled political life in Parliament, a few days before his 'Statement of Responsibility' which Parliament rejected (Bugis historian, confidential personal communication, 4 February 2000). Following Pelras (1996a), the city of Makassar and the Makassar ethnic group retain the same spelling here.

2 I am aware of the post-colonial and post-modern debates concerning the use of the term 'developing country', and the dualisms that its use reinforces. However, for the purposes of this work I will use this term since numerous Indonesians I talked to (both key informants and small-scale entrepreneurs), believed this best described their country's position within the world economy. It appears that the concept has become internalised and that, as Rigg (1997: 37) suggests, 'the language of the indigenous is framed in terms which are part and parcel of the development discourse'.

3 I use 'Government' when specifically implying the central state Government of the Republic of Indonesia, and 'government' when discussing regional or local government apparatus.

4 The Indonesian *Departemen Perindustri* (Department of Industry, which merged with the Department of Trade to become the *Departemen Perindustrian dan Perdagangan,* Department/Ministry of Industry and Trade in 1996/97) has defined small-scale and cottage industries since 1990 (Ministerial Decree No. 13/M/SK-1/3/1990) as those owned by an Indonesian citizen with a total asset value not exceeding *Rupiah* (Rp.) 600 million (equivalent to £1660 in 1996), excluding the value of housing and land (Dawam Rahardjo, 1994; Syamsuddin, 1995; Husaini *et al.*, 1996). This broad definition differs from those used by other government departments. The Indonesian Ministry of Finance defines 'weak economic group' as those enterprises with assets of not more than Rp. 300 million or turnover per annum of not more than Rp. 300 million (van Diermen, 1997). The *Biro Pusat Statistik (BPS)* (Central Bureau of Statistics) categorises enterprises with up to 100 workers into three groups: household/cottage enterprises which employ one to four people; small-scale enterprises which employ five to nineteen people; medium-scale enterprises which employ twenty to ninety-nine people; and large-scale enterprises which employ 100 people or more (Grijns *et al.*, 1994: 4). Again, within these categories there is considerable variation. As Sandee *et al.* (1994) found in Central Java, many of the medium and some large-scale firms, as defined by worker numbers, still had assets of less than Rp. 600 million and hence would have been classified as 'small-scale industries' by the Department of Industry. In

1995 the Small Business Act No. 5/1995 was passed by the Indonesian Government with the aim of strengthening the contribution of small and medium enterprises to the national economy. The Act defines small enterprises as having assets up to Rp. 200 million (excluding land/buildings) or revenue less than Rp. 1000 million (*Departemen Koperasi dan Pembinaan Pengusaha Kecil*, 1995; Competency Based Economies through Formation of Enterprise (CEFE), 1996). This definition, significantly different again from those used previously, was supposed to supersede all previous definitions, yet when field work was undertaken few government departments were employing this definition at the local level.

5 The exchange rate when field work was being undertaken varied from US$1=Rp.2330 and £1=Rp.3612 (26 July 1996) to US$1=Rp.2415 and £1=Rp.3956 (2 May 1997, prior to the general elections) (*Asiaweek*, 1996, 1997).

6 'General tailors' refers to those sewing batches of one type of item, such as shirts, Muslim headscarves or bedspreads, while 'personal tailors' comprise those sewing specific items to the requirements of the individual customer.

7 See Turner (1998) for details of the questionnaires and interview schedules used.

8 Key informants (KI) are identified in this book by the number assigned to them in Appendix 1, the date given being that when the cited information was obtained. For example (KI 1, 14/4/97).

9 I define 'survivalism' as referring to people's preoccupation with immediate economic and social survival. 'Survivalism' is characterised more by 'treading water' than socio-economic advancement (Parnwell and Turner, 1998).

2 Approaches to small enterprise research

1 See Turner (1998) for a more detailed critique of the dualistic framework.

2 Although there has been work examining the 'informal sector' from a dependency theory and neo-liberal approach, these have been critiqued in detail elsewhere (for dependency theory see Dos Santos, 1979, 1984; and critiques of the approach in McGee, 1978; Seligson, 1984; Lipietz, 1993. For the neo-liberal approach see de Soto, 1989; and critiques of the approach in Murphy, 1990; Mann, 1993; Bromley, 1997). These are not included in this discussion as I have focused on the approaches that have been the most prominent when looking specifically at small enterprises, rather than at 'development' *per se* (DiGregorio, 1994; van Diermen, 1997).

3 The classical examples of technology used in such craft production systems are the Jacquard loom used by silk weavers of Lyon, and the Zurich ribbon loom, styled on the former. These looms used perforated cards to control the raising and lowering of the threads in the sequence required. This reduced the time required to set up a new pattern and cut labour costs. Batches of goods could also be made in amounts too small to be profitable under a mass production regime. Although the Lyon industrial district was to be a casualty of the French Government's state campaign of economic modernisation in the 1960s, parts of it still survive, albeit now located in Italy (Piore and Sabel, 1984).

4 The term *Fordism* is often used interchangeably with mass production. Specifically, 'Fordism' relates to an assembly line model of production, developed in the first two decades of the 1900s in the United States of America, by Henry Ford. 'Fordism' has been generalised thereafter to describe the period in the United States (or globally) typified by mass production for mass consumption (Hirst and Zeitlin, 1991).

5 Here I am referring to the 'new NICs' or 'NIEs' (newly industrialising economies) of the four 'little tigers', 'little dragons' or 'gang of four' – Hong Kong, Singapore, South Korea and Taiwan – which proved (until mid-1997) to be spectacular examples of export-led growth (Schlossstein, 1991: 4). These four are sometimes referred

to as the 'first generation' NICs, with the 'second generation', or 'ASEAN Four' including the South East Asian countries of Indonesia, Malaysia, Thailand and the Philippines (Douglass, 1992; Dixon and Drakakis-Smith, 1993). Although these countries have experienced severely reduced levels of economic growth since mid-1997, the concept of the NIC still stands as a phenomenon. Even if one was to argue that it was a historical one, a report after the 'economic crisis' maintains that the countries concerned may be able to reach better balanced and more sustainable growth in the future, with positive economic results (*The Economist*, March 1998).

6 See Amin (1994: 25) for a concise summary of the views of a number of leading theorists in this field, and Kelly (1999) for an overview of recent associated debates.

7 The terms in bold print are those which a number of people who subsequently adopted this approach have argued to be the most important characteristics of flexible specialisation (see Rasmussen *et al.*, 1992; Smyth *et al.*, 1994; Galhardi, 1995). I subsequently focus upon those connected with the *small firm variant* in my small enterprise integrative framework.

8 Nonetheless, Schmitz (1989) does say that the distinction between mass production and flexible specialisation is now becoming blurred as new programmable automation technologies are increasing the 'flexibility' of mass production systems.

9 See Turner (1998) for case studies of flexible specialisation applied to small enterprises in the developed world, including the 'Third Italy', and parts of Japan and former West Germany.

10 Growth has been defined by proponents of flexible specialisation as the ability to make profit-maximising adjustments to obtain economic success (Sabel and Zeitlin, 1997).

11 For studies based in Africa, also of interest because many economies there have simple technologies and significant labour markets which, to a certain extent mirror the conditions for small enterprises in Indonesia, see Aeroe (1992) who focused on the relevance of the flexible specialisation paradigm to the development of small enterprises in Makambako, Tanzania, Dawson (1992) writing on a similar theme in Kumasi, Ghana, and Rasmussen (1992) looking to the southeast to Zimbabwe. Furthermore, Sverrisson (1992) studied woodworking enterprises in Mutare, Zimbabwe and Nakuru, Kenya, and the extent to which they resembled 'ideal type' flexible specialisation, and van Dijk (1992) researched small enterprises in Ouagadougou, Burkina Faso. Pedersen (1994a) examined small towns in Zimbabwe, and in a second paper the same year (1994b) used case studies from Tanzania, Zimbabwe and Uganda to draw conclusions regarding the ability of small enterprises to gain collective efficiency (see Turner (1998) for more details of these case studies).

12 My continued use of the term 'developing countries' needs to be justified in light of discussions regarding post-colonial discourse. The initial flexible specialisation paradigm advanced by Piore and Sabel (1984) was supported in their seminal work by a range of case studies from developed, industrialised countries. In this book I look at the operations of small enterprises in Makassar, Indonesia (a 'developing country' as defined by the small-scale entrepreneurs and many key informants I talked to, as explained in Chapter 1). Accordingly, in the next chapter, the conceptual framework developed is an attempt to design an approach to examine small enterprises in locations that *do not share the industrialising history* of Piore and Sabel's case study locations (see also Hettne's discussion regarding 'Development ideologies in Western history' (1995: 21–35)). Yet I am not implying that the experiences of these regions, here called 'developing countries' (for want of a better term, and in keeping with the preferred terminology of the entrepreneurs I talked to), are the same or even similar. I am, hence, problematising and destabilising the traditional, dichotomised relationship between

'developed' and 'developing' countries, and stressing the differences found within and among countries, as reasoned by post-colonial discourse. In Chapter 3 I stress the importance of deconstructing and examining, in detail, all possible components of the small enterprises' *own* socio/economic/political/cultural local and regional environments, factors which are all influenced by and have influenced the particular history of their location.

13 By insisting on allowing abstraction I am aware that I am engaging the post-modernism debate concerning whether individual actors are the only valid unit of analysis. While being opposed to the reconstruction of metatheory, I follow Schuurman (1993: 30) in considering that space must be left for 'a universalistic emancipation discourse', and I therefore believe that the search to find an appropriate conceptual framework concerning small enterprises should not be restricted to stressing only 'diversity', albeit an important component.

14 Such decision-making choices bring to mind Weber's *The Protestant Ethic and the Spirit of Capitalism* (1991) in which he suggested that early Puritans developed certain virtues like honesty and thrift, which were then beneficial in the accumulation of capital (Fukuyama, 1996). However, on the evidence presented by small-scale entrepreneurs, such as those studied in Makassar, I do not believe that they necessarily reflect Weber's suggestions. Although, as will be seen in Chapter 5, it could be argued that by frequently undertaking actions that were not directly related to the profit motive (such as a desire for prestige and social standing, and obligations towards family) the entrepreneurs were still undertaking actions helpful to the accumulation of capital, the latter process did not always transpire (see also Alatas, 1963; Upadhya, 1997; Upadhya and Rutten, 1997). However, this is not to reject the possibility that Weberian studies may be useful when examining small-scale entrepreneurs elsewhere in the developing world context.

3 Small enterprise research in developing countries: new directions

1 For discussions and critiques of the 'impasse' concept see Booth (1993), Corbridge (1993), Schuurman (1993), Crush (1994, 1995), Watts (1995) and Rigg (1997). Alternatively, it might be argued, following the post-modern distrust of 'grand theory' that a total move away from such an evolution is required.

2 Although Makassar was an urban field work location, no distinction is made in the following conceptual framework between rural and urban. This echoes Rigg's (1997: 278) argument that 'urban bias, core–periphery and other similar models may have had some validity a decade or two ago, and may still in some specific areas, but recent economic changes have made them increasingly irrelevant'.

3 See Turner (1998) for a detailed discussion concerning the politics of field work and representation.

4 Trust is taken to mean a 'reliance on and confidence in the truth, worth, reliability, etc., of a person or thing; faith' (*Collins Concise Dictionary*, 1988: 1271), or more specifically 'the expectation that arises within a community of regular, honest, and cooperative behavior, based on commonly shared norms, on the part of other members of that community' (Fukuyama, 1996: 26).

4 Setting the scene: the context of production

1 President Sukarno announced Indonesian independence on 17 August 1945, although fighting against the Dutch was to continue until 1949 (Drake, 1989). The turmoil of the years before 1966 means that the economic growth which Indonesia has experienced in recent years can be traced more readily from the birth of President Suharto's New Order regime in 1965 to 1966, which lasted until 1998. Ricklefs (1993), Vatikiotis (1993), Hill (1994, 1996), Hill and Mackie (1994), and

Schwarz (1999) all elucidate well the major trends in the Indonesian economy between 1966 and 1997.

2 In the 1997 elections, the sixth to be held under Suharto's New Order Government since 1971, the general population voted for 425 members for the House of Representatives, which also had seventy-five seats reserved for representatives of the Armed Forces whose members did not vote. The 1997 elections were contested by the *Partai Rakyat Demokrasi (PDI)* (Indonesian Democratic Party), the *Partai Persatuan Pembangunan (PPP)* (United Development Party) and *Golkar*, the ruling 'party' since 1971 (*Jakarta Post*, 4 March 1997). The House of Representatives then formed part of the Assembly or *Mejelis Permusyawaratan Rakyat (MPR)* (People's Consultative Congress), also including another 500 members appointed by the President. The vast majority of these were *Golkar* members, as well as serving and retired military personnel. The *MPR* convened every five years to elect a president and vice-president and on 10 March 1998 Suharto was sworn in for a seventh five-year term as President, brought to an abrupt end on 21 May 1998 with his resignation (Ricklefs, 1993; Mackie and MacIntyre, 1994; *Reuters*, 8 April 1998; *Guardian*, 22 May 1998). Chapter 8 details changes in the Government structure since that time.

3 While the interim Habibie Government passed Laws 22/1999 and 25/1999 detailing plans for increased autonomy at the district level and giving provinces greater control over their revenues, the degree of *real* autonomy provided is still up for debate (Bourchier, 2000; Sadli, 2000).

4 The total population of Indonesia was 204 million in mid-1998 (Economic and Social Commission for Asia and the Pacific (ESCAP), 1998); rising to 209 million by October 2000 (*Asiaweek*, 13 October 2000).

5 The benchmark for minimum physical needs in 1997 was determined using criteria which included the cost of a daily intake of 3000 calories for a single worker. The criteria raised criticisms from the 'All Indonesian Workers Union' which argued that the minimum physical needs had been calculated using wholesale prices, not retail prices (*New Zealand Herald*, 27 January 1997).

6 See Chapter 8 for a discussion of minimum wage rates since the economic crisis.

7 The 'Malari' affair refers to serious riots that took place in Jakarta in late 1974 to protest against Japanese investments in Indonesia. The riots occurred during a visit by the Japanese Prime Minister, Kakuei Tanaka, with protestors initially alleging that Japanese investments were causing growing economic inequality. The target of the attacks then shifted to also include domestic targets, especially Chinese-Indonesian partners of Japanese firms (Chalmers, 1997a).

8 The Department of Industry was merged with the Department of Trade in late 1996/early 1997 to become the Department of Industry and Trade.

9 There were also other programmes promoted by various government departments that were more localised in their approach, such as the 'Business Incubation Programme', which was heavily focused on Java (Lalkaka, 1996), and 'Venture Capital Company Programmes' that were unevenly distributed around Indonesia (*Jakarta Post*, 11 Marcy 1997). Due to the regional biases found in such programmes, they are not covered in this discussion, unless based in Makassar.

10 Eastern Indonesia is defined to include the islands of Sulawesi, the Nusa Tenggaras, Maluku and Irian Jaya. In Indonesian it is often referred to as *Kawasan Timor Indonesia* [the eastern region of Indonesia] (Barlow, 1996a).

11 The small enterprises in Makassar operated in a context where the nominal Gross Regional Product (GRP) of South Sulawesi in 1992 was Rp.6071 billion (JICA, 1996). This gave a nominal GRP per capita of Rp.840,000 (US$391 at 1992 exchange rates), which was 51 per cent of the country's per capita Gross National Product (GNP) levels. The productivity of human resources in South Sulawesi, as calculated by the GRP per capita, placed the region in the twenty-first position

out of the twenty-seven Indonesian provinces, well below the national average (*BAPPEDA*, 1996; JICA, 1996). It was therefore not a surprise that of the 7 per cent of the total population of Indonesia classified as 'poor' in 1992, 20.3 per cent lived in Sulawesi (JICA, 1996).

12 One of these was later imprisoned on corruption charges however, and was rumoured to have left the country (KI 14, 24/11/96).

13 See Sutherland (1986) for a detailed history of social change within Makassar city during colonial rule.

14 The Central Indonesian Government controls 60 per cent of the shares in *KIMA*, the Regional Government 30 per cent, and the City Government 10 per cent (South Sulawesi Chamber of Commerce and Industry, 1996).

15 See Silvey (2000) for a history of KIMA and a discussion of the effects of the economic crisis on women workers there.

16 This was calculated by combining the unemployed, those working fewer than thirty-five hours a week and willing to work longer, and those earning under Rp.1500 per week (Forbes, 1979).

17 The exchange rate at this time was one pound sterling = 750 Rupiah (Forbes, 1981b).

18 When distinguishing between culture and ethnicity, Kwen Fee and Rajah (1993: 244) state that: 'One can claim ethnic distinctiveness on the basis of 'cultural' criteria such as religion, language and nation', and continue to comment that the critical elements of self-identification of ethnicity include 'a collective name, a common myth of descent, a shared history, a distinctive shared culture, an association with a specific territory and a sense of solidarity' (Kwen Fee and Rajah, 1993: 244). See also Mitchell (1987), Brown (1989), Rogers and Vertovec (1995), and Fukuyama (1996) for more comprehensive discussions of these concepts.

19 Indeed, the last census to enumerate the population by ethnic group was the 1930 Census of the Netherland East Indies (Lineton, 1975).

20 Khan (1980: 25) maintains that the term *adat* is highly ambiguous as it can be used to refer to local traditions, as well as 'the way' a certain ethnic group does things, closer to the anthropological term 'culture'.

21 Detailed information concerning Chinese business relationships in Indonesia may be found in Mackie (1976), Robison (1986), MacIntyre (1991), and Schwarz (1999), among others.

22 Although considered new immigrants, the *totok* had been arriving in Indonesia since the late 1800s (Robison, 1986).

23 In this discussion I use the term 'social relations' rather than 'class' to examine the social organisation and relationships among those involved with the small enterprise sector in Makassar. This is because of the extreme 'class' differences that are apparent in the wider Indonesian context, as in many developing countries. In this book I wish to focus on the similarities and differences among members of what could be considered, in the Marxist sense, one 'class' of this diverse population (Lineton, 1975; Kahn, 1980). Historically, 'class' in South Sulawesi has been used to refer to 'three broad classes: the aristocracy, free persons and slaves' (Harvey, 1974: 25). The entrepreneurs I studied would have been historically considered 'free persons'. Nonetheless, this classification is not subtle enough to capture the nuances of the more recent social relations among small-scale entrepreneurs in the region.

5 Small enterprises in Makassar: internal dynamics

1 Much of the quantitative information in this chapter was gained from data analysis using SPSS, version 7.51 for Windows '95. The percentages used are the 'percentage of responses' (that is, not including 'no answer' results), unless stated otherwise. Although both bivariate correlation and bivariate regression analyses

were undertaken where appropriate, it was often found that scattergrams, produced to confirm the strength and direction (positive or negative) of relationships, and cross-tabulations, were the most suitable statistical methods for use with the data collected. When cross-tabulation methods were utilised, the chi-square test of independence was applied, unless only raw frequencies were required (Bryman and Cramer, 1990; Chapman McGrew and Monroe, 1993).

2 Information from interviews is labelled with the interview number, group and the date the interview was undertaken. For example, for Group A (23a, 15/10/96); for Group B (46b, 3/2/97); and for the information gained from the interviewed shop owners (24c, 24/4/97). These three groups were mutually exclusive.

3 It was difficult to locate entrepreneurs of small enterprises that had ceased to operate to gain an understanding of the causes of their decline. For this reason general information regarding such changes in the city was gained from discussions with a number of key informants instead.

4 Cook and Binford (1990: 236) discuss the difference between family and non-family labour in terms of the petty commodity production approach. They state that those enterprises that have under half the value of output created by waged, non-family labourers are called 'petty commodity producers' and those with over half the value of output created by such labourers are called 'petty capitalist producers'. My research did not study the value of output created by individual workers *per se* (because of the extreme flexibility within the workforce), but I have followed this same approach to a certain extent in examining the importance of family labour or non-family labour to the success of the enterprises (see also Arghiros, 1996).

5 These numbers were for the day the entrepreneur was interviewed and must be taken as a 'rough' guide rather than absolute because of the fluidity of the workforce.

6 People operating enterprises fully within subcontracting systems are called 'enterprise subcontractors' here, while those only partly operating within such arrangements, or undertaking independent production are called 'independent entrepreneurs', as they were able to make considerably more autonomous decisions concerning their enterprises. In sections of the analysis where this distinction is not crucial, the percentages used are for the two groups combined, and the term 'entrepreneur' is used.

7 See Turner (1998) for more details.

8 Similar findings were found in a study of thirty small enterprises by *Pusat Pembinaan Pengusaha Kecil (PPPK)* in 1995. In this the most significant barriers to the enterprises were found to be marketing, followed by funding, levels of investment, productivity and raw materials.

9 The Department of Industry and Trade product categories were not used past the initial interviewing stage because the categories were too broad to be useful in analysis.

10 For Group B specific details concerning only the entrepreneur or enterprise subcontractor were asked (except for the gender of the workers), as the workforce was continuously 'fluid' and 'flexible' due to the numbers of family members involved. The subcontracting enterprises here refer to the 23 per cent detailed in Table 5.4.

11 This area was broadly defined by the entrepreneurs encompassing the town of Rappang and the Lake Sidenreng area, to the north of Makassar (see Chapter 4, Figure 4.2).

12 This was also found to be the case in a five-Asian country survey of the attitudes and behaviours of entrepreneurs (see Yin, 1995).

13 The goldsmiths operated a payment system based on *kaca*, with one *kaca* being the equivalent of one-tenth of a gram of gold.

14 See Turner (1998) for other relevant case studies.

15 Chayanov used this model to look at peasant families operating in an environment

where 'no hired labor or opportunity to work outside the household for wages exist' (Netting, 1993: 301). These opportunities did exist in Makassar, and hence the model needs to be used with caution. Nonetheless, some form of 'self-exploitation' was clearly occurring in enterprises with labour costs of family members far below those of enterprises with non-family labour (see also Scott, 1976; Alexander, 1987; van Diermen, 1997).

16 *BPS South Sulawesi* (1996) has calculated the minimum monthly wage as being based on the daily wage x 30, in accordance with Government regulations introduced in 1996 (*Jakarta Post*, 23 January 1997). However, as the majority of the waged workers in the enterprises studied worked a six-day week, and were not paid for the day they did not work, I have adjusted the calculations accordingly.

17 See Alexander (1987: 88) for a detailed description of the Javanese production method for *tempe*. The Javanese migrants producing *tempe* in Makassar were using the same methods as Alexander described for those in central Java.

18 One important factor was that shipping routes to Eastern Indonesia were not considered to be of strategic importance. Shipping schedules were often unreliable, causing many delays for the delivery of raw materials for small enterprises as well as for marketing (KI 20, 12/5/97).

6 Small enterprises in Makassar: inter-firm dynamics

1 In the context of her study in Quito, Equador, Teltscher (1994) similarly identified family-style loans as being especially important for small-scale entrepreneurs, since they usually came interest-free and were therefore inexpensive in comparison with commercial loans and loan shark agreements.

2 Kahn (1980: 110) describes a very similar pattern of production and interaction with merchants for female seamstresses in West Sumatra.

3 Answers to how problems with raw material supplies might be overcome were grouped into three categories: survivalist-style answers; neutral; and positive and/or innovative answers. These were then individually analysed in clustered bar graphs against product type and then ethnicity, with raw frequencies gained from cross-tabulation.

4 The following information came mostly from twenty-eight interviews with retailers who had shops or stalls in the city, with small enterprises supplying (at least some of) their products. Many of these retailers then also acted as middlepeople, supplying retailers in other regions.

5 This 50 per cent payment system was also found to be used between blacksmiths and merchants in Bukit Tinggi market, by Kahn (1980: 87).

6 See Davis (1997: 13) for a similar discussion, highlighting the importance of family linkages to expanding trading networks from Minangkabau, Sumatra.

7 Pelras (1996b) has suggested that Sulawesi silver filigree work developed in South Sulawesi in the eighteenth century and is called 'Kendari filigree'.

8 I reject the use of Weberian location theory here. Although the small enterprises were located in a cost-minimising way regarding the supply of raw materials, labour and marketing, the production systems were much more complex and broader than this. They also encompassed different internal structures of enterprises as well as inter-firm linkages and interactions, influenced by historical and socio-cultural factors (Walker, 1989).

9 Such findings reflected a study of twenty enterprises (large and small) in Makassar in 1992 by McMahon and *KADIN* employees, in which the most significant barrier the entrepreneurs interviewed faced in improving their enterprises was a lack of capital and interest rates, followed by: human resources/skills; supply or quality of raw materials; government policies; lack of information; and the weak economy (McMahon, 1992).

7 Constraints to small enterprise growth

1 Similar results amongst informal traders in Central Java were found by Evers and Mehmet (1993: 13), with 73 per cent of the traders using their own capital (including daily income) as their main source of working capital.

2 At the time of this discussion, the key informant was the manager of an environmental project. He worked with a Bugis man, who had the Indonesian equivalent to a B.Sc. in soil chemistry, as the leader of the 'soil team'. The soil team also included a professor from a local University with much less practical experience than the leader. Nonetheless the professor was overheard saying to the latter, 'you can't tell me I'm wrong because I'm a professor here and you're not. Don't tell me what to do.' The key informant reported that this was one of many 'don't buck the system' incidents he had witnessed (KI 21, 11/5/97).

3 This suggestion was supported by Professor Macknight, a Sulawesi historian and Professor of Humanities, University of Tasmania (personal communication, 21 May 1998).

4 This was also found by Lineton (1975) in her case study of Bugis household incomes in Ana'banua, near Sengkang, South Sulawesi.

5 See also Rutten (1997) for a discussion of similar conspicuous consumption amongst small-scale iron foundry entrepreneurs in Central Java.

6 A very similar situation was found by Brenner (1998) amongst the merchant community in Laweyan, Java. Brenner (1998: 215) explains how the Arab and Chinese merchants, critical of the Javanese and their tendency towards conspicuous consumption, claimed that the latter were 'spending too much on fancy cars, expensive rituals, and lavish homes . . . the Javanese were letting their capital be 'eaten' . . . instead of investing it in business'.

7 Another goldsmith believed these links were already in trouble. He reported difficulties gaining access to working capital, as the gold in the city was largely controlled by what he called a 'syndicate' of gold shops – the Chinese shops discussed in Chapter 6 – most of which were located on Jalan Somba Opu. Directly or indirectly, they supplied the majority of the gold to Bugis goldsmiths in the city. Thus a goldsmith who did not have linkages with a retailer/supplier in the 'syndicate', or 'fell out' with them, could be placed in a highly detrimental position. The Chinese shop-owners discussed amongst themselves who were the most industrious and reliable goldsmiths, and if a goldsmith fell out with one shop-owner, word soon spread amongst the others (27a, 20/8/96).

8 Bureaucracy is defined here to mean 'any administration in which action is impeded by unnecessary official procedures', thus including privately owned banks and credit-lending agencies, as well as government-operated institutions (*Collins Concise Dictionary*, 1988: 145). Corruption is defined broadly as the act of being 'open to or involving bribery or other dishonest practices' (*Collins Concise Dictionary*, 1988: 252), whilst the definition 'the use of public office for private gain' (Transparency International, reported in *Asiaweek*, 9 October 1998) is also applicable here.

9 The Government departments in the city did not distinguish between independent small enterprises and subcontracting enterprises, the licenses required by both being the same.

10 Similar findings were found by Berry (1999: 21) who reported that in Central Java small entrepreneurs were found to be making legal and illegal payments to various government officials that were reaching 10-20 per cent of an enterprise's profits. The payments were 'frequently an ever larger burden for small enterprises than these figures suggest because payments . . . tend to come together at specific points in time, such as the end of the fasting month and Christmas'.

11 See Schwarz (1999) for an in-depth discussion of the 'big corruption' in Indonesia.

12 A high proportion of civil servants pay or bribe their way into such employment,

which often also requires family connections with current or former civil servants. The cost of obtaining such employment has been reported to be as high as Rp.5 million and ensures that civil servants will then spend a large part of their working lives trying to obtain funds from people requiring their services, to refund their initial 'investment' (*Jakarta Post*, 27 March 1997).

13 For example, this was documented in a 1997 survey by Hong Kong-based Political and Economic Risk Consultancy Ltd, reported in the *Jakarta Post* (1 April 1997).

14 See Chapter 8 for details of credit programmes initiated after the economic crisis concerning small enterprises. The focus and methods of implementation of newer programmes have not altered significantly from earlier ones.

15 This was also found to be the case amongst small enterprises in Java with many producers being unaware that assistance was available (Joseph, 1987).

8 Shifting fortunes of small enterprises

1 The impacts of the economic crisis have been diverse throughout the Indonesian archipelago. The details discussed in this chapter are those deemed the most significant in terms of the small enterprises in Makassar. For more general literature on the Indonesian economic crisis see e.g. Arndt and Hill (1999), Firman (1999), Forrester (1999), Hill (1999b), New Zealand Asia Institute (1999), Schwarz (1999), and Manning and van Diermen (2000).

2 The *result* of the restructuring was a House of Representatives (DPR) consisting of 462 elected members (231 from the outer islands and 231 from Java), and thirty-eight appointed Armed Forces members. The People's Consultative Assembly (MPR) included these 500 DPR members as well as 135 appointees from newly elected provincial legislatures (five from each of the provinces) and sixty-five functional group representatives (Zenzie, 1999: 244). The final results of the elections gave the following division of seats in the elected section of the DPR: Indonesian Democratic Party of Struggle (PDI-P) 153; Golkar 120; United Development Party (PPP) 58; National Awakening Party (PKB) 51; National Mandate Party (PAN) 34; Moon and Star Party (PBB) 13; Justice Party (PK) 7. The remaining twenty-six seats were won by a total of fourteen different parties, each gaining five seats or less each (Bourhier, 2000: 21).

3 The exchange rate in February 2000 when the minimum wage levels were set for that year was US $1= Rp.7255 and £1=Rp.11,514 (*Asiaweek*, 25 February 2000). Compare this with the exchange rate when field work was undertaken initially in 1996, US$1=Rp.2330 and £1=Rp.3612 (26 July 1996); and 1997, US$1=Rp.2415 and £1=Rp.3956 (2 May 1997, prior to the General elections) (*Asiaweek*, 26 July 1996; 2 May 1997).

4 For 1998 one interpretation of the Indonesian poverty line was those unable to reach 'the level of expenditure associated with a daily consumption of 2100 calories' (Cameron, 1999: 38). More precisely, Islam (1998: online) noted that for Indonesia: 'The concept of "poverty line" is based on the daily minimum requirement of 2,100 calories per capita plus a minimum requirement of non-food items (e.g. clothing, education, transportation, and other basic household and individual needs)'.

9 Retrospect and prospect

1 It is not my intention here to move into micro-level policy recommendations. This area has already been covered thoroughly by van Diermen (1997), Berry *et al.* (1999), and Tambunan (2000). Although in agreement with a number of the suggestions they propose, I would argue that in the future, by adopting the small enterprise integrative framework, policy-makers can make recommendations even more in line with localised, emic needs.

Bibliography

Adams, K. 1997a: Touting Touristic 'Primadonas': Tourism, Ethnicity, and National Integration in Sulawesi, Indonesia. In M. Picard and R. E. Wood (eds) *Tourism, Ethnicity, and the State in Asian and Pacific Societies*. University of Hawai'i Press, Honolulu, 155–180.

—— 1997b: Ethnic Tourism and the Renegotiation of Tradition in Tana Toraja (Sulawesi, Indonesia). *Ethnology*, 36 (4), 309–320.

Aeroe, A. 1992: New Pathways to Industrialisation in Tanzania: Theoretical and Strategic Considerations. *Flexible Specialisation: A New View on Small Industry?* IDS Bulletin, 23 (3),15–20.

Aglietta, M. 1979: *A Theory of Capitalist Regulation*. Verso, London.

Ahmed, I. 1999: Additional Insights on Indonesia's Unemployment Crisis. Paper presented at 'The Mini Workshop on Food and Nutrition', Jakarta. 10–12 May.

Alatas, S. H. 1963: The Weber Thesis and South East Asia. *Archives de Sociologie des Religions*, 8 (15), 21–34.

Alexander, J. 1987: *Trade, Traders and Trading in Rural Java*. ASAA Southeast Asia Publications Series, Oxford University Press, Oxford.

Amin, A. 1989: Flexible Specialisation and Small Firms in Italy: Myths and Realities. *Antipode*, 21 (1), 13–34.

—— 1994: Post-Fordism: Models, Fantasies and Phantoms of Transition. In A. Amin (ed.) *Post-Fordism. A Reader*. Blackwell, Oxford, 1–40.

Amin, A. and Robins, K. 1990: The Re-emergence of Regional Economies? The Mythical Geography of Flexible Accumulation. *Environment and Planning D: Society and Space*, 8, 7–34.

Andaya, L. Y. 1995: The Bugis–Makassar Diasporas. *Journal of the Malaysian Branch of the Royal Asiatic Society*, 73 (1), 119–138.

Antweiler, C. 1994: South Sulawesi: Towards a Regional Ethnic identity? Current Trends in a 'Hot' and Historic Region. In I. Wessel (ed.) *Nationalism and Ethnicity in Southeast Asia*. Proceedings of a Conference held at Humboldt University. Volume 1, Berlin, Germany, 87–105.

Arghiros, D. 1996: *Towards an Holistic Approach to Rural Industry: Differentiation and Paternalism in Provincial Thailand*. Occasional Paper 03/96, Centre for Development Studies, University of Bath, Bath.

Arndt, H. W. and Hill, H. (eds) 1999: *Southeast Asia's Economic Crisis. Origins, Lessons, and the Way Forward*. St Martin's Press, New York, and Institute of Southeast Asian Studies, Singapore.

Asia Pulse 1999: Anti Monopoly Law can Protect Small Biz: Expert. *Asia Pulse*, 21

September.

Asian Development Bank, 1999: *Fewer Rules, Better Environment, Business Urges Indonesian Government*. Asian Development Bank News Release, 28 December.

—— 2002: *Developing Small and Medium Enterprises in Indonesia*. Asian Development Bank News Release, 17 April.

Asiaweek 1996: Asiaweek Currencies, 26 July, 72–73.

—— 1997: Asiaweek Currencies,. 2 May, 70–71.

—— 1998: The Essential Crisis Guide, 17 July, 36–67.

—— 1998: Ten Days that Shook Indonesia, 24 July, 30–41.

—— 1998: Monitor. In the Eye of the Beholder, 9 October, 14.

—— 2000: Asiaweek Currencies. 25 February, 46–47.

—— 2000: The Bottom Line, 13 October. (Accessed through Internet site: <http://www.cnn.com/ASIANOW/asiaweek/magazine/2000/1013/bottomline..html>).

Atkinson, J. S. 1985: Flexibility: Planning for an Uncertain Future. *Man Power, Policy and Practice*, 1, summer, 26–38.

Azis, I. J. 1996: Eastern Indonesia in the Current Policy Environment. In C. Barlow and J. Hardjono (eds) *Indonesia Assessment 1995. Development in Eastern Indonesia*. Institute of Southeast Asian Studies, Singapore National University, Singapore, and Research School of Pacific and Asian Studies, Australian National University, Canberra, 75–122.

Babcock, T. 1990: Economy. Fisheries, Farms and Forests. In T. A. Volkman and I. Caldwell (eds) *Sulawesi. The Celebes*. Periplus Editions, Singapore. 38–41.

Bank of Indonesia 2000: *Financial Statistics*. (Accessed through Internet site: <http://www.bi.go.id/ind/datastatistik/index.htm>).

BAPPEDA 1996: Jumlah Investasi, Ujung Pandang [Total Investment, Ujung Pandang]. Unpublished data. Nine pages.

Barlow, C. 1996a: Introduction. In C. Barlow and J. Hardjono (eds) *Indonesia Assessment 1995. Development in Eastern Indonesia*. Institute of Southeast Asian Studies, Singapore National University, Singapore, and Research School of Pacific and Asian Studies, Australian National University, Canberra, 1–17.

—— 1996b: Conclusions. In C. Barlow and J. Hardjono (eds) *Indonesia Assessment 1995. Development in Eastern Indonesia*. Institute of Southeast Asian Studies, Singapore National University, Singapore, and Research School of Pacific and Asian Studies, Australian National University, Canberra, 253–268.

Bernard, H. R. 1995: *Research Methods in Anthropology. Qualitative and Quantitative Approaches*. Alta Mira Press, California.

Berry, A., Rodriguez, E. and Sandee, H. 1999: Firm and Group Dynamics in the Role of the SME Sector of Indonesia. Paper presented to the World Bank Project on 'The Role of Small and Medium Enterprises in Development', 1 November 1999.

Best, M. H. 1990: *The New Competition. Institutions of Industrial Restructuring*. Polity Press, Cambridge.

Biro Pusat Statistik (BPS) Republic of Indonesia [Central Bureau of Statistics] 2002: *Statistics Indonesia*. (Accessed through Internet site: <http://www.bps.go.id/>).

Biro Pusat Statistik (BPS) Kotamadya Ujung Pandang [Central Bureau of Statistics, Municipal Government, Ujung Pandang] 1996: *Kotamadya Ujung Pandang Dalam Angka 1995* [Ujung Pandang in Figures]. *Biro Pusat Statistik (BPS) Kotamadya Ujung Pandang*, Ujung Pandang.

Biro Pusat Statistik (BPS) Sulawesi Selatan [Central Bureau of Statistics, South Sulawesi Region] 1996: *Sulawesi Selatan Dalam Angka 1995* [South Sulawesi in

Figures]. *Biro Pusat Statistik (BPS) Sulawesi Selatan*, Ujung Pandang.

Blackwood, E. 1995: Senior Women, Model Mothers, and Dutiful Wives: Managing Gender Contradictions in a Minangkabau Village. In A. Ong and M. Peletz (eds) *Bewitching Women, Pious Men. Gender and Body Politics in Southeast Asia.* University of California Press, Berkeley, 124–158.

Boeke, R. T. 1953: *Economics and Economic Policy of Dual Societies as Exemplified by Indonesia.* International Secretariat of Pacific Relations, New York.

Booth, A. 1994: Repelita VI and the Second Long-Term Development Plan. *Bulletin of Indonesian Economic Studies*, 30 (3), 3–39.

—— 1999: Impact of the Crisis on Poverty and Equity. In H. W. Arndt and H. Hill (eds) *Southeast Asia's Economic Crisis. Origins, Lessons, and the Way Forward.* St Martin's Press, New York, and Institute of Southeast Asian Studies, Singapore, 128–141.

Booth, D. 1993: Development Research: From Impasse to a New Agenda. In F. J. Schuurman (ed.) *Beyond the Impasse. New Directions in Development Theory.* Zed Books, London, 49–76.

Bourchier, D. 2000: Habibie's Interrugnum: Reformasi, Elections, Regionalism and the Struggle for Power. In C. Manning and P. van Diermen (eds) *Indonesia in Transition.* Institute of Southeast Asian Studies, Singapore, 15–38.

Boyle, J. S. 1994: Styles of Ethnography. In J. M. Morse (ed.) *Critical Issues in Qualitative Research Methods.* Sage Publications, California 159–186.

Bradach, J. L. and Eccles, R. G. 1991: Price, Authority and Trust: From Ideal Types to Plural Forms. In G. Thompson, J. Frances, R. Levacic and J. Mitchell (eds) *Markets, Hierarchies and Networks. The Coordination of Social Life.* Sage Publications, London, 277–292.

Breman, J. 1999: Politics of Poverty and a Leaking Safety Net. *Economic and Political Weekly*, 34 (20), 1177–1178.

Brenner, S. A. 1998: *The Domestication of Desire. Women, Welath, and Modernity in Java.* Princeton University Press, New Jersey.

Bromley, R. 1978: Introduction – The Urban Informal Sector: Why is it Worth Discussing? *World Development*, 6 (9/10), 1033–1039.

—— 1997: Working in the Streets of Cali, Colombia: Survival Strategy, Necessity, or Unavoidable Evil? In J. Gugler (ed.) *Cities in the Developing World. Issues, Theory, and Policy.* Oxford University Press, Oxford 124–138.

Brown, D. 1989: Ethnic Revival: Perspectives. *Third World Quarterly*, 11 (4), 1–16.

Bryman, A. and Cramer, D. 1990: *Quantitative Data Analysis for Social Scientists.* Routledge, London.

Business Advisory Indonesia, 1991: *Study of the Development of Indonesian Business Organisations.* P. T. Yasa Monindo Perdana, Jakarta.

Cameron, L. 1999: Survey of Recent Developments. *Bulletin of Indonesian Economic Studies*, 35 (1), 3–40.

Castells, M. 1989: *The Informational City.* Basil Blackwell, New Work.

Castells, M. and Portes, A. 1989: World Underneath. The Origins, Dynamics and Effects of the Informal Economy. In A. Portes, M. Castells and L. A. Benton (eds) *The Informal Economy. Studies in Advanced and Less Developed Countries.* Johns Hopkins University Press, Baltimore, 11–37.

Chalmers, I. 1997a: The 'Society-First' Critics. Introduction. In I. Chalmers and V. R. Hadiz (eds) *The Politics of Economic Development in Indonesia. Contending Perspectives.* Routledge, London, 56–60.

—— 1997b: The Continued Appeal to State-Nationalism. Introduction. In I. Chalmers and V. R. Hadiz (eds) *The Politics of Economic Development in Indonesia. Contending Perspectives*. Routledge, London, 163–167.

Chapman McGrew, J. and Monroe, C. 1993: *An Introduction to Statistical Problem Solving in Geography*. Wm C. Brown Publishers, Iowa.

Chauvel, R. 1996: Beyond the Wallace Line. In C. Barlow and J. Hardjono (eds) *Indonesia Assessment 1995. Development in Eastern Indonesia*. Institute of Southeast Asian Studies, Singapore National University, Singapore, and Research School of Pacific and Asian Studies, Australian National University, Canberra, 61–74.

Chayanov, A. V. 1966: *The Theory of Peasant Economy* (trans. D. Thorner). The American Economic Association, Illinois.

Chickering, A. and Salahdine, M. 1991: Introduction. In A. Chickering and M. Salahdine (eds) *The Silent Revolution. The Informal Sector in Five Asian and Near Eastern Countries*. International Center For Economic Growth, California, 1–14.

Childs, P. and Williams, P. 1997: *An Introduction to Post-Colonial Theory*. Prentice Hall, Hertfordshire.

Christopherson, S. 1989: Flexibility in the US Service Economy and the Emerging Spatial Division of Labour. *Transactions of the Institute of British Geographers*, 14, 131–143.

Clairmonte, F. and Cavanagh, J. 1983: Transnational Corporations and The Struggle For The Global Market. *Journal of Contemporary Asia*, 13 (4), 446–481.

Cohen, M. 1998a: Funeral Rights. *Far Eastern Economic Review*, 161 (3), 36–38.

—— 1998b: Moving Targets. A City's Ethnic Chinese Community Shelters its Assets. *Far Eastern Economic Review*, 161 (8), 51.

Cohen, M. and Murphy, D. 1999: Indonesia. Swept Away. *Far Eastern Economic Review*, 8 April (internet edition).

Cohen, S. and Zysman, J. 1987: *Manufacturing Matters: The Myth of the Post-Industrial Economy*. Basic Books, London.

Collins Concise Dictionary 1988. Collins, London.

Competency Based Economies through Formation of Enterprise (CEFE), 1996: *CEFE in Indonesia*. CEFE, Jakarta.

Cook, S. and Binford, L. 1990: *Obliging Need. Rural Petty Industry in Mexican Capitalism*. University of Texas Press, Austin.

Corbridge, S. 1986: *Capitalist World Development. A Critique of Radical Development Geography*. Macmillan Education, London.

—— 1993: Marxisms, Modernities, and Moralities: Development Praxis and the Claims of Distant Strangers. *Environment and Planning D: Society and Space*, 11, 449–472.

Cox, K. R. 1993: The Local and the Global in the New Urban Politics: A Critical View. *Environment and Planning D: Society and Space*, 11, 433–448.

—— 1995: Globalisation, Competition and the Politics of Local Economic Development. *Urban Studies*, 32 (2), 213–224.

Crush, J. 1994: Post-colonialism, De-colonization, and Geography. In A. Godlewska and N. Smith (eds) *Geography and Empire*. Blackwell, Oxford, 333–350.

—— 1995: Introduction. Imaging Development. In J. Crush (ed.) *Power of Development*. Routledge, London, 1–26.

Curry, J. 1993: The Flexibility Fetish. A Review Essay on Flexible Specialisation. *Capital and Class*, 50, Summer, 99–126.

Dahles, H. 1999: Tourism and Small Entrepreneurs in Developing Countries. A Theoretical Perspective. In H. Dahles and K. Bras (eds) *Tourism and Small Entrepreneurs: Development, National Policy, and Entrepreneurial Culture: Indonesian Cases.* Cognizant Communication Corporation, New York, 1–19.

Das, S. K. and Panayiotopoulos, P. 1996: Flexible Specialisation. New Paradigm for Industrialisation for Developing Countries? *Economic and Political Weekly*, 31 (52), L57–61.

Davies, R. 1979: Informal Sector Or Subordinate Mode of Production? A Model. In R. Bromley and C. Gerry (eds) *Casual Work and Poverty in Third World Cities.* John Wiley and Sons, Chichester, 87–104.

Davis, C. 1997: *Women's Conversations in a Minangkabau Market: Toward an Understanding of the Social Context of Economic Transactions.* Occasional Paper No 33, Centre for South-East Asian Studies, University of Hull, Hull.

Dawam Rahardjo, M. 1994: Small Scale Business in the Indonesian Economy. In M. Dawam Rahardjo (ed.) *Small Business in the Indonesian Economy.* The Ministry of Cooperatives and Small Enterprises, Jakarta, ix–xli.

Dawson, J. 1992: The Relevance of the Flexible Specialisation Paradigm for Small-Scale Industrial Restructuring in Ghana. *Flexible Specialisation: A New View on Small Industry?* IDS Bulletin, 23 (3), 34–38.

De Koninck, R. 1994: *L'Asie du Sud-Est.* Masson, Paris.

Departemen Koperasi dan Pembinaan Pengusaha Kecil [Department of Co-operatives and Small Enterprises] 1995: *Undang-Undang Republik Indonesia. Nomor 9 Tahun 1995 Tentung Usaha Kecil* [Law of the Republic of Indonesia. No. 9 1995 regarding small enterprises]. Department of Co-operatives and Small Enterprises, Jakarta.

Departemen Koperasi dan Pembinaan Pengusaha Kecil, Sulawesi Selatan [Department of Co-operatives and Small Enterprises, South Sulawesi] 1997: *Rapat Konsultasi Nasional Bidang Pembinaan Pengusaha Kecil Tanggal, 10–11 April 1997 di Jakarta* [National Consultation Report regarding Small Enterprise Establishment, 10–11 April 1997, Jakarta]. South Sulawesi Department of Co-operatives and Small Enterprises, Ujung Pandang.

Departemen Perindustrian Dan Perdagangan, Kotamadya Ujung Pandang [Department of Industry and Trade, Ujung Pandang] 1995: *Data Perkembangan Industri Kecil Tahun* 1995 [Development Data for Small Industries Year 1995]. Ujung Pandang Department of Industry and Trade, Ujung Pandang.

De Soto, H. 1989: *The Other Path. The Invisible Revolution in The Third World.* Harper and Row, New York.

Dewar, D. and Watson, V. 1990: *Urban Markets: Developing Informal Retailing.* Routledge, London.

Dicken, P. 1993: The Changing Organisation of The Global Economy. In R. J. Johnston (ed.) *The Challenge For Geography. A Changing World: A Changing Discipline.* Blackwell, Oxford, 31–53.

—— 1994: The Roepke Lecture in Economic Geography. Global–Local Tensions: Firms and States in the Global Space-Economy. *Economic Geography*, 70 (2), 101–128.

Dicken, P. and Yeung, H. W. 1999: Investing in the Future: East and Southeast Asian Firms in the Global Economy. In K. Olds, P. Dicken, P. F. Kelly, L. Kong and H. W. Yeung (eds) *Globalisation and the Asia-Pacific.* Routledge, London, 107–128.

Dieleman, F. M. and Hamnett, C. 1994: Globalisation, Regulation and the Urban System: Editors' Introduction To the Special Issue. *Urban Studies*, 31 (3), 357–364.

DiGregorio, M. R. 1994: *Urban Harvest: Recycling as a Peasant Industry in Northern Vietnam.* East-West Center Occasional Papers, No. 17. East-West Center, Hawaii.

Dixon, C. and Drakakis-Smith, D. 1993: The Pacific Asia Region. In C. Dixon and D. Drakakis-Smith (eds) *Economic and Social Development in Pacific Asia.* Routledge, London, 1–21.

Dodd, T. 2000: Indonesians in for Belt Tightening as Prices Escalate. *Australian Financial Review.* 26 February (Assessed through internet listserve: <joyo@aol.com>).

Dos Santos, M. 1979: *The Shared Space. The Two Circuits of the Urban Economy in Underdeveloped Countries.* Methuen, London.

—— 1984: The Structure of Dependence. In M. A. Seligson (ed.) *The Gap Between Rich and Poor. Contending Perspectives On the Political Economy of Development.* Westview Press, Colorado, 95–104.

Douglass, M. 1992: Global Opportunities and Local Challenges for Regional Economies. *Regional Development Dialogue,* 13 (2), 3–21.

—— 1998: The Global–Local Context of Work and Urban Poverty in Asia. In B. Helmsing and J. Guimaraes (eds) *Locality, State and Development.* Institute of Social Studies, The Hague, 295–311.

—— 2001: Urban and Regional Policy After the Era of Naïve Globalism. In Asfaw Kumssa and T. G. McGee (eds) *New Regional Development Paradigms, Volume 1.* Greenwood Publishing Group, Westport, CT, 33–56.

Drake, C. 1989: *National Integration in Indonesia. Patterns and Policies.* University of Hawaii Press, Honolulu.

Echtner, C. M. 1995: Entrepreneurial Training in Developing Countries. *Annals of Tourism Research,* 22 (1), 119–134.

Economic and Social Commission for Asia and the Pacific (ESCAP) 1993: *Small Industry Bulletin for Asia and the Pacific,* 28. United Nations, New York.

—— 1998: *Population Data Sheet.* United Nations, New York.

Economist, The. 1998a: Survey. East Asian Economies, 7 March, 3–20.

—— 1998b: Asia goes to the Dole, 25 April, 79–83.

Economist Intelligence Unit Limited 1995: *Indonesia.* Economist Intelligence Unit Limited, New York.

Errington, S. 1990: Recasting Sex, Gender, and Power. A Theoretical and Regional Overview. In J. M. Atkinson and S. Errington (eds) *Power and Difference. Gender in Island Southeast Asia.* Stanford University Press, California, 1–58.

Evans, G. 1993: Introduction: Asia and the Anthropological Imagination. In G. Evans (ed.) *Asia's Cultural Mosaic. An Anthropological Introduction.* Prentice Hall, Singapore, 1–29.

Evers, H. D. and Mehmet, O. 1993: *The Management of Risk: Informal Trade in Indonesia.* Working Paper 186, Sociology of Development Research Centre, University of Bielefeld, Bielefeld, Germany.

—— 1994: The Management of Risk. Informal Trade in Indonesia. *World Development,* 22 (1), 1–9.

Fagan, R. H. and Le Heron, R. B. 1994: Reinterpreting the Geography of Accumulation: The Global Shift and Local Restructuring. *Environment and Planning D: Society and Space,* 12, 265–285.

Far Eastern Economic Review 1996: Indonesia Trade and Investment. Focus/Cover Story, 16 May, 39–57.

Feridhanusetyawan, T. 1999: Security Implication of the Economic Crisis for

Indonesian Workers. Paper presented at the CCSEAS-NWRCSEAS Conference, Vancouver, 22–24 October.

Fernandez Kelly, M. P. 1989: International Development and Industrial Restructuring: The Case of Garment and Electronics Industries in Southern California. In A. MacEwan and W. Tabb (eds) *Instability and Change in the World Economy*. Monthly Review Press, New York.

Firman, T. 1999: Guest Editorial. Indonesian Cities under the 'Krismon'. *Cities*, 16 (2), 69–82.

Forbes, D. 1978: Urban–Rural Interdependence: The Trishaw Riders of Ujung Pandang. In P. J. Rimmer, D. W. Drakakis-Smith and T. G. McGee (eds) *Food, Shelter and Transport in Southeast Asia and the Pacific*. Australian National University, Canberra, 219–236.

——1979: *The Pedlars of Ujung Pandang*. Working Paper No 17, Centre of Southeast Asian Studies, Monash University, Melbourne.

——1981a: Production, Reproduction, and Underdevelopment: Petty Commodity Producers in Ujung Pandang, Indonesia. *Environment and Planning A*, 13, 841–856.

——1981b: Petty Commodity Production and Underdevelopment: The Case of Pedlars and Trishaw Riders in Ujung Pandang, Indonesia. *Progress in Planning*, 16 (2), 105–178.

——1986: Spatial Aspects of Third World Multinational Corporations' Direct Investment in Indonesia. In M. Taylor and N. Thrift (eds) *Multinationals and the Restructuring of the World Economy. The Geography of Multinationals, Volume 2*. Croom Helm, Kent, 105–141.

——1988: Getting By in Indonesia: Research in a Foreign Land. In J. Eyles (ed.) *Research in Human Geography. Introductions and Investigations*. Basil Blackwell, Oxford, 100–120.

Forrester, G. 1999: Introduction. In G. Forrester (ed.) *Post-Soeharto Indonesia. Renewal or Chaos? Indonesia Assessment 1998*. Australian National University, Canberra, 1–18.

Fukuyama, F. 1996: *Trust. The Social Virtues and the Creation of Prosperity*. Free Press Paperbacks, New York.

Galhardi, R. M. A. A. 1995: Flexible Specialisation, Technology and Employment. Networks in Developing Countries. *Economic and Political Weekly*, 30 (34), m124–m128.

Gartman, D. 1998: Postmodernism; or, the Cultural Logic of Post-Fordism? *The Sociological Quarterly*, 39 (1), 119–137.

Geertz, C. 1963: *Peddlers and Princes. Social Change and Economic Modernization in Two Indonesian Towns*. University of Chicago Press, Chicago.

Gerry, C. 1987: Developing Economies and the Informal Sector in Historical Perspective. *The Annals of the American Academy of Political and Social Science. The Informal Economy*, 493, 100–119.

Gertler, M. 1992: Flexibility Revisited: Districts, Nation-States, and the Forces of Production. *Transactions of the Institute of British Geographers*, 17, 259–278.

——1994: Post-Fordism. In R. J. Johnston, D. Gregory and D. Smith (eds) *The Dictionary of Human Geography* (3rd edn). Blackwell, Oxford, 459.

Gilbert, A. and Gugler, J. 1992: *Cities, Poverty and Development. Urbanization in the Third World*. Oxford University Press, Oxford.

Goody, E. N. (ed.) 1982: *From Craft to Industry. The Ethnography of Proto-Industrial*

Cloth Production. Cambridge Papers in Social Anthropology, Cambridge University Press, Cambridge.

Gordon, D. M. 1988: The Global Economy: New Edifice Or Crumbling Foundations? *New Left Review*, 168, 24–64.

Government of Indonesia 1998: *Memorandum of Economic and Financial Policies*. Government of Indonesia, Jakarta (accessed through internet site: <www.imf.org/external/np/loi /011598.htm>).

Grabher, G. 1993: Rediscovering the Social in the Economics of Interfirm Relations. In G. Grabher (ed.) *The Embedded Firm. On the Socioeconomics of Industrial Networks*. Routledge, London, 1–31.

Graham, J. 1991: Fordism/Post-Fordism, Marxism/Post-Marxism: The Second Cultural Divide? *Rethinking MARXISM*, 4 (1), 39–58.

——1992: Post-Fordism As Politics: The Political Consequences of Narratives On The Left. *Environment and Planning D: Society and Space*, 10, 393–410.

Grieco, M. 1995: Transported Lives: Urban Social Networks and Labour Circulation. In A. Rogers and S. Vertovec (eds) *The Urban Context. Ethnicity, Social Networks and Situational Analysis*. Berg, Oxford, 189–212.

Grijns, M., Smyth, I. and van Velzen, A. 1994: Introduction. In M. Grijns, I. Smyth, A. van Velzen, S. Machfud and P. Sayogyo (eds) *Different Women, Different Work. Gender and Industrialisation in Indonesia*. Avebury, Aldershot, 1–8.

Grijns, M., Machfud, S., Smyth I. and van Velzen, A. 1994: The Sectors and Branches Studied. In M. Grijns, I. Smyth, A. van Velzen, S. Machfud and P. Sayogyo (eds) *Different Women, Different Work. Gender and Industrialisation in Indonesia*. Avebury, Aldershot, 95–122.

Gugler, J. 1997: Patterns of Political Integration and Conflict. Introduction. In J. Gugler (ed.) *Cities in the Developing World. Issues, Theory, and Policy*. Oxford University Press, Oxford, 307–313.

Guinness, P. 1986: *Harmony and Hierarchy in a Javanese Kampung*. ASAA Southeast Asia Publications Series, Oxford University Press, Oxford.

——1993: People in Cities. Anthropology in Urban Asia. In G. Evans (ed.) *Asia's Cultural Mosaic. An Anthropological Introduction*. Prentice Hall, Singapore, 307–323.

——1994: Local Society and Culture. In H. Hill (ed.) *Indonesia's New Order. The Dynamics of Socio-Economic Transformation*. University of Hawaii Press, Honolulu, 267–305.

Hakim, C. 1988: Homeworking in Britain. In R. E. Pahl (ed.) *Work, Historical, Comparative and Theoretical Approaches*. Blackwell, New York, 609–632.

Hancock, P. J. 1996: Labour and Women in Java: A New Historical Perspective. *The Indonesian Quarterly*, 24(3), 290–302.

Hart, K. 1973: Informal Income Opportunities and Urban Employment in Ghana. *The Journal of Modern African Studies*, 11 (1), 61–89.

Harvey, B. S. 1974: *Tradition, Islam and Rebellion: South Sulawesi 1950–1965*. Ph.D. Thesis, Cornell University, University Microfilms, Ann Arbor, Michigan.

Harvey, D. 1989: *The Condition of Postmodernity*. Blackwell, Oxford.

Hatta, M. 1957: *The Co-operative Movement in Indonesia*. Cornell University Press, New York.

Hays-Mitchell, M. 1993: The Ties that Bind. Informal and Formal Sector Linkages in Streetvending: The Case of Peru's *Ambulantes*. *Environment and Planning A*, 25, 1085–1102.

Hayter, R. 1997: *The Dynamics of Industrial Location. The Factory, the Firm and the Production System.* John Wiley and Sons, Chichester.

Healy, T. and Tesoro, J. M. 1998: Judging Habibie. *Asiaweek*, 4 September. 18–22.

Hemmer, H. R. and Mannel, C. 1989: On the Economic Analysis of the Urban Informal Sector. *World Development,* 17 (10), 1543–1552.

Hettne, B. 1995: *Development Theory and the Three Worlds* (2nd edn). Longman Scientific and Technical, Essex.

Heyzer, N. 1986: *Working Women in South-East Asia. Development, Subordination and Emancipation.* Open University Press, Milton Keynes.

Hill, H. 1990: Indonesia's Industrial Transformation. Part I. *Bulletin of Indonesian Economic Studies*, 26 (2), 79–120.

—— 1993: *Where is the Indonesian Economy Headed?* Occasional Paper Series No. 3, Centre for Southeast Asian Studies, Northern Territory University, Australia.

—— 1994: The Economy. In H. Hill (ed.) *Indonesia's New Order. The Dynamics of Socio-Economic Transformation.* University of Hawaii Press, Honolulu, 54–122.

—— 1996: *The Indonesian Economy since 1966. Southeast Asia's Emerging Giant.* Cambridge University Press, Cambridge.

—— 1997a: Myths About Tigers: Indonesian Development Policy Debates. *The Pacific Review*, 10 (2), 256–273.

—— 1997b: *Indonesia's Industrial Transformation.* Institute of Southeast Asian Studies, Singapore.

—— 1998: Introduction. In H. Hill and K. W. Thee (eds) *Indonesia's Technological Challenge.* Institute of Southeast Asian Studies, Singapore National University, Singapore, and Research School of Pacific and Asian Studies, Australian National University, Canberra, 1–54.

—— 1999a: An Overview of the Issues. In H. W. Arndt and H. Hill (eds) *Southeast Asia's Economic Crisis. Origins, Lessons, and the Way Forward.* St Martin's Press, New York, and Institute of Southeast Asian Studies, Singapore 1–15.

—— 1999b: *The Indonesian Economy in Crisis. Causes, Consequences and Lessons.* Allen and Unwin, Australia.

Hill, H. and Mackie, J. 1994: Introduction. In H. Hill (ed.) *Indonesia's New Order. The Dynamics of Socio-Economic Transformation.* University of Hawaii Press, Honolulu, xxii–xxxv.

—— 2001: Small and Medium Enterprises in Indonesia: Old Policy Changes for a New Administration. *Asian Survey*, 41 (2), 248–270.

Hirst, P. and Zeitlin, J. 1991: Flexible Specialization verses Post-Fordism: Theory, Evidence and Policy Implications. *Economy and Society*, 20 (1), 1–56.

Holmes, J. 1986: The Organization and Locational Structure of Production Subcontracting. In A. J. Scott and M. Storper (eds) *Production, Work, Territory. The Geographical Anatomy of Industrial Capitalism.* Allen and Unwin, London, 80–106.

Holmstrom, M. 1993: Flexible Specialisation in India? *Economic and Political Weekly*, 28 (35), m82–m86.

Howard, S. 1994: Methodological Issues in Overseas Fieldwork: Experiences from Nicaragua's Northern Atlantic Coast. In E. Robson and K. Willis (eds) *Postgraduate Fieldwork in Developing Areas: A Rough Guide.* Monograph No. 8. Developing Areas Research Group, Institute of British Geographers, London, 19–35.

Hugo, G. 1993: International Labour Migration. In C. Manning and J. Hardjono (eds)

Indonesia Assessment 1993. Labour: Sharing the Benefits of Growth? Proceedings of Indonesia Update Conference, August, Research School of Pacific Studies, Australian National University, Canberra, 108–123.

Huq, M. and Sultan, M. 1991: 'Informality' in Development: The Poor As Entrepreneurs in Bangladesh. In A. Chickering and M. Salahdine (eds) *The Silent Revolution. The Informal Sector in Five Asian and Near Eastern Countries.* International Center For Economic Growth, California, 145–184.

Husaini, M., Hardjosoekarto, S., Nurasa H. and Mariman, T. 1996: Small-Scale Enterprises Development in Indonesia. In M. Pangestu (ed.) *Small-Scale Business Development and Competition Policy.* Centre for Strategic and International Studies, Jakarta, 7–19.

Hutagalung, N. K., Grijns, M. and White, B. 1994: Women as Wage Workers. In M. Grijns, I. Smyth, A. van Velzen, S. Machfud and P. Sayogyo (eds) *Different Women, Different Work. Gender and industrialisation in Indonesia.* Avebury, Aldershot, 147–172.

Ibrahim, I. 1999: Donggala Cacao Farmers Savor Robust Business Amid Crisis. *The Jakarta Post,* 28 January.

Institut Studi Arus Informasi [Study Institute for the Flow of Information] 1998: *Amuk Makassar* [Makassar Run Amuck], *Institut Studi Arus Informasi,* Jakarta.

International Labour Office 1972: *Employment, Incomes and Equality: A Strategy For Increasing Productive Employment in Kenya.* International Labour Organisation, Geneva.

—— 1995: *Gender, Poverty and Employment: Turning Capabilities into Entitlements.* International Labour Organisation, Geneva.

—— 1998a: *Employment Challenges of the Indonesian Economic Crisis.* ILO and United Nations Development Programme, Jakarta.

—— 1998b: *The Social Impact of the Asian Financial Crisis.* Technical Report for Discussion at the High-Level Tripartite Meeting on Social Responses to the Financial Crisis in East and South-East Asian Countries, 22–24 April. ILO, Bangkok.

Islam, R. 1998: *Indonesia: Economic Crisis, Adjustment, Employment and Poverty.* Issues In Development. Discussion Paper 23. International Labour Organisation (accessed through internet site: <http://www.ilo.org/public/english/employment/strat/poldev/publ/iddp23.htm>).

Jackson, J. C. 1978: Trader Hierarchies in Third World Distributing Systems: The case of Fresh Food Supplies in Kuala Lumpur. In P. J. Rimmer, D. W. Drakakis-Smith and T. G. McGee (eds) *Food, Shelter and Transport in Southeast Asia and the Pacific.* Australian National University, Canberra, 33–61.

Jacobs, J. 1996: *Edge of Empire. Postcolonialism and the City.* Routledge, London.

James, J. and Bhalla, A. 1993: Flexible Specialization, New Technologies and Future Industrialization in Developing Countries. *Futures,* 25 (6), 713–732.

Japan International Cooperation Agency (JICA) 1996: *Master Plan and Feasibility Study on Wastewater and Solid Waste Management for the City of Ujung Pandang in the Republic of Indonesia. Final Report. Supporting Report.* JICA, Tokyo.

Jellinek, L. 1978: Circular Migration and the Pondok Dwelling System: A Case Study of Ice-Cream Traders in Jakarta. In P. J. Rimmer, D. W. Drakakis-Smith and T. G. McGee (eds) *Food, Shelter and Transport in Southeast Asia and the Pacific.* Australian National University, Canberra, 135–154.

—— 1997: Displaced by Modernity: The Saga of a Jakarta Street-Trader's Family from the 1940s to the 1990s. In J. Gugler (ed.) *Cities in the Developing World. Issues, Theory, and Policy*. Oxford University Press, Oxford, 139–155.

Jemadu, A. 1997: Indonesia's Nation-Building Process at the Crossroads. *Jakarta Post*. 4 March, 5.

Jones, G. 1994: Labour Force and Education. In H. Hill (ed.) *Indonesia's New Order. The Dynamics of Socio-Economic Transformation*. University of Hawaii Press, Honolulu, 145–178.

Jones, G. and Supraptilah, B. 1976: Underutilisation of Labour in Palembang and Ujung Pandang. *Bulletin of Indonesian Economic Studies*, 12 (2), 30–57.

Joseph, R. 1987: *Worker, Middlewomen, Entrepreneur: Women in the Indonesian Batik Industry*. The Population Council, Bangkok.

Kabra, K. N. 1995: The Informal Sector: A Reappraisal. *Journal of Contemporary Asia*, 25 (2), 197–232.

Kahn, J. S. 1974: Imperialism and the Reproduction of Capitalism. Towards a Definition of the Indonesian Social Formation. *Critique of Anthropology*, 2, 1–35.

—— 1978: Ideology and Social Structure in Indonesia. *Comparative Studies in Society and History*, 20, 103–122.

—— 1980: *Minangkabau Social Formations. Indonesian Peasants and the World-Economy*. Cambridge University Press, Cambridge.

Kalla, M. J. 1995: *Hadji Kalla Group*. NV. Hadji Kalla Trd. Coy. Ujung Pandang.

Kaplinsky, R. 1991: *From Mass Production to Flexible Specialisation: A Case Study from a Semi-Industrialised Economy*. Institute of Development Studies Discussion Paper 295, University of Sussex, Brighton.

—— 1994: From Mass Production to Flexible Specialization: A Case Study of Microeconomic Change in a Semi-industrialized Economy. *World Development*, 22 (3), 337–353.

Kelly, P. F. 1999: The Geographies and Politics of Globalization. *Progress in Human Geography*, 23 (3), 379–400.

Kindon, S. 1995: Balinese Gender Relations and the State: National Transformation of a Local System. In J. DeBernardi, G. Forth and S. Niessen (eds) *Managing Change in Southeast Asia. Local Identities, Global Connections*. Proceedings of the Twenty-first Meeting of the Canadian Council for Southeast Asian Studies, Canadian Asian Studies Association, Montreal, 59–73.

Kingsbury, D. 1998: *The Politics of Indonesia*. Oxford University Press, Melbourne.

Kingsley, D. 2000: Developing Indonesia's SMEs in the Digital Era. *Jakarta Post*, 21 February (accessed through internet site: <http//:www.thejakartapost.com>).

Knorringa, P. 1996: Operationalisation of Flexible Specialisation. Agra's Footwear Industry. *Economic and Political Weekly*, 31 (52), L50–L56.

Kristanto, K., Parenta, T. and Sturgess, N. 1989: South Sulawesi: New Directions in Agriculture? In H. Hill (ed.) *Unity and Diversity. Regional Economic Development in Indonesia Since 1970*. Oxford University Press, Oxford, 386–407.

Kwen Fee, L. and Rajah, A. 1993: The Ethnic Mosaic. In G. Evans (ed.) *Asia's Cultural Mosaic. An Anthropological Introduction*. Prentice Hall, Singapore, 234–259.

Lal, J. 1996: Situating Locations: The Politics of Self, Identity, and 'Other' in Living and Writing the Text. In D. L. Wolf (ed.) *Feminist Dilemmas in Fieldwork*. Westview Press, Colorado, 185–214.

Lalkaka, R. 1996: *Action Plan for Expansion of Business Incubation Program in Indonesia*. Business and Technology Development Strategies, New York.

Latanro, H. 1994: *Usulan Pengembangan Usaha Kecil di Kawasan Timur Indonesia*

[Proposal for the Development of Small Businesses in the East Indonesian Region]. YAPSAKTI, Ujung Pandang.

Leborgne, D. and Lipietz, A. 1988: New Technologies, New Modes of Regulation: Some Spatial Implications. *Environment and Planning D: Society and Space*, 6, 263–280.

Lindsey, T. 2000: Black Letter, Black Market and Bad Faith: Corruption and the Failure of Law Reform. In C. Manning and P. van Diermen (eds) *Indonesia in Transition. Social Aspects of Reformasi and Crisis*. Institute of Southeast Asian Studies, Singapore, 278–292.

Lineton, J. A. 1975: An Indonesian Society and its Universe. A Study of the Bugis of South Sulawesi (Celebes) and their Role within a Wider Social and Economic System. Ph.D. Thesis. School of Oriental and Asian Studies, University of London, London.

Lipietz, A. 1986: New Tendencies in the International Division of Labor: Regimes of Accumulation and Modes of Regulation. In A. Scott and M. Storper (eds) *Production, Work, Territory. The Geographical Anatomy of Industrial Capitalism*. Allen and Unwin, London, 16–40.

—— 1993: The Local and the Global: Regional Individuality or Interregionalism? *Transactions of the Institute of British Geographers*, 18 (1), 8–18.

Lomnitz, L. 1997: The Social and Economic Organization of a Mexican Shanty-Town. In J. Gugler (ed.) *Cities in the Developing World. Issues, Theory, and Policy*. Oxford University Press, Oxford, 204–217.

Lorenz, E. H. 1991: Neither Friends nor Strangers: Informal Networks of Subcontracting in French Industry. In G. Thompson, J. Frances, R Levacic and J. Mitchell (eds) *Markets, Hierarchies and Networks. The Coordination of Social Life*. Sage Publications, London, 183–192.

—— 1992: Trust, Community, and Cooperation. Toward a Theory of Industrial Districts. In A. J. Scott and M. Storper (eds) *Pathways to Industrialization and Regional Development*. Routledge, London, 195–204.

Loveard, K. 1996: A New Dilemma in Dili. As the Army Backs off, is Autonomy the Answer? *Asiaweek*, 13 December, 24–25.

Lubell, H. 1991: *The Informal Sector in the 1980s and 1990s*. Development Centre of the Organisation for Economic Co-Operation and Development, Paris.

Luke, T. W. 1994: Placing Power/Siting Space: the Politics of Global and Local in the New World Order. *Environment and Planning D: Society and Space*, 12, 613–628.

McBeth, J. 1998: The Empire Strikes Back. *Far Eastern Economic Review*, 9 July, 20–21.

McDowell, L. 1991: Life Without Father and Ford: The New Gender Order of Post-Fordism. *Transactions of the Institute of British Geographers*, 16, 400–419.

MacEwen Scott, A. 1979: Who Are the Self-Employed? In R. Bromley and C. Gerry (eds) *Casual Work and Poverty in Third World Cities*. John Wiley and Sons, Chichester, 105–129.

McGee, T. G. 1976: The Persistence of the Proto-Proletariat: Occupational Structures and Planning of the Future of Third World Cities. *Progress in Geography*, 9, 3–38.

—— 1978: An Invitation To the 'Ball': Dress Formal Or Informal? In P. J. Rimmer, D. W. Drakakis-Smith and T. G. McGee (eds) *Food, Shelter and Transport in Southeast Asia and the Pacific*. Australian National University, Canberra, 3–27.

—— 1979: The Poverty Syndrome: Making Out in the Southeast Asian City. In R. Bromley and C. Gerry (eds) *Casual Work and Poverty in Third World Cities*. John

Wiley and Sons, Chichester, 45–68.

—— 1991: Presidential Address: Eurocentrism in Geography-The Case of Asian Geography. *The Canadian Geographer*, 35 (4), 332–344.

—— 1995: Eurocentrism and Geography. Reflections on Asian Urbanization. In J. Crush (ed.) *Power of Development*. Routledge, London, 192–210.

McGee, T. G. and Yeung, Y. M. 1977: *Hawkers in Southeast Asian Cities. Planning For the Bazaar Economy*. International Development Research Centre, Ottawa.

McIndoe, A. 2000: Asian Development Bank Grants $200M Industry Loan in Indonesia. *Dow Jones Newswires*, 16 March.

MacIntyre, A. 1991: *Business and Politics in Indonesia*. ASAA Publication Series, Allen and Unwin, Sydney.

Mackie, J. A. (ed.) 1976: *The Chinese in Indonesia*. Thomas Nelson, Melbourne.

Mackie, J. A. and MacIntyre, A. 1994: Politics. In H. Hill (ed.) *Indonesia's New Order. The Dynamics of Socio-Economic Transformation*. University of Hawaii Press, Honolulu, 1–53.

Macknight, C. 1998: Professor of Humanities, University of Tasmania, informal discussion, 21 May.

McMahon, L. 1992: *Final Report. An Analysis of South Sulawesi KADIN Activities and Operations*. KADIN, Ujung Pandang.

Machfud, S., van Velzen A. and Smyth, I. 1994: Women as Entrepreneurs. In M. Grijns, I. Smyth, A. van Velzen, S. Machfud and P. Sayogyo (eds) *Different Women, Different Work. Gender and industrialisation in Indonesia*. Avebury, Aldershot.

Mann, C. 1993: Book Review: The Silent Revolution in Five Asian and Near Eastern Countries. *The Journal of Asian Studies*, 52 (1), 112–114.

Manning, C. 1993: Examining Both Sides of the Ledger: Economic Growth and Labour Welfare Under Soeharto. In C. Manning and J. Hardjono (eds) *Indonesia Assessment 1993. Labour: Sharing the Benefits of Growth?* Proceedings of Indonesia Update Conference, August, Research School of Pacific Studies, Australian National University, Canberra, 61–87.

—— 1998: *Indonesian Labour in Transition. An East Asian Success Story?* Cambridge University Press, Cambridge.

Manning, C. and van Diermen, P. 2000 (eds) *Indonesia in Transition. Social Aspects of Reformasi and Crisis*. Institute of Southeast Asian Studies, Singapore.

Massey, D. 1983: Industrial Restructuring as Class Restructuring: Production Decentralization and Local Uniqueness. *Regional Studies*, 17 (2), 73–89.

Mathew, P. M. 1997: From Beautiful 'Small' to Flexible Specialisation. Asian Experiences of Small Enterprise Development. *Economic and Political Weekly*, 32 (3), 84–86.

Mazumdar, D. 1976: The Urban Informal Sector. *World Development*, 4 (8), 655–679.

Mboi, B. 1996: The Socio-economic Development of Eastern Indonesia: The Role of Government. In C. Barlow and J. Hardjono (eds) *Indonesia Assessment 1995. Development in Eastern Indonesia*. Institute of Southeast Asian Studies, Singapore National University, Singapore, and Research School of Pacific and Asian Studies, Australian National University, Canberra, 123–140.

Millar, S. B. 1983: On Interpreting Gender in Bugis Society. *American Ethnologist*, 3 (10), 477–493.

—— 1989: *Bugis Weddings. Rituals of Social Location in Modern Indonesia*. Monograph 29. Center for South and Southeast Asia Studies, University of California, Berkeley.

Mingione, E. 1994: Life Strategies and Social Economics in the Postfordist Age.

International Journal of Urban and Regional Research, 18 (1), 24–45.

Mitchell, J. C. 1987: *Cities, Society and Social Perception: A Central African Perspective*. Clarendon Press, Oxford.

Mittelman, J. H. 1995: Rethinking the International Division of Labour in the Context of Globalisation. *Third World Quarterly*, 16 (2), 273–295.

Mitter, S. 1994: On Organising Women in Casualised Work. A Global Overview. In S. Rowbotham and S. Mitter (eds) *Dignity and Daily Bread. New Forms of Economic Organising Among Poor Women in the Third World and the First*. Routledge, London, 14–52.

Morrell, E. 1998: Symbolism, Spatiality and Social Order. In K. Robinson and M. Paeni (eds) *Living through Histories. Culture, History and Social Life in South Sulawesi*. Australian National University (with National Archives of Indonesia), Canberra, 151–167.

Morris, A. S. and Lowder, S. 1992: Flexible Specialization: The Application of Theory in a Poor-Country Context: Leon, Mexico. *International Journal of Urban and Regional Research*, 16 (2), 190–201.

Morris, J. L. 1988: New Technologies, Flexible Work Practices, and Regional Sociospatial Differentiation: Some Observations from the United Kingdom. *Environment and Planning D: Society and Space*, 6, 301–319.

Moser, C. O. N. 1978: Informal Sector or Petty Commodity Production: Dualism or Dependence in Urban Development? *World Development*, 6 (9/10), 1041–1064.

Mubyarto (no initial) 1979: Koperasi dan Ekonomi Pancasila [Cooperatives and the Pancasila Economy]. *Kompas*, 3 May. Translated and reprinted in I. Chalmers and V. R. Hadiz (eds) 1997: *The Politics of Economic Development in Indonesia. Contending Perspectives*. Routledge, London, 119–122.

Murdoch, J. 1995: Actor-Networks and the Evolution of Economic Forms: Combining Description and Explanation in Theories of Regulation, Flexible Specialization, and Networks. *Environment and Planning A*, 27, 731–757.

Murphy, M. 1990: The Need for a Re-Evaluation of the Concept 'Informal Sector': The Dominican Case. In M. Estellie Smith (ed.) *Perspectives On the Informal Economy*. Monographs in Economic Anthropology, 8, University Press of America, Maryland 161–181.

Nadvi, K. and Schmitz, H. 1994: *Industrial Clusters in Less Developed Countries: Review of Experiences and Research Agenda*. Institute of Development Studies Discussion Paper 339, University of Sussex, Brighton.

Nasution, A. 1998: Professor of Economics, University of Indonesia, Jakarta, Conference Discussion 9/9/98. 'Indonesia after Soeharto'. New Zealand Asia Institute Conference, Auckland, 9–10 September.

Netting, R. McC. 1993: *Smallholders, Householders. Farm Families and the Ecology of Intensive, Sustainable Agriculture*. Stanford University Press, Stanford, CA.

New Zealand Asia Institute (ed.) 1999: *Indonesia after Soeharto*. New Zealand Asia Institute, The University of Auckland, Auckland.

Oey-Gardiner, M. 1993: A Gender Perspective in Indonesia's Labour Market Transformation. In C. Manning and J. Hardjono (eds) *Indonesia Assessment 1993. Labour: Sharing the Benefits of Growth?* Proceedings of Indonesia Update Conference, August, Research School of Pacific Studies, Australian National University, Canberra, 203–213.

Ong, A. and Peletz, M. 1995: Introduction. In A. Ong and M. Peletz (eds) *Bewitching Women, Pious Men. Gender and Body Politics in Southeast Asia*. University of

California Press, Berkeley, 1–18.

Oxford English Dictionary 1989. Clarendon Press, Oxford.

Pangestu, M. 1996: Financing Small-Scale Business: The Indonesian Experience. In M. Pangestu (ed.) *Small-Scale Business Development and Competition Policy.* Centre for Strategic and International Studies, Jakarta, 27–46.

Panjatapda TK. I Prop. Sulawesi Selatan [Permanent Committee for Export Development of South Sulawesi], 1988, Makassar Special Economic Zone. Permanent Committee for Export Development of South Sulawesi, Ujung Pandang.

Parnwell, M. and Turner, S. 1998: Sustaining the Unsustainable? City and Society in Indonesia. *Third World Planning Review*, 20 (2), 147–163.

Peattie, L. 1987: An Idea in Good Currency and how it Grew: The Informal Sector. *World Development*, 15 (7), 851–860.

Peck, J. and Tickell, A. 1994a: Jungle Law Breaks Out: Neo-Liberalism and Global–Local Disorder. *Area*, 26 (4), 317–326.

——1994b: Searching for a New Institutional Fix: the *After*-Fordist Crisis and the Global–Local Disorder. In A. Amin (ed.) *Post-Fordism. A Reader.* Blackwell, Oxford, 280–315.

Pedersen, P. O. 1994a: Structural Adjustment and the Economy of Small Towns in Zimbabwe. In P. O. Pedersen, A. Sverrisson and M. P. van Dijk (eds) *Flexible Specialization. The Dynamics of Small-scale Industries in the South.* Intermediate Technology Publications, London, 21–41.

——1994b: *Clusters of Enterprises Within Systems of Production and Distribution. Collective Efficiency, Transaction Costs and the Economies of Agglomeration.* Center for Development Research Working Paper 94.14, Centre for Development Research, Denmark.

Pedersen, P. O., Sverrisson, A. and van Dijk, M. P. (eds) 1994: *Flexible Specialization. The Dynamics of Small-scale Industries in the South.* Intermediate Technology Publications, London.

Pelras, C. 1996a: *The Bugis.* Blackwell, Cambridge.

——1996b: Considerations about the Continuity of Bugis Identity from Age to Age. *Renungan Tentang Kesinambungan Identitas Bugis dari Masa ke Masa.* Paper presented at the *Seminar Internasional Sejarah Kebudayaan Dan Masyarakat Sulawesi Selatan* [International Seminar on South Sulawesi Culture and History], Ujung Pandang, 16–17 December.

Permerintah Daerah Tingkat I Sulawesi Selatan [Regional Government of South Sulawesi] 1996: *Pertemuan III, Saudagar Bugis Makassar. Proceedings. Ujung Pandang, 2–3 March, 1996* [Proceedings of the Third Meeting of Large Scale Bugis and Makassar Merchants. Ujung Pandang, 2–3 March, 1996], Regional Government of South Sulawesi, Ujung Pandang.

——1997: *Pertemuan IV, Saudagar Bugis Makassar. Proceedings. Ujung Pandang, 21–22 Februari, 1997* [Proceedings of the Fourth Meeting of Large Scale Bugis and Makassar Merchants. Ujung Pandang, 21–22 February, 1997], Regional Government of South Sulawesi, Ujung Pandang.

Phizacklea, A. 1990: *Unpacking The Fashion Industry.* Routledge, London.

Piore, M. and Sabel, C. 1984: *The Second Industrial Divide: Possibilities for Prosperity.* Basic Books, New York.

Pollert, A. 1988: Dismantling Flexibility. *Capital and Class: Bulletin of the Conference of Socialist Economists*, 34, 42–75.

Poot, H., Kuyvenhoven, A. and Jansen, J. 1991: *Industrialisation and Trade in*

Indonesia. Gadjah Mada University Press, Yogyakarta.

Potter, L. 2000: Rural Livelihoods and the Environment at the Time of Uncertainty: The Situation Outside Java. In C. Manning and P. van Diermen (eds) *Indonesia in Transition. Social Aspects of Reformasi and Crisis*. Institute of Southeast Asian Studies, Singapore, 239–252.

Powell, W. W. 1991: Neither Market nor Hierarchy: Network Forms of Organization. In G. Thompson, J. Frances, R. Levacic and J. Mitchell (eds) *Markets, Hierarchies and Networks. The Coordination of Social Life*. Sage Publications, London, 265–276.

Preston, P. W. 1998: *Pacific Asia in the Global System*. Blackwell, Oxford.

Pusat Pembinaan Pengusaha Kecil (PPPK), Tim Peneliti, Universitas Hasanuddin [Centre for the Establishment of Small Entrepreneurs, Research Team, Hasanuddin University] 1995: *Kebutuhan Pembinaan Bagi Usaha Kecil di Sulawesi Selatan* [Establishment Needs for Small Businesses in South Sulawesi: Survey Report]. PPPK, Ujung Pandang.

Pusat Pengembangan Usaha Kecil Kawasan Timur Indonesia (PUKTI) [Centre for Development of Small Enterprises, East Indonesia] 1995: *Dampak Ekonomi Kemitraan badan Usaha Milik Negara dan Usaha Kecil Di Kawasan Timur Indonesia: Suatu Studi Kasus* [Economic Impacts of Relationships between State Enterprises and Small Enterprises in Eastern Indonesia: Case Study]. PUKTI, Ujung Pandang.

Rahim, R. 1957: Introduction. In G. McT. Kahin (ed.) *The Co-operative Movement in Indonesia*. Cornell University Press, New York, xv–xxxiv.

Ranis, G. and Stewart, F. 1994: Decentralisation in Indonesia. *Bulletin of Indonesian Economic Studies*, 30 (3), 41–72.

Rasmussen, J. 1992: The Small Enterprise Environment in Zimbabwe: Growing in the Shadow of Large Enterprises. *Flexible Specialisation: A New View on Small Industry?* IDS Bulletin, 23 (3), 21–27.

Rasmussen, J., Schmitz, H. and van Dijk, M. P. (eds) 1992: *Flexible Specialisation: A New View on Small Industry?* IDS Bulletin, 23 (3).

Rattansi, A. 1997: Postcolonialism and its Discontents. *Economy and Society*, 26 (4), 480–500.

Regional Investment Co-ordinating Board of the Regional Government for South Sulawesi 1995: *Investment Opportunities*. Regional Government of South Sulawesi Province, Ujung Pandang.

—— 1996a: *Business Opportunities*. Regional Government of South Sulawesi Province, Ujung Pandang.

—— 1996b: *How to Invest in South Sulawesi, Indonesia*. Regional Government of South Sulawesi Province, Ujung Pandang.

Reid, A. 1990a: Dutch Hegemony. The Fall of Mighty Makassar. In T. A. Volkman and I. Caldwell (eds) *Sulawesi. The Celebes*. Periplus Editions, North America, 32–35.

—— 1990b: Independence. The Rocky Road to Nationhood. In T. A. Volkman and I. Caldwell (eds) *Sulawesi. The Celebes*. Periplus Editions, Singapore, 36–37.

—— 1990c: Ujung Pandang. Gateway to the Eastern Isles. In T. A. Volkman and I. Caldwell (eds) *Sulawesi. The Celebes*. Periplus Editions, Singapore, 68–73.

Ricklefs, M. C. 1993: *A History of Modern Indonesia Since c.1300*. MacMillan, London.

Rigg, J. 1997: *Southeast Asia. The Human Landscape of Modernization and*

Development. Routledge, London.

—— 1998: Geographies of Crisis: Ordinary people in a Globalizing World. Paper presented at the Southeast Asian Geography Association Conference, Singapore, 30 November to 4 December.

Roberts, B. 1990: The Informal Sector in Comparative Perspective. In M. Estellie Smith (ed.) *Perspectives On the Informal Economy.* Monographs in Economic Anthropology, 8, University Press of America, Maryland, 23–48.

—— 1994: Informal Economy and Family Strategies. *International Journal of Urban and Regional Research*, 18 (1), 6–23.

Robinson, K. 1999: Revisiting Inco. *Inside Indonesia*, 60 (October to December) (internet edition).

Robison, R. 1986: *Indonesia: The Rise of Capital.* Allen and Unwin, Sydney.

Robison, R., Beeson, M., Jayasuriya, K. and Hyuk-Rae Kim (eds) 2000: *Politics and Markets in the Wake of the Asian Crisis.* Routledge, London.

Rogers, A. and S. Vertovec, 1995: Introduction. In A. Rogers and S. Vertovec (eds) *The Urban Context. Ethnicity, Social Networks and Situational Analysis.* Berg, Oxford, 1–33.

Rudiyanto (no initial) 2000: Top Retails Get Post-Crisis Cheer. *Indonesian Observer*, 6 March.

Rustin, M. 1989: The Trouble with 'New Times'. In S. Hall and M. Jacques (eds) *New Times. The Changing Face of Politics in the 1990s.* Lawrence and Wishart in Association with *Marxism Today*, London, 303–320.

Rutten, M. 1997: Cooperation and Differentiation: Social History of Iron Founders in Central Java. In M. Rutten and C. Upadhya (eds) *Small Business Entrepreneurs in Asia and Europe. Towards a Comparative Perspective.* Sage Publications, New Delhi, 173–207.

Sabel, C. F. and Zeitlin, J. 1997: Stories, Strategies, Structures: Rethinking Historical Alternatives to Mass Production. In C. F. Sabel and J. Zeitlin (eds) *World of Possibilities. Flexibility and Mass Production in Western Industrialisation.* Cambridge University Press, Cambridge, 1–33.

Sadli, M. 1999: The Indonesian Crisis. In H. W. Arndt and H. Hill (eds) *Southeast Asia's Economic Crisis. Origins, Lessons, and the Way Forward.* St Martin's Press, New York, and Institute of Southeast Asian Studies, Singapore, 16–27.

—— 2000: Establishing Regional Autonomy in Indonesia: The State of the Debate. Paper presented at a workshop, University of Leiden, Holland, 15–16 May.

Said, E. 1979: *Orientalism.* Vintage Books, New York.

Sandarupa, S. 1984: *Life and Death of the Toraja People.* CV. Tiga Taurus, Ujung Pandang.

Sandee, H. 1994: The Impact of Technological Change on Inter-firm Linkages: A Case Study of Clustered Rural Small-scale Roof Tile Enterprises in Central Java. In P. O. Pedersen, A. Sverrisson and M. P. van Dijk (eds) *Flexible Specialization. The Dynamics of Small-scale Industries in the South.* Intermediate Technology Publications, London, 84–96.

Sandee, H. and van Hulsen, S. C. 2000: Business Development Services for Small and Cottage Industry Clusters in Indonesia: A Review of Case Studies from Central Java. Paper presented at the 'Business Services for Small Enterprises in Asia: Developing Markets and Measuring Performance' Conference, Hanoi, 3–6 April.

Sandee, H., Andadari, R. K. and Sulandjari, S. 2000: Small Firm Development

During Good Times and Bad: The Jepara Furniture Industry. In C. Manning and P. van Diermen (eds) *Indonesia in Transition*. Institute of Southeast Asian Studies, Singapore, 184–198.

Sandee, H., Rietveld, P., Supratikno, H. and Yuwono, P. 1994: Promoting Small Scale and Cottage Industries in Indonesia: An Impact Analysis for Central Java. *Bulletin of Indonesian Economic Studies*, 30 (3), 115–142.

Sarwono, J. 1999: Recycling Business Keeps on Going. *The Jakarta Post*, 7 August.

Schlossstein, S. 1991: *Asia's New Little Dragons. The Dynamic Emergence of Indonesia, Thailand and Malaysia*. Contemporary Books, Chicago, IL.

Schmitz, H. 1989: *Flexible Specialisation – A New Paradigm of Small-Scale Industrialisation?* Institute of Development Studies Discussion Paper 261, University of Sussex, Brighton.

—— 1992: On the Clustering of Small Firms. *Flexible Specialisation: A New View on Small Industry?* IDS Bulletin, 23 (3), 64–69.

Schmitz, H. and Nadvi, K. 1999: Clustering and Industrialization: Introduction. *World Development*, 27 (9), 1503–1514.

Schoenberger, E. 1988: From Fordism to Flexible Accumulation: Technology, Competitive Strategies, and International Location. *Environment and Planning D: Society and Space*, 6, 245–262.

Schuurman, F. J. 1993: Introduction: Development Theory in the 1990s. In F. J. Schuurman (ed.) *Beyond the Impasse. New Directions in Development Theory*. Zed Books, London, 1–48.

Schwarz, A. 1994: *A Nation in Waiting. Indonesia in the 1990s*. Allen and Unwin, Australia.

—— 1998: Press Fellow at the Council on Foreign Relations, Washington, Conference Discussion 9/9/98. 'Indonesia after Soeharto'. New Zealand Asia Institute Conference, Auckland, 9–10 September.

—— 1999: *A Nation in Waiting. Indonesia's Search for Stability*. Allen and Unwin, Australia.

Scott, A. J. 1983: Industrial Organization and the Logic of Intra-Metropolitan Location: A Theoretical Consideration. *Economic Geography*, 59 (3), 233–250.

—— 1988: *Metropolis, From the Division of Labor to Urban Form*. University of California Press, Los Angeles.

Scott, A. J. and Cooke, P. 1988: Guest Editorial. The New Geography and Sociology of Production. *Environment and Planning D: Society and Space*, 6, 241–244.

Scott, A. J. and Storper, M. 1992: Industrialization and Regional Development. In A. J. Scott and M. Storper (eds) *Pathways to Industrialization and Regional Development*. Routledge, London, 3–17.

Scott, J. C. 1976: *The Moral Economy of the Peasant. Rebellion and Subsistence in Southeast Asia*. Yale University Press, New Haven, CT.

Seda, F. 1990: Dampak Pertemuan Tapos [Impact of the Tapos Meeting]. *Kompas*, 8 and 9, June (two-part article). Translated and reprinted in I. Chalmers and V. R. Hadiz (eds) 1997: *The Politics of Economic Development in Indonesia. Contending Perspectives*. Routledge, London, 242–246.

Seligson, M. A. 1984: Foreword to T. Dos Santos. The Structure of Dependence. In M. A. Seligson (ed.) *The Gap Between Rich and Poor. Contending Perspectives On the Political Economy of Development*. Westview Press, Boulder, Colorado, 95.

Semlinger, K. 1993: Small Firms and Outsourcing as Flexibility Reservoirs of Large Firms. In G. Grabher (ed.) *The Embedded Firm. On the Socioeconomics of*

Industrial Networks. Routledge, London, 161–178.

Setiawan, B. 1999: Survival Strategies by the Poor: the Importance of the 'Social Capital'. Paper presented at the CCSEAS-NWRCSEAS Conference, Vancouver, 22–24 October.

Silvey, R. 2000: Stigmatized Spaces: Gender and Mobility under Crisis in South Sulawesi, Indonesia. *Gender, Place and Culture*, 7 (2), 143–161.

Simanjuntak, P. J. 1993: Manpower Problems and Policies. In C. Manning and J. Hardjono (eds) *Indonesia Assessment 1993. Labour: Sharing the Benefits of Growth?* Proceedings of Indonesia Update Conference, August, Research School of Pacific Studies, Australian National University, Canberra, 45–60.

Simon, D. 1998: Rethinking (Post)Modernism, Postcolonialism, and Posttraditionalism: South–North Perspectives. *Environment and Planning D: Society and Space*, 16, 219–245.

Sjahrir (no initial) 1993: The Indonesian Economy: A Case of Macro Success and Micro Challenge. In C. Manning and J. Hardjono (eds) *Indonesia Assessment 1993. Labour: Sharing the Benefits of Growth?* Proceedings of Indonesia Update Conference, August, Research School of Pacific Studies, Australian National University, Canberra, 13–25.

Sjaifudian, H. 1992: Women as Family Workers. In M. Grijins, S. Machfud, P. Sayogyo, I. Smyth and A. van Velzen (eds) *Gender, Marginalisation and Rural Industries. Female Entrepreneurs, Wage Workers and Family Workers in West Java.* Akatiga Foundation, Bandung, 175–191.

Slater, D. 1973: Geography and Underdevelopment – 1. *Antipode*, 5 (3), 21–32.

Smyth, I. 1992: Collective Efficiency and Selective Benefits: The Growth of the Rattan Industry of Tegalwangi (Indonesia). *Flexible Specialisation: A New View on Small Industry? IDS Bulletin*, 23 (3), 51–56.

Smyth, I., Saptari, R. and Maspiyati, 1994: *Flexible Specialization and Small-scale Industries: An Indonesian Case Study*. World Employment Programme Research Working Paper, International Labour Office, Geneva.

Soesastro, H. 1996: The Economy: A General Review. In C. Barlow and J. Hardjono (eds) *Indonesia Assessment 1995. Development in Eastern Indonesia.* Institute of Southeast Asian Studies, Singapore National University, Singapore, and Research School of Pacific and Asian Studies, Australian National University, Canberra, 22–42.

Sondakh, L. 1996: Agricultural Development in Eastern Indonesia: Performance, Issues and Policy Options. In C. Barlow and J. Hardjono (eds) *Indonesia Assessment 1995. Development in Eastern Indonesia.* Institute of Southeast Asian Studies, Singapore National University, Singapore, and Research School of Pacific and Asian Studies, Australian National University, Canberra, 141–162.

South Sulawesi Chamber of Commerce and Industry 1996: *South Sulawesi Business Guide 1995/1996.* South Sulawesi Chamber of Commerce and Industry, Ujung Pandang.

Spath, B. 1992: The Institutional Environment and Communities of Small Firms. *Flexible Specialisation: A New View on Small Industry? IDS Bulletin*, 23 (3), 8–14.

Sri Mulyani, I. and Winoto, A. 1999: Indonesian Economic Reconstruction. In New Zealand Asia Institute (ed.) *Indonesia after Soeharto.* New Zealand Asia Institute, The University of Auckland, Auckland, 55–70.

Storper, M. 1990: Industrialization and the Regional Question in the Third World: Lessons of Postimperialism; Prospects of Post-Fordism. *International Journal of*

Urban and Regional Research, 14 (3), 423–443.

Storper, M. and Scott, A. J. 1989: The Geographical Foundations and Social Regulation of Flexible Production Complexes. In J. Wolch and M. Dear (eds) *The Power of Geography. How Territory Shapes Social Life.* Unwin Hyman, Boston, MA, 21–40.

—— 1995: The Wealth of Regions. Market Forces and Policy Imperatives in Local and Global Context. *Futures*, 27 (5), 505–526.

Storper, M. and Walker, R. 1989: *The Capitalist Imperative: Territory, Technology and Industrial Growth.* Blackwell, Oxford.

Sudibjo (no initial) and Edwin, D. 1996: The Increasing Challenge of Regime's Legitimacy [*sic*]. *The Indonesian Quarterly*, 24(3), 226–232.

Sukamdi (no initial) 1996: Urbanization and the Structure of Urban Employment in Indonesia. *Sojourn*, 11 (1), 52–75.

Sundrijo, S. S. 1997: Female Labor Force in Indonesia: Opportunities and Challenges. *Proceedings of the International Conference on Women in the Asia-Pacific Region: Persons, Powers and Politics*, 11–13 August 1997. National University of Singapore, Singapore, 578–591.

Sunley, P. 1992: Marshallian Industrial Districts: The Case of the Lancashire Cotton Industry in the Inter-War Years. *Transactions of the Institute of British Geographers*, 17, 306–320.

Suryakusuma, J. 1991: State Ibuism: The Social Construction of Womanhood in the Indonesian New Order. *New Asian Visions*, 6(2), 46–71.

Sutherland, H. 1986: Ethnicity, Wealth and Power in Colonial Makassar. A Historical Reconsideration. In P. Nas (ed.) *The Indonesian City. Studies in Urban Development and Planning.* Foris Publications, Holland, 37–55.

Sutton, R. A. 1995: Performing Arts and Cultural Politics in South Sulawesi. *Bijdragen Tot de Taal-Land-en Volkenkunde*, 151–iv, 672–699.

Sverrisson, A. 1992: Flexible Specialisation and Woodworking Enterprises in Kenya and Zimbabwe. *Flexible Specialisation: A New View on Small Industry?* IDS Bulletin, 23 (3), 28–33.

—— 1994: Gradual Diffusion of Flexible Techniques in Small and Medium-Size Enterprise Networks. In P. O. Pedersen, A. Sverrisson and M. P. van Dijk (eds) *Flexible Specialization. The Dynamics of Small-scale Industries in the South.* Intermediate Technology Publications, London, 43–54.

Syamsuddin, A. 1995: *Mulai dengan Usaha Kecil. Merintis Karir Kewirausahaan Anda* [Beginning with Small Enterprises. Short Cuts for Your Business Career]. *PUKTI*, Ujung Pandang.

Tambunan, T. T. H. 2000: *Development of Small-Scale Industries During the New Order Government in Indonesia.* Ashgate, Aldershot.

Teltscher, S. 1994: Small Trade and the World Economy: Informal Vendors in Quito, Ecuador. *Economic Geography*, 70 (2), 167–187.

Thamrin, J. 1993: Labour in Small Scale Manufacturing: The Footwear Industry in West Java. In C. Manning and J. Hardjono (eds) *Indonesia Assessment 1993. Labour: Sharing the Benefits of Growth?* Proceedings of Indonesia Update Conference, August, Research School of Pacific Studies, Australian National University, Canberra, 139–154.

Thompson, M. 1995: Trade Unionism and Atypical Employment in Australia and New Zealand: An Examination of Labour Market Theory by Comparative Analysis. M.Soc.Sc. thesis, Centre for Labour and Trade Union Studies, University of Waikato, Hamilton, New Zealand.

Thrift, N. 1989: The Geography of International Economic Disorder. In R. J. Johnston and P. J. Taylor (eds) *A World In Crisis? Geographical Perspectives.* Blackwell, Oxford, 16–78.

Tickell, A. and Peck, J. A. 1995: Social Regulation *After* Fordism: Regulation Theory, Neo-Liberalism and the Global–Local Nexus. *Economy and Society,* 24 (3), 357–386.

Tirtosudarmo, R. 1996: Human Resources Development in Eastern Indonesia. In C. Barlow and J. Hardjono (eds) *Indonesia Assessment 1995. Development in Eastern Indonesia.* Institute of Southeast Asian Studies, Singapore National University, Singapore, and Research School of Pacific and Asian Studies, Australian National University, Canberra, 198–212.

Transparency International 2000: *1999 Corruption Perceptions Index* (accessed through internet site: <http://www.transparency.de/documents/cpi/index.html>).

Turner, S. 1994: The Impact of Globalisation on the Informal Sector in Malaysia, South East Asia. Unpublished M.Soc.Sc. thesis, Department of Geography, University of Waikato, Hamilton, New Zealand.

—— 1998: An Applicable Paradigm? Flexible Specialisation and Small Scale Enterprises in Ujung Pandang, Indonesia. Unpublished Ph.D. thesis, Centre for Southeast Asian Studies, University of Hull, England.

—— 2000: Globalisation, the Economic Crisis, and Small Enterprises in Makassar, Indonesia: Focusing on the Local Dimensions. *Singapore Journal of Tropical Geography,* 21 (3), 336–354.

Turner, S. and Seymour, R. 2002: Ethnic Chinese and the Indonesian Crisis. In R. Starrs (ed.) *Nations under Siege: Globalisation and Nationalism in Asia.* Palgrave, MacMillan Press, New York, 169–194.

United States Department of State, 2000: *1999 Country Reports on Human Rights Practices. Indonesia.* Bureau of Democracy, Human Rights and Labour, Washington, DC.

Upadhya, C. 1997: Culture, Class and Entrepreneurship: A Case Study of Coastal Andhra Pradesh, India. In M. Rutten and C. Upadhya (eds) *Small Business Entrepreneurs in Asia and Europe. Towards a Comparative Perspective.* Sage Publications, New Delhi 47–80.

Upadhya, C. and Rutten, M. 1997: In Search of a Comparative Framework: Small-scale Entrepreneurs in Asia and Europe. In M. Rutten and C. Upadhya (eds) *Small Business Entrepreneurs in Asia and Europe. Towards a Comparative Perspective.* Sage Publications, New Delhi, 13–43.

Utrecht, A. and Sayogyo, P. 1994: Policies and Interventions. In M. Grijns, I. Smyth, A. van Velzen, S. Machfud and P. Sayogyo (eds) *Different Women, Different Work. Gender and Industrialisation in Indonesia.* Avebury Publishing, Aldershot, 47–70.

van Diermen, P. 1995: Systems of Enterprises: A Study of Small-Scale Garment and Wood Furniture Enterprises in Jakarta. Ph.D. Thesis, Australian National University, Canberra.

—— 1997: *Small Business in Indonesia.* Ashgate Publishing, Aldershot.

van Diermen, P., Thee, K. W., Tambunan, M. and Tambunan, T. 2000: *The IMF Agreements and SMEs. Evaluating the Likely Impact of Economic Reforms on Small and Medium Enterprises in Indonesia.* The Asia Foundation, Jakarta.

van Dijk, M. P. 1992: How Relevant is Flexible Specialisation in Burkino Faso's Informal Sector and the Formal Manufacturing Sector? *Flexible Specialisation: A*

New View on Small Industry? IDS Bulletin, 23 (3), 45–50.

—— 1993: Industrial Districts and Urban Economic Development. *Third World Planning Review*, 15 (2), 175–186.

—— 1994: New Competition and Flexible Specialization in Indonesia and Burkina Faso. In P. O. Pedersen, A. Sverrisson and M. P. van Dijk (eds) *Flexible Specialization. The Dynamics of Small-scale Industries in the South.* Intermediate Technology Publications, London, 55–67.

Vatikiotis, M. R. J. 1993: *Indonesian Politics Under Suharto. Order, Development and Pressure for Change.* Routledge, London.

Volkman, T. A. and Muller, K. 1990: People. An Island of Great Ethnic Diversity. In T. A. Volkman and I. Caldwell (eds) *Sulawesi. The Celebes.* Periplus Editions, Singapore, 42–47.

Wah Chu, Y. 1992: Informal Work in Hong Kong. *International Journal of Urban and Regional Research*, 16 (3), 420–441.

Walker, R. 1989: A Requiem for Corporate Geography. New Directions in Industrial Organization, the Production of Place and the Uneven Development. *Geografiska Annaler*, 71B (1), 43–68.

Wallace, I. 1990: *The Global Economic System.* Unwin Hyman, London.

Wallerstein, I. 1980: *The Modern World System. Mercantilism and the Consolidation of the European World-Economy. 1600–1750.* Academic Press, New York.

Wanandi, S. 1999: The Post-Soeharto Business Environment. In G. Forrester (ed.) *Post-Soeharto Indonesia. Renewal or Chaos? Indonesia Assessment 1998.* Australian National University, Canberra, 128–134.

Wardhana, A. 1996: Economic Reform in Indonesia: The Transition from Resource Dependence to International Competitiveness. *The Indonesian Quarterly*, 24(3), 257–272.

Watts, M. 1995: 'A New Deal in Emotions'. Theory and Practice and the Crisis of Development. In J. Crush (ed.) *Power of Development.* Routledge, London, 44–62.

Weber, M. [1930] 1991: *The Protestant Ethic and the Spirit of Capitalism.* HarperCollins, London.

Weijland, H. 1994: Trade Networks for Flexible Rural Industry. In P. O. Pedersen, A. Sverrisson and M. P. van Dijk (eds) *Flexible Specialization. The Dynamics of Small-scale Industries in the South.* Intermediate Technology Publications, London, 97–110.

Wilson, F. 1992: Modern Workshop Industry in Mexico: on its Way to Collective Efficiency? *Flexible Specialisation: A New View on Small Industry?* IDS Bulletin, 23 (3), 57–63.

—— 1993: Workshops as Domestic Domains: Reflections on Small-Scale Industry in Mexico. *World Development*, 21 (1), 67–80.

Wolf, D. L. 1992: *Factory Daughters: Gender, Household Dynamics, and Rural Industrialisation in Java.* University of California Press, Berkeley.

—— 1993: Women and Industrialization in Indonesia. In J. Dirkse, F. Husken and M. Rutten (eds) *Indonesia's Experiences Under the New Order. Development and Social Welfare.* KITLV Press, Leiden, 135–155.

Wolf-Phillips, L. 1979: Why the Third World? *Third World Quarterly*, 1 (1), 105–109.

World Bank 1994: *Indonesia: Environment and Development. A World Bank Country Survey.* The World Bank, Washington, DC.

—— 1998: *Indonesia in Crisis. A Macroeconomic Update.* The World Bank, Washington, DC.

Yamashita, S. 1994: Manipulating Ethnic Tradition: The Funeral Ceremony, Tourism, and Television among the Toraja of Sulawesi. *Indonesia*, 58, 69–82.

Yin, H-W. S. 1995: Attitudes and Behaviours of Entrepreneurs in Five Asian Countries. *Journal of Small Business and Entrepreneurship*, 12 (4), 19–26.

Yuwono, P., Supramono (no initial) and Rietveld, P. 1994: Subcontracting in Small Scale Industry Clusters; The Case of the Copper Industry of Tumang, Indonesia. *Ekonomi dan Keuangan Indonesia*, 42 (4), 355–372.

Zenzie, C. U. 1999: Indonesia's New Political Spectrum. *Asian Survey*, 39 (2), 243–264.

Newspaper Articles*

Guardian

27 July 1996. A First Family Affair.

14 May 1998. From out of the Slums, a Seething Anger Takes Grip.

18 May 1998. Chinese Traders' Dreams Turned to Ashes.

22 May 1998. Suharto Goes With a Whisper.

Guardian Weekly

1 February 1998. Indonesian Chinese Made Scapegoat of Crisis.

Indonesian Observer

20 July 1999. New Financial Institution for UKMK unnecessary.

Jakarta Post

27 December 1996. Govt Policy on Women's Role 'Poses Setback'.

20 January 1997. Fruit Farmers Need Banking Facilities.

23 January 1997. Minimum Wage to be Raised by 10%.

25 January 1997. Wages and Efficiency. (Reported in *Jakarta Post* from *Bisnis Weekly*.)

23 February 1997. Workers and Employers Still Play Tug-Of-War.

4 March 1997. PPP Edict Draws Mixed Responses.

11 March 1997. Nurturing Small Firms.

24 March 1997. 'Oligopolistic Distribution Harms Consumers'.

27 March 1997. Bribery in Indonesia.

29 March 1997. Partnership Program Ineffective: Analyst.

1 April 1997. Most Corrupt in Asia.

7 April 1997. Toll Road a Blow for S. Sulawesi Administration.

8 April 1997. New Ruling for Foreign Banks.

10 April 1997. Quotas Worry Foreign Banks.

21 April 1997. Working Women Criticized.

24 April 1997. Poverty is Chiefly Government's Problem: Sofyan.

28 April 1997. Govt. Asked to Give Additional Power to Provinces.

15 May 1997. US$2.9b. in Loans Pledged for Small, Medium Firms.

* Newspaper feature articles where the author's name are given are listed in the main bibliography under the author's name.

17 May 1997. Military Gives Safety Assurance.
27 May 1997. 'Small Businesses Need Good Marketing': Mar'ie.
30 May 1997. Civil Servants' Salaries Increased.
3 June 1997. Small Businesses and Cooperatives (Letter to the Editor).
18 September 1997. Ujungpandang Under Control.
19 September 1997. Business Yet to Resume in Ujungpandang.
18 August 1998. Wheat Price Increase Kills Small Bread Producers.
31 July 1999. New Assistance Program. Business Brief.
21 September 1999. Antimonopoly Law Helps Small Enterprises.
19 January 2000. Demonstrators Clash with Troops on Makassar Campus.
22 January 2000. Indonesia Signs New Letter of Intent with IMF.
22 February 2000. Minimum Wage Set to Rise 15% to 55%.
23 February 2000. The Minimum Wage Riddle.
3 March 2000. A Token of Care.
22 June 2002. BI Says Loan Program for SMEs Running Well.

New Zealand Herald

27 January 1997. Wage Increase Leaves Poorest Underfed.
4 June 1998. Jakarta Toll Double that Given by the Military.
24 September 1998. NZ Counted Clean in Dirty World.

Reuters

8 April 1998. Finance Crisis Chronology
(accessed through internet site: <http://iias.leidenuniv.nl/cgi-bin/Daily Report 9/4/98>).

South China Morning Post

24 February 2000: Indonesia. Unrest Fears Grow as Unemployment Reaches 40%.

The Straits Times

23 September 1997. 600 Arrested in Sulawesi after Ethnic Riots.
29 July 1998. Habibie Extolls Value of Small Businesses.

Internet sites and list servers

Asiahouse: <http://www.asienhaus.org/links/crisis.htm>
Joyo News Service: <Joyo@aol.com>
Nourial Roubini: <http://www.stern.nyu.edu/~nroubini/asia/AsiaHomepage.html>
Van Zorge Report: <http://www.vanzorgereport.com/scripts/body.cfm>

Index

purchasing power 191
*Pusat Pengembangan Usaha Kecil
Kawasan Timur Indonesia (PUKTI)*
see Centre for Development of Small
Enterprises, East Indonesia
putting-out system 46

raw materials 138–42, 146, 155, 158, 201
reciprocity 27, 47, 50, 138
recycling 192
refrigeration 200
regime of accumulation 24–5
regional inequalities 69–71, 197
registration 175; *see also* licences
Regulation School 23–5
regulation theory 8, 23, 34
Repelita VI *see* Five-Year Plan
retailers 137, 139, 149
riots 90, 184
Rupiah 184, 191, 193

safety net 105; *see also kampung*
Sandee, H. 30
savings 110, 139, 164, 167, 192
Schmitz, H. 2, 27
Schwartz, A. 89, 171, 176
seasonal variations 133–4, 158
Second Industrial Divide 26
Second World War 71
self-exploitation 114, 115, 221
self-reliance 164
sentra 6, 65, 73, 174, 180; *see also*
clusters
sewing entrepreneurs *see* tailors
shipping costs 142; *see also*
transportation
shoe-making entrepreneurs 103, 124
Sidenreng Rappang 108, 137
silversmiths 97, 102, 123, 137, 149–50
Singapore 141
siri 86
sistem kekeluargaan 132, 190, 199
slum areas 77
Small Business Act (1995) 64
small enterprise integrative framework
8, 38–40, 94, 154, 194, 196–9
small enterprise parameters 27, 170
small enterprise production *see*
production
small enterprise registration 175; *see
also* licences
small enterprise taxation 175
Smyth, I. 30
Smyth, I., Saptari, R. and Maspiyati 30

social relations 34, 90, 109, 136, 170,
198, 219
social security 60, 121
social status 91, 122–3, 136, 173, 192;
see also conspicuous consumption
songkok 133, 150, 174
Soppeng 154
South Korea 183
South Sulawesi 71–5; Rebellion 71, 96
Southeast Asia 11, 16, 19, 183, 197; *see
also* Asia-Pacific
Southeast Asian NICs 21
specialisation 103, 135, 158, 200
speculation 183–84
srikaya 142
State Address (1995) 71
status symbols 139, 173; *see also*
conspicuous consumption
sub-contracting: 30, 45–7, 51, 97–8, 220,
and ethnicity 98–9, 136; furniture
makers 134–5; and gender 98, 107;
goldsmiths 137– 9, 175; networks
134–40; payment 113; tailors 112, 137
success 28, 36, 121, 167, 200–1
Suharto 57–8, 67, 70, 184, 193, 202; *see
also* Government of Indonesia
Sukarnoputri, Megawati 184; *see also*
Government of Indonesia
Sulawesi 7, 56, 70, 150, 189, 198; *see
also* South Sulawesi
Sumatra 70, 95, 141–2
suppliers 140–3
Surabaya, Java 70, 75, 124, 174, 197
Surat Izin Tempat Usaha 6, 66, 175; see
also *licences*
Surat Izin Untuk Perusahaan 66, 175; *see
also* licences
survivalism 80, 94, 147, 172, 197,
199–200; competition 104; during
economic crisis 190; labour 106, 120;
and networking 153; raw materials
143

tahu entrepreneurs 116, 132, 152, 172
tailors: clustering 155; economic crisis
191; gender 107, 125–6; general 98,
103, 112, 163, 215; personal 101, 103,
114, 115, 126, 163, 215; seasonal
demand 133–4; subcontracting 112,
136; trust 140
Takalar 142
Tambunan, T. 2, 193
Technical Assistance and Training
Programme 187